T0353683

MARY, MARY; QUITE THE CONTRARY

JOEY MASSANG

WestBow Press books may be ordered through booksellers or by contacting:

WestBow Press
A Division of Thomas Nelson & Zondervan
1663 Liberty Drive
Bloomington, IN 47403
www.westbowpress.com
844-714-3454

ISBN: 979-8-3850-4177-0 (sc)
ISBN: 979-8-3850-4178-7 (hc)
ISBN: 979-8-3850-4179-4 (e)

Library of Congress Control Number: 2025900706

Print information available on the last page.

WestBow Press rev. date: 03/31/2025

To all who seek to know God and discern between that which is of God and that which is not. May the Spirit of God lead you on your journey.

CONTENTS

ACKNOWLEDGMENTS

I wish to thank the following who read and checked my manuscript: my friend Sonny Tan, my pastor David Warwick of Real Life Church in Gosnells and his father, John Warwick, who pastored the church before him. I also wish to thank the following missionaries who kindly allowed me to include some of their stories: Ivan and Jane Mills, Hans Hansma, Geoff Kingsford, and the unnamed one who ministers in dangerous lands.

If anyone takes offense at the contents of this book, then let such offense rest upon me as none of those I acknowledge here have researched Mariolatry or had any prior interest or involvement in the creation of the material. The research and writing are mine alone.

PREFACE

Mary, the mother of Jesus and wife of Joseph, occupies a unique place in Christianity. She was literally with Jesus from the moment He entered into this world as the Son of Man. She was chosen by God for the role that she took on. Her example of servanthood was all-encompassing, from the moment she acceded to the will of God, through raising Jesus as her child, up to the events at the cross and beyond. She was even there in the upper room when the church was born at Pentecost.

Mary in Scripture

What is written of her in scripture, however, is fairly brief compared to the volumes of material added through the ages since the Gospels were written. What was written in scripture is summarized below and can be examined in detail in Appendix 1: Mary as She Appears in the Holy Bible:

- The prophet Isaiah foretold of her as the virgin who would bring forth the child who would be named Immanuel.
- The archangel Gabriel was sent to announce to Mary news of her unique role chosen by God and of her cousin Elizabeth's pregnancy.

- After the encounter with the angel, she went to visit her elder cousin.
- The Gospel of Matthew told of how Joseph came to accept the child of Mary, his betrothed.
- The Gospel of Luke told of the birth of Jesus in Nazareth during the Roman census.
- The apostle Matthew mentioned Mary in his genealogy of Jesus, the visit of the Magi, the warning about King Herod, the consequent flight to Egypt, and the subsequent return.
- The Gospel of Luke told of the presentation of Jesus as an infant at the temple.
- Luke also wrote of the later loss of Jesus when He stayed back at Jerusalem after a festival when His parents had left for Galilee.
- At the wedding at Cana, when the water was turned into wine.
- The Gospels describe an event that revealed how the family of Jesus doubted His divine calling and also told elsewhere of the disbelief of His townspeople and immediate family.
- Jesus's relationship with His family was foretold by King David in one of his psalms.
- Luke's Gospel related the story of the woman who called out to Jesus and His reply.
- Mary was shown to have been present at the Crucifixion and with the believers at Pentecost.
- Saint Paul, when writing to believers in Galatia, mentions that God sent His Son born of a woman.

Mary in Tradition

The Roman Catholic Church and many Orthodox churches go beyond scripture in their approaches to Mary. Mary has become the go-to for mercy, pardon for sin, guidance through this life, source of

God's gifts and grace, and more. She has become God's advocate, one to pray to, to honor, to give oneself completely over to, to be imitated, and to seek, especially at the hour of death.

Many of the positions and attributes reserved solely for God have become shared with her in this view of Mary. There is clearly a vast difference between the Mary of scripture and the Mary who has become created over time. The positions and attributes given to her are the result of beliefs and teachings about her promoted by the church.

For Protestants—and perhaps even to the less Mary-inclined of the traditional churches—it might appear to be almost inconceivable that so many beliefs have developed over time. However, it will be shown that each is nonetheless a taught belief that has become rooted in both dogma and practice.

The dangers and consequences of such beliefs will also be examined in this brief study, which is by no means exhaustive.

Scripture as the Basis of Understanding

Our understanding of Mary must derive primarily if not wholly from scripture.

St. Paul wrote to his disciple Timothy, *"All Scripture is God-breathed and is useful for teaching, rebuking, correcting and training in righteousness, so that the servant of God may be thoroughly equipped for every good work"* (2 Tim 3:16). This means that not only can we learn from scripture but are also able to find correction through scripture.

In the letter to the Hebrews, it is written, *"For the Word of God is alive and active. Sharper than any double-edged sword, it penetrates even to dividing soul and spirit, joints and marrow; it judges the thoughts and attitudes of the heart"* (Heb 4:12).

Writing of faithfulness and integrity, St. Paul wrote to the Corinthian church, *"I have applied these things to myself and Apollos for your benefit, so that you may learn from us the meaning of the saying, 'Do not go beyond what is written'"* (1 Cor 4:6).

As we are limited in our understanding, we must call upon the Holy Spirit who is able to bring understanding when we read scripture. For as Jesus taught, "***But the Advocate, the Holy Spirit, whom the Father will send in my name, will teach you all things and will remind you of everything I have said to you***" (John 13:26).

Who This Book Is Written For

This book is written for those who have devoted their lives to Mary. It is also written for the many who wonder why so many in the traditional churches even spend time "honoring" Mary and the saints in the way and measure that they do.

Finally, it is written for those who believe that the first group lives in bondage and who want to reach out to them but don't know how to.

Helpful Tips

The following will be helpful for the reader:

- an accurate translation of the Bible[1]
- having the heart of the Bereans who, St. Paul wrote, would listen to him and then nightly check what he had said against scripture to verify the truth (Acts 17:11)
- abiding with the few tips from scripture such as "*do not go beyond the word*" (1 Cor 4:6) and to "*test everything*" (1 Thess 5:21)

[1] All scripture in this book, unless otherwise stated, is taken from the New International Version (NIV), which is one of a number of accurate translations.

- having a sincere heart to call to God who gives His Holy Spirit to guide the reader in understanding His word and discerning truth from anything else.
- read at a slow to moderate pace due to the nature of this material. Scripture and related material do not readily lend themselves to speedy reading.

PART I

BELIEFS AND THEIR ORIGINS

This section is divided into numerous chapters, each covering a particular belief about Mary. The bulk of the material being examined is taken from *The Glories of Mary* by Alphonsus Liguori.

Alphonsus Liguori and *The Glories of Mary*

Alphonsus Liguori (1696–1787) was an Italian Catholic bishop, theologian, and late Renaissance man. Besides being a musician, lawyer, poet, and composer, he was also a writer whose writings included numerous works on Mary. His most famous work was *The Glories of Mary* (*The Glories*), and his most lasting achievement was perhaps his founding of the Congregation of the Most Holy Redeemer, now better known as the Redemptorists.

Liguori was especially dedicated to Mary, and this reflects in both his writings and the congregation he founded being especially dedicated to Our Mother of Perpetual Help. As a result of the latter, Pope Pius X appointed the Redemptorists as both custodians and missionaries of the icon bearing that title. Later in life, Liguori was dismissed from the very congregation he founded. In 1816, a mere twenty-nine years after his passing, he was beatified by Pope Pius VII, and in 1839, he was canonized by Pope Gregory XVI.

His work *The Glories,* published in 1888, is a sizable compilation of the Marian legends and the thoughts and teachings of the major Catholic influencers regarding Mary up until his time. These influences have permeated into the Church at large, and studying *The Glories* gives us an understanding of both the dominant Marian thoughts and, in some cases, the origins of those thoughts. The work has the imprimatur of the church, confirming that what he wrote is not the work of some fringe group but is central to the beliefs of the highest clergy.

In *The Glories*, Liguori divides his discourses into numerous chapters and then into sections within those chapters. The first ten chapters focus on various attributes of Mary and the benefits she brings to those who would be her followers. Subsequent chapters cover prayers dedicated to her, discourses on her feasts and trials, her virtues, novenas, meditations, more prayers, and acclamations.

Throughout his work, Liguori puts forward numerous beliefs about Mary and often repeats the scriptural citations to back them up so that, by the end, the reader might be convinced by the justification of these ideas.

In *Catholicism Volume 2,* Richard P. McBrien wrote,

> As popular Eastern legends (e.g., the story of Theophilus, who "sells" his soul to the devil only to have it saved by Mary) were translated and circulated in the West, and as theology in the West became increasing divorced from the Bible and the Fathers, Mariology took a turn toward some measure of exaggeration. The principle of fittingness or convenience became important: If God *could* do something and it seemed *fitting* that it should be

> done, then God *must have* done it (*potuit, decuit, fecit*).[2]

Liguori's work is peppered with the principle of fittingness, and he reveals this when describing various dogmas.

The following chapters list some of the many tenets about Mary that Liguori put forward as *truth,* and each is examined using guidelines given by God in scripture. Of necessity, each is described in some of the detail that Liguori used when he often quoted one source and then "confirmed" the truth of the tenet by quoting another source when all they were doing was agreeing with each other and not necessarily with God's written word.

Liguori did not come up with most of the ideas presented in his book. Rather, he compiled the many existing beliefs about Mary and shared in these beliefs, agreeing with those who promoted them and promoting them himself.

The Glories is no small work and consists of more than eight hundred pages with two hundred thousand words, excluding the contents and index pages. Like the Bereans who were commended by St. Paul for their diligent checking of his teachings to verify if they lined up with God's scripture (Acts 17:11), so too should we examine every spiritual teaching in the light of scripture.

***

In examining each belief, the passages from *The Glories* will be shown in this font with the page number in parenthesis, such as (). Where scripture or other references are quoted, these are shown in italics unless they are the very words of Christ, in which case they appear in bolded italics.The scriptural sources are shown in parenthesis. In both *The Glories* and scripture, any underlining that appears is mine for emphasis. Underlining appears neither in Liguori's work nor in scripture.

[2] *Catholicism Volume Two,* Richard P. McBrien, 1980.

It would have been nice to have each chapter cover a single belief, but many of these beliefs developed over the ages are interrelated, as Liguori's writings show. The material compiled is extensive as reflected in the size of *The Glories*. Some of the "excess" material for each chapter appears in the appendixes. These are for those who either wish to explore the beliefs further or wish to check that I have not exaggerated the extent and depths to which such beliefs have been taken.

Mary, Full of Grace

One key belief born in the fourth century that has persisted and has been the foundation of many other beliefs was that Mary was "full of grace." This belief arose when St. Jerome translated scripture into what became known as the Latin Vulgate Bible. Jerome took the Greek of the original New Testament canon when he translated the account of the annunciation of St. Gabriel to Mary, where he told her that God had chosen her for the role of mother of the Messiah.

A verse from the Gospel of Luke 1:28 is today rendered in English: "*The angel went to her and said, 'Greetings, you who are highly favoured! The Lord is with you'*" (Luke 1:28).

However, Jerome translated this as "*Ave Maria, gratia plena, Dominus tecum,*"[3] which when translated into English is "*Hail Mary, full of grace, the Lord is with you.*"

There was no "full of grace" written or inferred in the original Greek Gospel text. However, because of this mistranslation, which became used in the Catholic Bible, the idea that Mary was abounding in supernatural grace became a belief that soon gathered strength as can be seen in the following passages written or recorded by Liguori:

> *The angel, therefore, before she was the mother of God, already found her full of grace, and thus saluted*

[3] University of Dayton, udayton.edu/ imri/mary/a/ave-maria-translation.php.

> *her: Hail, full of grace: "Ave gratia plena." Commenting upon which words, Sophronius*[4] *writes, that to the other saints grace is given in part, but to the Virgin it was given in fulness.* (Liguori 360)

The correct translation "highly favoured" speaks of God's favor onto her by His choice in her for the mother of our Savior. Jerome's mistranslation turned the emphasis from God to Mary and endowed her with qualities not written about but claimed as having come from scripture. It may have been that Jerome took "grace" to be unmerited favor of God and meant that God was exceedingly gracious toward Mary.

However, his translation birthed a range of beliefs and doctrines that can be seen in the following passages, none of which would likely have appeared had it not been for his choice of words:

> *St. Thomas says the most holy Virgin was full of grace in three ways: 1st, She was full of grace in soul, so that from the beginning her holy soul belonged entirely to God. 2d, She was full of grace in body, so that she merited to clothe the eternal Word with her pure flesh. 3d, She was full of grace for the common benefit, so that all men might share it. Some saints, adds the angelic Doctor, have so much grace, that not only is it enough for themselves but also to save many others, not, however, all men; only to Jesus Christ and Mary was given so great a grace that it was sufficient to save all men. If any one had enough for the salvation of all, that would be the greatest; and this was in Jesus Christ and the blessed Virgin. Thus St. Thomas writes. Hence what St. John said of Jesus—"And of his fulness we all have received—" the saints say of Mary.* (Liguori 387–388)

[4] Sophronius was the patriarch of Jerusalem from AD 638.

Liguori emphasized this "fullness" that Mary was said to have been given:

> *The Angelic Doctor, St. Thomas, says, that Mary received grace sufficient to save all men; and therefore St. Bernard calls Mary a channel so full that we can all partake of its fulness.* (Liguori 758)

St. Thomas (either perhaps of Villanova or Aquinas but not the apostle Thomas) based his ideas on the "full of grace" fully on the mistranslation and thereafter added much to it, including attributing to Mary what is exclusive to Jesus, which was the ability to save. Liguori's claim of what the saints said of Mary does not include any of the apostles or early disciples of Jesus. If Mary as he asserts had "*grace that it was sufficient to save all men,*" then the sacrifice of Jesus Christ at the cross would not have been necessary showing the assertion is completely without basis.

> *He* (the Archangel Gabriel) *enters and salutes her, saying: "Hail, full of grace, the Lord is with thee; blessed art thou among women." Hail, oh Virgin, full of grace, for thou wast always rich in grace, above all the other saints. The Lord is with thee because thou art so humble. Thou art blessed among women, for all others have incurred the curse of original sin; but thou, because thou art to be the mother of the Blessed One, hast been and wilt always be blessed, and free from every stain.* (Liguori 412–413)

The archangel's address told Mary of the grace of God in favoring her, who undoubtedly was special in His eyes. Mary herself then said that all generations would call her blessed because "*the Mighty One has done great things for me*" (Luke 1:49) in *choosing her* for His mother—not as Liguori says, because she was free from every stain.

For Mary herself said, "*My soul glorifies the Lord and my spirit rejoices in God my Saviour*" (Luke 1:46–47), telling us that she herself knew she needed the salvation offered and given by her Savior.

Mary: The Source of Grace and Gifts from God

From initially being led to believe Mary was "full of grace," and then that her grace could somehow save, believers were later taught that she is the storehouse and dispenser of all divine graces. This meant that they were to go to her to receive the grace needed to live the Christian life.

> *Mary is the treasurer of all the divine graces. Therefore to who desires graces should have recourse to Mary; and he who has recourse to Mary, should be secure of obtaining the graces he wishes.* (Liguori 436)

> *St. Bernard says that God had bestowed all graces on Mary, that men, through her as through a channel, may receive whatever goods is in store for them. Moreover, the saint here makes an important reflection, and says that before the birth of the most holy Virgin there flowed no such current of grace for all, since this desired channel did not yet exist. But for this end, he adds. Mary has been given to the world, that through this channel the divine graces might continually flow down upon us.* (Liguori 175–176)

Scripture, however, tells a very different story. St. Peter wrote that God has "*given us everything we need for a godly life through our knowledge of him who called us by his own glory and goodness*" (2 Pet 1:3). The apostle Paul wrote many times of the gifts of God given to us. In Romans 12 and 1 Corinthians 12, he described these gifts and then tells us the channel by which we receive these precious gifts: "*All these are the work of one and the same Spirit, and he distributes them to each one, just as he determines*" (1 Cor 12:11).

It was not that the birth of Mary brought about "*this desired channel*" but rather the sacrifice of our Savior, Jesus Christ, who paid the price of sin and who bore all our infirmities and sicknesses. Through His sacrifice on the cross, "*all the promises of God in Him are Yes, and in Him Amen, to the glory of God through us*" (2 Cor 1:20). This is why we can receive all that God has for us. It is not insignificant that the apostles quoted in the above scriptures knew Mary, but not once said she was the keeper or dispenser of grace and gifts of God. On the contrary, they wrote of the Holy Spirit being for us the channel of these divine gifts.

However, it was apparently not enough that the Holy Spirit was given to us with all the gifts required to live this life for God. Some writers and teachers proceeded to teach that Mary was the only source from which we were to receive gifts from God.

> *Also the Idiot[5] remarks, that every blessing, every help, every grace that men have received or will receive from God, to the end of the world, has come to them, and will come to them, through the intercession and by means of Mary.* (Liguori 119)
>
> *St. Bernard also affirms that the Lord has placed in the hands of Mary all the graces that he wishes to dispense to us, that we may know that whatever of good we receive, we receive it all from her hands. And of this Mary herself assures us when she says: In me is all grace of the way and of the truth: "In me gratia omnis vise et veritatis."* (Liguori 440–441)

[5] "The Idiot" appears to have been one Raimondo Giordano, a fourteenth-century French mystic who, in humility, referred to himself as such.

The Holy Spirit is the true dispenser of gifts and graces.

He even works within us to bring us to perfection in Christ. Writing of the Holy Spirit, Paul wrote, "*I thank my God every time I remember you. In all my prayers for all of you, I always pray with joy because of your partnership in the Gospel from the first day until now, being confident of this, that he who began a good work in you will carry it on to completion until the day of Christ Jesus*" (Phil 1:3–6). The verse in Latin, on the other hand, quoted by Liguori and attributed to Mary as proof was taken from Ecclesiasticus 24, which was written about the subject of Wisdom and not Mary.

> *She gives us to know that she has with her all the riches of God, that is, the divine mercies, that she may dispense them for the benefit of those who love her. "With me are riches and glory, that I may enrich them that love me"* (Prov 8:18–21). (Liguori 120–121)

In this passage too, Liguori made the claim that Mary has and dispenses according to her wishes using his paraphrased version from Proverbs 8: 18–21 as proof. Here, as elsewhere where he has quoted from Proverbs and Ecclesiasticus, the verses were written about wisdom, including the very first verse of Proverbs 8: "*Does not wisdom call out? Does not understanding raise her voice?*" (Prov 8:1). Verse 12 reiterates this: "*I, wisdom, dwell together with prudence, I possess knowledge and discretion*" (Prov 8:12).

Liguori emphasized that the spiritual gifts from God come only through Mary:

> *FINAL perseverance is a divine gift so great, that … all the graces which are bestowed on us by God pass through the hands of Mary, it must also be true that only through Mary can we hope for and obtain this great gift of perseverance.* (Liguori 89–90)

> *spiritual strength is necessary to resist all the enemies of our salvation. Now, this strength can only be obtained by means of Mary.* (Liguori 90)

Liguori, and others whom he quoted in *The Glories*, often misquoted scripture to refer to Mary when those scriptures refer to the Holy Spirit as well as to attributes of God such as wisdom. These writers quote from the books of Proverbs, Ecclesiasticus, and Ecclesiastes, among others, when each of those books clearly states that the subject of the verses quoted is wisdom, an attribute of God. Those same verses state that the subject of the writings, wisdom, was formed even before creation, which further confirms that the subject was never Mary.

Where scripture was not used as proof of the beliefs they professed as true of Mary, they often resorted to the "*it was fitting*" argument: that God *could have* done so—and so *must have* done so.

Further, Liguori often cited one writer's opinion and then "confirmed" that using the opinion of another writer instead of ever checking against scripture.

> *If, then, we desire graces, we must go to this treasurer and dispensatrix of graces; for this is the sovereign will of the Giver of every good, as St. Bernard himself assures us, that all graces are dispensed by the hands of Mary. All, all, Totum, totum; he who says all, excludes nothing.* (Liguori 443)

St. Bernard, whom Liguori often quoted, taught that Mary was both treasurer and dispenser of the graces:

> *It cannot be doubted, therefore, except by those who are deficient in faith, that it is a useful and holy thing to have recourse to the intercession of Mary. But the point that we here propose to prove*

> *is, that the intercession of Mary is even necessary for our salvation: necessary, to speak properly, not indeed absolutely, but morally. And we affirm that this necessity arises from the will of God itself, who has ordained that all the favors which he dispenses should pass through the hands of Mary, according to the opinion of St. Bernard, which may well be considered at the present day the common opinion of doctors and divines, as the author of "The kingdom of Mary" has already called it. It is embraced by Vega, Mendoza, Paciucchelli, Segneri, Poire, Crasset, and innumerable other learned authors.*
>
> *Even Father Noel Alexander, an author usually very reserved in his assertions, declares it to be the will of God that we receive all favors through the intercession of Mary. In confirmation of this, he quotes the celebrated passage of St. Bernard: This is the will of him who would have us receive all things through Mary.* (Liguori 170–171)

Having asserted that all graces and favors pass through the hands of Mary, Liguori admitted that this is not found in scripture when he wrote that this was the *opinion* of St. Bernard and others. This opinion goes against all scriptures which tell us that we have everything we need through His Spirit: "*His divine power has given us everything we need for a godly life through our knowledge of him who called us by his own glory and goodness*" (2 Pet 1:3).

If having God through His Holy Spirit in us and living by His Spirit is not enough, then <u>*nothing*</u> is.

> *Mary is called the co-operatrix with her Son in our justification, because God has committed to her keeping all the graces that he has destined for us. Wherefore St. Bernard affirms, that <u>all men, past,</u>*

> *present, and to come, should regard her as the medium and negotiator of the salvation of all ages.* (Liguori 186)

There is no "*negotiator of the salvation.*" Negotiation is only possible in any transaction if a price has not yet been paid. Jesus Christ paid the price *in full* for our salvation, and His life was the price paid for it. His body and His blood were the "medium" of payment.

> *The glorious St. Cajetan said that we could ask for graces, but we could never obtain them without the intercession of Mary. And St. Antoninus confirms this, expressing himself thus beautifully: Whoever asks and wishes to obtain graces without the intercession of Mary, attempts to fly without wings; for, as Pharaoh said to Joseph, "The land of Egypt is in thy hand" and as he sent all those to Joseph who applied to him for assistance, saying: Go to Joseph "Ite ad Joseph;" so God, when we supplicate him for favors, sends us to Mary: Go to Mary—"Ite ad Mariam;" for he has decreed, says St. Bernard, that he will grant no favors except through the hands of Mary. Hence Richard of St. Laurence says: Our salvation is in the hands of Mary, and we Christians can more justly say to her than the Egyptians to Joseph, our salvation is in thy hand. The venerable Idiot says the same thing: Our salvation is in her hands—"Salus nostra in manuillius est." Cassian asserts the same thing, but in stronger language. He absolutely affirms that the salvation of the whole world depends upon the favor and protection of Mary. St. Bernardine of Sienna thus addresses her: Oh Lady, since thou art the dispenser of all graces, and we must receive the grace of salvation*

> *through thy hand alone, then our salvation depends on thee.* (Liguori 189–190)

This passage sums up the extent to which the belief in Mary being "full of grace" was taken. From the mistranslation by St. Jerome, it was built up until no believer could hope for salvation without going through Mary.

Confirm as each did what the others of like mind believed, yet none of these beliefs were based on anything given in the revealed Word of God. If all they wrote was true, then this negated the very reason why God in His infinite wisdom and love gave us His Holy Spirit to be our intercessor (Rom 8:27), dispenser of graces (1 Cor 12), guarantee of what is to come (2 Cor 1:22; Eph 1:13–14), and the means of our ongoing salvation (Titus 3:5–7). Instead, what those quoted by Liguori taught was that all those roles belong to Mary.

Jesus did not teach that one day what was explicitly written of the Holy Spirit and His roles would be taken over by Mary. Instead, He said that God (in the person of the Holy Spirit) would be with us "***to the very end of the age***" (Matt 28:20).

Jesus also said the following:

- ***Whatever you ask in my name the Father will give you.*** (John 15:16)
- ***In that day you will no longer ask me anything. Very truly I tell you, my Father will give you whatever you ask in my name.*** (John 16:23)
- ***In that day you will ask in my name. I am not saying that I will ask the Father on your behalf. No, the Father himself loves you because you have loved me and have believed that I came from God. I came from the Father and entered the world; now I am leaving the world and going back to the Father.*** (John 16:26–28)

In every case of the above, Jesus told His disciples to ask the Father in His name. He never told His disciples that they were to ask Mary.

The following scriptures, which are not exhaustive, relate the same eternal truths:

On Intercession

> *And he* (God) *who searches our hearts knows the mind of the Spirit, because the Spirit intercedes for God's people in accordance with the will of God.* (Rom 8:27)

Regarding the Source and Dispenser of Gifts/Graces

> *There are different kinds of gifts, but the same Spirit distributes them. There are different kinds of service, but the same Lord. There are different kinds of working, but in all of them and in everyone it is the same God at work.*
>
> *Now to each one the manifestation of the Spirit is given for the common good. To one there is given through the Spirit a message of wisdom, to another a message of knowledge by means of the same Spirit, to another faith by the same Spirit, to another gifts of healing by that one Spirit, to another miraculous powers, to another prophecy, to another distinguishing between spirits, to another speaking in different kinds of tongues, a and to still another the interpretation of tongues. All these are the work of one and the same Spirit, and he distributes them to each one, just as he determines.* (1 Cor 12:4–11)

> *This salvation, which was first announced by the Lord, was confirmed to us by those who heard him. God also testified to it by signs, wonders and various miracles, and by gifts of the Holy Spirit distributed according to his will*. (Heb 2:3–4)

Regarding Our Helper in Salvation

> *But when the kindness and love of God our Savior appeared, he saved us, not because of righteous things we had done, but because of his mercy. He saved us through the washing of rebirth and renewal by the Holy Spirit, whom he poured out on us generously through Jesus Christ our Savior, so that, having been justified by his grace, we might become heirs having the hope of eternal life*. (Titus 3:4–7)

Scripture never taught that our salvation was in the hands of Mary or that the roles of the Holy Spirit would one day be turned over to Mary. Instead, it taught that from the Day of Pentecost, the Holy Spirit would inhabit those who belong to God until the completion of all things:

> ***And surely I am with you always, to the very end of the age.*** (Matt 28:20)
>
> ***And I will ask the Father, and he will give you another advocate to help you and be with you forever—the Spirit of truth.*** (John 14:16–17)
>
> ***I will not leave you as orphans; I will come to you.*** (John 14:18)

While Jesus sits at the right hand of God until all His enemies are made His footstool,[6] His Spirit[7] works in believers to guide, lead, and make them to be made more and more into the image of Christ.[8]

Gifts and Graces

It might be argued that the graces attributed to Mary are not the same as the gifts of Holy Spirit, such as the "grace of perseverance" or the "grace of a happy death" that appear in Liguori's writings.

However, nowhere in scripture does Jesus or the apostles speak of these "graces" either as gifts or in the terms argued as being *indispensable* by Liguori and others. If these were indispensable, they would have been taught by the apostles. St. Paul wrote that he had taught everything that disciples needed to know (Acts 20:20).

Two of these "graces" that come from Mary are described below from Liguori and alternatively from scripture.

Perseverance

Liguori describes perseverance as a gift—one of many graces available from God only through Mary:

> *FINAL perseverance is a divine gift so great, that... all the graces which are bestowed on us by God pass through the hands of Mary, it must also be true that only through Mary can we hope for and obtain this great gift of perseverance.* (Liguori 89–90)

[6] Matt 22:44; Mark 16:19; Luke 22:69; Acts 2:33; 7:55–56; 8:34; Eph 1:20; Col 3:1; Heb 1:3; 8:1, 10:12: 2; 1 Pet 3:22.

[7] Phil 1:19.

[8] John 14:25–27; 16:13; Rom 8:13–14; Gal 4:6–7; 5:16–18; 2 Cor 3:17–18; Eph 1:13–14; Col 3:10; Tit 3:4–7.

Scripture, on the other hand, writes of the gift of faith. The apostle Paul, in his letter to the Romans, wrote much of this gift. He wrote of the righteousness through faith (chapter 3), the justification through faith (chapter 4), and our peace with God (chapter 5):

> *Therefore, since we have been justified through faith, we have peace with God through our Lord Jesus Christ, through whom we have gained access by faith into this grace in which we now stand. And we boast in the hope of the glory of God. Not only so, but we also glory in our sufferings, because we know that suffering produces perseverance; perseverance, character; and character, hope. And hope does not put us to shame, because God's love has been poured out into our hearts through the Holy Spirit, who has been given to us.* (Rom 5:1–5)

St. Paul neither describes perseverance as a gift nor a grace; instead, it is part of a *process* of the growth in faith we go through in life as believers. If it is simply part of a process, then it cannot be a gift.

St. James teaches a similar lesson in his letter:

> *Consider it pure joy, my brothers and sisters, whenever you face trials of many kinds, because you know that the testing of your faith produces perseverance. Let perseverance finish its work so that you may be mature and complete, not lacking anything.* (Jas 1:2–4)

The apostle Peter shared a similar lesson:

> *For this very reason, make every effort to add to your faith goodness; and to goodness, knowledge; and to*

> *knowledge, self-control; and to self-control, perseverance; and to perseverance, godliness; and to godliness, mutual affection; and to mutual affection, love.* (2 Pet 1:5–6)

He did not describe it as a gift or grace but again as part of the process of maturing in faith.

The Holy Spirit molds us into the image of Christ Jesus and uses the challenges that believers face and turns them into stepping stones on the road to perfection: "*And we know that in all things God works for the good of those who love him, who have been called according to his purpose*" (Rom 8:28).

As for *Final* perseverance, St. Paul describes how we are to acquire it, which once again involves working with the Holy Spirit and allowing Him and his gifts to work in our lives:

> *Finally, be strong in the Lord and in his mighty power. Put on the full armor of God, so that you can take your stand against the devil's schemes. For our struggle is not against flesh and blood, but against the rulers, against the authorities, against the powers of this dark world and against the spiritual forces of evil in the heavenly realms. Therefore put on the full armor of God, so that when the day of evil comes, you may be able to stand your ground, and after you have done everything, to stand. Stand firm then, with the belt of truth buckled around your waist, with the breastplate of righteousness in place, and with your feet fitted with the readiness that comes from the Gospel of peace. In addition to all this, take up the shield of faith, with which you can extinguish all the flaming arrows of the evil one. Take the helmet of salvation and the sword of the Spirit, which is the Word of God.* (Eph 6:10–17)

And through all things, we are to focus on our Creator:

> *Therefore, since we are surrounded by such a great cloud of witnesses, let us throw off everything that hinders and the sin that so easily entangles. And let us run with perseverance the race marked out for us, fixing our eyes on Jesus, the pioneer and perfecter of faith.* (Heb 12:1–2)

A Blessed Death

Liguori wrote much of the "grace of a good death." He wrote a "Prayer to the Blessed Virgin to obtain a good death" as well as much on how "Mary renders death sweet to her servants." Some of that material is examined in the chapter on "Special Powers" in this book.

Scripture does not teach us to seek a good death. Jesus warned that, as His followers, we would be considered enemies by the world. Our desire should be to please our Father in heaven to do His will and to pray His will on earth as it is in heaven. We are only to trust God that He knows best as to where we will be at the end of our time on earth. When our eyes are on the Lord, we do not look or plan for how our lives will conclude this side of eternity; instead, we await His welcome on the "other side."

If the reader wishes to read more on this topic, additional teachings from Liguori's *The Glories,* as well as the comparisons against scripture, appear in appendix 2: "Additional Material for Mary: The Source of Grace and Gifts from God."

Mary as Our Mother

In *The Glories*, Liguori presented reasons we should turn to Mary in three sections, totaling forty pages, which were named as follows:

- how much greater should be our confidence in Mary because she is our mother
- how great is the love of our mother for us
- how Mary is also mother of penitent sinners

These were written based on the belief and teaching that Mary is our mother. This belief is claimed by a few orthodox and traditional denominations who use, as justification, the following passages from the Gospel of John:

> *Near the cross of Jesus stood his mother, his mother's sister, Mary the wife of Clopas, and Mary Magdalene.*
>
> *When Jesus saw his mother there, and the disciple whom he loved standing nearby, he said to her, **"Woman, here is your son,"** and to the disciple, **"Here is your mother."***
>
> *From that time on, this disciple took her into his home.* (John 19:25–27)

Liguori concludes:

> *After that he said to the disciple: **"Behold thy mother."** Let it be remarked that Jesus Christ did not say this to John, but to <u>the disciple</u>, to signify that the Saviour appointed Mary for common mother of all those who, being Christians, bear the name of his disciples.* (Liguori 44)

The Gospel account from which these verses are quoted is that of John, written by the apostle John.

Jesus did not call John "*the disciple,*" but John himself did. In fact, John always referred to himself in his Gospel in the third person, and this instance was no exception. The following are all the references John made of himself in his Gospel:

- *The next day John* (the Baptist) *was there again with two of his disciples.* (John 1:35)
- *One of them, the disciple whom Jesus loved, was reclining next to him. Simon Peter motioned to this disciple and said, "Ask him which one he means."* (John 13:23–24)
- *Simon Peter and another disciple were following Jesus. Because this disciple was known to the high priest, he went with Jesus into the high priest's courtyard, but Peter had to wait outside at the door. The other disciple, who was known to the high priest, came back, spoke to the servant girl on duty there and brought Peter in.* (John 18:15–16)
- *The man who saw it has given testimony, and his testimony is true. He knows that he tells the truth, and he testifies so that you also may believe.* (John 19:35)
- *So she came running to Simon Peter and the other disciple, the one Jesus loved, and said, "They have taken the Lord out of the tomb, and we don't know where they have put him!" So Peter and the other disciple started for the tomb. Both were running, but the other disciple outran Peter and reached the tomb first. He bent over and looked in at the strips of linen lying there but did not go in. Then Simon Peter came along behind him and went straight into the tomb. He saw the strips of linen lying there, as well as the cloth that had been wrapped around Jesus' head. The cloth was still lying in its place, separate from the linen. Finally the other disciple, who had reached the tomb first, also went inside. He saw and believed.* (John 20:2–8)
- *Then the disciple whom Jesus loved said to Peter, "It is the Lord!"* (John 21:7)

- *Peter turned and saw that the disciple whom Jesus loved was following them. (This was the one who had leaned back against Jesus at the supper and had said, "Lord, who is going to betray you?")* (John 21:20)
- *Because of this, the rumour spread among the believers that this disciple would not die. This is the disciple who testifies to these things and who wrote them down. We know that his testimony is true.* (John 21:23–24)

As can be seen in the above passages, each and every time John wrote of himself, he described himself in the "third person" as either "he," "his," "the man," "the disciple," "the other disciple," or "the disciple whom Jesus loved."

So, John, in writing the crucifixion account, did not imply that Jesus meant for all disciples to take Mary as their mother.

That the account of the conversation with John at the cross does not appear in any other Gospel account seems to point to it having been an instruction specific to John and to him alone.

Further, Jesus did return at His resurrection shortly after and was seen by at least five hundred believers. It is not recorded anywhere in the New Testament that He taught any of them to consider His mother as their mother even though He would, more than likely, have met her again.

> *The same opinion is held by Father Contensone who, explaining the words of Jesus Christ of the cross to John, behold thy mother, "Ecce matertua," says: It is as if he said, no one shall partake of my blood except by the intercession of my mother. My wounds are fountains of grace, but to none can their streams be conveyed except by the channel of Mary.* (Liguori 171)

To extrapolate "*My wounds are fountains of grace, but to none can their streams be conveyed except by the channel of Mary*" from what Jesus on the cross said for John to take His mother as his own to care for her is to "go beyond what is written." This is warned against in 1 Corinthians 4:6 since it goes against the very reason why God gave us His Holy Spirit.

> *"The eyes of the Lord are upon the just," says David; but the eyes of our Lady are upon the just and upon sinners, as Richard of St. Laurence says; for he adds: The eyes of Mary are the eyes of a mother; and the mother not only guards her child from falling, but if he falls, she hastens to raise him.* (Liguori 241–242)

In another example of going beyond the Word, Richard of St. Laurence saw it fit to praise Mary higher than the Lord in regard to having eyes of mercy. Jesus, after all, was berated by the Pharisees for His practice of always being in the company of sinners to whom He reached out in love, grace and compassion.

> *And if the sacrifice of Abraham in offering up to him his son Isaac so pleased God that he promised, as a reward, to multiply his descendants as the stars of heaven: "Because thou hast done this thing, and hast not spared thy only begotten son for my sake, I will bless thee, and I will multiply thy seed as the stars of heaven;" we must certainly believe that the more remarkable sacrifice which this great mother made of Jesus was much more agreeable to the Lord; and, therefore, it has been granted her, that by her prayers, the number of the elect should be multiplied, that is, the favored succession of her children, for she holds and protects as such her devoted servants.* (Liguori 469–470)

There are two beliefs about Mary that are put forward in the above statement. Liguori first states that Mary made the sacrifice of Jesus at the cross. This belief will be looked at in the chapter "Mary Offered Up Jesus for Crucifixion." The second belief is that God granted Mary believers as her children.

The writers of the Gospels and the books of the New Testament made no such claim that Mary, by her obedience, was given the church as her children. Rather than Mary who "*holds and protects … her devoted servants*" as children, scripture tells us that we have been adopted into the family of Father God (Rom 8:15 and 8:23; Eph 1:5; Gal 4:5) and it is the Spirit of God who guides and protects us; not Mary.

Further, we are not slaves ("servants" in Liguori's words) of this Spirit:

> *For those who are led by the Spirit of God <u>are the children of God</u>. <u>The Spirit you received does not make you slaves</u>, so that you live in fear again; rather, the Spirit you received brought about your adoption to sonship. And by him we cry, "Abba, Father."* (Rom 8:14–15)

Liguori instead claims:

> *But the presence of Mary on Calvary, with her dying Jesus, is alone enough to show us how constant and sublime was her patience: There stood by the cross of Jesus, his mother: "Stabat juxta crucem Jesu mater ejus." Then, by the merit of this her patience, as blessed Albertus Magnus remarks, she became our mother, and brought us forth to the life of grace. If we desire then to be the children of Mary, we must seek to imitate her patience.* (Liguori 637)

Scripture tells us that <u>*when*</u> we have faith in the finished work of Christ Jesus and are led by the Spirit of God, we <u>*become*</u> children of God (1

John 3:10; Rom 9:8; 1 John 3:1; Heb 2:13; Rom 8:16; John 11:52; Phil 2:15; Luke 20:36; 1 John 3:2; Gal 3:26; Matt 5:9; Rom 8:14.)

It is revealing to then read the words of those who teach that the redeemed who are *already* God's children must then be *qualified before* we can *become* Mary's children i.e. "if we *desire* to be children of Mary, we *must* …."

For if we already are the children of God, why seek any other belonging?

Jesus neither taught nor demonstrated to His disciples the elevation of the role of earthly "motherhood" over anything divine in nature in any of His teachings.

> *As Jesus was saying these things, a woman in the crowd called out, "Blessed is the mother who gave you birth and nursed you." He replied, "**Blessed rather are those who hear the Word of God and obey it.**"* (Luke 11:27–28)

> "***Who are my mother and my brothers?"*** *he asked. Then he looked at those seated in a circle around him and said, "**Here are my mother and my brothers! Whoever does God's will is my brother and sister and mother.**"* (Mark 6:31–35)

In teaching about the resurrection, Jesus corrected the error of the Sadducees and revealed that, ***"At the resurrection people will neither marry nor be given in marriage; they will be like the angels in heaven"*** (Matt 22:30). As with marriage, it is likely so too with motherhood in being a relationship that exists only here on earth. There is no "motherhood of believers with Mary as mother over them," as Liguori and others have taught from beyond scripture. To those who have been saved into the kingdom, God is always

Father—and we are His adopted children as the result of our saving belief in Christ Jesus.

In scripture, God has made it clear that ***all*** we need, including the *mothering* some seek, is to be found in Him:

> *For this is what the Lord says:*
> *I will extend peace to her* (Jerusalem) *like a river,*
> *and the wealth of nations like a flooding stream;*
> *you will nurse and be carried on her arm*
> *and dandled on her knees.*
> *As a mother comforts her child,*
> *so will I comfort you; and you will be comforted over Jerusalem.* (Isa 66:12–13)

In speaking to the unbelieving in Jerusalem, Jesus echoed the above with these words:

> ***Jerusalem, Jerusalem, you who kill the prophets and stone those sent to you, how often I have longed to gather your children together, as a hen gathers her chicks under her wings, and you were not willing.*** (Matt 23:37; Luke 13:34)

Jesus uses the picture of mother hen to show us the love of God is so complete as to even cover any maternal love we may desire.

The love of God is all-encompassing, and there is no greater love than that which is of God—and all the words of man who elevate the love of a mother over the love of God will fall to the ground.

> *God is love. Whoever lives in love lives in God, and God in them.* (1 John 4:16)

God Himself contrasts the love of a mother to the love of God:

> *Can a mother forget the baby at her breast*

and have no compassion on the child she has borne?
Though she may forget, I will not forget you. (Isa 49:15)

Exiles and Orphans

Our alleged need for and dependence on Mary as "our mother" is further emphasized in Liguori's writings where attempts are made to paint a picture of believers being exiles of God and orphaned without Him.

> *The glorious St. Bonaventure, in order to revive in the hearts of sinners confidence in the protection of Mary, represents to us the sea in a tempest, in which sinners who have fallen from the bark of divine grace, tossed about by remorse of conscience, and by the fear of divine justice, without light and without a guide, have almost lost the breath of hope, and are nearly sinking in despair.* (Liguori 131)

A believer has to ask, "Why does this St. Bonaventure present a picture of a sea in tempest, sinners in fear of divine justice, without light and without a guide, and then point them to Mary as their hope?" The true believer has placed his trust in Jesus who has covered over all his sin and who will not fail him. Further, the Father has sent His Spirit to be the believer's guide and His word to be his light. The sinner who has turned to Jesus does *not* live in a sea of tempest.

Instead of turning the eyes of believers to look to God, our only hope, St. Bonaventure and Liguori turn the eyes of these to Mary after painting a false picture of abandonment. The freedom and grace given the believer, for which Jesus paid the price with His life, is simply ignored.

> *We poor children of the unhappy Eve, guilty before God of her sin, and condemned to the same punishment, go wandering through this valley of tears, exiles from our country, weeping and afflicted by innumerable pains of body and soul! But blessed is he who in the midst of so many miseries turns to the consoler of the world, to the refuge of the unhappy, to the great mother of God, and devoutly invokes her and supplicates her!* (Liguori 142)

Which believer, redeemed by the blood of Christ, born of and walking with the Spirit of God, would write that we remain "*guiltybefore God and condemned to the same punishment*"?

> *Whoever believes in the Son has eternal life, but whoever rejects the Son will not see life, for God's wrath remains on them.* (John 3:36)

> ***Very truly I tell you, whoever hears my word and believes him who sent me has eternal life and will not be judged but has crossed over from death to life.*** (John 5:24)

> *Blessed are those whose transgressions are forgiven, whose sins are covered. Blessed is the one whose sin the Lord will never count against them.* (Rom 4:7–8)

> *Since we have now been justified by his blood, how much more shall we be saved from God's wrath through him! For if, while we were God's enemies, we were reconciled to him through the death of his Son, how much more, having been reconciled, shall we be saved through his life!* (Rom 5:9–10)

There are numerous other verses—all of which form part of the "good news" so that no one who is born again of the Spirit looks back and says that he remains under the judgment of God and in need of ***another*** savior to whom he turns to find refuge. The "*consoler of the world*" in scripture is not Mary; it is the Holy Spirit, who is many times referred to as "*The Comforter.*"[9]

> *Many authors assert, that before she died, by a divine miracle, the apostles and also some of the disciples came from the different places where they were dispersed, and all assembled in the apartmentof Mary, and that when she saw all these her dear children united together in her presence, she thus addressed them: My dear children, for love of you, and to help you, my Son left me on this earth. But now the holy faith is spread throughout the world, already the fruit of the divine seed is grown up; hence my divine Son, seeing that my assistance was no longer needed upon the earth, and compassionating me for the pain of separation, has graciously heard my desire to depart from this life, and go to see him in glory. If I leave you, my heart does not leave you; I will carry with me the great love I bear you, and it shall always remain with me. I am going to paradise to pray for you.*
>
> *At these sad tidings, who can realize how great were the tears and lamentations of these holy disciples, knowing that they were shortly to be separated from their mother? Then, they all in tears exclaimed, then, oh Mary, thou wilt leave us! It is true that this earth is not a worthy and fit place*

[9] John 14:16; 14:26; 15:26; 16:7 NIV.

for thee, and that we are not worthy to enjoy the society of a mother of God; but remember that thou art our mother; thou hast until now enlightened us in our doubts, consoled our sorrows, strengthened us in persecutions, and how canst thou now abandon us, leaving us alone without thy comfort in the midst of so many enemies and so many conflicts? We have already lost on earth Jesus, our master and our Father, who has ascended into heaven; we have since been consoled by thee, our mother; and now how canst thou leave us orphans, without father or mother? Oh remain with us, oh our Lady! or take us with thee.

Thus writes St. John Damascene. "No, my children (thus sweetly the loving queen began to speak) this is not according to the will of God; content yourselves to do what lie has appointed for you and for me. To you it yet remains to labor on the earth for the glory of your Redeemer, and to perfect your eternal crown. I do not leave you to abandon you, but to help you more by my intercession with God in heaven. Be satisfied. I commend to you the holy Church; I commend to you the souls redeemed by my Son; let this be my last farewell, and the only remembrance that I leave you. If you love me, labor for souls, and for the glory of my Son; for we shall one day meet again in paradise, never more to separate throughout eternity." (Liguori 486–487)

In summary, the "authors" assert the following:

1. By a divine miracle, the apostles and some disciples assembled together at Mary's apartment.

2. She then gave a speech in which she said that she was left on earth to help them, but as the faith was now spreading and "*the fruit of the divine seed is grown up*," her presence was no longer required.
3. The followers lamented that they had lost Jesus and had since been consoled by Mary as mother and were now in danger of losing her—to be left as "*orphans, without father or mother*."
4. Mary then told them to be content with their task of labor. She said, "*I do not leave you to abandon you, but to help you more by my intercession with God in heaven.*" She commended to them the holy Church and the redeemed souls.

A Spirit-led believer will immediately recognize that nowhere in the above "dialogues" between Mary and the disciples is there any mention of the Holy Spirit whose presence created and empowered the church. This is the same Spirit who filled every one of the believers, including Mary, at Pentecost and every new believer since. It is He who was left on earth to help them (us). It is He who came to guide, enlighten, and console them in place of Jesus after He left to be with the Father so that they were not left as orphans as Jesus had promised.

Instead, the teaching of these "authors" is that Mary was the presence left by Jesus with no place for the Holy Spirit. The teachings of these "authors" then are deceiving and do not convey truth as the dialogues would not have been as they reported—if, indeed, they existed at all—for none of the apostles would have considered himself an orphan and without help.

Finally, these believers *were* the church and the redeemed. There was no other church to whom Mary could have commended to them.

The following is a *"Meditation . . . on the Feast of the Assumption of Mary into Heaven."*

> *Oh holy mother, thou hast already left the earth; do not forget us, miserable pilgrims, who remain in this valley of tears struggling against so many enemies, who desire to see us lost in hell. Ah, by the merits of thy precious death, obtain for us detachment from earthly things, pardon of our sins, love to God, and holy perseverance; and, when the hour of our death shall arrive, assist us from heaven with thy prayers, and obtain for us to come and kiss thy feet in paradise.* (Liguori 755–756)

Believers have not been left as *miserable pilgrims* on earth.

The Holy Spirit raised Christ up from the dead, raised and empowered the church at Pentecost, and remains with us to the end of time—perhaps except when we ignore Him and turn our eyes to *another* for the very things that He is here to give us. There are no "*merits of (her) precious death*" that can be used to obtain for us the many things Liguori claims. With the Holy Spirit, we are the redeemed and mighty if we walk in His ways, and we have been given all we need. As Jesus said to Paul, "***My grace is sufficient***" (2 Cor 12:9).

How abundant that grace is to us when we recognize and live in its fullness. It is the very "fullness of life" that Jesus spoke of (John 10:10).

Mary Was Born without Original Sin

Original sin is that which all humankind inherited from Adam and

Eve. Scripture teaches that all their descendants are born with the sin, which is what separates us from God. It is because we cannot redeem ourselves from both the sin and the curse of the sin that God sent His only begotten Son to pay the price for our sin.

Liguori compiled a list of reasons as to why Mary was said to have been born without original sin. These foundations fall into the following categories:

- it was meet and fitting that God did so
- the nobility of birth
- Jesus was separate from Sin
- the consensus of the Church

Meet and Fitting

The "it was meet" and "fitting" arguments are based on beliefs that God could have done so—and, hence, it *must* have been so. Being neither omniscient nor omnipresent, we are never qualified to make these arguments since we never have all the facts (past, present, and future) at hand, the wisdom or the grace to be able to make proper judgments on anything—much less what God could or should do.

In all the following passages, where the "meet and fitting" arguments have been used, they have been highlighted for easy identification. For someone to say that God *should* have done something is for them to have elevated themselves to God-likeness.

> *In the first place, it was fitting that the eternal Father should create Mary free from the original stain, because she was his daughter, and his first-born daughter, as she herself attests: "I came out of the mouth of the Most High, the first-born before all creatures."* (Liguori 337–338)

The verse quoted from Ecclesiasticus 24:5 (see appendix 3: "The Apocrypha") clearly states that the subject is wisdom.

Verse 6: "*I made that in the heavens there should rise light that never faileth, and as a cloud I covered all the earth.*"

Verse 14: "*From the beginning, and before the world, was I created, and unto the world to come I shall not cease to be, and in the holy dwelling place I have ministered before him.*"[10]

Since Mary was not the firstborn of all creation, did not call forth light in heaven, and did not exist before the world, Liguori's premise is without merit.

> *Moreover, it was meet that the eternal Father should create her in his grace, since he destined her for the restorer of the lost world, and mediatrix of peace between man and God.* (Liguori 338)

> *For there is one God and one mediator between God and mankind, the man Christ Jesus, who gave himself as a ransom for all people. This has now been witnessed to at the proper time. And for this purpose I was appointed a herald and an apostle—I am telling the truth, I am not lying—and a true and faithful teacher of the Gentiles.* (1 Tim 2:5–7)

> *Besides, it was fitting that God should preserve her from original sin, since he destined her to bruise the head of the infernal serpent, who, by seducing our first parents, brought death upon all men, as our Lord predicted: "I will put enmities between thee and the woman, and thy seed and her seed; she shall crush*

[10] Ecclesiasticus: The Book of Sirach.

> *thy head." Now, if Mary was to be the strong woman brought into the world to crush Lucifer, surely it was not fitting that she should first be conquered by Lucifer, and made his slave, but rather that she should be free from every stain, and from all subjection to the enemy.* (Liguori 340)

The argument fails because Genesis speaks of Jesus—and not Mary—who will crush the head of Satan:

> *And I will put enmity between you and the woman, and between your offspring and hers; he will crush your head, and you will strike his heel.* (Gen 1:15)

The version that renders the "she" and "her heel" is from Jerome's Latin Vulgate Bible, which was written in the fourth century AD. The earlier Greek Septuagint, which was compiled around the second century BC, renders "he and his," which the apostles—and perhaps Mary herself—would have been familiar with. As with all messianic prophecies, scripture foretold of a *Son* of David who would accomplish our salvation and to rule—a Man and not a woman.

> *But it was especially fitting that the eternal Father should preserve his daughter from the sins of Adam, because he destined her for the mother of his only begotten Son. Thou wast preordained in the mind of God, before every creature, to bring forth God himself made man. If for no other reason, then, at least for the honor of his Son, who was God, the Father would create her pure from every stain.* (Liguori 341)

Liguori's argument here is that it was *meet* that God chose a sinless vessel into which His sinless Son should be made incarnate. However, Mary was a *type* of the post-Pentecost Spirit-filled Christian. She carried the Word made flesh in her just as the Spirit-filled believer at and after Pentecost carries God in Spirit in them. No one would claim that it is especially fitting that the Spirit-filled believer should have been and therefore must have been preserved from the sins of Adam in order to carry the Holy Spirit:

> *All have sinned and fall short of the glory of God, and all are justified freely by his grace through the redemption that came by Christ Jesus.* (Rom 3:23–24)
>
> *[*Jesus*] gave himself as a ransom for all people.* (1 Tim 2:5–6)

These scriptures were written by St. Paul, who would have known Mary, and he would have known to not to have written "*all*" if she was indeed known to have been sinless.

Nobility of Birth

> *It is acknowledged to be the greatest glory of sons to be born of noble parents. The glory of children are their fathers: "Gloria filiorum, patres eorum." So that in the world the imputation of small fortune and little science is more endurable than that of low birth; for the poor man may become rich by industry, the ignorant learned by study, but he who is of low birth can hardly become noble; and if ever this occurs, the old and original reproach is liable always to be revived. How can we then believe that- God, when he was able to give his Son a noble mother, by preserving her from sin, would have consented that he should be born of a mother defiled with sin, and permit Lucifer to reproach him with the opprobrium of being born of a mother who once was his slave and an enemy of*

> *God! No, the Lord has not permitted this, but he has well provided for the honor of his Son, by ordaining that his mother should always be immaculate, that she might be a fit mother for such a Son.* (Liguori 342–343)

Few today might subscribe to this notion that those of low birth can hardly become noble. This is not a teaching from scripture; it is the product of a class-based world that is opposed to the will of God:

> *There is neither Jew nor Gentile, neither slave nor free, nor is there male and female, for you are all one in Christ Jesus. If you belong to Christ, then you are Abraham's seed, and heirs according to the promise.* (Gal 3:28–29)

Scripture does not indicate that Mary was born immaculate. The chapter continues with much what God *could have* done and so *must have done* in relation to coming "*into the world immaculate.*" Jesus did not say such a thing:

> ***I tell you, among those born of women there is no one greater than John; yet the one who is least in the kingdom of God is greater than he.*** (Luke 7:28)

No one claims that John the Baptist was born free of Adam's sin, yet Jesus said that John was the greatest born thus far. This means that—even with Adam's sin—John was still greater than Mary, who Liguori said was born free of sin.

> **Second Point**. *In the second place, it was befitting the Son that Mary, as his mother, should be preserved from sin. It is not permitted to other children to select a mother according to their good pleasure; but if this were ever granted to anyone,*

> *who would choose a slave for his mother when he might have a queen? who a peasant, when he might have a noble? who an enemy of God, when he might have a friend of God? If, then, the Son of God alone could select a mother according to his pleasure, it must be considered as certain that he would choose one befitting a God. Thus St. Bernard expresses it: The Creator of men to be born of man must choose such a mother for himself as he knew to be most fit.* (Liguori 345–346)

Once again, Liguori turned to what he considered "fitting" for what God should have done. Yet, God chose humble rather than kingly beginnings for His life on earth. It was for the Father to choose who the earthly mother would be but not perhaps according to the criteria St. Bernard thought "*fit.*" For God's ways are not man's ways, and deciding that God must have done according to man's ideas of ideal puts God on man's level:

> *And as it was, indeed, fitting that a most pure God should have a mother pure from all sin, such was she created, as St. Bernardine of Sienna says, in these words: The third kind of sanctification is that which is called maternal, and this removes every stain of original sin. This was in the blessed Virgin. God, indeed, created her, by the nobility of her nature as well as by the perfection of grace, such as it was be fitting that his mother should be.* (Liguori 346)

The concept of "maternal sanctification" is not one that comes from scripture; it comes from the mind of man. Again, Liguori appealed to what he determined was fit for God to do.

Jesus Was Separate from Sin

> *And here the words of the apostle may be applied: "For it was fitting that we should have such a high priest, holy, innocent, undefiled, separated from sinners," (Heb 7:26) &c [etc.]. Here a learned author remarks, that according to St. Paul, it was meet that our Redeemer should not only be separated from sin, but also from sinners, as St. Thomas explains it: It was meet that he who came to take away sins, should be separate from sinners as far as concerns the sin of which Adam was guilty. But how could it be said of Jesus Christ that he was separate from sinners if his mother was a sinner?* (Liguori 346–347)

The St. Thomas written of here is not the apostle Thomas; it was possibly Thomas Aquinas (1225–1274). Jesus was separate from sinners in that He was not a sinner. This does not mean that *He kept Himself separate from sinners*. Jesus said, "***I have not come to call the righteous but sinners to repentance***" (Luke 5:32).[11] For Jesus to have been born without the stain of original sin did not require that His mother to have been free of such sin since the seed planted in Mary by the Holy Spirit could have been complete in Itself.

The dogma of the Immaculate Conception of Mary (i.e. Mary born without sin) was created to show Mary was free from original sin, but it does provide the solution for Jesus not inheriting Adam's sin through Mary. This is because Mary's mother would also have had to have been immaculately conceived and her mother before her—all the way back to Eve.

> *The Holy Spirit says, that the honor of the Father is the glory of the Son, and the dishonor of the Father is the shame of the Son. And St. Augustine*

[11] See also Paul's comment in 1 Cor 5:9–11 about being apart from the sinful.

> *says, that Jesus preserved the body of Mary from being corrupted after death, since it would have dishonored him if corruption had destroyed that virginal flesh from which he had clothed himself. Corruption is the reproach of the human condition, from which the nature of Mary was exempted, in order that Jesus might be exempt from it, for the flesh of Jesus is the flesh of Mary. Now, if it were a dishonor for Jesus Christ to be born of a mother whose body was subject to the corruption of the flesh, how much greater would be the shame had he been born of a mother whose soul was corrupted by sin!* (Liguori 348)

The verse attributed to the Holy Spirit is from Ecclesiasticus (see appendix 3: "The Apocrypha"), which writing isn't attributed to the Holy Spirit. Further, a fuller reading of the verse and those that precede and follow it renders:

> *The father's blessing establisheth the houses of the children: but the mother's curse rooteth up the foundation. Glory not in the dishonour of thy father: for his shame is no glory to thee. For the glory of a man is from the honour of his father, and a father without honour is the disgrace of the son. Son, support the old age of thy father, and grieve him not in his life.*

These verses do not speak of heavenly things but earthly. The remainder of Liguori's argument is based on the dogma of the Assumption, and one dogma cannot be used to support another. Instead, any appeal must be made from scripture.

Consensus of the Church

The final arguments documented by Liguori appear below:

> *But there are two arguments which conclusively prove the truth of this opinion. The first is the universal consent of the faithful on this point. Father Egidius, of the Presentation, asserts that all the religious orders follow the same opinion: and although in the order of St. Dominic, says a modern author, there are ninety-two writers who are of the contrary opinion, yet one hundred and thirty-six are of ours.* (Liguori 364–365)

The first of the two "final and conclusive" arguments then is that all the faithful believe it, and by this, he states that the religious orders in Catholicism are of this opinion. The above writing does not sound like there even was consensus in the numbers quoted.

Richard P. McBrien, in his *Catholicism, Volume Two,* said of the dogma of Immaculate Conception:

> *The former was described as a "pious doctrine" by the Council of Basel in its thirty-sixth session (1439), but by that time the council was no longer in communion with the pope and, therefore, its decrees were not regarded as binding. Ten years later, however, all members of the University of Paris were required to take an oath to defend it, and other universities followed suit. In 1476 the feast of the Immaculate Conception was approved by Pope Sixtus IV (d. 1484), and the Council of Trent in the next century explicitly excluded Mary from its decree on the universality of Original Sin (Decree on Original Sin, Session V, 1546). In 1661 Pope Alexander VII*

> *(d. 1667) forbade any attacks on the doctrine, so that even the Dominicans, who had originally opposed it, began to change sides, taking pains to establish that perhaps St. Thomas had not really been opposed to it in the first place.*[12]

The religious orders followed this "opinion" because they were forced to in the days when disagreeing with the pope had dire consequences.

> *But what should especially persuade us; that our pious opinion is conformable to the common opinion of Catholics, is the declaration of Pope Alexander VII., in the celebrated bull, "Sollicitudo omnium ecclesiarum," issued in the year 1661, namely: "This devotion and worship to the mother of God again increased and was propagated, … so that the universities having embraced this opinion (that is, the pious one), almost all Catholics embrace it." … The learned Petavius rests his proof of the immaculate conception mainly upon this argument of the common consent of the faithful.* (Liguori 365)

Liguori's argument was that if the *common believers* believed it, then it must be true. This is a poor argument given that the common believers did not have access to scripture until around the time of the Reformation. There was no Bible available to the common folk in their vernacular until the likes of Tyndale and others translated it—for which "crime," a number of them were burned at the stake.

Since the ecclesiastical authorities prevented the common folk from having access to scripture, what the common folk believed did not line up with scripture. Instead, they were told from the pulpits

[12] *Catholicism, Volume Two,* by Richard P. McBrien, Google Books, 879.

and in the hymns what and why to believe as described in this section. What the clergy heard from the common folk was only a reflection of what they had taught them in the first place—beliefs far removed from scripture.

> *By another reason, still stronger than the first, we are assured of the truth of the fact, that the Virgin is exempt from the original stain, namely, the festival instituted by the universal Church in honor of her immaculate Conception. And with regard to this I see, on the one hand, that the Church celebrates the first moment when her soul was created and infused into the body, as Alexander VII. declares in the bull above quoted, in which it is expressed that the Church prescribes the same veneration for the conception of Mary, as the pious opinion concedes to her, which holds her to be conceived without original sin.* (Liguori 366)

His final argument is that the church has determined that it is so—and only because the masses believe it so. The second argument then reverts to the first as its "proof."

Whether or not Mary was conceived without original sin, however, is of less consequence than the fact that, having established such a belief, she became elevated to heights of the divine in the minds of the believers. Along with it came all the prayers, songs, and every other praise that rightly belonged only to the Divine—God Himself.

Further material on this topic can be found in Appendix 4: "Additional Material for Mary Was Born without Original Sin."

Mary Understood the Plan of God as to Why Jesus Was Here

Liguori and those he quoted in his work made the case that Mary fully understood the plan of God as to the mission of Jesus on Earth. They even went so far as to assert that she offered up Jesus at the cross to God and would have sacrificed Him herself if His enemies had not done so. A straightforward reading of the scriptures does not lead one to agree, and in Mark's Gospel, she appears to not only not understand what Jesus is doing but even tried to stop Him at one stage.

Liguori firstly built his case for her understanding as starting from a supernatural grace given at the time of her conception in the womb of her mother (the *Immaculate Conception*):

> ***First Point***. *Mary offered herself to God promptly. From the first moment when this heavenly infant was sanctified in the womb of her mother (which was at the first moment of her immaculate conception), she received the perfect use of reason, that she might from thenceforth begin to merit, as the Doctors universally agree.* (Liguori 394)

Given that there is no other source for such teachings than apocryphal texts such as the *Protoevangelium of James* (see appendix 3: "The Apocrypha"), the good "*Doctors universally agree*" on something based on material that even their pope (Pope Innocent I in AD 405) and church councils condemned as being non-scriptural and hence unreliable. Liguori then followed this with a number of "it was meet" arguments as to the grace given to Mary and that Mary must have had all graces for Jesus to then have had them. Supernatural grace, however, is not something transferred from parent to children; it is given by the Holy Spirit to those who seek God and yearn to both obey and receive.

> ***Point Second.*** *The enlightened infant well knew that God does not accept a divided heart, but wishes it entirely consecrated to his love, according to the precept he has given: "Thou shalt love the Lord thy God with thy whole heart." Hence, from the first moment of her existence, she began to love God with all her strength, and gave herself wholly to him.* (Liguori 399)

There is nothing in scripture to say that Mary understood God's wishes or plan. Liguori again based any discussion on the *Protoevangelium of James*. He and others then elaborated and added more to the apocryphal Gospel without any scriptural basis; instead, they used what they *chose* to believe, including "revelations" to St. Bridget and others. These write of her life of being brought up at the temple, her temperament, her habits, practices, manner of speech, and even daily timetable there without there being any evidence in scripture. Rightly does scripture warn us to not go beyond the written Word.

The Gospel of Mark on the other hand points to Mary not knowing Jesus's mission:

> *Then Jesus entered a house, and again a crowd gathered, so that he and his disciples were not even able to eat. When his family heard about this, they went to take charge of him, for they said, "He is out of his mind."* (Mark 6:20–21)

> *Then Jesus's mother and brothers arrived. Standing outside, they sent someone in to call him. A crowd was sitting around him, and they told him, "Your mother and brothers are outside looking for you."*
>
> ***"Who are my mother and my brothers?"*** *he asked.*

> *Then he looked at those seated in a circle around him and said, "**Here are my mother and my brothers! Whoever does God's will is my brother and sister and mother.**"* (Mark 6:31–35)

In the above passage, the family of Jesus went to try to stop Him from doing what He was doing for they believed He was "out of His mind." The family then appears, and it is made clear that these were His mother and brothers. If Mary knew His divine plan, she would likely have dissuaded the brothers from going to stop Him instead of following them in their endeavor.

> *Jesus left there and went to his hometown, accompanied by his disciples. When the Sabbath came, he began to teach in the synagogue, and many who heard him were amazed.*
>
> *"Where did this man get these things?" they asked. "What's this wisdom that has been given him? What are these remarkable miracles he is performing? Isn't this the carpenter? Isn't this Mary's son and the brother of James, Joseph, a Judas and Simon? Aren't his sisters here with us?" And they took offense at him.*
>
> *Jesus said to them, "**A prophet is not without honor except in his own town, among his relatives and in his own home.**" He could not do any miracles there, except lay his hands on a few sick people and heal them. He was amazed at their lack of faith.* (Mark 6:1–5)

Mark's Gospel continues with a different episode where the people of His hometown did not believe in Him or His authority. Jesus then makes it clear that it was not just the townsfolk; it was the very relatives in His own home.

> *The blessed Amadeus says, that in the heart of Mary two kinds of love to her Jesus were united: the supernatural love with which she loved him as her God, and the natural love with which she loved him as her son; so that, of these two loves, one only was formed, but a love so immense that William of Paris even said, that the blessed Virgin loved Jesus to such a degree that a pure creature could not love him more.* (Liguori 529)

Scripture does not tell us that Mary fully understood that her Son was God Incarnate, and so the belief here that she loved Him as God is not based on scripture but on the Protoevangelium of James. William of Paris lived in the twelfth century. The blessed Amadeus would have been one of two people referred to by that name, and both of whom lived in the fifteenth century. All these lived long after Mary.

> *For St. Simeon in the temple, after having received the divine child in his arms, predicted to her that this child was to be the mark for all the opposition and persecution of men; "Set for a sign which shall be contradicted" and that therefore the sword of sorrow should pierce her soul: "And thy own soul a sword shall pierce."*
>
> *The holy Virgin herself said to St. Matilda, that at the announcement of St. Simeon all her joy was changed into sorrow. For, as it was revealed to St. Theresa, the blessed mother, although she knew before this that the life of her Son would be sacrificed for the salvation of the world, yet she then learned more particularly and distinctly the sufferings and cruel death that awaited her poor Son. She knew that he would be contradicted in all things.* (Liguori 538)

Scripture does not tell us that Mary "*knew before this that the life of her Son would be sacrificed for the salvation of the world*." In Mark's Gospel, it appears that she did not understand His mission as she was with His brothers when they thought He was mad. So the idea that she knew comes from these "revelations," which are not tested as to their source (i.e. whether they are from God). At the temple, Luke simply writes that having heard the prophecies of the devout and righteous Simeon, Mary and Joseph "marveled" at what was spoken.

The belief that Mary understood the plan of God resulted in two consequences that Liguori then wrote much about:

- Mary suffered immeasurably all her life as a result of knowing what would happen to Jesus
- Mary offered up Jesus and would have sacrificed Him herself if necessary.

These related but separate beliefs are examined in the next two chapters.

The Immeasurable Suffering of Mary

This chapter is about the belief that Mary in her lifetime suffered immeasurably as a result of her knowledge that her Son, Jesus, was going to suffer exceedingly and give up His life at the cross.

Apart from non-scriptural written sources, some of the beliefs about Mary apparently had their beginnings in the cloistered monasteries where monks practiced contemplation. While monasteries produced some benefits, including the preservation of scripture and the production of some significant Church leaders, monastic life was not what Jesus or the apostles put forward as the life that believers were to live when He said, "***Go into all the world and preach the Gospel to all creation***" (Mark 16:15). The following is one of many examples in Liguori's work that tell of the product of such monastic contemplation:

> *Abraham suffered great affliction during the three days he passed with his beloved Isaac, after he knew that he was to lose him. Oh God! not for three days, but for thirty-three years, Mary had to endure a like sorrow. Like, do I say? A sorrow as much greater as the Son of Mary was more lovely than the son of Abraham. The blessed Virgin herself revealed to St. Bridget, that while she lived on the earth there was not an hour when this grief did not pierce her soul: As often, she continued, as I looked upon my Son, as often as I wrapped him in his swaddling clothes, as often as I saw his hands and his feet, so often was my soul overwhelmed as it were with a fresh sorrow, because I considered how he would be crucified. Rupert the Abbot, contemplating Mary, while she was suckling her Son, imagines her addressing him in these words: A bundle of myrrh is my beloved to me, he shall abide between my breasts. Ah, my Son, I clasp the (sic) in my arms, because thou art so dear to me; but the dearer thou art to me, the more thou dost become to me a bundle of myrrh and of sorrow, when I think of thy sufferings.* (Liguori 541)

As shown before, scripture does not say that Mary understood the destiny of her Child. One has to ask, "Why did Rupert contemplate Mary suckling her Son?" Liguori then reiterated Rupert's (eleventh-to-twelfth-century AD) contemplation as though it were revelation when it was neither the dreams nor visions spoken of in scripture.

> *Ah, there has never been in the world, says St. Lawrence Justinian, a son more worthy of love than Jesus, nor a mother who loved her son more than Mary; if, then,*

> *there has never been in the world a love like the love of Mary, how can there be a grief like the grief of Mary? Therefore, St. Ildephonsus did not hesitate to affirm, that it was little to say that the sufferings of the Virgin exceeded all the torments of the martyrs, even were they united together... But St. Bonaventura, addressing the blessed Virgin, says: Oh Lady, why hast thou wished to go and sacrifice thyself also on Calvary? Was not a crucified God sufficient to redeem us, that thou his mother wouldst be crucified also? Indeed, the death of Jesus was more than enough to save the world, and also an infinity of worlds; but this good mother wished, for the love she bore us, likewise to aid the cause of our salvation with the merits of the sorrows which she offered for us on Calvary. And, therefore, says the blessed Albertus Magnus, as we are indebted to Jesus for what he suffered for love of us, we are also to Mary for the martyrdom which she, in the death of her Son, voluntarily suffered for our salvation.* (Liguori 530–532)

None of what was written has its source in scripture.

> *IN this valley of tears, every man is born to weep, and every one must suffer those afflictions that daily befall him. But how much more miserable would life be, if everyone knew also the future evils which are to afflict him! Too unhappy would he be, says Seneca, whose fate was such. The Lord exercises his compassion towards us, namely, that he does not make known to us the crosses that await us; that if we are to suffer them, at least we may suffer them only once. But he did not exercise this compassion with Mary, who, because God wished her to be the queen of dolors* (i.e. sufferings or sorrows), *and in all things like his Son, and to see always before her eyes,*

> *and to suffer continually all the sorrows that awaited her; and those were the sufferings of the passion and death of her beloved Jesus.* (Liguori 537–538)

The belief that Mary knew the "*afflictions that (would) daily befall*" her was not from scripture but from "revelations" that others would receive. However, God does not reveal Himself in scripture to be He who would wish anyone to be a "queen of dolors"—"*to see always before her eyes, and to suffer continually all the sorrows that awaited her; and those were the sufferings of the passion and death of her beloved Jesus.*"

When we read about Jesus in the Gospels, we do not get a picture that He would always see before His eyes and to suffer continually all the sorrow that would befall Him. We do not read in scripture a continual torment of soul—neither in Jesus nor in Mary ("in all thing like his Son"), yet this is exactly what Liguori and others propose.

The God described by Liguori and others is a very different God from He who is revealed in scripture. Our revealed God is He who, beyond taking our death, also took our afflictions, infirmities, shame, and guilt upon Himself and bore them to the cross to redeem humankind who had turned against Him even to the point of crucifying Him.

Jesus willingly came to die so the sin of man could be put on Him and the debt of sin, which is death, paid for. The reason He suffered as He did was so that, by His stripes, our sicknesses and infirmities are taken away. There was no purpose for Mary, His mother, to suffer or be made a "queen of dolors." This teaching is not from scripture.

God does not take delight in the suffering and death of fools or the wicked,[13] much less the suffering of those in whom His heart delights.

---

[13] Ezek 18:23; 33:11.

Apart from the contemplation of monks, other sources of ideas that would become beliefs were the "revelations" given to individuals. One such revelation was that received by St. Bridget:

> *Father Engelgrave writes, that it was revealed to the same St. Bridget, that the afflicted mother, knowing all that her Son would have to suffer, suckling him, thought of the gall and vinegar; when she swathed him, of the cords with which he was to be bound; when she bore him in her arms, she thought of him being nailed to the cross; and when he slept, she thought of his death. As often as she put on him his clothes, she reflected that they would one day be torn from him, that he might be crucified; and when she beheld his sacred hands and feet, and thought of the nails that were to pierce them, as Mary said to St. Bridget: "My eyes filled with tears, and my heart was tortured with grief."* (Liguori 542)

> *But if Jesus advanced in the esteem and love of others, how much more did he advance in Mary's love! But oh God, as love increased in her, the more increased in her the grief of having to lose him by a death so cruel. And the nearer the time of the passion of her Son approached, with so much greater pain did that sword of sorrow, predicted by St. Simeon, pierce the heart of the mother; precisely this the angel revealed to St. Bridget, saying: "That sword of sorrow was every hour drawing nearer to the Virgin as the time for the passion of her Son drew nearer."* (Liguori 543)

Revelations such as these will be examined separately. For the most part, if not entirely, the revelations and visions of Mary were always accepted on face value and tested to verify that they may have happened but ***not*** for whether they were of God and of His divine will.

> *As the stag, wounded by an arrow, carries the pain with him wherever he goes, because he carries with him the arrow that has wounded him; thus the divine mother, after the prophecy of St. Simeon, as we saw in our consideration of the first grief, always carried her sorrow with her by the continual remembrance of the passion of her Son. Ailgrin, explaining this passage of the Canticles, "The hairs of thy head as the purple of the king bound in the channel," says: These hairs of Mary were her continual thoughts of the passion of Jesus, which kept always before her eyes the blood which was one day to flow from his wounds.* (Liguori 545)

Song of Solomon (the *Canticles* as quoted) chapter 7 starts with the following passage:

> *How beautiful your sandaled feet,*
> *O prince's daughter!*
> *Your graceful legs are like jewels,*
> *the work of an artist's hands.*

It goes to praise each attribute of the maiden, and verse 5 adds the following passage:

> *Your head crowns you like Mount Carmel.*
> *Your hair is like royal tapestry;*
> *the king is held captive by its tresses.*

There is nothing in these verses to suggest that either Mary or her sufferings are alluded to in this or any of chapters in the Songs of Solomon.

> *Secondly. Mary well understood the cause and end of the other dolors, namely, the redemption of the world, the divine will; but in this she did not know the cause of the absence of her Son. The sorrowful mother was grieved to find Jesus withdrawn from her, for her humility, says Lanspergius, made her consider herself unworthy to remain with him any longer, and attend upon him on earth, and have the care of such a treasure.* (Liguori 555)

This claim that Mary understood the destiny and purpose of Jesus coming to the world is made many times throughout Liguori's very wordy book, but there is nothing in scripture to back this claim. Liguori did not give any indication how Lanspergius, a monk, could have known what Mary thought fifteen centuries earlier. Whatever the source, it was not of scripture.

> *If a mother should see a servant redeemed by a beloved son of hers, by twenty years of imprisonment and suffering, for this reason alone how much would she esteem that servant! Mary well knows that her Son came upon earth solely to save us miserable sinners, as he himself declared: "I have come to save what was lost."* (Liguori 56)

One only has to remember that God sent His Son, Jesus, to die for all humankind, which includes Mary, to realize that the above analogy is meaningless because Mary was not outside those sent to be saved. She herself was very much the "servant" (for she called herself that[14]) her Son was sent to save.

[14] Luke 1:38, 48.

Mary Offered Up Jesus for Crucifixion

Taking the line even further from Mary understanding the plan of God in Jesus and then her immeasurable suffering, Liguori and the writers he quoted then claimed that she offered up the life of Jesus.

> *In three ways, says Father Suarez, the divine mother shared in the work of our salvation: first, by having merited, that is, with merit of congruity, the Incarnation of the Word. Secondly, by praying much for us while she lived on the earth. Thirdly, by willingly sacrificing to God the life of her Son for our salvation; and therefore the Lord has justly ordained that as Mary has, with so much love for man, aided in the salvation of all, and thereby so greatly promoted the glory of God, all through her intercession shall obtain salvation.* (Liguori 186)

Father Suarez's Three Ways

Firstly, Mary did cooperate with God to bear His Son, but to take it beyond what was God's grace that she was offered this role is to go beyond the written word. Secondly, there is no scriptural evidence that she prayed much for us while she lived on earth. The Gospel of Mark in chapter 3 appears to show that Mary did not understand His mission, which primarily was to save us.

> *Then Jesus entered a house, and again a crowd gathered, so that he and his disciples were not even able to eat. When his family heard about this, they went to take charge of him, for they said, "He is out of his mind."* (Mark 3:20–21)

Thirdly, the Gospels do not indicate that she "*willingly sacrificed to God, the life of her Son for our salvation.*" Indeed, as Mark's Spirit-led observations reveal, she did not appear to understand His mission. If Mary had indeed understood the mission of Jesus, she would have dissuaded the family from interfering with Him. Instead, she was there with them when they went to try to get him.

> *He* (God) *sent him therefore on the earth to become man, destined for him a mother, and chose the Virgin Mary; but as he did not wish his divine Word to become her Son before she accepted him by her express consent, so he did not wish that Jesus should sacrifice his life for the salvation of men without the concurrence of the consent of Mary, that together with the sacrifice of the life of the Son, the heart of the mother might be sacrificed also. St. Thomas teaches, that the relation of mother gives an especial right over her children; hence Jesus, being innocent in himself and not deserving any punishment for his own sins, it seemed fitting that he should not be destined to the cross as the victim for the sins of the world without the consent of his mother, by which she should voluntarily offer him to death.* (Liguori 459)

Scripture neither says that God revealed the divine purpose of His Son to Mary nor that He asked for "*the concurrence of the consent of Mary*" for His sacrifice. Nowhere in scripture is God shown to ask the consent of mothers for the missions He gave to their offspring. Liguori then, instead of quoting scripture to back up this proposition, tells us another of his "*it seemed fitting that*" God should have acted in such a way.

> *But although Mary, from the moment she was made mother of Jesus, gave her consent to his death, yet the Lord wished her, on this day, to make, in the temple, a solemn sacrifice of herself, by offering solemnly her Son, and sacrificing to the divine justice his precious life. Hence St. Epiphanius called her a priest: "Virginem appello velut sacerdotem." Now we begin to see how much this sacrifice cost her, and what heroic virtue she was obliged to practise when she had herself to sign the sentence of condemnation of her dear Jesus to death.* (Liguori 459–460)

There is likewise nothing in scripture to base the assumption that Mary "*from the moment she was made mother of Jesus, gave her consent to his death.*" Where Liguori could not find support in scripture, he quoted instead the words of man in Latin as though these have the weight of scripture.

> *She enters the temple, approaches the altar, and there, filled with modesty, humility, and devotion, she presents her Son to the Most High. At this moment St. Simeon, who had received the promise from God that he should not die before seeing the expected Messias, takes the divine child from the hands of the Virgin, and, enlightened by the Holy Spirit, announces to her how much sorrow this sacrifice must cause her, this sacrifice which she was about to make of her Son, with whom must her blessed soul also be sacrificed. Here St. Thomas of Villanova contemplates the holy old man, who, when he had come to announce the fatal prophecy to this poor mother, is agitated and silent. Then the saint considers Mary, who asks: Why, oh Simeon, in the time of so great consolation, are you thus disturbed? "Unde tanta turbatio?" To whom he*

> *answers: Oh, noble and holy Virgin, I wished not to announce to thee such bitter tidings, but since the Lord wishes it thus, for thy greater merit, hear what I say to thee. This infant who now causes thee, and with reason, so much joy, oh God, shall one day bring thee the most cruel suffering that any creature has ever experienced in the world; and this will be when thou shalt see him persecuted by men of every sort, and placed on earth as the mark of their sneers and derision, even until he is put to death before thy eyes. Know that after his death there will be many martyrs who, for love of this thy Son, will be tormented and slain; but if their martyrdom will be of the body, thy martyrdom, oh divine mother, will be of the heart.* (Liguori 460–461)

While Liguori and St. Thomas of Villanova (a fifteenth-century Spanish friar of the Order of St. Augustine who later became an archbishop) *claim* to know many things of this exchange between Mary and Simeon, scripture instead simply tells us the following:

> *Now there was a man in Jerusalem called Simeon, who was righteous and devout. He was waiting for the consolation of Israel, and the Holy Spirit was on him. It had been revealed to him by the Holy Spirit that he would not die before he had seen the Lord's Messiah. Moved by the Spirit, he went into the temple courts. When the parents brought in the child Jesus to do for him what the custom of the Law required, Simeon took him in his arms and praised God, saying:*
>
> *"Sovereign Lord, as you have promised,*
> *you may now dismissed your servant in peace.*
> *For my eyes have seen your salvation,*
> *which you have prepared in the sight of all nations:*

> *a light for revelation to the Gentiles,*
> *and the glory of your people Israel."*
> *The child's father and mother marveled at what was said about him. Then Simeon blessed them and said to Mary, his mother: "This child is destined to cause the falling and rising of many in Israel, and to be a sign that will be spoken against, so that the thoughts of many hearts will be revealed. And a sword will pierce your own soul too."* (Luke 2:25–35)

Scripture, unlike any other word, cannot be broken and rightly warns us to not go beyond the written word. It tells us the parents *marveled* at Simeon's words, which does not sound like the kind of response they would give if the contemplation of St. Thomas of Villanova was true.

> *As Jesus is called King of sorrows and King of martyrs, because he suffered in his life more than all the other martyrs, so is also Mary called, with reason, queen of the martyrs, having merited this title by suffering the greatest martyrdom that could be suffered, next to that of her Son. Hence she was justly named by Richard of St. Laurence the martyr of martyrs: "Martyr martyrum." And to her may be applied what Isaias said: He will crown thee with the crown of tribulation: "Coronans coronabit tetribulatione." For that suffering itself which exceeded the suffering of all the other martyrs united, was the crown by which she was shown to be the queen of martyrs ... Mary was a martyr, says St. Bernard, not by the sword of the executioner, but by the bitter sorrow of her heart. If her body was not wounded by the hand of the executioner, yet her blessed heart was pierced by grief at the passion of her Son; a grief sufficient to cause her not only one, but a thousand deaths. And*

> *from this we shall see that Mary was not only a true martyr, but that her martyrdom surpassed that of all the other martyrs, for it was a longer martyrdom, and, if I may thus express it, all her life was a long death.* (Liguori 516–517)

Firstly, a search of the book of Isaiah shows there are verses with the word "crown." None of these refer to any crown of tribulation; instead, they are crowns of glory, joy, beauty, and splendor. The remaining two verses add neither positive nor negative connotations to the crown.

Secondly, Liguori and others base much of their teaching of Mary's suffering exceeding "*the suffering of all the other martyrs united*" on the belief that Mary understood her Son's mission even before He was born. This is not born out in scripture. Further, Jesus told His disciples before His crucifixion that they would grieve, but that their grief would in a short time turn to joy that no one could take away from them (John 16:19–22). This joy would apply to Mary as well. To say then that all Mary's life was a long death is plainly untrue.

> *My life was wholly passed in grief and tears; for my grief, which was compassion for my beloved Son, never departed from before my eyes, seeing, as I did, continually the sufferings and death that he was one day to endure. The divine mother herself revealed to St. Bridget, that even after the death—and ascension of her Son into heaven, the memory of his passion, whether she ate or worked, was deeply impressed and ever recent in her tender heart. Taulerus therefore says, that Mary passed her whole life in perpetual sorrow; for her heart was always occupied with thoughts of sadness and of suffering.* (Liguori 520)

There is no precedent in scripture of anyone whom God showed from beginning to end what their suffering was to be, and nothing in scripture backs up the revelations of St. Bridget. In scripture, those whose lives are blessed have at time undergone suffering, but anyone whose life is suffering from beginning to end can hardly be called "*blessed*," yet scripture calls her blessed. This is just one indicator that revelations such as those to St. Bridget should be called into question and not taken at face value. Scripture tells us to "test all things" (1 Thess 5:21) and judge a tree by its fruit (Matt 7:15–23). The fruit of these *revelations* and beliefs will be examined in a later chapter.

If it was not enough that writers claimed that Mary suffered all her life knowing the fate to befall Jesus, these same writers went even further to claim that she would have sacrificed Him at the cross for the salvation of the world.

> *But no, Mary would not utter even one word in favor of her Son, to prevent his death, upon which our salvation depended; finally, she gave him to us again at the foot of the cross, in those three hours when she was witnessing his death; because then, at every moment, she was offering up for us his life, with the deepest grief, and the greatest love for us, at the cost of great trouble and suffering, and with such firmness, that if executioners had been wanting, as St. Anselm and St. Antoninus tell us, she herself would have crucified him in obedience to the will of the Father, who had decreed he should die for our salvation.*
>
> *And if Abraham showed a similar fortitude in consenting to sacrifice his son with his own hands, we must believe that Mary would certainly have done the same, with more resolution, as she was holier, and more obedient than Abraham.* (Liguori 55)

> *But above all, she showed her heroic obedience, when, in order to obey the divine will, she offered her Son to death with so much firmness that, as St. Ildephonsus says, she would have been ready to crucify him, if executioners had been wanting.* (Liguori 634–635)

The source of the above belief is shown to be yet another argument of what she "would have done" and not scripture. Scripture did not say that Mary was holier or more obedient than Abraham; it simply said that she was blessed to have been chosen by the Father.

> *But that we may better understand this last dolor, let us return to Calvary, again to look upon the afflicted mother, who still holds, clasped in her arms, the lifeless body of her Son … Thus St. Bernard speaks in her name: Oh truly begotten of God, thou wast to me a father, a son, a spouse; thou wast my life! Now I am deprived of my father, my spouse, and my Son, for with my Son whom I have lost, I lose all things.* (Liguori 586)

From Liguori's writings, it would seem that St. Bernard was often in the practice of putting words into the mouths of others, which others then took to be akin to gospel truth. Liguori himself taught that Mary understood the plan of God all through her life. If that were so, she would not have said "*for with my Son whom I have lost, I lose all things*" for—understanding the plan of God—she would have known that He was not to be lost for long.

Beyond the death of Jesus, Liguori then claimed that Mary accompanied the soul of Jesus to heaven:

> *A devout author says, that when our Redeemer was dead, the heart of the great mother was first engaged in accompanying the most holy soul of the Son, and*

> *presenting it to the eternal father. I present thee, oh my God, Mary must then have said, the immaculate soul of thy and my Son, which has been obedient to thee even unto death: receive it, then, in thy arms.* (Liguori 578)

Mary of the Gospels was as human as we are. She was not a heavenly spirit who could follow the soul of her Son and present it to God in heaven. In the Gospel of John, after Jesus had arisen on the third day after He had died, He met Mary Magdalene. When she went toward Him, He said, ***"Do not hold on to me, for I have not yet ascended to the Father. Go instead to my brothers and tell them, 'I am ascending to my Father and your Father, to my God and your God'"*** (John 20:17).

So, Jesus did not rise to heaven as soon as He died as the *devout author* claimed, and Mary could not have presented His soul to the Father. The apostle Peter wrote that upon His death, Jesus was made alive in the Spirit and went to make proclamation to the imprisoned spirits in Hades (1 Pet 3:18–20).

Scripture tells us of when Jesus subsequently entered heaven alone to present His sacrifice and both comparing and contrasting this to the high priest entering the holy of holies:

> *It was necessary, then, for the copies of the heavenly things to be purified with these sacrifices, but the heavenly things themselves with better sacrifices than these. For Christ did not enter a sanctuary made with human hands that was only a copy of the true one he entered heaven itself, now to appear for us in God's presence.* (Heb 9:23–24)

Liguori's claim is contrary to scripture, and this is one of many instances compiled in *The Glories* of writers putting words into the mouth of Mary and then treating it as truth.

> *Thy justice is now satisfied, thy will accomplished; behold, the great sacrifice to thy eternal glory is consummated. And then turning to the lifeless members of her Jesus: Oh wounds, she said, oh loving wounds, I adore you, I rejoice with you, since through you salvation has been given to the world. You shall remain open in the body of my Son, to be the refuge of those who will have recourse to you. Oh how many, through you, shall receive the pardon of their sins, and then through you shall be inflamed to love the Sovereign Good!* (Liguori 578–579)

Scripture does not indicate that Mary understood the sacrifice of her Son, but it seems to indicate the opposite. Liguori and others would have one believe that even the young Mary (before the angelic visitation) understood the plan of God thoroughly—by diligent study of scripture and special enlightenment of the Holy Spirit. If this were true, the apostles should not have been surprised by the death or resurrection of Jesus since Mary would have told them what to expect, but this is clearly not the case.

> *She could in no way show greater charity than by offering her Son for our salvation; so that St. Bonaventure says: Mary so loved the world as to give her only-begotten Son.* (Liguori 612–613)

It was not enough that scripture tells us that <u>*God*</u> loved the world so much that He gave His only Son (John 3:16). Instead, St. Bonaventure tried to compare or compete Mary against God—but using those same words and applying them to Mary. This reveals how far these teachers, including Liguori, had strayed from scriptural truth. Rather than searching scripture and seeking the help of the Holy Spirit to enlighten them on scripture, these writers apparently turned to contemplation and the words of others—even when they contradicted scripture.

In summary, the arguments against Mary having understood the plan of God as to why Jesus was on earth and that she offered up Jesus for crucifixion are:

- These teachings have no basis in scripture and are not even hinted at.
- God does not delight in the suffering of people—even the wicked—how much less those in whom He delights,
- If Mary was indeed blessed, this does not equate to the lifetime of torment that God was said to have chosen for her.

Special Powers

One reason that many follow Mary is because of the special powers ascribed to her. None of these powers appear in scripture; instead, they derive from the teachings of men and the "revelations" of spirits. Many follow her on account that they or their loved ones might be "saved" by her in one or more ways as the beliefs teach.

The claims compiled by Liguori are numerous, and summarized below are a few categories of these powers with a sampling of his writings for each of the claims.

Protection against Demons and Enemies

> *It is well known that the palm is the emblem of victory, and for this reason our queen has been placed on a high throne in the sight of all potentates, as a palm, the sign of certain victory, which all can promise themselves who have recourse to her. "I was exalted like a palm-tree in Cades." That is, for a defence as blessed Albertus Magnus says: Oh, my children, Mary seems to say to us with these*

> *words, when the enemy assails you, lift your eyes to me, behold me and. take courage; for in me, who defends you, you will behold, at the same time, your victory. So that recourse to Mary is the most certain means of overcoming all the assaults of hell; for she, as St. Bernardine of Sienna says, is queen over hell, and ruler of the spirits of evil, for she controls and conquers them.* (Liguori 157–158)

How Albertus Magnus derived so much from this short verse ("palm-tree in Cades"), taken from Ecclesiasticus 24:18, is not explained when the chapter clearly states that it refers to "wisdom" and not to a created being. If, as St. Bernadine says, Mary is "*queen over hell, ruler of the spirits of evil for she controls and conquers them,*" then she would not also be the woman crowned with twelve stars in Revelation who has to hide and flee from the dragon, which is also claimed by Liguori in other sections of his book.

> *We should understand that the protection of Mary, as St. Germanus says, is greater and more powerful than we can comprehend. And how is it that the same Lord, who was under the old law so severe in punishing, exercises so great mercy towards the greatest sinners? Thus asks the author del Pomerio; and he also answers: He does all this for the love and merits of Mary. Oh, how long since would the world have been destroyed, says St. Fulgeiitius, if Mary had not preserved it by her intercession!* (Liguori 299)

The preservation of the world is unlikely to have been due to Mary since God had already purposed from the very beginning that He would send His Son to die for all, including Mary herself. When speaking to the serpent, He promised the Savior who "*will crush your head, and you will strike his heel*" (Gen 3:15).

Prophesized long before the birth of Mary, this was followed by many prophecies regarding the Lamb and Messiah who would take away the sins of the world right from the time of Abraham. All these point to the saving plan of God for humankind from the earliest of times—long before any prospect of her intercession.

Rendering Sweet Death with the Devil and Demons in Fear of Her

In *The Glories*, Liguori wrote an entire section entitled "*Mary Renders Death Sweet to Her Servants*" (101–114). In it, he wrote of many clergy who, dedicated to Mary, were assailed by demonic forces at the time of their deaths and how turning to Mary caused these forces to flee.

> *"Oh, how the devils in hell," says St. Bonaventure, "tremble at Mary and her great name!" The saint compares these enemies to those of whom Job makes mention and says: "He diggeth through houses in the dark ... If the morning suddenly appear, it is to them the shadow of death." Thieves enter houses in the dark to rob them, but when the dawn comes they flee, as if the image of death appeared to them. In the same manner, as St. Bonaventure expresses it, the demons enter into the soul in times of darkness, that is, when the soul is obscured by ignorance; they dig through the houses of our minds in the darkness of ignorance; but then, he adds, as soon as the grace and the mercy of Mary enter the soul, this beautiful aurora dissipates the darkness, and the infernal enemies flee as at the approach of death. Oh, blessed is he who always, in his conflicts with hell, invokes the beautiful name of Mary!*

> *In confirmation of this it was revealed to St. Bridget that God has given Mary such power over all evil spirits, that whenever they assail any of her servants who implore her aid, at the slightest sign from her they flee far away in terror, preferring that their pains should be redoubled rather than that Mary should domineer over them in this manner.* (Liguori 159–160)

This teaching is similar to all the other teachings about Mary that say we should turn to her. Scripture, on the other hand, clearly tells us that Jesus overcame the world as well as the principalities and powers of darkness. Having ascended to heaven, God gave His Holy Spirit, who is greater than he who is in the world[15] (i.e. the devil), to indwell believers, and so we need not fear any evil spirit. Every teaching of Jesus about His kingdom, of which every spirit-filled believer is a part, is one of being given all the powers and grace to overcome with the victory He won at the cross. By living Spirit-led lives, we are the salt of the earth, the lights on the hills and His body, to do His will here on earth.

> *On the other hand, the devils, as Thomas Kempis affirms, are in such fear of the queen of heaven that at the sound of her great name they flee from him who pronounces it as from burning fire. The Virgin herself revealed to St. Bridget that there is no sinner living so cold in divine love, that if he invokes her holy name, with the resolution to amend, the devil will not instantly depart from him. And she at another time assured her of this, telling her that all the demons so greatly venerate and fear her name, that when they hear it pronounced they immediately release the soul which they held in their chains.* (Liguori 311)

[15] 1 John 4:4.

Jesus demonstrated to His disciples how to cast out demons. He also taught that some demons are only cast out with much prayer and fasting. Never did He teach that the name of His earthly mother was to be used to cast out demons. Even after He left, the book of Acts records how demons were cast out, and never is it recorded that the name of Mary was used nor did the apostles teach such a thing.

> *"As the vine I have brought forth a pleasant odor." "I, like the vine, as the Holy Spirit puts it in her mouth to say, have given fruit of sweet odor." "It is said," adds St. Bernard, on this passage, "that every venomous reptile shuns the flowering vines." As from vines all poisonous serpents flee, thus the demons flee from those fortunate souls in whom they perceive the odor of devotion to Mary.* (Liguori 158)

The verse comes from Ecclesiasticus 24:23 (see appendix 3: "The Apocrypha"), which plainly says it refers to wisdom and not Mary. To then have claimed that "*the Holy Spirit puts it in her mouth to say*" is inaccurate to say the least. The assertion that "*demons <u>flee</u> from those fortunate souls in whom they perceive the odor of devotion to Mary*" contradicts what Liguori and others teach that demons gather at the imminent passing of a soul as is shown below.

> *When any one is at the point of death, his house is filled with demons, who unite to accomplish his ruin.* (Liguori 102)

Strikingly, every example he wrote of demons filling houses featured servants loyal to Mary. If demons fled at the mere perception of the odor of devotion to Mary, how could it be then that they appeared to congregate at the deaths of those who were devoted to her?

> *Blessed is he, says St. Bonaventure, who love thy sweet name, oh mother of God. Thy name is so glorious and*

> *admirable, that those who remember to invoke it at the moment of death, do not then fear all the assaults of the enemy.* (Liguori 316)

The only name one should remember is that of Jesus—whether in life or in death. This is amply demonstrated in scripture:

- *And this is his command: to believe in the name of his Son, Jesus Christ, and to love one another as he commanded us.* (1 John 3:23)
- *And everyone who calls on the name of the Lord will be saved.* (Joel 2:32 and Acts 2:21)
- *Salvation is found in no one else, for there is no other name under heaven given to mankind by which we must be saved.* (Acts 4:12)
- ***And I will do whatever you ask in my name, so that the Father may be glorified in the Son. You may ask me for anything in my name, and I will do it.*** (John 14:13–14)

That this is the only name to turn to was amply demonstrated at the cross when the thief was promised that he would be with Jesus that very day because he had turned to Him in faith.

The spirit who appears as Mary instead teaches that we are to ignore the words of Jesus and the Holy Spirit <u>at the very time</u> when we should call on Him; instead, we should turn our eyes to her. It is not the assaults of the enemy that we should fear but instead that we might foolishly turn our eyes away from Jesus at such a time. We can only hold one thought in our minds at any one time; the very thing we need at such a time is the very thing we are asked to turn away from. This chapter of Liguori's book is filled with examples of devout men who "died with the name of Mary on his lips" because they heeded such teachings.

Liguori provided a number of examples of clergy who at the point of death apparently had been much assailed by demons, some even having been seen. These clergy then turn to Mary as their hope and then *"an army of devils was seen taking flight in despair, crying: 'Alas! we have no power, for she who is without stain defends him'"* (Liguori 104).

Given that these demons take their lead from one (the devil) whom Jesus called the "***liar and the father of lies***" (John 8:44), should it not be obvious that the appearances of these legions were to have believers place their trust not in God but in Mary, especially at their dying? After all, how often do we otherwise see demons—whose primary weapons are both fear and deception? These were the very weapons shown to have been wielded by the enemy when these followers of Mary lay on their deathbeds.

Instead of turning to Jesus, they turn to Mary as Liguori would have his readers do.

Despoiling Hell and Saving Souls

This belief is that Mary has power over hell to redeem souls from its clutches and destiny.

> *Richard of St. Laurence gives a beautiful explanation to these words of Proverbs: "The hearts of her husband trusteth in her, and he shall have no need of spoils." Richard says: The heart of her husband, that is, Christ, trusts in her, and he shall have no need of spoils, for she will endow him with the spoils which she has taken from the devil. If God has intrusted the heart of Jesus, as a Lapide expresses it, to the care of Mary, that she may procure for it the love of men; and thus he will not be in need of spoils, that is, of the conquest of souls, for she will enrich him with those souls of which she despoils hell, and which she has rescued from the demons from her powerful aid.* (Liguori 157)

If Mary is the mother, then she is not the spouse and not the subject of Proverbs 31:11, which clearly states that it simply describes a wife of noble character. In Matthew 12: 24–29, Jesus speaks of *Himself* when He describes how He binds Satan and plunders his house. He does not say that Mary is the one who despoils hell.

> ***If Satan drives out Satan, he is divided against himself. How then can his kingdom stand? And if I drive out demons by Beelzebul, by whom do your people drive them out? So then, they will be your judges. But if it is by the Spirit of God that I drive out demons, then the kingdom of God has come upon you. Or again, how can anyone enter a strong man's house and carry off his possessions unless he first ties up the strong man? Then he can plunder his house.*** (Matt 12:26–29)

If there are any spoils from victory, then it is *we* who are the spoils when Christ conquered over sin and death and redeemed us by the finished work of His blood. In each succeeding generation, it is the Gospel going out by the Spirit that saves by the word that goes out and does not return void.[16]

> *When you were dead in your sins and in the uncircumcision of your flesh, God made you alive with Christ. He forgave us all our sins, having cancelled the charge of our legal indebtedness, which stood against us and condemned us; he has taken it away, nailing it to the cross. And having disarmed the powers and authorities, he made a public spectacle of them, triumphing over them by the cross*. (Col 2:13–15)

[16] Isa 55:11.

As a result of the finished work of Christ Jesus, Spirit-filled and led believers have been given authority to reach those who are lost and who still belong to the world where Satan blinds them to the truth. All who come to the saving faith in Christ are not immediately taken to glory because they have the mandate and privilege to remain on earth as the hands and feet of Jesus to carry out the will of God. This mandate is to ***"Therefore go and make disciples of all nations, baptizing them in the name of the Father and of the Son and of the Holy Spirit, and teaching them to obey everything I have commanded you"*** (Matt 28:19–20).

Jesus taught that the church would be built and that ***"gates of hell shall not prevail against it'*** (Matt 16:18), meaning that it is the body of Spirit-filled and led believers who would despoil hell and snatch out the souls still living on earth who would otherwise be destined to an eternity there. This is *our mandate* as believers, not Mary's, who having been saved, went to be with the Lord in the first century.

> *Thou, oh great mother, art the beginning, the middle, and the end of our felicity, says St. Methodius. The beginning, because Mary obtains for us the pardon of our sins; the middle, because she obtains for us perseverance in divine grace; the end, because she finally obtains for us paradise. By thee, St. Bernard continues, heaven has been opened by thee hell has been emptied by thee paradise has been restored by thee, in a word, eternal life has been given to many sinners who have merited eternal death.* (Liguori 284)

"Felicity" is a source of happiness, bliss, and good fortune. One has to ask why any believer would make the statement that Mary is the beginning, middle, and end of our happiness, which mimics the statement that Christ is the beginning and end, the "Alpha and Omega," of all things (Rev 1:8; 21:6, 22:13).

It is Jesus who was the propitiation of our sin. It is the Holy Spirit who both guides and enables us to live the commands of our God to love Him and to love our neighbor as ourselves. It is the Holy Spirit who is the seal of our salvation. We have an "open heaven" only because Christ both made the way and is the Way. Hell, on the other hand, has not been emptied nor will it be. None of the words written in this extract from Liguori's book line up with scripture, but they are opposed to it.

Pardon from Judgment and Mercy for Sinners

> *Look upon us, then, we will conclude with the words of Euthymius, look upon us, then, with thine eyes of compassion, oh our most merciful mother, for we are thy servants, and in thee we have placed all our hope.* (Liguori 123)

These few words reveal so much. Firstly, they tell us why the followers look to her—for their hope is for mercy from or through her. Mercy can only be sought from one who has the right to judge and dispense justice. This can only be God and, more precisely, Jesus Christ to whom has been given the right to judge.[17] For He alone who took our punishment for sin can and will both dispense judgment and mercy.

Secondly, faithful believers are servants only to one who is lord over them—again God alone.

Finally, in God alone can we rightly place all our hope who is always faithful to meet us in our need.

> *Hence the Abbot Adam Persenius, considering the great compassion that Mary has for all, full of confidence says to her: Oh mother of mercy, thy power is as great as thy pity. As thou art powerful to obtain, so thou art merciful to pardon.*

[17] John 5:22.

> *And when, he adds, dost thou ever fail to have compassion on sinners, being the mother of mercy; or art thou unable to help them, being mother of omnipotence? Ah, thou canst as readily obtain whatever thou wilt, as thou canst listen to our woes.* (Liguori 249–250)

While the faith these have in Mary is admirable, it is nonetheless misplaced since such faith ought to be placed in God alone whom we know has the great compassion, willingness, mercy, and power to help us. All scripture testifies that He wants to help us and wants us to come to Him for that help.

> *I hope, oh Lady, through the merits of Jesus Christ and thy intercession to secure my salvation. In these I trust; and so entirely do I trust in thee, that if my eternal salvation were in my own hands, I would wish to place it in thine; for in thy mercy and protection I would trust far more than in my own works.* (Liguori 126)

The writer seemingly has not the faith nor the understanding that the atoning sacrifice of Jesus has covered his sin. Instead, he says he chooses to place his faith in Mary's hands above his *own* works. Neither by works[18] nor by any other means is our salvation secure except through faith in the finished work of Christ[19] and walking by His Spirit[20] who is the seal of our salvation.

> *St. Antoninus asserts the same thing in nearly the same words: As it is impossible that those from whom*

---

[18] John 6:27–29, 47; Acts 16:29–34; Rom 1:16–17; 3:20–21; 9:30–33; 11:3–7; Eph 2:4–5, 8–9.

[19] John 3:36; 5:24; 6:47; 7:37–39; Acts 2:21; 16:29–34; Rom 3:24–25, 27–31; 5:1–2; 10:13; Gal 2:15–16, 21; Phil 3:7–9.

[20] John 3:3–5; 16:8–11, 13; Rom 8:1–4, 9–14, 27; 2 Cor 1:21–22; 4:14; Gal 5:16–18; 2 Thess 2:13; Phil 1:6; 1 Pet 1:2.

> *Mary turns away her eyes of compassion should be saved, so it must be that all those towards whom she turns her eyes, and for whom she intercedes, shall be saved and glorified.* (Liguori 255)

Mary is not omnipresent or omniscient. To say then that those from whom her "eyes of compassion" are turned away should not be saved is unfounded. This is a teaching not of God nor revealed by His Holy Spirit:

> *Every one invoking this mother of mercy may then say, with St. Augustine: "Remember, oh most compassionate Lady! that since the beginning of the world there never has been any one abandoned by thee. Therefore pardon me if I say that I do not wish to be the first sinner who has sought thy aid in vain."* (Liguori 151)

That St. Augustine should have said this is remarkable as it implies that Mary has been around since the beginning of the world, which clearly is not the case.

> *She is the mother of mercy, and there would be no occasion for mercy, if there were no wretchedness to be relieved. Therefore, as a good mother does not hesitate to apply a remedy to her child, however loathsome its disease, although the cure may be troublesome and disgusting; thus our good mother does not abandon us, when we recur to her however great may be the filth of our sins, which she comes to cure. This sentiment is taken from Richard of St. Laurence.* (Liguori 146)

Our "mother" cannot cure us of any sin. Neither did Jesus come to "cure" us since sin cannot be "cured" when the only punishment and remedy for sin is death:

> *For the wages of sin is death, but the gift of God is eternal life in Christ Jesus our Lord.* (Rom 6:23)

> *In fact, the law requires that nearly everything be cleansed with blood, and without the shedding of blood there is no forgiveness.* (Heb 9:22)

> *God presented Christ as a sacrifice of atonement, through the shedding of his blood—to be received by faith.* (Rom 3:25)

Jesus came to take away our sins by taking our place in death, thus paying its price in full.

Having washed us of our sin, we need no further "*cure,*" and the Holy Spirit is with us not to cure us but to guide us so that we may no longer fall into sin but walk in the victory of Christ.

It is God, not a "mother of mercy," who does not abandon us.

> *The prophet Isaias predicted that by the great work of human redemption, a great throne of divine mercy would be prepared for us: "A throne shall be prepared in mercy." Who is this throne? St. Bonaventure answers: This throne is Mary, in whom all, both the just and sinners, find the consolations of mercy; and he afterwards adds: As the Lord is full of compassion, so also is our Lady; and as the Son, so the mother cannot withhold her mercy from those who ask it. (Liguori 248)*

Contrary to the interpretation of St. Bonaventure, scripture says:

> *In love a throne will be established; in faithfulness a man will sit on it—one from the house of David—one who in judging seeks justice and speeds the cause of righteousness.* (Isaiah 16:5)

This passage says "a man" from the house of David shall sit on the throne. It also says "one who in judging seeks justice," which clearly reveals that the one who sits on the throne is the one who is the judge. The One can only be Christ—our Judge and Advocate—and not Mary. She cannot be our judge.

> ***Moreover, the Father judges no one, but has entrusted all judgment to the Son, that all may honor the Son just as they honor the Father.*** (John 5:22–23)

It is our just judge, Christ Jesus, who dispenses both judgment and mercy.

> *If our sins ever throw us into despair, let us say with William of Paris: Oh Lady, do not bring forward my sins against me, for I shall bring forward thy mercy in opposition to them. And let it never be said that my sins can rival, in the judgment, thy mercy, which is more powerful to obtain my pardon, than my sins are to obtain my condemnation.* (Liguori 250)

The statement of William somewhat resembles the following verse from Romans:

> *The law was brought in so that the trespass might increase. But where sin increased, grace increased all the more, so that, just as sin reigned in death, so also grace might reign through righteousness to bring eternal life through Jesus Christ our Lord.* (Romans 5:20–21)

Where there was sin, all the more the grace of Jesus Christ (and not Mary) proved greater than the sin.

> *Not even those who deserve hell should despair of attaining the kingdom of the blessed, if they faithfully devote themselves to the service of this queen. Sinners, says St. Germanus, have sought to find God by thy means, oh Mary and have been saved!* (Liguori 281–282)

Liguori appears to believe that there are those who deserve hell and those who do not. Scripture tells us something else:

> *For all have sinned and fall short of the glory of God, and all are justified freely by his grace through the redemption that came by Christ Jesus. God presented Christ as a sacrifice of atonement, through the shedding of his blood—to be received by faith. He did this to demonstrate his righteousness, because in his forbearance he had left the sins committed beforehand unpunished—he did it to demonstrate his righteousness at the present time, so as to be just and the one who justifies those who have faith in Jesus.* (Rom 3:23–26)

Liguori and these writers teach a different Gospel that faithful devotion to "the service of this queen" will result in "attaining the kingdom of the blessed." If this were so, there would have been no need for Jesus to have endured the cross and death.

There is no means of finding God other than through Jesus who said, ***"I AM the way, the truth and the life. No one comes to the Father except through Me"*** (John 14:6).

There is much written by these authors about Mary's mercy, and those who wish to explore more can find material in Appendix 5: "Additional Material for Pardon from Judgment and Mercy for Sinners."

Power to Overcome Temptation and Sin

> *Especially is it everywhere known, and the servants of Mary daily experience, that her great name gives strength to overcome temptations against chastity. The same author* (Richard of St. Laurence), *remarking on the words of St. Luke: And the name of the Virgin was Mary: "Et nomen Virginis Maria," says, that these two names, of Mary and of Virgin, are united by the evangelist to show that the name of this most pure Virgin can never be separated from chastity.* (Liguori 313)

Jesus and His apostles never taught that different temptations require different sources of power in order to overcome them:

> *Therefore, since Christ suffered in his body, arm yourselves also with the same attitude, because whoever suffers in the body is done with sin. As a result, they do not live the rest of their earthly lives for evil human desires, but rather for the will of God. For you have spent enough time in the past doing what pagans choose to do—living in debauchery, lust, drunkenness, orgies, carousing and detestable idolatry.* (1 Pet 4:1–3)

Scripture tells each of us what we are to do instead:

> *Submit yourselves then to God, resist the devil and he will flee from you.* (Jas 4:7)

> *Because he* (Jesus) *himself suffered when he was tempted, he is able to help those who are being tempted.* (Heb 2:18)

> *No temptation has overtaken you except what is common to mankind. And God is faithful; he will*

> *not let you be tempted beyond what you can bear. But when you are tempted, he will also provide a way out so that you can endure it.* (1 Cor 10:13)

The Holy Spirit always provides a way if we are willing to trust and lean on Him as the apostles Paul, John and Peter write:

> *So I say, walk by the Spirit, and you will not gratify the desires of the flesh.* (Gal 5:16)

> *We know that anyone born of God does not continue to sin; the One who was born of God keeps them safe, and the evil one cannot harm them.* (1 John 5:18)

> *His divine power has given us <u>everything</u> we need for a godly life through our knowledge of him who called us by his own glory and goodness.* (2 Pet 1:3)

And having been tempted but if we still fail:

> *If we confess our sins, he is faithful and just and will forgive us our sins and purify us from all unrighteousness.* (1 John 1:9)

God has given us all we need to overcome sin, and He instructed us on how to deal with temptation and even our falls when we fail to heed the instruction. However, it seems that not all agree with God's righteous word:

> *St. Bonaventure said that the name of Mary cannot be invoked without profit to him who invokes it. But more than all, this name has the power to overcome the temptations of hell.* (Liguori 729)

Neither Jesus nor the apostles taught such a thing—that the name of Mary has the power to overcome temptations. In fact, all of scripture teaches us that God alone is the One who keeps us from all harm and ruin when we abide in Him as our Stronghold:

> *Everyone who calls on the name of the Lord will be saved.* (Joel 2:32; Acts 2:21; Rom 10:13)
> *Salvation is found in no one else, for there is <u>no other name</u> under heaven given to mankind by which we must be saved.* (Acts 4:12)

Salvation is not just the final destiny to which we go; it is a daily victory over sin, temptation, attacks of the enemy, and the obstacles and challenges we face in this life.

Liguori and others, on the other hand, teach a different gospel of salvation and living not by the Spirit and by the power of the name of Jesus but instead by Mary.

Able to Command God

> *St. Antoninus says that the prayer of Mary has the force of a command with Jesus Christ: "Oratio Virginis habet rationem imperil;" and hence he adds, that it is impossible for this mother to ask a favor of the Son that the Son will not grant her: "Impossibile est Deiparam non exaudiri." Therefore St. Bernard exhorts us to ask through Mary for every grace that we wish from God: "Quaerarnus gratiam, et per Mariam quseramus;" ... Oh great mother of God, pray to Jesus for me. Look upon the miseries of my soul, and have pity on me. Pray, and never cease to pray for me until thou seest me safe in paradise. Oh Mary, thou art my hope; do not abandon me. Holy*

> *mother of God, pray for us; "Sancta Dei genitrix, ora pro nobis."* (Liguori 729–730)

Regardless of whether these claims have any merit, approaching Mary for favors instead of God is trying to get around God. They are also prayers that are not of faith since, in essence, they distrust the mercy of God and raise Mary to a higher level of mercy and efficacy.

> *Without faith, it is impossible to please God, because anyone who comes to him must believe that he exists and that he rewards those who earnestly seek him.* (Heb 11:6)

Jesus opened for us the way to God by His sacrifice on the cross. Liguori and others teach instead that we should go to Mary because it is apparently a "better and more effective way."

> *Virgo potens: Virgin most powerful. And who among the saints is so powerful with God as his most holy mother? She obtains whatever she wishes, as St. Bernard has said: It is enough that thou dost wish, and all things are done: "Velis tu et omnia fient." St. Peter Damian even says that when Mary asks graces from God she does not pray, but in a certain manner commands ... Oh, Mary thou canst make me holy; in thee I trust.* (Liguori 735–736)

None of the apostles would have written either of the above statements about "commanding" and "*thou* (Mary) *can make me holy.*" Only the Holy Spirit can make one holy if one submits to, walks with, and allows the Spirit to do His molding and refining work in us.

> *God chose you as firstfruits to be saved through the sanctifying work of the Spirit and through belief in the truth.* (2 Thess 2:13)

> *Who have been chosen according to the foreknowledge of God the Father, through the sanctifying work of the Spirit, to be obedient to Jesus Christ and sprinkled with his blood.* (1 Pet 1:2)

Liguori's prayer instead is:

> *Oh mother of holy love, oh our life, our refuge, and our hope, thou knowest that thy Son Jesus Christ, not content with making himself our perpetual intercessor with the eternal Father, would have thee also engaged in obtaining for us, by thy prayers, the divine mercy. He has ordained that thy prayers should aid in our salvation, and has given such power to them that they obtain whatever they ask; I, a miserable sinner, turn to thee then, oh hope of the wretched.* (Liguori 126)

There is no testimony in scripture that Jesus has ordained such a thing. Scripture makes no such claim and does not label anyone redeemed of God, by the sacrifice of Jesus, a "miserable sinner."

Health and Healing

> *Salus infirmorum: Health of the weak. Mary is called by St. Simon Stock: The medicine of sinners: "Peccatorum medicina;" and by St. Ephrein, not only medicine, but health itself: Firm health for those who have recourse to her: "Salus firma recurrentium ad eam." For he who has recourse to Mary not only finds medicine, but he finds health, as she herself promises to him who seeks her: "He that shall find me shall find life, and shall have salvation from the Lord."* (Liguori 745–46)

It is not known where the idea that Mary dispenses health came from. However, the scripture attributed to Mary from Proverbs 8:35 is about *Wisdom*, not Mary, speaking these promises of life and salvation.

Throughout the Gospels, Jesus principally healed by praying and laying His hands on those who needed healing. He also spoke the word of healing as an active powerful command as when He called the dead to life.

> *At sunset, the people brought to Jesus all who had various kinds of sickness, and laying his hands on each one, he healed them*. (Luke 4:40)

> *Then he put his hands on her, and immediately she straightened up and praised God.* (Luke 13:13)

He then commanded that we do the same even as He commissioned the disciples just before His ascension:

> *He said to them,* ***"Go into all the world and preach the Gospel to all creation. Whoever believes and is baptized will be saved, but whoever does not believe will be condemned. And these signs will accompany those who believe: In my name they will drive out demons; they will speak in new tongues; they will pick up snakes with their hands; and when they drink deadly poison, it will not hurt them at all; they will place their hands on sick people, and they will get well."*** (Mark 16:15–18)

In obedience, the apostles performed miracles of healing by the laying of hands:

> *In a vision he has seen a man named Ananias come and place his hands on him to restore his sight.* (Acts 9:12)
>
> *Paul went in to see him and, after prayer, placed his hands on him and healed him.* (Acts 28:8)
>
> *Is anyone among you in trouble? Let them pray. Is anyone happy? Let them sing songs of praise. Is anyone among you sick? Let them call the elders of the church to pray over them and anoint them with oil in the name of the Lord.* (James 5:13–14)

The anointing with oil involved the use of hands.

The ministry of healing, as taught by Jesus, involved prayer to God and the laying of hands. This is very different from going to Mary and asking her for healing, and nowhere in scripture is it recorded that Mary healed anyone. We can either choose to listen to the clear instruction and mandate from Jesus or ignore it to find another way.

Consoling and Freeing Souls from Purgatory

Those who follow Mary closely devote much of their energies toward praying to her in the hope of obtaining her help with regard to purgatory. They have been led to believe that she has powers in the following areas:

- the power to free the souls already in purgatory—mostly their loved ones
- the power to help those in purgatory lessen their pain and to console them
- the power to help themselves avoid purgatory or at the very least to lessen their own time or punishment there

> *St. Bernardine of Sienna says, that in that prison of souls who are spouses of Jesus Christ, Mary has a certain dominion and plenitude of power to relieve them, as well as deliver them from their pains. And, in the first place, as to relieving them, the same saint, applying the words of Ecclesiaticus: I have walked in the waves of the sea: "In fluctibus maris ambulavi," adds, visiting and relieving the necessities and sufferings of my servants, who are my children.*
> *St. Bernardine says, that the pains of purgatory are called waves, because they are transitory, unlike the pains of hell, which never end: and they are called waves of the sea, because they are very bitter pains. The servants of Mary tormented by those pains are often visited and succored by her. See, then, how important it is, says Novarino, to be a servant of this good Lady; for she never forgets such when they are suffering in those flames. And although Mary succors all the souls in purgatory, yet she always obtains more indulgences and alleviations for those who have been especially devoted to her.* (Liguori 267–268)

The verse from Ecclesiasticus (see appendix 3: "The Apocrypha") was taken from chapter 24, which clearly states that the "I" it refers to is Wisdom and not to Mary.

Verse 1 reads: "*Wisdom shall praise her own self, and shall be honoured in God, and shall glory in the midst of her people.*" The other relevant verses read, "*Alone, I have made the circuit of the heavens and walked through the depths of the abyss. Over the waves of the sea and over the whole earth, and over every people and nation I have held sway.*"

The subject is Wisdom who speaks, and it says that Wisdom has alone walked through the heavens, the earth and seas, and the depths of the abyss. Instead of referring to Mary, the verse appears to echo Job:

> *He alone stretches out the heavens and treads on the waves of the sea.* (Job 9:8)

The *substitution* of God with Mary in the writings of Liguori and those he quoted will be explored in greater depth in a later chapter in part III of this book.

> *This divine mother, in her revelations to St. Bridget, said: "I am the mother of all the souls in purgatory; and all the sufferings which they merit for the sins committed in life are every hour, while they remain there, alleviated in some measure by my prayers."* (Liguori 268)

> *This kind mother sometimes condescends even to enter into that holy prison, to visit and console these her afflicted children. I have penetrated into the bottom of the deep: "Profundum abyssi penetravi," as we read in Ecclesiasticus; and St. Bonaventure, applying these words, adds: I have penetrated the depth of this abyss, that is, of purgatory, to relieve by my presence those holy souls.* (Liguori 268–269)

This verse from chapter 24 of Ecclesiasticus refers not to Mary but to Wisdom.

> *But not only does Mary console and succor her servants in purgatory; she also releases them from this prison, and delivers them by her intercession. From the day of her glorious assumption, in which that prison is said to have been emptied, as Gerson writes; and Novarino confirms this by saying, that many weighty authors relate that Mary, when about to ascend to paradise, asked this favor of her Son, that she might take with her all the souls that were*

> *then in purgatory; from that time, says Gerson, the blessed Virgin has possessed the privilege of freeing her servants from those pains. And this also is positively asserted by St. Bernardine, who says that the blessed Virgin has the power of delivering souls from purgatory by her prayers and the application of her merits, especially if they have been devoted to her.* (Liguori 270)

> *And Novarino says the same thing, believing that by the merits of Mary, not only the torments of these souls are assuaged, but also abridged, the time of their purgation being shortened by her intercession: and for this it is enough that she presents herself to pray for them.* (Liguori 270–271)

> *St. Peter Damian relates, that a certain lady, named Marozia, after death, appeared to her godmother, and told her that on the day of the Assumption of Mary she had been released by her from purgatory, with a multitude of souls exceeding in number the whole population of Rome. St. Denis the Carthusian relates, that on the festivals of the birth and resurrection of Jesus Christ, Mary descends into purgatory, accompanied by troops of angels, and releases many souls from their torments. And Novarino believes that the same thing happens on every solemn festival of the holy Virgin.* (Liguori 271)

These are examples of Liguori confirming the authenticity of one teaching by quoting others who agree with him. None of these learned teachers turn to scripture as the source of their teachings. On the other hand, we are warned in scripture to not listen to deceiving spirits.[21] It seems that the appearance of any spirit that attests to Mary is believed and never questioned.

> *Every one has heard of the promise made by Mary to Pope John, to whom she appeared, and ordered him to make known to all those who should wear the sacred scapular of Carmel, that on the Saturday after their death they should be released from purgatory. And this was proclaimed by the same pontiff, as Father Crasset relates, in a bull which he published. It was also confirmed by Alexander V., Clement VIL, Pius V., Gregory XIII. and Paul V., who, in 1612, in a bull said: "That Christians may piously believe that the blessed Virgin will aid by her continual intercession, by her merits and special protection, after death, and principally on Saturday, which is a day consecrated by the Church to the blessed Virgin, the souls of the members of the confraternity of holy Mary of Mount Carmel, who shall have departed this life in the state of grace, worn the scapular, observing chastity according to their state of life, recited the office of the Virgin, and if they have not been able to recite it, shall have observed the fasts of the Church, abstaining from flesh-meat on Wednesdays, except on Christmas-day."* (Liguori 271–272)

Those who teach about purgatory tell us that it is good for the souls to go there. That by being there, they are somehow purified. If that were true, then why should Mary offer the scapular as an early way out? What then of the purification? Why even go to purgatory if that is the case? And why should her "merits" be

[21] 1 Kgs 22:22–23; 2 Chr 18:21–22; 1 Tim 4:1; Rev 20:3,

used for such a purpose if it shortcuts the benefits of a stay at purgatory?

> *And in the solemn office of the feast of holy Mary of Mount Carmel, we read that it is piously believed, that the holy Virgin, with a mother's love consoles the members of the confraternity of Mount Carmel in purgatory, and by her intercession conducts them to their heavenly country.*
>
> *Why should we not also hope for the same graces and favors, if we are devoted to this good mother? And if with more special love we serve her, why cannot we hope to obtain the grace of going immediately after death to paradise, without entering into purgatory? as we read that the holy Virgin said to the blessed Godfrey, through brother Abondo, in these words: "Go and tell brother Godfrey to advance in virtue, for thus he will be a child of my Son, and mine also; and when his soul quits the body, I will not permit it to go to purgatory, but I will take it and present it to my Son.* (Liguori 272–273)

From this, it appears that the *real* reason for the belief in purgatory and the scapular is simply that we should turn to Mary for graces and favors and serve *her*.

And this is simply because she is seemingly <u>alone</u> in offering the release from purgatory since we hear nothing of God or Jesus securing the release of these "prisoners." These "revelations" have their end in turning our attention and prayers to Mary.

That her followers turn to her for all is evident in the following passage:

> *From thee, oh Lady, I await <u>all my blessings</u>. Thou must obtain the pardon of all my sins, thou must obtain for me perseverance, succor in death, deliverance*

> *from purgatory, in a word, thou must conduct me to paradise. All this thy lovers hope from thee, and they are not deceived.* (Liguori 275)

The apostle Paul and others believed and wrote that to be out of this body is to be with Christ—not in purgatory waiting for His mother to deliver them.

The book of Maccabees (see appendix 3: "The Apocrypha") alludes to purgatory, but this book was not part of the accepted Hebrew Bible and was included in the early Christian Bible only as supplemental historical text but not inspired scripture. Maccabees covers the revolt led by Judas Maccabeus against the Romans. It alludes to purgatory as the leader makes offerings to fallen soldiers. However, this book is part of the Apocrypha, and even biblical scripture makes mention of practices by the Jews (such as the building of high places and worship of Baal) that occurred but were never part of God's will or direction for His people.

It is beyond the scope of this book to adequately address the question of purgatory. The non-scriptural beliefs in Mary, however, which developed over time inevitably assigned to her powers over purgatory. Those powers, however, are only accessible to the follower of Mary if he or she persists in performing certain practices of devotion and worship toward her that only rightly should instead be given to God.

In contrast, God fully forgives all who accept and confess the substitutionary sacrifice of Jesus, repent of their sin, and develop in their relationship with God through the Holy Spirit. He does not mandate a set of must-do practices of devotion and worship.

Examples of practices of devotion to Mary include the following:

- *To celebrate, or cause to be celebrated, or at least to hear Mass in honor of the holy Virgin.*
- *To reverence the saints who are most closely united to Mary, as St. Joseph, St. Joachim, and St. Ann. The Virgin herself recommended to a nobleman the devotion to St. Ann her mother.*

- *To read every day some book which treats of the glories of Mary. To preach, or at least recommend to all, particularly to one's relatives, devotion to the divine mother.* (Liguori 670–671)

Approved examples for lessening the time in purgatory include the following:

- *To those who say: "Blessed be the holy and immaculate conception of the blessed Virgin Mary," an indulgence of one hundred years is granted; and when after the word "immaculate," the word "most pure" is added, according to Father Crasset, other indulgences are granted, applicable to the souls in purgatory.* (Liguori 672)
- *For the "Salve Regina," forty days.*
- *Litanies, two hundred days.*
- *To those who bow the head at the names of Jesus and of Mary, twenty days.*
- *To those who repeat five "Our Fathers" and "Hail Marys" in honor of the passion of Jesus and the dolors of Mary, ten thousand years.* (Liguori 671)

Why recite the Salve Regina and litanies if the five "Our Fathers" and "Hail Marys" will return a much better result? Liguori lists other indulgences:

- *To those who recite fifteen "Our Fathers" and "Hail Marys," for sinners, remission of the third part of their sins.*
- *Those who kneel before the most holy Sacrament gain two hundred days.*
- *Those who kiss the cross, one year and forty days.*
- *To those who kiss the regular scapular, five years.* (Liguori 672)

Laity who practice these acts are sometime excused as acting out of ignorance. However, Liguori demonstrated in his writings *why* they perform these acts—because they have been taught by their clergy to worship images, icons, and things made by human hands at churches dedicated to Mary:

> *But if we also desire the happy visits of this queen of heaven, it will greatly aid us if we often visit her before some image, or in some church dedicated to her.* (Liguori 453)

True scripture tells us that believers are the living stones of the temple of God dedicated to His will (1 Pet 2:5). In scripture, "church" always refers to those who belong to Christ and not buildings.

Once believers are given to turning to Mary for all their hopes and expectations, there isn't much of a way out of the devotions and other practices that have become part of their routine. To do so is to suffer the loss of all that was promised:

> *Thomas a Kempis, when a young man, was accustomed daily to have recourse to the Virgin with certain prayers; one day he omitted them, then he omitted them for some weeks, then he gave them up entirely. One night he saw Mary in a dream, who embraced his companions, but having come to him, said: "What do you expect, who have given up your devotions? Depart, for you are unworthy of my favors." Terrified by these words, Thomas awoke, and resumed his accustomed prayers. Richard therefore with reason says: He who is perseveringly devoted to Mary will be blessed with the hope, that all his desires may be gratified. But as no one can be secure of this perseverance, no one can be sure of salvation before his death.* (Liguori 655–645)

In contrast, God's love is unconditional. It is the love of the father who runs to meet and forgive his wayward son who is still a distance away and who has not had the chance to even deliver his prepared speech of repentance (Luke 15:11–32). This is the love of a God who would give up His only begotten Son to cover the punishment of the unworthy.

Some who choose to believe in purgatory use scripture where the criminal on one side of Jesus asks to be remembered by Jesus when He appears in His kingdom. It appears they do so believing that the criminal still has punishment to be meted out to him after this life. However, Jesus plainly says that the criminal would be with Him in paradise that very day. Paradise is hardly purgatory, and this shows that every sin is blotted out by the blood of the Lamb for those who believe and confess.

The belief in purgatory causes many to spend time praying for the release of souls of the dead from that domain:

- Devotional time to Mary that might otherwise be spent communicating with God and having His will done in the lives of those who pray.
- A focus on the dead and not on the living where the kingdom of God should be made to manifest. The harvest is ready, but instead of being in the fields, the workers are found at the cemetery—whether physical or in the mind.
- Meanwhile, the living continue to die in sin, and the kingdom is not advanced in the *only* arena where it can be advanced—among the living.

Extraordinary Miracles

Liguori included accounts of numerous unusual and extraordinary miracles to demonstrate the power of Mary. A few of the shorter stories will be examined here.

> *A certain nobleman who was despairing of his eternal salvation on account of his sins, was encouraged by a religious to have recourse to the most holy Virgin, by visiting her sacred image which was in a certain church. The nobleman went to the church, and on seeing the figure of Mary he felt himself, as it were, invited by her to cast himself at her feet and trust. He hastens to do so, kisses her feet, and Mary, from that statue, extended her hand for him to kiss, and on it he saw these words written: "I will deliver thee from them that afflict thee." As if she had said to him: My son, do not despair, for I will deliver thee from thy sins, and from the fears that oppress thee. It is related that on reading these sweet words, that sinner felt such sorrow for his sins, and conceived such a love for God, and for his sweet mother that he died there at the feet of Mary.* (Liguori 232–233)

How can this story be believed when the only one who could relate it, especially the sorrow and love he conceived for God as a result, is the very one who died and thus cannot vouch for its truthfulness? In any case, scripture warns us to never bow to any work of human hands whether representing things on earth or in heaven. It is also a different Gospel that says that anyone or anything but God can deliver one from their sins.

> *Pelbart, moreover, relates, that in his time, when the Emperor Sigismund was crossing the Alps with his army, a voice was heard, proceeding from a dead body, of which only the bones remained, asking for confession, and saying, that the mother of God, to whom he had been devoted whilst he was a soldier, had obtained for him that he should live in those*

> *bones until he had made his confession. Having confessed, he died.* (Liguori 262)

Scripture warns us not to listen to spirits. That this was most likely a deceiving spirit was not considered all because of the belief in the efficacy of Mary. The bones attest to the fact that the person had already long before died.

> *It is sufficient for us to mention the compassion which she showed to that bandit chief, who on account of this devotion, was permitted to remain alive, although his head had been cut off, and although he was under the displeasure of God, and was enabled to make his confession before dying. He afterwards declared that the holy virgin, for this fasting which he had offered her, had preserved him in life, and he then suddenly expired.* (Liguori 656)

This man was said to have been a bandit chief, yet he practiced this devotion of fasting, which likely meant he was very dedicated to Mary since fasting is something not taken lightly on account of the sacrifice it entails. It is interesting that he could have been so devoted while leading such an ungodly life. A Spirit-filled believer would live a life where God and His purposes come first and so would hardly make a career out of banditry. The result of this and the other stories is that people turn to Mary instead of to God for their needs.

Miracles are a sign of the manifestation of the supernatural. They are not necessarily signs of the presence of God or His will being done. Scripture records many signs having been done that were not of God. These include the signs conjured by the magicians of Egypt at the time of Moses, the storm at the lake that threatened to capsize the ship that the disciples were in, and the conjuring up of the prophet Elijah by the sorceress at the request of King Saul.

As believers, Christians are told to test the signs and their fruit to see what the sources of them are. On account of the belief in the efficacy of Mary, the mention of her name is often sufficient for many to neglect to do the testing we are commanded to do.

Merits of Mary

Within Liguori's *The Glories*, Mary has the powers she is claimed to have for three reasons:

- She was born with merits.
- She accumulated them on account of the works done in her life.
- She was given them when she was crowned queen of heaven.

This chapter will look briefly at the first two reason for Mary's claimed merits.

> *And at the same time she was the creature most full of love for God that until that time had appeared in this world; so that Mary, had she been born immediately after her most pure conception, would have come into the world more rich in merits, and more holy, than all the saints united.* (Liguori 383)

Holiness in scripture is being set aside for God and His purposes. As it is the lessening of things and attachments to the world, to say that it can then be quantified so that one could measure the holiness of one against the sum of the holiness of all others seems unconvincing. Scripture also does not teach of anyone's "merits" as counting for anything. St. Paul addressed this concept:

> *But whatever were gains to me I now consider loss for the sake of Christ. What is more, I consider everything*

> *a loss because of the surpassing worth of knowing Christ Jesus my Lord, for whose sake I have lost all things. I consider them garbage, that I may gain Christ and be found in him, not having a righteousness of my own that comes from the law, but that which is through faith in Christ—the righteousness that comes from God on the basis of faith.* (Phil 3:7–9)

Liguori on the other hand writes:

> *We should understand that the protection of Mary, as St. Germanus says, is greater and more powerful than we can comprehend. And how is it that the same Lord, who was under the old law so severe in punishing, exercises so great mercy towards the greatest sinners? Thus asks the author del Pomerio; and he also answers: He does all this for the love and merits of Mary. Oh, how long since would the world have been destroyed, says St. Fulgeiitius, if Mary had not preserved it by her intercession!* (Liguori 299)

It is unlikely due to Mary since God had already purposed from the very beginning that He would send His Son to die for all, including Mary herself. When speaking to the serpent in the Garden, He promised the Savior who "*will crush your head, and you will strike his heel*" (Gen 3:15). This was then followed all through the Old Testament by many prophecies regarding the Lamb of God—who is our salvation—long before Mary appeared.

Her merits are said to partly have been a consequence of her understanding the plan of God and participating in it even to the sacrificing her Son, as previously examined in the chapter "Mary Understood the Plan of God as to Why Jesus Was Here."

> *The divine mother then, on account of the great merit she acquired in this great sacrifice, which she made to God for the salvation of the world, was justly called by St. Augustine: The restorer of the human race: "Reparatrix generis humani." By St. Epiphanius: The redeemer of captives: "Redemptrix captivorum." By St. Ildephonsus: The restorer of the ruined world: "Reparatrix perditi orbis." By St. Germanus: The consolation of our miseries: "Restauratio ealamitatum nostrarum." By St. Ambrose: The mother of all believers: "Mater omnium credenti urn." By St. Augustine: The mother of the living:" Mater viventium." By St. Andrew of Crete: The mother of life: "Mater vitse." For, as St. Arnold Carnotensis says: In the death of Jesus, Mary united her will to that of her Son in such a manner, that both offered the same sacrifice; and therefore the holy abbot says, that thus the Son and the mother effected human redemption, obtaining salvation for men. Jesus by satisfying for our sins, Mary by obtaining for us that this satisfaction should be applied to us. And hence blessed Denis the Carthusian likewise affirms, that the divine mother may be called the salvation of the world, since by the pain she endured in commiserating her Son (voluntarily sacrificed by her to divine justice), she merited that the merits of the Redeemer should be communicated to men.* (Liguori 468–469)

It is easier to see then why these believe her to be the "co-redemptrix"—based on the belief that she knew everything that was to happen to Jesus even though it is not from scripture. However, this does not explain why they believe that Mary obtained "*for us that this satisfaction should be applied to us.*" There is certainly nothing in the scriptures to back this up either.

Instead, scripture says something else:

> *This is how God showed his love among us: He sent his one and only Son into the world that we might live through him. This is love: not that we loved God, but that he loved us and sent his Son as an atoning sacrifice for our sins.* (1 John 4:9–10)

The jailer who had Paul and Silas imprisoned:

> *"Sirs, what must I do to be saved?" They replied, "Believe in the Lord Jesus, and you will be saved—you and your household."* (Acts 16:30–31)

> *Jesus answered, "**The work of God is this: to believe in the one he has sent.**"* (John 6:29)

There is no mention or hint in the New Testament that Mary is the one through whom salvation is obtained for us. Rather, it is our loving God who prepared and worked out our salvation even when we were his enemies:

> *But God demonstrates his own love for us in this: While we were still sinners, Christ died for us.* (Rom 5:8)

We receive our salvation when we believe in the One God sent and confess Him as our Savior.[22] This salvation received is complete—no merit should or even can be added to it.

> *Prayer. Ah, mother, the most afflicted of all mothers, thy Son, then, is dead; thy Son so amiable, and who loved thee so much! Weep, for thou hast reason*

[22] John 3:36; 5:24; 8:24; Acts 2:21; 3:19; 4:12; 16:29–34; Rom 3:20–25; 2 Cor 5:14–15; Eph 1:7–8, 13–14; 2:4–5, 8–9, 14–18; 3:12; Col 1:22–23; 2:13–15; Heb 8:12; 1 Pet 2:6; 2 Pet 1:9; 1 John 2:2.

> *to weep. Who can ever console thee? Nothing can console thee but the thought that Jesus, by his death, hath conquered hell, hath opened paradise which was closed to men, and hath gained so many souls. From that throne of the cross he was to reign over so many hearts, which, conquered by his love, would serve him with love. Do not disdain, oh my mother, to keep me near to weep with thee, for I have more reason than thou to weep for the offences that I have committed against thy Son. Ah, mother of mercy, I hope for pardon and my eternal salvation, first through the death of my Redeemer, and then through the merits of thy dolors* (sufferings). *Amen.* (Liguori 576–577)

The notable things about this prayer are those things that are in common in all such prayers.

Firstly, they are prayed to Mary and not to God.

Secondly, they constantly go back to a time of pain and suffering that Mary experienced for three days as though such pain and sorrow is still suffered by Mary in heaven. In doing so, these prayers also turn the eyes of the one who prays away from today and what the Spirit wants to do this day. The Spirit was given that we may be Jesus's hands and feet today, and prayer in the Spirit enables us to be the salt and light in the world today—not dwelling on an event of long ago and wasting today in trying to console one who is already in the presence of God.

What consolation is there if one in heaven close to God still requires the prayers of those comparatively far from Him?

Thirdly, such prayer fails to attribute full worth of salvation to the sacrifice of Jesus but instead turns to "*the merits of* (Mary's) *dolors.*" After hours hanging on the cross, His body already brutally disfigured by the beating and scourging, Jesus died. His last words were "***It is finished.***" *With that, he bowed his head and gave up his spirit* (John 19:30).

> *Therefore, there is now no condemnation for those who are in Christ Jesus, because through Christ Jesus the law of the Spirit who gives life has set you free from the law of sin and death. For what the law was powerless to do because it was weakened by the flesh, God did by sending his own Son in the likeness of sinful flesh to be a sin offering. And so he condemned sin in the flesh, in order that the righteous requirement of the law might be* <u>*fully met*</u> *in us, who do not live according to the flesh but according to the Spirit.* (Rom 8:1–4)

> *He did not enter by means of the blood of goats and calves; but he entered the Most Holy Place once for all by his own blood, thus obtaining eternal redemption. The blood of goats and bulls and the ashes of a heifer sprinkled on those who are ceremonially unclean sanctify them so that they are outwardly clean. How much more, then, will the blood of Christ, who through the eternal Spirit offered himself unblemished to God, cleanse our consciences from acts that lead to death, so that we may serve the living God!* (Heb 9:12–14)

> *In fact, the law requires that nearly everything be cleansed with blood, and without the shedding of blood there is no forgiveness.* (Heb 9:22)

Scripture is clear that only the blood[23] (i.e., the life) of Jesus cleanses us and provides for the forgiveness of sin. Nothing humankind, including Mary, can ever do can add *anything* to the finished work

[23] "The life of a creature is in the blood" (Lev 17:11). "The life of every creature is its blood" (Lev 17:14).

of Christ Jesus for our salvation. As scripture confirms, the righteous requirements of the law have been fully met through Christ Jesus and our obedience to the Holy Spirit.

> *If he who prays, says St. Anselm, does not deserve to be heard, the merits of Mary, to whom he commends himself, will cause him to be heard. Hence St. Bernard exhorts every sinner to pray to Mary, and to feel great confidence in praying to her; because if he does not deserve what he demands, yet Mary obtains for him, by her merits, the graces which she asks of God for him.* (Liguori 70–71)

Scripture teaches a very different Gospel:

- That the blood of Jesus obtains for us all we need in life.
  I have come that they may have life, and have it to the full (John 10:10).
  For no matter how many promises God has made, they are "Yes" in Christ (2 Cor 1:20).
- That Jesus is our Intercessor in heaven.
  For there is one God and one mediator between God and mankind, the man Christ Jesus, who gave himself as a ransom for all people (1 Tim 2:5–6).
  If you remain in me and my words remain in you, ask whatever you wish, and it will be done for you (John 15:7).
- The Holy Spirit makes available all the gifts we need.
  All these are the work of one and the same Spirit, and he distributes them to each one, just as he determines (1 Cor 12:4–11).

Liguori claims instead:

> *Wherefore St. Anselm well remarks, that when we implore the holy Virgin to obtain graces for us, it is*

> *not that we distrust the divine mercy, but rather that we distrust our own unworthiness, and commend ourselves to Mary that her merits may compensate for our unworthiness.* (Liguori 170)

It is rather that they ***do*** distrust the mercy of He, who speaking of the New Covenant in the blood of Christ, said, "***For I will forgive their wickedness and will remember their sins no more***" (Heb 8:12).

> *Therefore, there is now no condemnation for those who are in Christ Jesus, because through Christ Jesus the law of the Spirit who gives life has set you free from the law of sin and death.* (Rom 8:1–2)

The following verses from scripture summarize the position of followers of Christ:

> *Once you were alienated from God and were enemies in your minds because of your evil behaviour. But now he has reconciled you by Christ's physical body through death to present you holy in his sight, without blemish and free from accusation— if you continue in your faith, established and firm, and do not move from the hope held out in the Gospel. This is the Gospel that you heard and that has been proclaimed to every creature under heaven, and of which I, Paul, have become a servant."* (Col 1:21–23)

Our *unworthiness* was always a given; Christ died to take our place because we could *never* be worthy. Christ came not only to save *us*—but also all humankind, including Mary—for "*all have sinned and fall short of the glory of God, and all are justified freely by his grace through the redemption that came by Christ Jesus*" (Rom 3:23–24).

However, rather than looking to Jesus and fully trusting in His finished work, they look to their unworthiness and to the "merits of Mary." The opposite—believing and trusting in the finished work of Jesus—is called "faith" and by that faith (which we are given), we are saved:

- *Jesus answered, "**The work of God is this: to believe in the one he has sent**"* (John 2:29).
- ***Very truly I tell you, the one who believes has eternal life*** (John 6:47).
- *But where sin increased, grace increased all the more, so that, just as sin reigned in death, so also grace might reign through righteousness to bring eternal life through Jesus Christ our Lord* (Rom 5:21–22).

Looking to our unworthiness is to turn our eyes away from our Lord and Savior and to believe that the sin in us is greater than the price paid and the redemption won at the cross. If that were true, then Jesus might as well have never paid that price. But He did, and the victory He won far exceeds the sin we have.

When we trust in Jesus and His finished work, we rest in the peace that is given us. We do not implore any created being to obtain for us the divine mercy that has already been promised and given.

The Master said, "***Come to me, all you who are weary and burdened, and I will give you rest***" (Matt 11:28).

Queen of Heaven

In the previous chapter about the "Merits of Mary," one source of Mary's power, authority, and merits was claimed by Liguori to have been that she received them upon becoming crowned queen of heaven. The belief in her exalted heavenly position is one of the justifications given as to why it is good and acceptable for believers to exalt her—because Jesus first exalted her in heaven.

Liguori devoted six pages in *The Glories* to writing of the welcome Mary was given when she entered heaven after Jesus "*really did come from heaven to meet his mother*" and take her there (499–505). The account, which includes conversations in heaven between Mary and the angels, Adam and Eve, Joseph, her husband, the apostle James, Simeon, Zechariah and Elizabeth, her parents, the archangel Gabriel, and the holy Trinity appear to have been based entirely on a contemplation (the imagination) of St. Peter Damian, a Benedictine monk of the eleventh century.

The following are some of the writings compiled by Liguori regarding Mary being the queen of heaven:

> *If the Son is king, says St. Athanasius, his mother must necessarily be considered and entitled queen. From the moment that Mary consented, adds St. Bernardine of Sienna, to become the mother of the Eternal Word, she merited the title of queen of the world and all creatures. If the flesh of Mary, says St. Arnold, abbot, was the flesh of Jesus, how can the mother be separated from the Son in his kingdom? Hence it follows that the regal glory must not only be considered as common to the mother and the Son, but even the same.*
>
> *If Jesus is the king of the whole world, Mary is also queen of the whole world: therefore, says St. Bernardine of Sienna, all creatures who serve God ought also to serve Mary; for all angels and men, and all things that are in heaven and on earth being subject to the dominion of God, are also subject to the dominion of the glorious Virgin. Hence Guerric, abbot, thus addresses the divine mother: Continue, Mary, continue in security to reign; dispose, according to thy will, of every thing belonging to thy Son, for*

> *thou, being mother and spouse of the King of the world, the kingdom and power over all creatures is due to thee as queen.* (Liguori 26)

The above is an example of simply applying worldly principles onto the heavenly realm. God is not bound to follow the ideas and practices of man. King David's mother was not a queen, and scripture tells us that the flesh counts for nothing.[24]

> *Kings should then principally occupy themselves with works of mercy, but not to the neglect of the exercise of justice towards the guilty, when it is required. Not so Mary, who, although queen, is not queen of justice, intent upon the punishment of the guilty, but queen of mercy, solely intent upon compassion and pardon for sinners. Accordingly, the Church requires us explicitly to call her queen of mercy. The High Chancellor of Paris, John Gerson, meditating on the words of David, "These two things have I heard, that power belongeth to God, and mercy to thee, O Lord," says, that the kingdom of God consisting of justice and mercy, the Lord has divided it: he has reserved the kingdom of justice for himself, and he has granted the kingdom of mercy to Mary, ordaining that all the mercies which are dispensed to men should pass through the hands of Mary, and should be bestowed according to her good pleasure. St. Thomas confirms this in his preface to the Canonical Epistles, saying that the holy Virgin, when she conceived the divine Word in her womb, and brought him forth, obtained the half of the kingdom of God by becoming queen of mercy, Jesus Christ remaining king of justice.* (Liguori 26–27)

[24] John 6:63.

Gerson (d. 1429) used a quote from the book of Psalms:

> *One thing God has spoken,*
> *two things I have heard:*
> *"Power belongs to you, God,*
> *and with you, Lord, is unfailing love";*
> *and, "You reward everyone*
> *according to what they have done."* (Ps 62:11–12)

The power and mercy (unfailing love) are clearly with God. There is no separation of dispensation that can be inferred from this scripture.

In the Old Testament, mercy was firstly represented by the sacrificial lamb of the first Passover whose blood delivered the children of Israel from the angel of death at the end of their time at Egypt. It was God's mercy that delivered the Israelites from their bondage to Egypt. This prefigured the actual Lamb of God, our Messiah, who was to come.

Mercy was also represented by the mercy seat on the Ark of the Covenant in the most sacred place: the holy of holies in both the tabernacle and later the temple. This seat was occupied only by presence of God, and from this seat flowed God's merciful dealings with Israel.

In the New Testament, the mercy was represented by the Lamb of God, Jesus Christ, whose one-time sacrifice at the cross took away the sin of the world and its punishment. The mercy seat of the ark was symbolic of the actual throne of grace described in the book of Hebrews:

> *Therefore, since we have a great high priest who has ascended into heaven, Jesus the Son of God, let us hold firmly to the faith we profess. For we do not have a high priest who is unable to empathize with our weaknesses, but we have one who has been tempted in*

> *every way, just as we are—yet he did not sin. Let us then approach God's throne of grace with confidence, so that we may receive mercy and find grace to help us in our time of need.* (Heb 4:14–16)

Our High Priest in heaven, Jesus, occupies God's throne of grace from which we receive the mercy and grace we so need—not just for salvation but for our every need.

While God says, "*I will have mercy on whom I have mercy, and I will have compassion on whom I have compassion*" (Ex 33:19 and Rom 9:15), Liguori would have that it is, instead, Mary who dispenses mercy:

> *Oh my God, what a consolation must it be in that last hour of life, when our lot for eternity is to be decided, to find close by our side the queen of heaven, who sustains and comforts us by promising us her protection!* (Liguori 110)

This expectation for Mary to come for her servants is, in fact, practiced and promoted by groups such as the Legion of Mary who will attend to the dying and have them turn their eyes to look to Mary instead of Jesus.

Contrary to Liguori advising believers to hope for, pray for, and expect their "queen" to be with them at their last moments to walk them into eternity, Jesus told of a different expectation for believers:

> ***My Father's house has many rooms; if that were not so, would I have told you that I am going there to prepare a place for you? And if I go and prepare a place for you, I will come back and take you to be with me that you also may be where I am.*** (John 14:2–3)

Liguori instead would have us believe:

> *NOT only most holy Mary is queen of heaven and of the saints, but also of hell and the devils, for she has bravely triumphed over them by her virtues.* (Liguori 155)
>
> *For she, as St. Bernardine of Sienna says, is queen over hell, and ruler of the spirits of evil, for she controls and conquers them.* (157–158)

If, as St. Bernadine says, Mary is "*queen over hell, ruler of the spirits of evil for she controls and conquers them,*" then she could not also be the woman described in the book of Revelation (Rev 12). The woman of Revelation has to hide and flee from the dragon with the help of God—clearly not the behavior of one who controls and conquers "devils."

However, Liguori claims the woman of Revelation to be Mary, whereas the vision describes Israel. The apostle John, who wrote Revelation, would have said she was Mary if it were her since he knew her well. See also "The Apostle John's End-Time Vision" in appendix 1.

> *Victories were gained in Judea by means of the ark. Thus Moses conquered his enemies. "When the ark was lifted up, Moses said, Arise, oh Lord, and let thy enemies be scattered." Thus Jericho was conquered; thus were the Philistines conquered; "for the ark of God was there."*
>
> *It is well known that this ark was the type of Mary. As the ark contained the manna, thus Mary contained Jesus, whom the manna also prefigured, and by means of this ark, victories were gained over the enemies of earth and over hell. Wherefore St. Bernardine of Sienna says that when Mary, the*

> *ark of the New Testament, was crowned queen of heaven, the power of hell over men was weakened and overthrown.* (Liguori 159)

The victories won with the ark were because the Lord was with His people and fought their battles just as He had promised—likely not because the ark itself was victorious. If the ark brought about victory, it was because the Holy Spirit rested above the holy seat—again not because the ark—itself made by man's hands—was the source of power.

If Mary was the ark when she was carrying the child Jesus in her, then Spirit-filled believers since Pentecost have been and are the ark today as they carry within them the Spirit of God. As long as we continue to look back to Mary, we are not fulfilling our purpose as the arks of today.

Scripture makes clear that Jesus's victory at the cross (and not Mary's said crowning) is what overthrew the powers of Satan over mankind:

> *When you were dead in your sins and in the uncircumcision of your flesh, God made you alive with Christ. He forgave us all our sins, having cancelled the charge of our legal indebtedness, which stood against us and condemned us; he has taken it away, nailing it to the cross. And having disarmed the powers and authorities, he made a public spectacle of them, triumphing over them by the cross.* (Col 2:13–15)

It is puzzling to say the least why anyone said to be a believer would take away from the clear writing of scripture that it was Jesus who broke the power of Satan and hell to instead glorify Mary.

> *And is there any mother who would not rescue her child from death, if she could do it by praying his judge for mercy? And can we believe that Mary, the most loving mother possible to her servants, would fail to rescue one of them from eternal death, when she can do it so easily? Ah, devout reader, let us thank the Lord if we find that he has given us the love of the queen of heaven, and confidence in her; for God, as St. John Damascene says, does not grant this grace except to those whom he wishes to save.* (Liguori 259)

Instead of looking to God and setting our hearts onto Him who created and saved us, this philosophy of man uses human thinking and emotions regarding motherly love and then puts these as requirements for God to follow. When Peter met the Roman Cornelius, he did not put forward such a gospel of motherly love to save this Gentile—and neither did any of the apostles and believers in the accounts of the New Testament. St. John Damascene would claim however that they had put forward such an idea.

> *To serve Mary and to belong to her court, adds St. John of Damascus, is the greatest honor we can attain; for to serve the queen of heaven is to reign already in heaven, and to live in obedience to her commands is more than to reign. On the other hand, he says that those who do not serve Mary will not be saved; whilst those who are deprived of the support of this great mother, are deprived of the succor of the Son, and of all the celestial court.* (Liguori 280–281)

To love and serve <u>our God</u> is our highest calling, and it is also our duty. When asked what the greatest commandment is, Jesus said, ***"Love the Lord your God with all your heart and with all***

your soul and with all your mind. This is the first and greatest commandment" (Matt 22:37–38).

Scripture does not teach that to not serve Mary is to not be saved, and anyone teaching this is adding to scripture, which is warned against in scripture. St. Paul wrote the following in his letter to the Ephesians declaring we already reign in heaven with Christ, for He has given us His authority here on earth (Matt 18:18–19):

> *But because of his great love for us, God, who is rich in mercy, made us alive with Christ even when we were dead in transgressions—it is by grace you have been saved. And God raised us up with Christ and seated us with him in the heavenly realms in Christ Jesus, in order that in the coming ages he might show the incomparable riches of his grace, expressed in his kindness to us in Christ Jesus.* (Eph 2:4–7)

Jesus Christ is the Alpha and Omega, the beginning and end of all things, including our salvation. He is the Author and Finisher of our faith. It is for Him that we were created, by Him that we are saved, and through Him that we reign.

Anyone who teaches instead that our highest calling is to serve Mary—that to serve Mary is to reign in heaven and that we are not saved if we do not serve her—is teaching from a different gospel.

> *Father Kierembergh still further remarks, that the servants of the mother of God not only are more privileged and favored in this world, but also in heaven will be more especially honored. And he adds, that in heaven they will have a peculiarly rich device and livery, by which they will be known as servants of the queen of heaven and as the people of her court, according to those words of Proverbs:*

> *"All her domestics are clothed with double garments."* (Liguori 286)

The only reference given to support the idea that Mary's servants will be more highly favored and privileged in heaven is the verse from Proverbs 31:21, which describes "a wife of noble character" in verse 10. How this can be taken to be Mary is not explained.

> *And why not? because, as St. Anselm answers: To say of Mary this alone, that she was the mother of a God, transcends every glory that can be attributed to her, in thought or word, after God. Peter of Celles adds, remarking on this same thought: By whatever name you may wish to call her, whether queen of heaven, ruler of the angels, or any other title of honor, you will never succeed in honoring her so much as by calling her only the mother of God.* (Liguori 424)

It was not God who called Mary "the mother of God." It was man—and not until the Council of Ephesus in 431 was this title formally given and then against some objection. In His *human nature,* Jesus did not have an earthly father, and in His *divine nature,* Jesus did not have a heavenly mother.

> *I omit other devotions, which are to be found in other books, as the seven joys, the twelve privileges of Mary, and the like, and let us terminate this work with the beautiful words of St. Bernardine: Oh woman, blessed among all women, thou art the honor of the human race, the salvation of our people. Thou hast a merit that has no limits, and an entire power over all creatures. Thou art the mother of God, the mistress of the world, the queen of heaven. Thou art the dispenser of all graces, the glory of the holy Church. Thou art the example of*

> *the just, the consolation of the saints, and the source of our salvation. Thou art the joy of paradise, the gate of heaven, the glory of God. Behold, we have published thy praises. We supplicate thee then, oh mother of mercy, to strengthen our weakness, to pardon our boldness, to accept our service, to bless our labors, and impress thy love upon the hearts of all, that after having honored and loved thy Son on earth, we may praise and bless him eternally in heaven. Amen.* (Liguori 678)

Almost every word of St. Bernadine's prayer should be directed to God instead of to Mary.

Having seen some of the many references Liguori and those he quoted made about Mary being queen of heaven and indeed, at times, the queen of the universe (384), it is time to examine scripture on this subject.

Every vision of heaven recorded in scripture does not include Mary or the queen of heaven.

We have already looked briefly at the vision of the woman that the apostle John received and described in the book of Revelation. The vision was not that of heaven; it was a span of time. The vision revealed the birth of the Messiah to Israel depicted by the woman crowned with twelve stars, the stars representing the tribes of Israel. The vision also revealed the persecution of the woman representing Israel and God's protection over her. This has happened throughout history. One such event happened during the reign of the Hellenistic King Antiochus IV Epiphanes, around 168 BC, who also prefigures the final Antichrist yet to come and the events then.

In every scripture where heaven is revealed whether by the Old or New Testament prophets and apostles, nowhere do we see a queen in the revealed heaven—not even in the throne room (where, as Liguori would have it, she sits on a throne to the right of Jesus).[25]

Scripture does, however, speak of the queen of heaven, but when it does, it does not speak of Mary. Instead, the queen of heaven is a deceptive principality or power that the prophet Jeremiah warned the sons of Israel against exalting. In the following scripture, God tells Jeremiah not to pray for the remnant of the children of Israel who had fled the Babylonians by going to Egypt where they worshipped the queen of heaven.

> *So do not pray for this people nor offer any plea or petition for them; do not plead with me, for I will not listen to you. Do you not see what they are doing in the towns of Judah and in the streets of Jerusalem? The children gather wood, the fathers light the fire, and the women knead the dough and make cakes to offer to the Queen of Heaven. They pour out drink offerings to other gods to arouse my anger.* (Jer 7:16–18)

In chapter 44 of the same book, Jeremiah wrote of the remnant refusing still to stop burning incense, pouring out drink offerings, and making and sacrificing cakes to her. God then spoke His judgment upon them that they would never return to the Promised Land and would all die by the sword and by famine for their sin.

This is what scripture says of the queen of heaven and of her followers.

Advocate

In Liguori's *The Glories*, Mary is said to have the role of our advocate to God. The advocate is one who represents us to God the Father and who speaks on our behalf in order that we might receive mercy

[25] Isa 6; Rev 4–8, 11, 15, 19, 20, 22 NIV.

rather than the judgment we deserve. This title is also sometimes described as intercessor or mediator. In Liguori's writings, Mary's role is exalted even above the advocate role of Jesus when Mary is said to be an advocate *preferable* to Jesus for our needs.

Chapter VI of *The Glories* comprises of three sections:

- Ah, then, our advocate! Mary is an advocate, powerful to save all.
- Mary is a merciful advocate who does not refuse to defend the cause of the most miserable sinners.
- Mary is the peacemaker between sinners and God.

The following paragraphs show how the role of advocate was proposed, then restricted to only Mary, and finally her advocacy being taught as preferable to that of the Lamb of God.

Jesus is our advocate in heaven, and the Holy Spirit is our advocate on earth. No mention is made of the Holy Spirit's role as our advocate in Liguori's book—even though this role of His is clearly described many times in the New Testament.

Mary as Advocate and Intercessor

> *Those who hope for some favor from the king, hope for it from the king as sovereign, and hope for it from his minister or favorite as intercessor. If the favor is granted, it comes in the first place from the king, but it comes through the medium of his favorite; wherefore, he who asks a favor justly calls that intercessor his hope.*
>
> *The king of heaven, because he is infinite goodness, greatly desires to enrich us with his graces; but, because confidence is necessary on our part, in order to increase our confidence, he has given his own mother for our mother and advocate, and has*

> *given her all power to aid us; and hence he wishes us to place in her all our hopes of salvation, and of every blessing.* (Liguori 115–116)

While the above sounds sensible from an earthly perspective, there are many references in the New Testament that identify Jesus as our *only* mediator in heaven. Perhaps the following verse is the clearest:

> *For there is one God and one mediator between God and mankind, the man Christ Jesus, who gave himself as a ransom for all people.* (1 Tim 2:5–6)

What greater advocate can we have than the One who by His actions said He was willing to take our punishment and pay our penalty?

Liguori's assertion that God gave His own mother to be our mother and advocate and that *He "wishes us to place in her all our hopes of salvation and of every blessing"* comes only from the apparitions and words of a spirit who claims to be Mary.

> *Console yourselves, then, oh ye faint of heart, I will say with St. Thomas of Villanova, take heart, oh miserable sinners; this great Virgin, who is the mother of your judge and God, is the advocate of the human race. Powerful and able to obtain whatever she wishes from God; most wise, for she knows every method of appeasing him; universal, for she welcomes all, and refuses to defend none.* (Liguori 223–224)

"*Advocate of the human race*" and "*most wise*" are terms reserved only for members of the Holy Trinity.

For further examples of Liguori's teaching on this subject, please see appendix 6: "Additional Material for Mary as Advocate and Intercessor."

Mary as Our Only Advocate

From being designated our advocate, Liguori then goes on to say that she is our *only* advocate:

> *Justly, then, does St. Lawrence Justinian call her the hope of evil-doers, "spes delinquentium," since she alone can obtain their pardon from God. (Liguori 83)*

> *St. Augustine rightly calls her the only hope of us sinners, since by her means alone we hope for the remission of all our sins. And St. John Chrysostom repeats the same thing, namely, that sinners receive pardon only through the intercession of Mary. (Liguori 83–84)*

> *Hence St. Ephrem says: Thou art the only advocate of sinners, and of those who are deprived of every help; and he thus salutes her: Hail! refuge and retreat of sinners, to whom alone they can flee with confidence. (Liguori 129)*

> *Let us say with St. Thomas of Villanova: Oh Mary, we poor sinners know no refuge but thee. Thou art our only hope; to thee we intrust our salvation. Thou art the only advocate with Jesus Christ; to thee we all have recourse.* (Liguori 130)

> *St. Augustine, contemplating the affection and earnestness with which Mary is continually occupied in interceding with the divine Majesty for us, that the Lord may pardon our sins, assist us with his grace, free us from dangers, and relieve us from our miseries, thus addresses the holy Virgin: Oh Lady! it is true that all the saints desire our salvation*

> *and pray for us; but the charity and tenderness which thou dost manifest for us in heaven, by obtaining with thy prayers so many mercies from God, obliges us to confess, that we have in heaven only one advocate, that is thyself, and that thou alone art the only true lover watchful of our welfare.* (Liguori 219)

> *Moreover, it was meet that the eternal Father should create her in his grace, since he destined her for the restorer of the lost world, and mediatrix of peace between man and God.* (Liguori 338)

St. Paul wrote the following in his letter to Timothy, his disciple:

> *For there is one God and one mediator between God and mankind, the man Christ Jesus, who gave himself as a ransom for all people. This has now been witnessed to at the proper time. And for this purpose I was appointed a herald and an apostle—I am telling the truth, I am not lying—and a true and faithful teacher of the Gentiles.* (1 Tim 2:5–7)

As to the claim that there are those who are deprived of every help, God has always been the Helper whether as Father, Son, or Holy Spirit. Those who say that there are any deprived of help choose to ignore scripture.[26]

> *Oh mother of God, thou art my joy and my hope, for thou dost refuse thy favor to none, and thou dost obtain from God whatever thou dost wish.* (Liguori 739)

[26] Here are a few examples of many: Ps 27:9; 37; 40; 46:1; John 14:16; 1 Cor 10:13; Rom 8:26; Heb 4:16; 2 Tim 1:14.

This belief—that it is through Mary that we should bring our petitions for God—excludes true faith. Jesus taught that we are to ask in His name and not doubt. Scripture also teaches that without faith (in all that He taught us), it is impossible to please God.

Jesus always taught His disciples to <u>come to Him</u>:

> ***And I will do whatever you ask in my name, so that the Father may be glorified in the Son. You may ask me for anything in my name, and I will do it.*** (John 14:13–14)

> ***You did not choose me, but I chose you and appointed you so that you might go and bear fruit—fruit that will last—and so that whatever you ask in my name the Father will give you.*** (John 15:16)

> ***In that day you will no longer ask me anything. Very truly I tell you, my Father will give you whatever you ask in my name.*** (John 16:23)

> ***Though I have been speaking figuratively, a time is coming when I will no longer use this kind of language but will tell you plainly about my Father. In that day you will ask in my name. I am not saying that I will ask the Father on your behalf. No, the Father himself loves you because you have loved me and have believed that I came from God.*** (John 16:25–27)

Jesus said we only have to ask the Father in His (Jesus's) name, and He clarifies this even further by saying we do not have to ask *through* Him:

> *Let us then approach God's throne of grace with confidence, so that we may receive mercy and find grace to help us in our time of need.* (Heb 4:16)

"Confidence" here means "in faith."

> *And without faith it is impossible to please God, because anyone who comes to him must believe that he exists and that he rewards those who earnestly seek him.* (Heb 11:6)

What Liguori and others teach instead is that you should not go to God for you don't know if, as Judge, He will reject you. Instead, you should turn to Mary whom you *can* trust. This is the very opposite of the faith Jesus tells us to have.

For additional details on this subject, please see appendix 7: "Additional Material for Mary as Our Only Advocate."

Advocate Preferable to Jesus

After having championed Mary as our advocate to God and then claiming that she is our only advocate with God, Liguori et al. then proposed that she is *the* advocate—even *preferable to Jesus.*

The following writings show that the belief that it is preferable to go to Mary as our advocate was taught from the highest levels so that many believers go to Mary instead of to Jesus or to the Holy Spirit.

There are several reasons for this claimed preference:

- Jesus is the Judge whom we should fear, but Mary is the advocate to appease Him.
- Mary has more compassion than *any* in heaven or on earth.
- As mother of Jesus, she has a certain *authority* over Him.

> *St. Bernard has said the same thing: If you would not be overwhelmed in the tempest, turn to this star, and call Mary to thy aid. The devout Blosius also says that she is the only refuge for those who have offended God: the asylum of all those who are tempted and afflicted. This mother of mercy is all kindness and all sweetness, not only with the just, but also with sinners and those who are in despair; so that when she beholds them turning towards her, and sees that they are with sincerity seeking her help, she at once welcomes them, aids them, and obtains their pardon from her Son.* (Liguori 131–132)

All these writers seem so eager to represent God as one who is offended and Mary as the mother of mercy who is all kindness and sweetness, when it was God who gave His Son for us. They glorify her and not God.

> *Sooner will heaven and earth be destroyed, says the devout Blosius, than Mary fail to aid those who, with a pure intention, recommend themselves to her and put their confidence in her. And to increase our confidence, St. Anselm adds, that when we have recourse to this divine mother, we may not only be sure of her protection, but that sometimes we shall be sooner heard and saved by invoking her holy name than that of Jesus our Saviour. And he gives this reason: Because it belongs to Christ, as our judge, to punish, but to Mary, as our advocate, to pity.* (Liguori 149)
>
> *By this he would give us to understand, that we sooner find salvation by recurring to the mother than the Son; not because Mary is more powerful than her Son to save us, for we know that Jesus is our only*

> *Saviour, and that by his merits alone he has obtained and does obtain for us salvation; but because when we have recourse to Jesus, considering him also as the judge to whom it belongs to punish the ungrateful, we may lose the confidence necessary to be heard; but going to Mary, who holds no other office than that of exercising compassion towards us as mother of mercy, and defending us as our advocate our confidence will be more secure and greater.* (Liguori 149–150)

These teachings are not scriptural and do not come from any revelation of God.

On the contrary, Jesus is our Judge *and* our Advocate and Intercessor as revealed in scripture. He who *alone* paid the price for our redemption is *alone able* to credit the resulting righteous grace for our benefit. This right and position can belong to no one else.

> *There is no doubt, says St. Bernard, that Jesus is the only mediator of justice between men and God, who in virtue of his merits can, and according to his promises will, obtain for us pardon and divine grace; but because men recognize and fear in Jesus Christ the divine majesty, which dwells in him as God, it was necessary that another advocate should be assigned to us, to whom we could have recourse with less fear and more confidence; and this is Mary, than whom we can find no advocate more powerful with the divine majesty and more compassionate towards us.* (Liguori 221)

It may be that some men recognize and fear in Jesus the divine majesty, but perfect love casts out all fear. God gave us this perfect love to live in us in His Spirit.

If we do not learn by the Spirit how to come to Jesus and place our whole trust in Him in *this life*, how can we expect to be free of fear of Him in the next?

The idea that it was necessary for God to assign another advocate is entirely unscriptural. We learn from numerous events in the Old Testament how necessary it is to overcome one's fear of God and to approach Him in the proper way. Even after Cain was judged by God for the murder of his brother, Abel, and told that any who came upon him would seek to kill him, he approached God instead of avoiding Him out of fear as Adam and Eve had done when they sinned. As a result of approaching God, He relented and provided protection for Cain so that he was able to prosper and even build a city in his long life.

Faith is to believe God in all that He says and to live accordingly.

God has said that we can approach the throne of grace without fear because of the covering of the blood of the Lamb, but Liguori and others teach that we should try to get *around* Him by approaching Mary and placing our trust in her. They choose to live outside of the faith that God seeks, and they command others to do the same:

> *Hence St. Idelbert remarks, that Mary is called fair as the moon: "Pulchra ut Luna:" because, as the moon illuminates and benefits the smallest bodies upon the earth, so Mary enlightens and helps the most unworthy sinners. And although the moon receives all her light from the sun, she moves more quickly than the sun; for, as a certain author remarks, what the sun does in a year, the moon does in a month. Hence, says St. Anselm: Our relief is sometimes more immediate when the name of Mary is invoked than when we invoke the name of Jesus.* (Liguori 297–298)

The verse pertaining to the moon is from Song of Solomon 6:10 and does not appear to refer to Mary who was not born then. A lack of faith in God causes many to turn to Mary for their needs when Jesus Himself said, "***Come to Me.***"

- ***Come to me, all you who are weary and burdened, and I will give you rest*** (Matt 11:28).
- ***All those the Father gives me will come to me, and whoever comes to me I will never drive away. For I have come down from heaven not to do my will but to do the will of him who sent me. And this is the will of him who sent me, that I shall lose none of all those he has given me, but raise them up at the last day. For my Father's will is that everyone who looks to the Son and believes in him shall have eternal life, and I will raise them up at the last day*** (John 6:37–40).

To then expect Jesus to answer them when they flee to Mary and, worse still, to compare what they expect of His response to supposedly her *preferable* relief is being disrespectful to our God who paid the ultimate price for our salvation.

> *Mary is that very throne of grace, says St. Antoninus, to which the apostle exhorts us to have recourse with confidence, that we may obtain the divine mercy, with all needed help for our salvation. To the throne of grace, that is, to Mary, as St. Antoninus remarks. Hence, Mary was called by St. Catherine of Sienna; The dispenser of divine mercy: "Administratrix misericordise."* (Liguori 300–301)
>
> *No, neither in heaven nor on earth can I find one who has more compassion for the miserable, or who can aid me more than you.* (Liguori 79)

Contrary to these saints, the throne of grace is what the Lion and the Lamb, Jesus Christ, occupies for both judgment and mercy.

Only the One seated in the place of judgment has the power to exercise mercy and grace whether in heaven or on earth. Scripture is clear on this.

> *St. Antoninus says, that the prayers of the blessed Virgin being the prayers of a mother, have a certain kind of authority, hence it is impossible that she should not be heard when she prays. On this account St. Germanus encourages sinners to recommend themselves to this advocate with these words; Thou, oh Mary, <u>having the authority of a mother with God,</u> dost obtain pardon for the vilest sinners; for the Lord, who in all things recognizes thee for his true mother, cannot refuse to grant thee whatever thou dost ask. St. Bridget, too, heard the saints in heaven saying to the Virgin: What is there that thou canst not do? Is it not, says St. Augustine, worthy of the goodness of the Lord thus to guard the honor of his mother? for he asserts that he has come on the earth, not to break, but to fulfil the law, which, among other things, commands us to honor our parents.* (Liguori 209–210)

While it may be possible that Mary could have the ear of her Son, the testimony of St. Brigit not being infallible, these believers have used it as a convenience to go past God and take their petitions to Mary for no other reason than that they trust in her "mercy" more than their Creator and Savior. God did not come to earth and die for our sins to establish for us a path to Mary but to Himself. If what St. Augustine said is true, then all the more believers should more closely follow our Father God and not try to *use* the *earthly* mother of His Son in order to bypass Him.

> *St. John Damascene addresses the Virgin in these words: Thou, then, oh Mary, being mother of God,*

> *canst save all men by thy prayers, which are enforced by a mother's authority.* (Liguori 211)

In the same way, this St. John Damascene teaches that we should approach Mary simply because he believes that she has authority over God instead of approaching God Himself who planned for and made the provision for us to be reconciled to Him through the blood of His Son.

To look past the sacrifice of the Son and His open invitation for us to come to Him and to instead approach the mother is an exercise in faithlessness.

> *In the Franciscan chronicles it is related of brother Leo, that he once saw a red ladder, upon which Jesus Christ was standing, and a white one, upon which stood his holy mother. He saw persons attempting to ascend the red ladder; they ascended a few steps and then fell; they ascended again, and again fell. Then they were exhorted to ascend the white ladder, and on that he saw them succeed, for the blessed Virgin offered them her hand, and they arrived in that manner safe in paradise.* (Liguori 279)

Did no one question whether the "vision" Leo saw was of God or from the enemy? If the vision were of God, then the apostles were apparently mistaken in all their teachings when they all taught us to have faith in Christ alone and never taught that we were meant to place our trust in Mary.

Scripture has the final word in all things, and scripture is the Word of God that stands forever:

> *But in fact the ministry Jesus has received is as superior to theirs as the covenant of which he is mediator is*

> *superior to the old one, since the new covenant is established on better promises.* (Heb 8:6)

The context in which the above verse was written was regarding the comparison between the Old and New Testament priesthood, it also establishes that in the New Covenant made in the blood of Christ, Jesus is not only the mediator; the ministry over which He is mediator is His alone. No one else has this ministry, and scripture confirms this:

> *Now there have been many of those priests, since death prevented them from continuing in office but because Jesus lives forever, he has a permanent priesthood. Therefore he is able to save completely those who come to God through him, because he always lives to intercede for them.* (Heb 7:23–25)

It is folly to go to another when God promises that Jesus is able to save *completely* those who come to God *through Him*.

Endnote: Part I: Beliefs and Their Origins

In this part of the book, some of the many beliefs about Mary were examined along with, where possible, a look at some of their apparent origins. In this section, we summarize these origins.

The Mistranslation of Scripture

The prime example of this was St. Jerome's Greek-to-Latin translation of God's abundant favor toward Mary, in which he described as her being "*full of grace,*" a meaning not derived from the original text. As we have seen, this birthed many other beliefs.

The Meditations and Contemplations of Monks

Jesus and the apostles did not advocate a monastic lifestyle for believers. There already were some who practiced this within sects of Judaism and in Eastern religions, but followers of Jesus were told to go *into* the world while not being *of* the world.

As a fruit of the monastic lifestyle, various beliefs arose and were developed about Mary through the contemplations of monks. Many examples from *The Glories* have been presented here, including the contemplation of Jesus suckling at the breast of Mary, her presenting Jesus to God the Father immediately upon His death at the cross, and her glorious entry into heaven.

Believers are told to pray to God and to meditate upon the Word of God (scripture), but it appears that many false teachings arose from the "contemplations" of monks who believed it was good and acceptable to ponder and imagine things outside of scripture. This may be one reason why scripture warns us to not go beyond what was written in scripture (1 Cor 4:6).

> *Finally, brothers and sisters, whatever is true, whatever is noble, whatever is right, whatever is pure, whatever is lovely, whatever is admirable—if anything is excellent or praiseworthy—think about such things.* (Phil 4:8)

St. Paul wasn't advocating allowing the mind to creatively generate beliefs that would go beyond scripture. Worse still was for clergy to teach these contemplations as revelations or truths—even when they contradicted the clear revelations and teachings of scripture.

Non-Scriptural Sources

These include the Protoevangelium of James and other books, such as those in the Apocrypha. Even though the Protoevangelium was dismissed by the church, it didn't stop some from spreading teachings found in it as though they were the Word of God.

Apparitions, Visions and Conversations of Heaven

A source of many of the beliefs were the encounters with spirits that claimed to have been Mary or Jesus as well as conversations apparently "overheard" in heaven between Jesus and Mary.

Likewise, there are many references in Liguori's writing to such revelations of the Blessed Virgin to various individuals, including St. Bridget. Nowhere was it questioned if the spirits who appeared to such individuals might not be Mary—despite there being clear disparities between the revelations to actual scripture:

> *It was revealed to St. Elizabeth, the nun, that Mary, from the time she was in the temple, was always praying that God would quickly send his Son to save the world.* (Liguori 447)

While this "revelation" lines up with the writings in the Protoevangelium of James, the book was apparently written in the second century AD and contained so many errors that it was condemned by the church. The idea that Mary could have been raised in or around the holy of holies in the temple is one such idea that cannot be believed if one understands the laws regarding the temple and the prohibitions even for priests. No one was allowed in the holy of holies (the innermost sanctum of the temple) except a priest chosen by God for the occasion.

> *The blessed Virgin herself revealed to St. Bridget, that no sinner in the world is so great an enemy to God, that if he has recourse to her and invokes her aid, does not return to God and is not restored to his favour. And the same St. Bridget heard one day Jesus Christ saying to his mother, that she could obtain the divine favor even for Lucifer, if he would humble himself so far as to ask her help. That proud spirit would never stoop to implore the protection of Mary, but if such a thing could happen, Mary would take pity upon him, and the power of her prayers would obtain from God his pardon and salvation.* (Liguori 135)

St. Bridget is described here and elsewhere as having the ability to eavesdrop on Jesus talking to His mother. This is unlikely, and scripture is clear about Lucifer. God lets us understand both His plans and Satan's destiny.

> *And as the rebel angels depart from sinners who invoke the name of Mary, thus, on the contrary, our Lady herself told St. Bridget, that the good angels draw more closely around those just souls who devoutly pronounce it.* (Liguori 312)

The teaching here is that believers should seek to have "good angels" surround them—and that the name of Mary enables this. Jesus never taught such a thing; instead, He taught that the Holy Spirit would come to us when He returned to the Father. This is the Spirit whom Jesus said would be *better for us to have than He Himself* (Jesus), He would guide, gift, and empower us, and He is greater than Satan and his cohorts in the world.

Instead, the spirit that purports to be Mary teaches a completely different theology around herself and the angels, completely ignoring the Spirit who gives life and who Alone prepares us for the day when we shall meet with God.

> *One day the most holy Mary appeared to the blessed Colletta, a Franciscan nun, and showed her the infant Jesus in a basin, torn in pieces, and then said to her: "Thus sinners continually treat my Son, renewing his death and my sorrows; oh, my daughter, pray for them that they may be converted." Similar to this is that other vision which appeared to the venerable sister Jane, of Jesus and Mary, also a Franciscan nun. As she was one day meditating on the infant Jesus, persecuted by Herod, she heard a great noise, as of armed people, who were pursuing someone; and then appeared before her a most beautiful child, who was fleeing in great distress, and cried to her: "My Jane, help me, hide me; I am Jesus of Nazareth, I am flying from sinners who wish to kill me, and who persecute me as Herod did: do thou save me."* (Liguori 551)

Scripture is clear that Jesus died *once* for our sins and that He sits at the right hand of the Father until all things are put under His feet. Anyone who teaches otherwise—such as that Jesus is renewed in His death, pursued, and in great distress, whether that one is from heaven—is not teaching the truth. Scripture warns about such teachings.

Jesus is neither the victim of sinners nor subject to them. Scripture tells us that no one can subject Jesus to any suffering even by their sins:

> ***I am the good shepherd. The good shepherd lays down his life for the sheep.*** (John 10:11)
>
> *He took up our infirmities and bore our diseases.* (Isa 53:4; Matt 8:17)
>
> ***The reason my Father loves me is that I lay down my life—only to take it up again. No one takes it from me, but I lay it down of my own accord.*** (John 10:17–18)
>
> *Unlike the other high priests, he does not need to offer sacrifices day after day, first for his own sins, and then for the sins of the people. He sacrificed for their sins once for all when he offered himself. For the law appoints as high priests men in all their weakness; but the oath, which came after the law, appointed the Son, who has been made perfect forever.* (Heb 7:27)

Jesus *chose* to come to this Earth and become the Lamb of God to take away our sin and all the punishment of sin in a once-for-all-time sacrifice at the cross. His death is not renewed, and neither is His sorrow—nor that of His mother, Mary. He is not an infant at the mercy of anyone; He is the King of kings and Lord of lords.

> *But even if we or an angel from heaven should preach a Gospel other than the one we preached to you, let them be under God's curse!* (Gal: 1:8)

Richard P. McBrien, the noted Catholic writer, addressed this idea:

> *Apparitions, visions, and other unusual occurrences attributed directly or indirectly to Mary may or may not be believed. None of them can ever be regarded as essential to Christian faith, whether they are approved by the official Church or not. If these phenomena do have any final authority, they are authoritative only for those who directly or immediately experience them. No one but the recipient(s) can be bound in conscience by whatever is communicated.*[27]

Attributing Scripture to Mean Mary When They Meant Otherwise

Numerous beliefs either arose from or were reinforced by taking the object of scripture to be Mary when they were either directly referring to God or to the attributes of God, such as Wisdom. The wrongful ascription of the character, position, and titles of God to Mary is examined in the section "Positions, Attributes and Titles of God" in part III.

Other wrongful credits to Mary include (page numbers from *The Glories* follow):

- The female person referred to in the Song of Solomon (as referred to as the Canticles): 41, 82, 144, 158, 207–208, 228, 231, 297–298, 306, 310–311, 358, 386, 394, 405, 411–412, 481, 545, 604, 740–741, 741–742, 757, 763
- The wife of noble character described in Proverbs 31: 31, 68, 157, 359
- The moon: 94, 127, 147, 176–177, 231, 244, 297–298, 324–325, 393, 445
- The sun: 92, 94, 244–245, 324–325, 378, 442, 509–510, 581

[27] *Catholicism, Volume Two* by Richard P. McBrien, 1980.

- Noah's Ark, the dove from the ark, the rainbow: 135–136, 229, 230–231
- The Ark of the Covenant and/or the Tabernacle: 118, 129–30, 159, 497–498
- The cities of refuge: 128–129, 445–446, 657–658
- Israel and Jerusalem: 521, 577

For examples of some of the above, please see appendix 8: "Additional Material for Attributing Scripture to Mean Mary when They Meant Otherwise."

PART II

THE VISITATIONS

The beliefs about Mary and the teachings that continued to propagate these beliefs set believers up to look to Mary as a divine being who remained accessible through prayer and even through personal experience.

Many different movements grew in the church that were aimed at prayer, devotion, dedication, and servanthood toward Mary. These movements grew even as the personal relationship with the Holy Spirit that began the early church became a thing of the past in the minds of believers. Miracles that testified of the Spirit and the power of the Gospel became thought of as something that belonged to an earlier age that had now passed. Gifts of the Spirit and His presence that powered the early church were replaced by the vaguer "*graces*" bestowed by Mary and long-dead saints.

"*Our* mother" seemed a more intimate and understandable relationship to that of "*the* Holy Spirit."

Over time, series of supernatural experiences of "Mary" began to manifest, albeit rarely enough to have each series identifiable usually by the location of the "visitation." These usually occurred to very small groups of children of remote rural communities. Their families had raised them up in religious settings where devotion to Mary was the norm and where knowledge of actual scripture was minimal if anything.

Many of these visitations, which occurred fairly recently, include those at Lourdes in France (1858), Fatima in Portugal (1917), Garabandal in northern Spain (1961), and Medjugorje in then Yugoslavia (1981).

The Fatima visitation is characteristic of these incidents. It will be used here to examine the encounter, the teachings and beliefs engendered, and the effects on the children as well as the communities of believers in general. Fatima is also insightful because a detailed account of the apparitions was written by the one surviving child who was present. The account includes details of the conversations the spirit had with those who were present.

It is a firsthand account, and the following details are taken from *Fatima: In Lucia's Own Words* (tenth edition, 1998). Such accounts are significant since they are less likely to have been embellished by introduced theology and justifications as to how and why these events occurred.

To make it easier to cross-check these references, instead of adding footnotes, the page numbers of the source are simply inserted after each quotation (as was done with Liguori's book).

Fatima: An Overview

The year was 1915 and the Great War raged in Europe. Three little country children, Lucia dos Santos (seven years old), Francisco (six years old), and Jacinta Marto (four years old) lived in Aljustrel, a hamlet of the parish of Fatima in rural Portugal, far from the fighting. Lucia was the youngest in a family of six girls and one boy. Living close by were her cousins Francisco, Jacinta, and their brothers. All are raised as devout Catholics.

Lucia later wrote that "*the first thing I learnt was the Hail Mary*"

(14). She was also taught by her confessor priest to "*kneel down before our Lady and ask her, with great confidence to take care of your heart, to prepare it to receive Her beloved Son worthily tomorrow* (first communion), *and to keep it for Him alone*" (56). She was also taught to pray the words "*Sweet heart of Mary, be my salvation*" (114). Lucia's sisters took care of the altar of Our Lady of the Rosary at their church.

Around 1915, when she first started tending sheep at the age of eight, Lucia and three young shepherd friends (not her cousins) experienced a series of visions on the pasture slopes. These visions were of a shrouded, hovering semitransparent white figure who looked like a boy of about fourteen years old and who later claimed to be the "*angel of peace,*" the guardian "*angel of Portugal.*"

Later, Lucia would shepherd her sheep in the company of her young cousins Francisco and Jacinta. They would regularly pray the Rosary and call out the name of Mary across the valleys to hear its echo. The apparition of the angel would appear to them and instruct them to recite certain prayers that this spirit would teach them. Later still, a seemingly different spirit, this time in the form of a "*mysterious lady,*" would appear to them. Initially, this lady would not reveal who she was, but she would reveal certain "*secrets*" to them and teach and ask them to do a number of things, including praying the Rosary and sacrificing themselves (self-mortification).

This mysteriously lady later claimed that she was the Blessed Virgin, revealing new teachings such as that sins are committed against the immaculate heart of Mary, that God wished to establish world devotion to her Immaculate Heart, and other teachings (which will be covered in detail when we compare them against the Word of God).

She also said that she would soon take the young cousins, Francisco and Jacinta, to heaven. Francisco and Jacinta, in fact, died soon after, amid great suffering from sickness, which the lady led them to believe was sent by God. This, in fact, happened even whilst "*Our Lady*," as they called her, would sometimes grace healing on others who, by then, had come in large numbers to adore and ask for healings and blessings at the location of her visitations.

In all, there were six such encounters which fell on the thirteenth day of the months of May through October 1917. Only the three young cousins were able to see this "Lady" each time, and of the three, only the two young girls could actually hear the words she spoke. Francisco could see her, but he could not hear her words.

On the last of these visits, the "Lady" appeared in different forms, sometimes appearing as they had known her, sometimes appearing as "*Our Lady of the Rosary*," "*Our Lady of Dolours,*" or "*Our Lady of Carmel*." Sometimes, too, she would appear with a "*Child Jesus*" and "*St. Joseph*."

Lucia would later become a nun of the Immaculate Heart, and she had further visions in the 1920s. Many of the teachings of "*the Lady*" have since become part of the established prayers and tradition of the Catholic Church.

Fatima: The Encounters

Early Encounters with "the Angel"

A mysterious presage appeared to Lucia and her three shepherd companions (not the cousins) in 1915—all of whom saw a "*figure poised in the air above the trees; it looked like a statue made of snow and rendered almost transparent by the rays of the sun*" (60–61).

In 1916, what appeared to Lucia to have been the same figure again appeared—this time to Lucia, Francisco, and Jacinta.

> *Above the olive trees, the figure I have already spoken about… As it drew closer, we were able to distinguish its features. It was a young man, about fourteen or*

> *fifteen years old, whiter than snow, transparent as crystal when the sun shines through it, and of great beauty. On reaching us, he said, "Do not be afraid! I am the Angel of Peace. Pray with me."* (63, 158)

He then taught them some new prayers to recite.

> *Some time passed* (between apparitions), *and summer came . . . One day we were playing. Suddenly, we saw beside us the same figure, or rather Angel, as it seemed to me.*
>
> *"What are you doing?" he asked. "Pray, pray very much! The most holy Hearts of Jesus and Mary have designs of mercy on you. Offer prayers and sacrifices constantly to the Most High."*
>
> *"How are we to make sacrifices?" I asked.*
>
> *"Make of everything you can a sacrifice, and offer it to God as an act of reparation for the sins by which He is offended, and in supplication for the conversion of sinners. You will thus draw down peace upon your country. I am its Angel Guardian, the Angel of Portugal. Above all, accept and bear with submission, the sufferings which the Lord will send you."* (63–64)

At this meeting too, an apparition of a suspended chalice and host appeared, and the "angel" taught the children a strange prayer of offering Christ's body and blood to the Holy Trinity. For more details, please see appendix 9: "Prayer Taught by the Angel at Fatima."

"*I don't know how I feel,*" Jacinta subsequently said. "*I can no longer talk, or sing or play. I haven't strength enough for anything.*"

Francisco: "*I love to see the Angel, but the worst of it is that, afterwards, we are unable to do anything. I couldn't even walk. I don't know what was the matter with me*" (129).

The First Meeting with "Our Lady"

The first appearance of the lady occurred on May 13, 1917. The three cousins were playing on a high slope while tending their flocks. They saw a flash that resembled lightning. As they hurried with the sheep to avoid what they thought to be a thunderstorm, another flash occurred. Before them, on a small holm oak tree, they "*beheld a Lady all dressed in white. She was more brilliant that the sun, and radiated a light more clear and intense than crystal glass*" (164). The lady told she would do them no harm and said she was from heaven.

When asked what she wanted, the lady said, "*I have come to ask you to come here for six months in succession, on the thirteenth day, at the same hour. Later on, I will tell you who I am and what I want. Afterwards, I will return here yet a seventh time.*"

When asked if they would go to heaven, the lady responded that the two girls would go to heaven, and Francisco "*will go there too, but he must say many Rosaries.*"

The lady then asked, "*Are you willing to offer yourselves to God and bear all the sufferings He wills to send you, as an act of reparation for the sins by which He is offended, and of supplication for the conversion of sinners?*"

When they agreed, the lady then said, "*Then you are going to have much to suffer, but the grace of God will be your comfort.*"

The children were overcome when the lady opened her hands and communicated to them "*a light so intense that, as it streamed from her hands, its rays penetrated our hearts and the innermost depths of our souls, making us see ourselves in God, Who was that light." They then fell on their knees, repeating in their hearts, "O most Holy Trinity, I adore You! My God, my God, I love you in the most Blessed Sacrament!*"

The lady spoke again saying, "*Pray the Rosary every day, in order to obtain peace for the world, and the end of the war." Then she began to rise serenely, going up toward the east, until she disappeared in the immensity of space* (166–168).

Second Meeting with "Our Lady"

By the thirteenth of June, many had heard of the apparitions and were starting to ask questions and follow the cousins. Within her own family, Lucia's own mother and siblings were contemptuous of what they believed to be her lies regarding the visitations. Lucia was distressed and bitter because they wanted her to admit she lied.

A number of people followed the cousins to the site of the prior vision:

> *We saw once more the flash … and the next moment, Our Lady was there on the holmoak, exactly the same as in May.*
>
> *"What do you want of me?" I asked.*
>
> *"I wish you to come here on thirteenth of the next month, to pray the Rosary every day, and to learn to read. Later, I will tell you what I want."*
>
> *"I would like to ask you to take us to heaven."*
>
> *"Yes, I will take Jacinta and Francisco soon. But you are to stay here some time longer. Jesus wishes to make use of you to make me known and loved. He wants to establish in the world devotion to my Immaculate Heart."*
>
> *"Am I to stay here alone?" I asked, sadly.* (168–169)

> *Our Lady, as though guessing what was going on* (regarding her distress)*, said to me: "Are you suffering a great deal? Don't lose heart. I will never forsake you. My Immaculate Heart will be your refuge and the way that will lead to God."* (69)

> *As she spoke these words, she opened her hands, and from them streamed a light that penetrated to our inmost hearts. From that day onwards, our hearts were*

filled with a more ardent love for the Immaculate Heart of Mary. (69)

Third Meeting with "Our Lady"

Lucia later wrote candidly that on July 12, the day before the promised third apparition, she had serious doubts as to whether these manifestations might be of the devil. By this time, the three cousins were well into "*making sacrifices and acts of mortification,*" but she was still doubtful of whether to go. "*If it's the devil, why should I go to see him?*" (71–72).

At the last moment, she felt impelled to go. Even larger crowds had gathered, so that the cousins had difficulty getting there. It was at this encounter that the "secret" was revealed to the cousins.

The conversation with "*the lady*" once again began with Lucia asking what she wanted of her:

> *I want you to come here on the thirteenth of next month, to continue to pray the Rosary every day in honour of Our Lady of the Rosary, in order to obtain peace for the world and the end of the war, because only she can help you.*
>
> *Continue to come here every month. In October, I will tell you who I am and what I want, and I will perform a miracle for all to see and believe.* (170)

When requests were made on behalf of the people gathered, "*Our Lady said it was necessary for such people to pray the Rosary in order to obtain these graces during the year.*" (170)

> *Sacrifice yourselves for sinners, and say many times, especially whenever you make some sacrifice: O Jesus, it is for love of You, for the conversion of sinners*

> *and in reparation for the sins committed against the Immaculate Heart of Mary*. (73, 170)

She then revealed a vision of "hell" to the cousins with *"a sea of fire. Plunged in this fire were demons and souls in human form … floating about in the conflagration."* (170)

> *You have seen hell where the souls of poor sinners go. To save them, God wishes to establish in the world devotion to my Immaculate Heart. If what I say to you is done, many souls will be saved and there will be peace. The war is going to end; but if people do not cease offending God, a worse one will break out during the pontificate of Pius XI. When you see a night illuminated by an unknown light, know that this is the great sign given you by God that his is about to punish the world for its crimes, by means of war, famine, and persecutions of the Church and of the Holy Father.*
>
> *To prevent this, I shall come to ask for the consecration of Russia to my Immaculate Heart, and the Communion of Reparation on the First Saturdays. If my requests are heeded, Russia will be converted, and there will be peace; if not, she will spread her errors throughout the world, causing wars and persecutions of the Church. The good will be martyred, the Holy Father will have much to suffer, various nations will be annihilated. In the end, my Immaculate Heart will triumph. The Holy Father will consecrate Russia to me, and she will be converted, and a period of peace will be granted to the world. In Portugal, the dogma of the Faith will always be preserved; etc. … Do not tell this to anybody. Francisco, yes, you may tell him.*

> *When you pray the Rosary, say after each mystery: "O my Jesus, forgive us, save us from the fire of hell. Lead all souls to heaven, especially those who are most in need."* (170–174)

Fourth Meeting with "Our Lady"

The meeting on the thirteenth of August was not to eventuate.

On the way to the Cova da Iria, as the location of the apparitions was called, the cousins were making their way through the crowds that had been pouring in from all parts when an order came from the local administrator to see him for interrogation regarding the phenomena.

The monthly encounter was delayed until Lucia's return on the fifteenth.

The message was then given once again:

> *I want you to continue going to the Cova da Iria on the thirteenth and to continue praying the Rosary every day. In the last month, I will perform a miracle so that all may believe.*

When asked, *"What do you want done with the money that the people leave in the Cova da Iria?"* the lady replied, *"Have two litters made. One is to be carried by you and Jacinta and two other girls dressed in white; the other one is to be carried by Francisco and three other boys. The money from the litters is for the 'fiesta' of Our Lady of the Rosary, and what is left over will help towards the construction of a chapel that is to be built here."*

> *"Pray, pray very much, and make sacrifices for sinners; for many souls go to hell, because there are none to sacrifice themselves and to pray for them."* (77, 175)

Fifth Meeting with "Our Lady"

Another message arrived on the thirteenth of September:

> *Continue to pray the Rosary in order to obtain the end of the war. In October, Our Lord will come, as well as Our Lady of Dolours and Our Lady of Carmel. Saint Joseph will appear with the Child Jesus to bless the world. God is pleased with your sacrifices. He does not want you to sleep with the rope on, but only to wear it during the daytime.*

When asked about healing the sick, she responded, "*Yes, I will cure some, but not others. In October, I will perform a miracle so all may believe*" (176–177).

Sixth Meeting with "Our Lady"

This was the last of the six successive meetings that "*the lady*" had asked the cousins to meet with her. There were now huge crowds kneeling and requesting favors in the mud and rain. This was also the date that she had promised "*a miracle so all may believe.*"

Another message arrived this time:

> *I want to tell you that a chapel is to be built here in my honour. I am the Lady of the Rosary. Continue always to pray the Rosary every day. The war is going to end, and the soldiers will soon return to their homes.*

When asked for healings, conversions, and other things, she responded, "*Some yes, but not others. They must amend their lives and ask forgiveness of their sins. Do not offend the Lord our God any more, because He is already so much offended.*"

She then was said to have opened her hands.

> *And made them reflect on the sun, and as she ascended, the reflection of her own light continued to be projected on the sun itself. After Our Lady had disappeared into the immense distance of the firmament, we beheld St. Joseph with the Child Jesus and Our Lady robed in white with a blue mantle, beside the sun. St. Joseph and the Child Jesus appeared to bless the world, for they traced the Sign of the Cross with their hands. When, a little later, this apparition disappeared, I saw Our Lord and Our Lady; it seemed to me that it was Our Lady of Dolours. Our Lord appeared to bless the world in the same manner as St. Joseph had done. This apparition also vanished, and I saw Our Lady once more, the time resembling Our Lady of Carmel.* (177, 178)

Only the cousins saw these apparitions.

Of the crowds, it is said that some had not seen anything unusual at all, but others—upon staring at the sun after Lucia had pointed toward it—saw the sun dancing in the sky. Outside of the immediate area, there was not reported to have been any unusual activity associated with the sun that day.

Subsequent Apparitions

December 10, 1925

Lucia subsequently entered the College of Porto, and in 1925, at the age of eighteen, she entered the Institute of St. Dorothy as a novitiate. While there, on December 10, 1925, she had further visions:

> *The most holy Virgin appeared to her, and by her side, elevated on a luminous cloud, was a child. The most holy Virgin rested her hand on her shoulder, and as she did so, she showed here a heart encircled by thorns, which she was holding in her right hand. At the same time, the Child said:*
>
> *"Have compassion on the Heart of your most holy Mother, covered with thorns, with which ungrateful men pierce it at every moment, and there is no one to make an act of reparation to remove them."*
>
> *Then the most holy Virgin said:*
>
> *"Look, my daughter at my Heart, surrounded with thorns with which ungrateful men pierce me every moment by their blasphemies and ingratitude. You at least try to console me and say that I promise to assist at the hour of death, with the graces necessary for salvation, all those who, on the first Saturday of five consecutive months, shall confess, receive Holy Communion, recite five decades of the Rosary, and keep me company for fifteen minutes while meditating on the fifteen mysteries of the Rosary, with the intention of making reparation to me."* (197)

February 15, 1926

On February 15, 1926, Lucia wrote that the Infant Jesus appeared to her again. He asked if she had already spread the devotion to His most holy Mother.

Lucia placed before Jesus the difficulty that some people had about confessing on Saturday, and she asked that it might be valid to go to confession within eight days. Jesus provided an answer:

> *Yes, and it could be longer still, provided that, when they receive Me, they are in the state of grace and have*

> *intention of making reparation to the Immaculate Heart of Mary.*
>
> *Resplendent Child: "It is true, my daughter, that many souls begin the First Saturdays, but few finish them, and those who do complete them do so in order to receive the graces that are promised thereby. It would please me more if they did Five (decades of the Rosary) with fervour and with the intention of making reparation to the Heart of your heavenly Mother, than if they did Fifteen, in a tepid and indifferent manner."* (197–200)

June 13, 1929

On this day, in the chapel of the convent at Tuy, Spain, Lucia reported she had heard the Blessed Virgin ask for the consecration of Russia to her Immaculate Heart under certain well-defined conditions.

> *Our Lady then said to me: "The moment has come in which God asks the Holy Father, in union with all the Bishops of the world, to make the consecration of Russia to my Immaculate Heart, promising to save it by this means. There are so many souls whom the Justice of God condemns for sins committed against me, that I have come to ask reparation: sacrifice yourself for this intention and pray."* (200–201)

Fatima: Effect of the Apparitions on the Cousins

The immediate effect of the encounters on the young children was the turning of their hearts to the lady of the visions. She had, after all, promised they would go to heaven, but for Francisco, it was conditional on him having to "say" many Rosaries. As a result, they began to spend considerably more time reciting the Rosary.

They also began to engage in various acts of mortification (self-inflicted pain) as sacrifice to please our Lord as the lady had said these are as *"acts of reparation for the sins by which He is offended, and of supplication for the conversion of sinners"* (68). These acts took many forms:

Dehydrating Themselves (32)

> *Occasionally also, we were in the habit of offering to God the sacrifice of spending nine days or a month without taking a drink.* (90, see appendix 10: "Dehydration Practiced by the Cousins at Fatima.")

Drinking Contaminated Water

> *We came to a pond beside the road and Jacinta said to me: "Oh I'm so thirsty, and my head aches so! I'm going to drink a drop of this water ... No, I don't want good water. I'd rather drink this, because instead of offering Our Lord our thirst, I could offer Him the sacrifice of drinking this dirty water." As a matter of fact, this water was filthy. People washed their clothes in it, and the animals came there to drink and waded right into it. That was why my mother warned her children not to drink this water.* (90)

Self-Inflicted Suffering: Using Nettles

> *While Jacinta was plucking these plants, she happened to catch hold of some nettles and stung herself. She no sooner felt the pain than she squeezed them more tightly in her hands, and said to us: "Look! Look! Here is something else with which we can mortify*

> *ourselves!" From that time on, we used to hit our legs occasionally with nettles, so as to offer to God yet another sacrifice.* (79)

Self-Inflicted Suffering: Rope Tying

> *I found a piece of rope that had fallen off a cart. I picked it up and, just for fun, I tied it around my arm. Before long, I noticed that the rope was hurting me. "Look, this hurts!" I said to my cousins. "We could tie it round our waists and offer this sacrifice to God."*
>
> *The poor children promptly fell in with my suggestion. We then set about dividing it between the three of us, by placing it across a stone and striking it with the sharp edge of another one that served as a knife. Either because of the thickness or roughness of the rope, or because we sometimes tied it too tightly, this instrument of penance often caused us terrible suffering. Now and then, Jacinta could not keep back her tears, so great was the discomfort this caused her.* (78)

The children would bleed as a result of the coarseness of the tightly bound rope.

Self-Inflicted Suffering: Pain and Lack of Sleep

> *"Last night," she (Jacinta) answered, "I had so much pain, and I wanted to offer Our Lord the sacrifice of not turning over in bed; therefore I didn't sleep at all."* (97)

The mortifications practiced by the children were not only condoned by Our Lady; they were actually taught and encouraged by her. The children believed that God desired their sufferings only because she had said so.

> *"God is pleased with your sacrifices. He does not want you to sleep with the rope on, but only to wear it during the daytime."* (80)
>
> *Once again the most Blessed Virgin recommended to us the practice of mortification, and ended by saying: "Pray, pray very much, and make sacrifices for sinners; for many souls go to hell, because there are none to sacrifice themselves and to pray for them."* (78)

Progressively, Francisco and his sister Jacinta became more and more ill. In the end, they were both hospitalized and died soon after—although they had appeared healthy before the visions. Jacinta had a large open wound in her chest, which had to be treated every day.

> She said, *"Our Lady wants me to go to two hospitals, not to be cured but to suffer more for love of Our Lord and for sinners."* (102)
>
> Sick and dying, when asked if she needed anything, she would answer, *""No, I don't, thank you." Then when they left the room, she said: "I'm so thirsty, but don't want to take a drink. I'm offering it to Jesus for sinners."* (47)
>
> *Of Our Lord and Our Lady: "Oh, how much I love to suffer for love of Them, just to give Them pleasure! They greatly love those who suffer for the conversion of sinners."* (45)

Francisco died on April 4, 1919, and his sister died on February 20, 1920. Did the self-mortifications cause or contribute to their illnesses?

Summary of the Teachings at Fatima

In the following sections, the primary teachings of the angel and "Our Lady" at Fatima are examined and compared against the Word of God.

The main points will be examined in detail:

- God desires our suffering and sacrifices.
- Sins are committed against Mary.
- The Rosary is instrumental in salvation.
- The Rosary is key to prayer.
- Jesus desires world devotion to the "Immaculate Heart of Mary."

Suffering, Sacrifices, and God

Both the angel and "the Lady" taught the children that God sent them sufferings and desired their sacrifices:

- It is God's will to sends sufferings which little children are to bear "*as an act of reparation for the sins by which He is offended*" (68).
- Such sufferings sent by Him are also "*supplication for the conversion of sinners*" (68).
  "*Once again, the most Blessed Virgin recommended to us the practice of mortification, and ended by saying: 'Pray, pray very much, and make sacrifices for sinners; for many souls go to hell,*

because there are none to sacrifice themselves and to pray for them'" (78).

- The sufferings were not trivial but were described by the children as "*much*" (68) and "*a great deal*" (44) and were to be borne with patient endurance.

  The angel had said *"Above all, accept and bear with submission, the sufferings which the Lord will send you"* (64, 159).

  "Our Lady came to see us," Jacinta said. "She told us she would take Francisco to heaven very soon, and she asked me if I still wanted to convert more sinners. I said I did. She told me I would be going to a hospital where I would suffer a great deal; and that I am to suffer for the conversion of sinners, in reparation for the sins committed against the Immaculate Heart of Mary, and for love of Jesus" (43–44).
- Self-mortification "pleases" God.

  Our Lady: *"God is pleased with your sacrifices, but He does not want you to sleep with the rope on; only wear it during the day"* (80).

  That the children were led to believe it was God who was sending the sufferings is evident in the following statements:

  Jacinta: *"Our Lady wants me to go to two hospitals, not to be cured but to suffer more for love of Our Lord and for sinners"* (102).

  Lucia: *"As the Angel had announced that God would send me sufferings, I always saw the hand of God in it all"* (76).

  Jacinta spoke *"of Our Lord and Our Lady: 'Oh, how much I love to suffer for love of Them, just to give Them pleasure! They greatly love those who suffer for the conversion of sinners'"*(45).

  Lucia: *"Such sufferings on my part must have been pleasing to Our Lord, because He was about to prepare*

> *a most bitter chalice for me which He was soon to give me to drink. My mother fell so seriously ill that, at one stage, we thought she was dying."* (94)
>
> Lucia: *"Our good Lord … once again came knocking on my door to ask yet another sacrifice, and not a small one either. My father was a healthy man, and robust; he said he had never known what it was to have a headache. But in less than 24 hours, an attack of double pneumonia carried him off to eternity … My God! My God! I never thought You had so much suffering in store for me! But I suffer for love of You, in reparation for the sins committed against the Immaculate Heart of Mary, for the Holy Father and for the conversion of sinners."* (95)
>
> Our Lady: *"The war (WW1) is going to end: but if people do not cease offending God, a worse one will break out during the pontificate of Pius XI. When you see a night illumined by an unknown light, know that this is the great sign given you by God that He is about to punish the world for its crimes, by means of war, famine, and persecutions of the Church and of the Holy Father."* (108–110)

The angel and Our Lady made several claims:

1. God sends sufferings, death, and destruction.
2. Sacrifices, such as mortifications and sufferings, count for something in the spiritual.
3. Jesus and God the Father would be pleased or comforted by such acts.
4. These acts are a means by which to bring about the "*conversion of sinners*" and save souls from going to hell.

What the Word of God Teaches about Suffering, Sacrifices, and God

"*God is love*," the apostle John wrote twice in his letter (1 John 4:8, 16), and Jesus is the perfect representation of God:

> *In the beginning was the Word, and the Word was with God, and the Word was God.* (John 1:1)
>
> *The Word became flesh and made his dwelling among us. We have seen his glory, the glory of the one and only Son, who came from the Father, full of grace and truth.* (John 1:14)
>
> *The Son is the radiance of God's glory and the exact representation of his being, sustaining all things by his powerful word.* (Heb 1:3)
>
> ***If you really know me, you will know my Father as well. From now on, you do know him and have seen him.*** (John 14:7)
>
> *Jesus answered:* ***"Don't you know me, Philip, even after I have been among you such a long time? Anyone who has seen me has seen the Father. How can you say, 'Show us the Father'?"*** (John 14:9)

> *The Son is the image of the invisible God, the firstborn over all creation.* (Col 1:15)
>
> What Jesus said and the way He lived then clearly demonstrated the will of our Father God toward us. Scripture also tells us that He is unchanging: "*Jesus Christ is the same yesterday and today and forever.*" (Heb 13:8).
>
> Looking then at the life of Jesus, we can compare to see if the testimony of the spirits at Fatima (the angel and the Lady)—about God and the sufferings He supposedly sent the children—line up with scripture.

Sickness and Sufferings: Their Source

Scripture reveals that when the disciples rebuked parents for bringing little children to Jesus for Him to place His hands on and pray for them:

> *Jesus said,* ***"Let the little children come to me, and do not hinder them, for the kingdom of heaven belongs to such as these."*** (Matthew 19:14; Mark 10:14; Luke 18:16)

He blessed them, loved them, healed them, and even brought those who had died back to life[28] instead of having inflicted any illness or suffering upon them.

In His encounters with adults too, He blessed them, fed them, healed them and brought the dead back to life.[29] Scripture shows how He revealed His ministry to us:

[28] Matthew 9:18–25.

[29] Luke 7:11–18; John 11:1–46.

> ***The Spirit of the Lord is on me, because he has anointed me to proclaim good news to the poor. He has sent me to proclaim freedom for the prisoners and recovery of sight for the blind, to set the oppressed free.*** (Luke 4:18)

God's purpose has never been to inflict sickness or death. These came only as a result of humankind's turning from living under His perfect will.

> ***The thief does not come except to steal, and to kill, and to destroy. I have come that they may have life, and that they may have it more abundantly.*** (John 10:10)

So, the sender of death and destruction is the evil one. However, the spirits who appeared to the children told them it was God who sent such.

Mortifications and Other Self-Inflicted Sufferings

What about mortifications (self-inflicted suffering)? The Bible speaks of self-inflicted suffering in chapter 18 of the first book of Kings.

At Mount Carmel, God had staged a showdown with the prophets of Baal who numbered 450 against His prophet Elijah.

Elijah had issued the challenge for the children of Israel, who had gathered there with King Ahab to choose: "*If the Lord is God, follow Him; but if Baal, follow him*" (1 Kings 18:21). He then gave instruction for two altars of burnt offerings to be built, with the wood and a bull for each altar. He challenged the prophets of Baal to call on their god first to bring down fire from heaven to consume the offering on their altar.

After much calling, crying, and self-inflicted cutting of

themselves with knives and lances, *"as was their custom … until their blood flowed"* (1 Kings 18:28), there was still no answer from Baal. However, when Elijah called on the name of the Lord, even after his altar had been liberally drenched with water, the fire came down from heaven and consumed not just the sacrifice but also all the water that had accumulated in the trench around the altar. So, the biblical reference to self-inflicted suffering describes the beliefs and actions of people opposed to God.

Another reference to self-imposed suffering was Judas Iscariot hanging himself on a tree after his betrayal of Jesus. These are hardly meant to have been examples for believers to follow.

Suffering for the Sake of the Gospel

The apostle Paul suffered much at the hands of those opposed to the Gospel, and he wrote much about suffering from personal experience. He had been imprisoned, beaten, lashed, and stoned so badly his persecutors had left him for dead. In each case, his suffering—like the suffering of others in the New Testament—resulted from his spreading the Gospel, which often led to resistance and opposition from people held in bondage to the enemy.

This led to suffering in the form of persecution for the sake of the Gospel. In every case, it was—and still is—the result of pushing against the gates of hell, and it was never self-inflicted suffering.

Further, what Paul wrote speaks of going out to proclaim the message of the kingdom, healing the sick (*from their* suffering), and setting the captives free *from their* bondages. It is in the exercise of the power of the Spirit to heal, loose *from sufferings* of various kinds, and restore that brings about the *conversion of sinners.*

Hence, the lost are saved as they experience the saving grace of God in their *release from suffering* and not the *imposition of suffering.* As scripture says, "*God's kindness … is intended to lead you to repentance*" (Rom 2:4). We live under God's grace, and the blood of the Lamb of God covers over our pain, shame, and guilt.

Jesus Bore Our Sufferings (Including Sickness and Shame)

Where sacrifice and suffering are concerned, the Son of God went through more than we will ever experience. At the cross, He took upon Himself the punishment we had deserved. His was thc *once-and-for-all-time sacrifice* so that we would be reconciled to God and not have to suffer for sin.

> *Unlike the other high priests, he (Jesus) does not need to offer sacrifices day after day, first for his own sins, and then for the sins of the people. He sacrificed for their sins once for all when he offered himself.* (Heb 7:27)

If this was not sufficient clear to the Hebrews to whom Paul wrote, he added the following:

> *We have been made holy through the sacrifice of the body of Jesus Christ once for all.* (Heb 10:10)

The apostle Peter wrote the same message:

> *For Christ also suffered once for sins, the righteous for the unrighteous, to bring you to God. He was put to death in the body but made alive in the Spirit.* (1 Pet 3:18)

True "Mortification" for Believers

The mortification that exists in the Christian walk is the putting to death of the flesh (*the self-will)* in order to live by the Spirit of God.[30] Examples of these teachings of these include the following:

---

[30] Mark 8:34–35; Matt 16:24–25; Luke 9:23–24; 1 John 3:16; Rom 8:13; Col 3:5; Matt 5:29–30; Gal 2:20, 5:24, 6:14; 1 Pet 2:11; Rom 6:6–7; Eph 4:22–23; 1 Cor 9:27.

> *Put to death, therefore, whatever belongs to your earthly nature: sexual immorality, impurity, lust, evil desires and greed, which is idolatry.* (Col 3:5)

> *For the grace of God has appeared that offers salvation to all people. It teaches us to say "No" to ungodliness and worldly passions, and to live self-controlled, upright and godly lives in this present age, while we wait for the blessed hope—the appearing of the glory of our great God and Savior, Jesus Christ.* (Titus 2:11–13)

The spirits at Fatima teach believers to sacrifice ourselves—but not in self-denial and going into all the world to preach the Gospel. Instead, they teach mortifications, which are based on the workings of and to the flesh and not of the Spirit.

Scripture warns us <u>against</u> such teaching:

> *Since you died with Christ to the elemental spiritual forces of this world, why, as though you still belonged to the world, do you submit to its rules: "Do not handle! Do not taste! Do not touch!"? These rules, which have to do with things that are all destined to perish with use, are based on merely human commands and teachings. <u>Such regulations indeed have an appearance of wisdom, with</u> their self-imposed worship, their false humility and <u>their harsh treatment of the body, but they lack any value in restraining sensual indulgence</u>.* (Col 2:20–23)

Mortifications taught by the spirits correspond to *penance* taught by some in the traditional churches. In these churches, penance is what you do when you try to atone for your own sin. However, every *penance* said and done is one that should never have been done because it is not in the will of God.

The mistranslation of scriptural references of "repentance" (a turning away from sin to God) into "penance" meant that—instead of trusting in the finished work of Christ and that He who started a good work in you will finish it—one trusts that such penance is efficacious toward forgiveness and right relations with God. This is not what scripture teaches.

These spirits of Fatima also taught the children to attribute the source of all manner of suffering that comes our way to our heavenly Father, which is patently untrue. This is blaming God for all our miseries.

The essence of the Gospel message is that Jesus sacrificed Himself for us so that we could have life and have it in abundance. Such a Gospel is not taught by those spirits.

The loving God of the Bible, who sent His only Son to die for us, is He who healed, restored, and even raised the dead. He is not a god who is pleased to have innocent children drink dirty water, dehydrate themselves until they are ill, and inflict pain on themselves, and He does not send disease or death. It is only the spirits of Fatima who claim that it is so.

Jesus bore our sufferings, but this is not to say believers are completely free from suffering. We live in a fallen world that will be redeemed. We also often make foolish choices that lead to unnecessary suffering—for ourselves and others. As believers, we have been given much grace from God through His Holy Spirit:

- protection from injury and suffering by following His loving guidance
- healing that we can claim for ourselves and for others—a direct gift of the Spirit
- a way out of suffering through the Spirit (1 Cor 10:13)

Sins Are Committed Against Mary

In their encounters with the Lady, the cousins were told many times that sins are committed against her, including blasphemy:

> *Sacrifice yourselves for sinners, and say many times, especially whenever you make some sacrifice: O Jesus, it is for love of You, for the conversion of sinners and in reparation for the sins committed against the Immaculate Heart of Mary.* (73)
>
> *Look, my daughter at my Heart, surrounded with thorns with which ungrateful men pierce me every moment by their blasphemies and ingratitude. You at least try to console me and say that I promise to assist at the hour of death, with the graces necessary for salvation, all those who, on the first Saturday of five consecutive months, shall confess, receive Holy Communion, recite five decades of the Rosary, and keep me company for fifteen minutes while meditating on the fifteen mysteries of the Rosary, with the intention of making reparation to me.* (197)
>
> *There are so many souls whom the Justice of God condemns for sins committed against me, that I have come to ask reparation: sacrifice yourself for this intention and pray.* (202)

Even "*Jesus,*" who appears firstly as an infant (199) and then as a "*resplendent child,*" said the following to Lucia:

> *It would please me more if they did First Saturdays with fervour and with intention of making reparation to the Heart of your heavenly Mother.* (200)

In summary:

1. Sins are committed against Mary, including blasphemy.
2. God condemns for sins against Mary.
3. We can make reparations for sin.

What Scripture Teaches Us about Sin

Sin Is Against God

Sin is invariably committed against God, and He alone is holy, righteous, and just.

King David had had an affair with Bathsheba, the wife of Uriah the Hittite. When she became pregnant, he tried to hide his guilt, but when he could not, he arranged for Uriah to die in battle. Later, after having repented, he wrote of his sin as being against God alone:

> *Have mercy upon me, O God,*
> *According to Your lovingkindness;*
> *According to the multitude of Your tender mercies,*
> *Blot out my transgressions.*
> *Wash me thoroughly from my iniquity,*
> *And cleanse me from my sin.*
> *For I acknowledge my transgressions,*
> *And my sin is always before me.*
> *Against You, You only, have I sinned,*
> *And done this evil in Your sight—*
> *That You may be found just when You speak,*
> *And blameless when You judge.* (Ps 51:1–4)

Sin might be aimed at another to whom one bears ill will, but in the end, it is to God to whom we must give account as our sin is a rejection of Him, His will, and the atoning grace He has provided through the suffering and death of His Son.

Blasphemy Is a Sin Committed against God Alone

Blasphemy in the Bible refers to speaking ill of God either in misrepresenting Him or in cursing Him. Speaking ill of persons or things other than God is not described as blaspheming them. Our Lady seems to say that the ungrateful blaspheme her, but unless she is God, this cannot be counted as blasphemy.

Our Reparation Against Sin Is Impossible

Unlike our Lady, God does not ask for *reparation* for sin. This is because there is *nothing* we can do to compensate for sin apart from accepting that Jesus came as our substitute for the punishment of sin and declaring His Lordship over us. After all, He redeemed us with His blood.

God does ask for *confession* (admission) and *repentance* (turning away from sin).

> *If we confess our sins, he is faithful and just and will forgive us our sins and purify us from all unrighteousness.* (1 John 1:9)

> Jesus said, "***I have not come to call the righteous, but sinners to repentance.***" (Luke 5:32)

> *Say to them, "As surely as I live, declares the Sovereign LORD, I take no pleasure in the death of the wicked, but rather that they turn from their ways and live. Turn! Turn from your evil ways! Why will you die, people of Israel?"… If a righteous person turns from their righteousness and*

> *does evil, they will die for it. And if a wicked person turns away from their wickedness and does what is just and right, they will live by doing so.* (Ezek 33:11, 18–19)[31]

> *The Lord is not slow in keeping his promise, as some understand slowness. Instead he is patient with you, not wanting anyone to perish, but everyone to come to repentance.* (2 Pet 3:9)

The Lady, in contrast, asks for *reparation* as though sin could somehow be recompensed through some activity of the sinner. She asks for *reparation*—and that the *reparation* be made *to her.*

The Word of God clearly states that "*the wages of sin is death*" (Rom 6:23) and "*without the shedding of blood* (signifying the loss of life), *there is no forgiveness*" (Heb 9:22). If the only thing that can pay for sin is death, then how can anyone "make reparation" since any such payment is worth nothing compared to life?

Fortunately, the full text of the Word of God says, "*For the wages of sin is death, but the gift of God is eternal life in Christ Jesus our Lord*" (Rom 6:23). Jesus was <u>*the*</u> reparation, having taken our punishment and death at the cross. There is neither any *other* reparation nor can any *other* life pay for sin since only the sinless can redeem the sinful just as only a credit can pay for a debt. One debt cannot pay for another. All we can do to clear our sin is *accept* the gift of eternal life in the manner described below:

> *Then they asked him, "What must we do to do the works God requires?" Jesus answered,* ***"The work of God is this: to believe in the one he has sent."*** (John 6:28–29)

> *And I am convinced that nothing can ever separate us from God's love. Neither death nor life, neither*

[31] For the full text, see Ezek 33:11–20.

> *angels nor demons, neither our fears for today nor our worries about tomorrow—not even the powers of hell can separate us from God's love.* (Rom 8:38)

There Is No Condemnation for Sin against Mary

The Lady says that sins are committed against her, that "*ungrateful men pierce (her heart) at every moment … by their blasphemies and ingratitude*" (197), and that "*the Justice of God condemns for sins committed against me*" (202).

However, scripture reveals a very different picture:

> *Therefore, there is now no condemnation for those who are in Christ Jesus, because through Christ Jesus the law of the Spirit who gives life has set you free from the law of sin and death.* (Rom 8:1)

Scripture teaches that "*you will know the truth and the truth will set you free*" (John 8:32) and "*if the Son sets you free, you will be free indeed*" (John 8:36). The message of Fatima, on the other hand, leads to a life of bondage to guilt and the never-ending efforts prescribed by the Lady to make reparations for sin *already atoned for* at the cross.

Our Lady's heaven isn't heaven if those already redeemed and at rest in heaven are subject to pains inflicted by humankind on earth.

Salvation and the Rosary

A core teaching of the Lady is that praying "the Rosary" plays a very important part in the life of a believer and is a key to "going to heaven." She who called herself "*Our Lady of the Rosary*" told the cousins at every encounter to pray the Rosary. The following are her own words.

First Meeting

> *Pray the Rosary every day, in order to obtain peace for the world, and the end of the war.* (168)

Second Meeting

> *I wish you to come here on thirteenth of the next month, to pray the Rosary every day, and to learn to read. Later, I will tell you what I want.* (169)

Third Meeting

> *I want you to come here on the thirteenth of next month, to continue to pray the Rosary every day in honour of Our Lady of the Rosary, in order to obtain peace for the world and the end of the war, because only she can help you.* (170)

When petitions (such as for healings and blessing) were made by the cousins on behalf of the people gathered, "*Our Lady said it was necessary for such people to pray the Rosary in order to obtain these graces during the year*" (170).

Fourth Meeting

> *I want you to continue going to the Cova da Iria on the thirteenth and to continue praying the Rosary every day.* (175)

Fifth Meeting

> *Continue to pray the Rosary in order to obtain the end of the war.* (176)

Last Meeting

> *Continue always to pray the Rosary every day.* (177)

Apparition of December 17, 1927

> *I promise to assist at the hour of death, with the graces necessary for salvation, all those who, on the first Saturday of five consecutive months, shall confess, receive Holy Communion, recite five decades of the Rosary, and keep me company for fifteen minutes while meditating on the fifteen mysteries of the Rosary, with the intention of making reparation to me.* (197)

For some, promises such as healings and various "graces" are made conditional upon praying the Rosary: "*Pray the Rosary every day in honour of Our Lady of the Rosary, in order to obtain peace for the world and the end of the war, because only she can help you.*"

For others, these are a requisite in order to get to heaven. When the cousins asked if they could go to heaven, she responded that the two girls would go to heaven and Francisco "*will go there too, but he must say many Rosaries.*"

What Scripture Teaches

The Way to Salvation

The apostle Paul wrote the following words in a letter to the church in Rome:

> *Everyone who calls on the name of the Lord will be saved. How, then, can they call on the one they have not believed in? And how can they believe in the one of whom they have not heard? And how can they hear without someone preaching to them?* (Rom 10:14)

He explains plainly that to be saved, which includes being sealed to go to heaven, the Gospel must firstly be preached and heard. This is so the listener, being moved by the Spirit of God, is convicted in his heart to accept by faith that God sent His Son to die for him and that God raised Christ from the dead.

After confessing Christ as Lord, the believer then lives a life of discipleship led by the Holy Spirit. As opposed to living for himself or herself, the life of a disciple is one of repentance (turning away from the old self). This life is lived out in relationship with the Father through His Spirit every day. Such a life led by the Spirit in strength, protection, and provision is described in Psalm 23, which begins with the words "*The Lord is my Shepherd.*"

We Already Have Been Given All We Need

Scripture does not describe such a life as one of one of mortification, reciting prayers, and pleading in order to obtain graces and entrance into heaven. Salvation is not earned but received; it is a gift. Just as a slave once freed is no longer a slave—salvation, once received, changes everything unless that slave chooses to go back to living in slavery to sin.

When the criminal who hung on the cross turned to Jesus and asked that He remember him when He would come to His kingdom, Jesus answered, "***Truly I tell you, today you will be with me in paradise***" (Luke 23:43). Jesus had declared him to have been justified by his faith in Him, and he was received as one forgiven of sin. Here was a criminal who admitted his crimes were deserving of the severest Roman punishment, yet Jesus pardoned him all his past, demonstrating that true repentance and turning to Him do not require reparation, mortifications, or the Rosary—things Our Lady and the angel repeatedly declared. Neither was there a working out of penances to reduce time in purgatory.

None of the salvations documented in the New Testament required mortifications, the Rosary, or the special graces that Our Lady alone is said to dispense—and no believer would doubt that the apostles and disciples saved in the book of Acts were welcomed to heaven. The New Testament church was, after all, the very church to which all believers trace their origins.

The apostle Paul, on one of his missionary journeys, traveled to Berea and wrote a good report of them. Luke wrote that:

> *They received the message with great eagerness and examined the Scriptures every day to see if what Paul said was true.* (Acts 17:11)

St. Paul cautioned the believers in Corinth as follows:

> *For if someone comes to you and preaches <u>a Jesus other than the Jesus we preached</u>, or if you receive <u>a different spirit from the Spirit you received</u>, <u>or a different Gospel from the one you accepted</u>, you put up with it easily enough.* (2 Cor 11:4)

For it is a different Gospel to what the apostles preached to say that mortifications, the Rosary, or graces from Our Lady are required for one to be saved. To say otherwise is to say that the early church and their Gospel must have somehow been deficient.

St. Paul emphasized the completeness of his teachings to the elders of the church at Ephesus:

> *You know that I have not hesitated to preach anything that would be helpful to you but have taught you publicly and from house to house.* (Acts 20:20)

For more on the Rosary, please see appendix 11: "The Rosary."

The Holy Spirit

The teachings of Our Lady and the angel *about* the Holy Spirit can be summed up in one word: *nil.*

There were *no* teachings and not even a mention of the Spirit who gives life to both us and to all living creation, including spirits.

Instead, the following ideas were taught. Firstly, it is the Lady (and not the Holy Spirit) who will never leave us:

> *Are you suffering a great deal? Don't lose heart, I will never forsake you*. (69)

Secondly, *she* is our refuge and the way that leads to God:

> *My Immaculate Heart will be your refuge and the way that will lead you to God*. (69)

These were spoken during the apparition of June 13, 1917.

Thirdly, graces and salvation conditionally come through her, and we must turn to her for them:

> *I promise to assist at the hour of death, with the graces necessary for salvation, all those who, on the first Saturday of five consecutive months, shall confess, receive Holy Communion, recite five decades of the Rosary, and keep me company for fifteen minutes while meditating on the fifteen mysteries of the*

> *Rosary, with the intention of making reparation to me*. (197)

In each case, the above teachings allude to certain concepts:

- Her role effectively replaces that given to the Holy Spirit whom scripture tells us is the source of God's gifts and who will be with us forever.[32]
- She is our refuge.
- We lack the necessary "graces" for salvation that she can provide.

What the Word Teaches

God Sent Us His Spirit to Be with and in Us

Scripture teaches us that, from the very beginning of creation, the Holy Spirit was there even as Jesus, the Son of God, called all things into being. As such, He has been witness to all things.

In the Old Testament, God repeatedly sent His Spirit to guide and help those whose hearts were turned to Him. He spoke through His prophet Ezekiel, however, that the day would come when His Spirit would not just be *with* or *on* but would *indwell* His people.[33] That day was to be the day of Pentecost when He poured out His Spirit upon the disciples of Jesus who had gathered and waited just as Jesus had instructed before His ascension into heaven.

Jesus Said His Spirit Would Be Forever with Us

When Jesus walked the earth, he told His disciples that He would never abandon them. This is despite knowing that, after His betrayal by Judas Iscariot, they would all abandon Him—even if for a while.

---

[32] Matt 28:20; John 14:16, 18; Rom 8:38–39; 2 Cor 1:22; Eph 1:13–14; Heb 13:5.

[33] Ezek 36:27.

Shortly before His death, resurrection and ascension to heaven, He said:

> ***And I will ask the Father, and he will give you another advocate to help you and be with you forever—the Spirit of truth. The world cannot accept him, because it neither sees him nor knows him. But you know him, for he lives with you and will be in you.*** (John 14:16–17)

Jesus Said His Spirit Is Better for Us than Even His Physical Presence

When the disciples wanted Jesus to remain with them, He said that it would be *better* for them that He returned to the Father for only then could the Spirit be given to them. He also said that His disciples would even do *greater works* with the presence of His Spirit than He Himself had done because He would go to be with His Father.

Jesus called the Holy Spirit, the "Advocate", the "Helper" and the "Spirit of Truth" who would teach them all things and bring to remembrance all the things He had said to them.

> ***But now I am going to him who sent me. None of you asks me, "Where are you going?" Rather, you are filled with grief because I have said these things. But very truly I tell you, it is for your good that I am going away. Unless I go away, the Advocate will not come to you; but if I go, I will send him to you. When he comes, he will prove the world to be in the wrong about sin and righteousness and judgment: about sin, because people do not believe in me; about righteousness, because I am going to the Father, where you can see me no longer; and about judgment, because the prince of this world now stands condemned.***

> ***I have much more to say to you, more than you can now bear. But when he, the Spirit of truth, comes, he will guide you into all the truth. He will not speak on his own; he will speak only what he hears, and he will tell you what is yet to come. He will glorify me because it is from me that he will receive what he will make known to you.*** (John 16:5–14)

The Holy Spirit is our Helper whom Jesus sent to shepherd us in this life so that we live as His in this life and into the next. The apostle Paul wrote a letter to the believers in Galatia:

> *Therefore, there is now no condemnation for those who are in Christ Jesus, because through Christ Jesus the law of the Spirit who gives life has set you free from the law of sin and death. For what the law was powerless to do because it was weakened by the flesh, God did by sending his own Son in the likeness of sinful flesh to be a sin offering. And so he condemned sin in the flesh, in order that the righteous requirement of the law might be fully met in us, who do not live according to the flesh but according to the Spirit.*
>
> *Those who live according to the flesh have their minds set on what the flesh desires; but those who live in accordance with the Spirit have their minds set on what the Spirit desires. The mind governed by the flesh is death, but the mind governed by the Spirit is life and peace. The mind governed by the flesh is hostile to God; it does not submit to God's law, nor can it do so. Those who are in the realm of the flesh cannot please God.*
>
> *You, however, are not in the realm of the flesh but are in the realm of the Spirit, if indeed the Spirit of God lives in you. And if anyone does not have the*

> *Spirit of Christ, they do not belong to Christ. But if Christ is in you, then even though your body is subject to death because of sin, the Spirit gives life because of righteousness. And if the Spirit of him who raised Jesus from the dead is living in you, he who raised Christ from the dead will also give life to your mortal bodies because of his Spirit who lives in you.* (Rom 8:1–11)

> *In the same way, the Spirit helps us in our weakness. We do not know what we ought to pray for, but the Spirit himself intercedes for us through wordless groans. And he who searches our hearts knows the mind of the Spirit, because the Spirit intercedes for God's people in accordance with the will of God.* (Rom 8:26–27)

> *At one time we too were foolish, disobedient, deceived and enslaved by all kinds of passions and pleasures. We lived in malice and envy, being hated and hating one another. But when the kindness and love of God our Savior appeared, he saved us, not because of righteous things we had done, but because of his mercy. He saved us through the washing of rebirth and renewal by the Holy Spirit, whom he poured out on us generously through Jesus Christ our Savior, so that, having been justified by his grace, we might become heirs having the hope of eternal life.* (Titus 3:3–7)

Scripture thus reveals that the Holy Spirit is *with* and *in* believers to intercede, convict, reveal, overcome, and give us the life that Jesus died to give us. This life is what Jesus had described as "***life in its fullness***." The Spirit is the One who will remain with us and never leave us. In Jesus's words, He will "***abide with you forever***."

Our Lady, instead, says that *she* is the one who will never forsake us.

God Alone Is Our Refuge

She also asks that believers look to her as their refuge and the way that will lead to God.

In doing as the Bereans did, to scripture check every claim of the apostle Paul, one finds the word "refuge" in scripture as follows:

- The "eternal God" who is the "God of Jacob" is our refuge. This accounts for more than half of these scriptures.
- God had designated that cities of refuge in the land of Israel be set up to which one who had accidentally killed another could flee so that justice might be administered. This accounts for about a third of the remaining scriptures.
- Other references to "refuge" in a more general sense account for about a tenth of the scriptures.
- The remaining scriptures warn of turning to lies and false gods as refuges.

Throughout scripture, God has revealed *Himself* as the only personal "refuge" to whom we, His creation, can turn. As for "*the way that will lead you to God*," the only personal references in scripture to "*the way leading to God*" are spoken by Jesus:

> ***I am the way and the truth and the life. No one comes to the Father except through me.*** (John 14:6)

For any person or spirit to claim otherwise is to deny the words of Christ.

We Do Not Lack Any "Graces Necessary for Salvation"

Our Lady made the following conditional promise:

> *I promise to assist at the hour of death, with the graces necessary for salvation*, (all those if), *on the*

> *first Saturday of five consecutive months, (they) shall confess, receive Holy Communion, recite five decades of the Rosary, and keep me company for fifteen minutes while meditating on the fifteen mysteries of the Rosary, with the intention of making reparation to me.*

This means that there are certain "graces" that believers need at the hour of death. That the promise is made to believers is clear because the only ones who might do all the things that her graces require (confession, receiving of Communion, and the recitation and meditation of the "mysteries" of the Rosary while "keeping her company") would be believers who adhere to these traditions.

The Word of God tells us that we already have *everything* we need in Christ Jesus, as evidenced in the apostle Paul's first letter to the believers in Corinth:

> *I always thank my God for you because of his grace given you in Christ Jesus. For in him you have been enriched in every way—with all kinds of speech and with all knowledge— God thus confirming our testimony about Christ among you. Therefore you do not lack any spiritual gift as you eagerly wait for our Lord Jesus Christ to be revealed. He will also keep you firm to the end, so that you will be blameless on the day of our Lord Jesus Christ.* (1 Cor 1:4–8)

Paul tells us that we already have all things we need, and this is especially so since we have the very Spirit of God in us. While we can write of all the gifts of the Holy Spirit as well as the fact that every believer saved in the New Testament did not require any additional "graces necessary for salvation" that were conditional on the practices recommended by Our Lady, Paul's scriptural exposition of truth is more than sufficient.

However, he addresses any who might still doubt in his letter to the Romans:

> *Therefore, there is now no condemnation for those who are in Christ Jesus, because through Christ Jesus the law of the Spirit who gives life has set you free from the law of sin and death.* (Rom 8:1)

Scripture

As they did with the Holy Spirit, the spirits at Fatima make no mention of scripture and neither refer to, teach from, nor advocate the teaching of scripture.

In contrast, the prophets, apostles, and Jesus Himself taught from scripture, quoted from scripture, and advocated its teaching.

Jesus Taught the Importance of Scripture

The following are but a few examples of Jesus teaching the importance of scripture:

> *Jesus answered,* ***"It is written: 'Man shall not live on bread alone, but on every word that comes from the mouth of God."*** (Matt 4:4)

> ***But the seed falling on good soil refers to someone who hears the word and understands it. This is the one who produces a crop, yielding a hundred, sixty or thirty times what was sown.*** (Matt 13:23)

> ***Sanctify them by the truth; your word is truth.*** (John 17:17)

> ***Do not think that I have come to abolish the Law or the Prophets; I have not come to abolish them but to fulfill them ... Therefore anyone who sets aside one of the least of these commands and teaches others accordingly will be called least in the kingdom of heaven, but whoever practices and teaches these commands will be called great in the kingdom of heaven.*** (Matt 5:17, 19)

Jesus and the Apostles Taught the Importance of Teaching Scripture

Jesus so often taught from scripture, that He was referred to numerous times as "*Teacher*" and even referred to Himself as that at least three times as recorded in the Gospels.[34] The following show that the apostles and disciples themselves followed the example of Jesus in teaching and promoting scripture:

> *Now the Berean Jews were of more noble character than those in Thessalonica, for they received the message with great eagerness and examined the Scriptures every day to see if what Paul said was true.* (Acts 17:11)

> *Now I commit you to God and to the word of his grace, which can build you up and give you an inheritance among all those who are sanctified.* (Acts 20:32)

> *By this gospel you are saved, if you hold firmly to the word I preached to you. Otherwise, you have believed in vain.* (1 Cor 15:2)

> *Like newborn babies, crave pure spiritual milk* (the Word of God), *so that by it you may grow up in your*

[34] Mark 14:14; Luke 22:11; John 13:13–14.

> *salvation, now that you have tasted that the Lord is good.* (1 Peter 2:2–3)
>
> *What you heard from me, keep as the pattern of sound teaching, with faith and love in Christ Jesus. Guard the good deposit that was entrusted to you—guard it with the help of the Holy Spirit who lives in us.* (2 Tim 1:13–14)
>
> *But as for you, continue in what you have learned and have become convinced of, because you know those from whom you learned it, and how from infancy you have known the Holy Scriptures, which are able to make you wise for salvation through faith in Christ Jesus. All Scripture is God-breathed and is useful for teaching, rebuking, correcting and training in righteousness, so that the servant of God may be thoroughly equipped for every good work.* (2 Tim 3:14–17)
>
> *So Paul stayed in Corinth for a year and a half, teaching them the Word of God.* (Acts 18:11)
>
> *For everything that was written in the past was written to teach us, so that through the endurance taught in the Scriptures and the encouragement they provide we might have hope.* (Rom 15:4)
>
> *Until I come, devote yourself to the public reading of Scripture, to preaching and to teaching.* (1 Tim 4:13)

As already stated, the spirits at Fatima neither taught nor advocated the teaching of scripture. Further, what they *did* teach was not what Jesus or the apostles taught.

The Spirits at Fatima

As a result of the extra-biblical teachings about Mary that were created and propagated within the church after the first century, believers had been praying to Mary and expecting to hear from her.

The biblical Mary did not ask for believers to come to her—unlike Jesus who always said, "***Come to Me.***" The Mary of scripture did not make promises, perform miracles, or claim that salvation came from her. Like the other disciples, she had no followers and did not ask for any. As with other disciples, she would have turned the eyes of others to her Son as she demonstrated at the wedding at Cana when she said, "*Do whatever He tells you*" (John 2:5).

The spirits behind the visitations, on the other hand, did all the things the biblical Mary did not do. Beyond seeking followers, she claimed that Jesus wanted world devotion and the dedication of all Russia to her.

Apart from when the children were "*repeating in their hearts, 'O most Holy Trinity, I adore You! My God, my God, I love you in the most Blessed Sacrament,*'" the prayers and activities she promoted appeared to be primarily directed toward prayer and worship of her. This included asking that a chapel and litters for the fiesta be built for devotion to her.

Other prayers the Lady asked the children to pray were to appease a God who desired the painful sacrifices of little children and who apparently sent sicknesses and even death. Like the teachings of Liguori and others, the picture painted of God by the spirits was one of an angry God—whereas Mary is portrayed as gentle, loving, and understanding.

New Testament disciples always directed believers to members of the Holy Trinity. Scripture testifies that each member of the Holy Trinity also always directed our prayers to other members of the Trinity. Examples of these include the following verses:

- God the Father exalting His Son: Matt 3:17; 17:5; Mark 1:11; 9:7; Luke 3:22; 9:35; Acts 2:22, 24–28, 32–36; 3:22–23; 4:30–31; 10:36–38, 40; 13:32–36

- Jesus exalting the Father: Matt 5:16; 6:9–10; 10:29; Luke 11:2; John 14:24, 28, 31; 15:1, 7–8; 16:5, 28; 17:1, 3–4, 6–8, 26; 20:24
- Jesus exalting the Holy Spirit: John 3:5–6; 15:26; 16:7–11, 13, 15; 20:22; Acts 1:4–5, 8; 9:17
- The Holy Spirit exalting Jesus: John 16:14; Acts 4:25–26, 30–31; 9:17–20, 31; 11:24
- The Holy Spirit exalting the Father: Acts 10:44–46
- All the prophets exalting Jesus: Acts 10:43

The spirit at Fatima spoke of Jesus only as her Son but does not appear to call Him Savior, Lord, Son of God, or any of the divine titles that rightly belong only to Him. The emphasis appears to be on her "divine motherhood" but not on Jesus, the Lord of Life. More than anything else, the spirits direct believers (always already Christian) to pray to Mary and to devote their prayer life to seeking her favor, miracles, and everything the New Testament church looked for in Christ Jesus.

Many in the traditional churches, which already subscribed to the beliefs covered in part I of this book, readily took the spirit who appeared as the Lady to be the Mary of the Bible simply because she said she was. That she could change appearance from moment to moment as demonstrated at the sixth meeting from Our Lady to Our Lady of Dolours and then to Our Lady of Carmel meant this spirit could—and did—take on any appearance she wanted.

Why This Spirit Cannot Be Mary

It is highly unlikely that the spirit behind the various visitations, including at Fatima, was Mary. In many of visitations, it is highly significant that the seers who saw or interacted with the spirit had long before dedicated themselves to Mary instead of to God Himself.

The following spheres are examined along with the reasons why this spirit cannot be Mary:

- in worship
- in servanthood
- in being a child of God
- in being dependent upon God's mercy
- in not being the dispenser of God's gifts and grace
- in the sacredness of the Sabbath
- idolatry

In Worship

The biblical Mary would not have wanted anyone to redirect their worship of God to herself. That is called "idolatry," and the biblical Mary was not idolatrous. While many in the churches that follow her use various terms instead of worship such as *honor* to describe what is clearly worship, Liguori and even Pope Alexander VII did not claim it was anything *less* than worship:

> *This devotion and worship to the mother of God again increased and was propagated … so that the universities having embraced this opinion (that is, the pious one), almost all Catholics embrace it.* (Liguori 365)

If, as her followers believe, she, being omniscient, is ever attentive to her servants and has her ear toward their requests, she would be fully aware of the many prayers that are prayed to her and that these exalt her equal to God.

Her followers also believe that she will answer their prayers and petitions. If that were so, and if she were the biblical Mary, she would, without doubt, have corrected them in their many unsound teachings, beliefs, and prayers that directly contradict scripture:

- the belief in her lifelong—and beyond—sufferings
- that sins are committed against her instead of God
- that we have to go through her to get to God
- that all the gifts of God come through and only through her hands
- that she is our advocate to God when she knew her Advocate in the Holy Spirit
- that salvation comes only through her

In Servanthood

The biblical Mary acknowledged herself simply as the handmaid (servant) of the Lord and would not have wanted anyone to be her servant. Indeed, what would such servanthood to her achieve other than to exalt her when God alone is to be exalted?

In the Lord's Prayer that Jesus taught, we pray "***Your*** (God's) ***will be done, on earth as it is in heaven***" (Matt 6:10) and not the will of any other.

She would have been very familiar with Jesus's teachings during her life and thereafter: "***Worship the Lord your God, and serve him only***" (Matt 4:10).

In Being a Child of God

Mary, as with all called by God, belongs to God's chosen family by virtue of faith in Christ Jesus and by the leading of the Holy Spirit:

> *So in Christ Jesus you are all children of God through faith, for all of you who were baptized into Christ have clothed yourselves with Christ.* (Gal 3:26–27)
>
> *For those who are led by the Spirit of God are the children of God.* (Rom 8:14)

> *And by him we cry, "Abba, Father." The Spirit himself testifies with our spirit that we are God's children. Now if we are children, then we are heirs—heirs of God and co-heirs with Christ, if indeed we share in his sufferings in order that we may also share in his glory.* (Rom 8:15–17)[35]

> *Jesus replied, "**The people of this age marry and are given in marriage. But those who are considered worthy of taking part in the age to come and in the resurrection from the dead will neither marry nor be given in marriage, and they can no longer die; for they are like the angels. They are God's children, since they are children of the resurrection.**"* (Luke 20:34–36)

Mary is a child of God, and nowhere in scripture is she described as being "*our mother.*" She does not represent herself as such except in the teachings and beliefs compiled by Liguori and the spirit of the visitations. This subject was covered in "Mary as Our Mother" in part I of this book.

In Being Dependent upon God's Mercy

The biblical Mary acknowledged her need for the mercy of God and did not consider herself the arm of God in the dispensation of His mercy:

> *My soul glorifies the Lord*
> *and my spirit rejoices in God my Saviour,*
> *for he has been mindful*
> *of the humble state of his servant.* (Luke 1:46–48)

[35] These are not self-inflicted sufferings; they are suffering for the sake of the Gospel.

In Not Being the Dispenser of God's Gifts and Grace

The Mary of scripture also acknowledged that it was God who had bestowed His grace upon her rather than her being the source or conduit of such grace. In her song of praise, she exclaimed the following:

> *From now on all generations will call me blessed, for the Mighty One has done great things for me—holy is his name.* (Luke 1:48–49)

In the Sacredness of the Sabbath

Being brought up in Judaism, the biblical Mary would have kept the Sabbath (from dusk Friday to sunset Saturday) holy and recognized it as not just a day to refrain from work but a special day dedicated to her relationship with her God. She would likely not have condoned Pope Paul V's Bull of 1612, which determined that Saturday is instead "consecrated by the Church to the blessed Virgin."

Idolatry

She would not have approved the creation of litters that carried an image of herself either; she would have been intimately familiar with the Commandments that say not to create images of things either in heaven or on earth and bow down before them.

Further, she would not have condoned anyone bowing down to her and dedicating their entire lives to her when she is already in the presence of Almighty God who alone deserves all praise and all we can offer.

Neither would she have approved of the practice of her followers calling her all the divine titles that belong exclusively to God.

Who Then Is This Spirit?

The spirit of the visitations is likely who she always said she was: *the queen of heaven*. At many of the different visitations in different locations and times, she called herself so. This subject was looked at briefly in the chapter "Queen of Heaven" in part I of this book when we examined scripture that told of this *queen* who led astray many of the children of Israel.

The queen of heaven was one of many "gods" that the peoples of the Near East worshipped. Scripture does not tell us if the queen of heaven was like the many other idols made of wood or metal that had neither ears to hear nor eyes to see or if it was a spiritual principality and power spoken of in both the Old and New Testaments.[36]

The followers of this spirit at the time of Jeremiah apparently believed in her presence and power since they refused to turn back to God even when His anointed prophet warned them time and again of the impending judgment that was shortly to visit them.

That any spirit would identify itself as the *queen of heaven*, given what scripture warns about her, says perhaps as much concerning the deficit in knowledge of scripture of those that follow her as about the spirit itself.

The spirit who manifests at the many visitations does a number of things:

- "She" diverts believers' attention away from the holy presence of God's Holy Spirit and all that He was given to do in the lives of believers. He will only do what believers allow Him to do.
  This restriction placed on the Spirit is similar to how the people of Jesus's hometown treated Him so that He did not do many miracles there.[37] Unlike the large crowds

[36] Isa 24:21; Dan 4:35; Rom 8:38; Eph 1:21; 3:10; 6:12; Col 1:16; 2:10, 15.

[37] Matt 13:53–58.

from near and far, as described in Matthew 4:23–25, these townspeople likely did not bring to Him all who needed His touch and so He could not heal them.

- "She" neither quotes scripture nor encourages any believer to read scripture. How important should scripture be in the lives of believers? This is answered in part IV.
- "She" promotes the practice of penance when scripture tells us that God instead seeks repentance. Penance implies two things that are contrary to the Gospel:
    - that sin can be atoned for by a means other than the blood of Christ
    - that God has not forgiven sin so that there remains a debt that has to be paid

    Both these ideas are contrary to the Gospel message that says that only the blood of Christ can wash away sin, God has forgiven our sin, and the debt was paid in full at the cross.

    Repentance, on the other hand, is a turning away from self or the world and turning to God, which Jesus always taught.[38]

    In teaching penance, "she" teaches a different way to that of turning to God.

- "She" has never corrected any of the incorrect teachings about her promoted by others.
    - The teaching that believers need to reach God through her instead of going to God directly through Christ and

[38] Matt 4:17; 11:20–24; 12:41; 21:32; Mark 6:12; Luke 5:32; 6:31–38; 10:13–15; 11:29–32; 13:2–5, 15; 16:30; 17:3–4; 24:47; John 5:14; 8:11.

His Spirit (both of whom are persons of the Trinity of God). On the contrary, "she" taught the children that she is the way to God

- the teaching that graces come through her instead of through the Holy Spirit
- sins are committed against her rather than that all sins are committed against God

There are many other practices that "she" promotes in the many visitations that go beyond Fatima, but this book would be too lengthy to cover them in the detail that would be required to do so.

In various areas around the world and at different times, what seems to be this same spirit has also appeared in remote villages and in grottos. Her followers call her the Goddess of Mercy, Guanyin, etc. They have also erected statues, worship her, and place their petitions before her. She teaches what appear to be "good" moral teachings—but without leading her followers to Jesus or God who is their Creator and Savior.

It would appear that she tailors her appearance and teachings based on what the local people would readily accept based on the prevailing local beliefs—whatever the religion.

Rather than following the one Holy Spirit who God has given us, scripture warns us:

> *The Spirit clearly says that in later times some will abandon the faith and follow deceiving spirits and things taught by demons.* (1 Tim 4:1)

PART III

THE FRUIT OF BELIEFS

In the previous two parts of this book, we have looked at the teachings of man and of spirits that have appeared and have examined these in the light of scripture.

Jesus taught us a simple way to discern both teachers and their teachings:

> ***Watch out for false prophets. They come to you in sheep's clothing, but inwardly they are ferocious wolves. By their fruit you will recognize them. Do people pick grapes from thornbushes, or figs from thistles? Likewise, every good tree bears good fruit, but a bad tree bears bad fruit. A good tree cannot bear bad fruit, and a bad tree cannot bear good fruit. Every tree that does not bear good fruit is cut down and thrown into the fire. Thus, by their fruit you will recognize them.***
> (Matt 7:15–20)

This testing by examining the fruit can be applied both to the teachings as compiled by Liguori and to those promoted at the visitations. So far, in this book, the teachings have only been compared against scripture, but now the fruit will be examined.

One fruit of the teachings and beliefs covered in part I was the expectation that Mary was and is accessible and that believers should actively pray to her and seek her. This likely opened up believers to the series of visitations of which the encounters at Fatima was one example, which was described in part II. Scripture warns us to beware of deceiving spirits that will appear at the end-times (Gal 1:6–9; 1 Tim 4:1) and that even Satan appears as an angel of light (2 Cor 11:14).

Nowhere are we told, in New Testament scripture, to follow ***any spirit*** when we have been given God's Holy Spirit to be with us and remain in us all our days.

The fruit examined in this section include the following:

- The belief that what we have been given is spiritually lacking, so that followers have to go to Mary to get that which they lack. This topic is addressed in "A Fruit: Belief in the Insufficiency of Our Salvation."
- A form of Christian theology different from what Jesus and the apostles taught is looked at in "A Fruit: Another Gospel."
- The belief that God is angry with us so we should instead go to Mary who is welcoming of us. This is addressed in "A Fruit: God Being Made to Appear Angry but Mary as Merciful."
- The belief that various positions, attributes, and titles that belong to God and Him alone belong also to Mary. This addressed in "A Fruit: Reassignment of the Positions, Attributes, and Titles of God."

The result of the above is:

- The substitution of God by Mary—addressed in "The End Fruit: The Substitution of God."
- Believers giving themselves completely over to Mary in ways that belong entirely to God—addressed in "The End Fruit: Giving Themselves Completely Over to Her."

Two other topics are examined in this section:

- the possibility of the teachings being "another Gospel" that New Testament scripture speaks of
- an examination of "The Spirit of the Visitations" in greater depth

Finally, "Why all of this has happened" concludes this part of the book. It looks at some of the possible reasons that God has, in His patience, allowed the church to have gone so far away from the teachings of Jesus and the apostles.

A Fruit: Belief in the Insufficiency of Our Salvation

The belief in our spiritual insufficiency is a fruit of many of the previously examined teachings about Mary. It is the belief that, without the continuing work of Mary in our lives, we are incomplete spiritually and that what God has given us is insufficient. This is not about the Mary who lived at the time of Christ; it is a Mary who is said to live now and to whom we should turn and give our allegiance to and become servants of.

This idea of insufficiency is best captured in the slogan "(Your country) *Needs Fatima,*" such as "America Needs Fatima," which is actively promoted by certain groups in a growing list of countries.

This teaching says that we actively *need* to seek from Mary *that* which we lack in order to be assured of our salvation. "*That*" ranges from any of the following things:

- graces
- "final perseverance"
- assurance of the forgiveness of the Father and our right standing with Him
- power to overcome temptation and more

In addition to the above, Liguori taught that we need to become "*servants of Mary*." Some examples from Liguori that speak of the insufficiency and required servanthood appear below:

> *If a soul loses her devotion to Mary, she will immediately be full of darkness, and that darkness of which the Holy Ghost says: "Thou hast appointed darkness, and it is night; in it shall the beasts of the woods go about."* (Liguori 92)

Examination of the scripture quoted, which is taken from Psalm 104, reveals it is written about the works of God and how He put everything in its proper place: night and day, seasons, animals, food, the sea, etc. It does not speak of Mary or devotion to her.

> *To serve Mary and to belong to her court, adds St. John of Damascus, is the greatest honor we can attain; for to serve the queen of heaven is to reign already in heaven, and to live in obedience to her commands is more than to reign. On the other hand, he says that those who do not serve Mary will not be saved; whilst those who are deprived of the support of this great mother, are deprived of the succor of the Son, and of all the celestial court.* (Liguori 280–281)

On the contrary, to serve God is our highest calling and our rightful response to He who both made us and saved us because of His great love. Scripture, which is the revealed Word of God, does not teach that to not serve Mary is to not be saved. The good news of the Gospel reveals that what Christ has done is completely sufficient as we shall see further along.

> *Thomas a Kempis, when a young man, was accustomed daily to have recourse to the Virgin with certain prayers; one day he omitted them, then he omitted them for some weeks, then he gave them up entirely. One night he saw Mary in a dream, who embraced his companions, but having come to him, said: "What do you expect, who have given up your devotions? Depart, for you are unworthy of my favors." Terrified by these words, Thomas awoke, and resumed his accustomed prayers. Richard therefore with reason says: He who is perseveringly devoted to Mary will be blessed with the hope, that all his desires may be gratified. But as no one can be secure of this perseverance, no one can be sure of salvation before his death.* (Liguori 644–645)

In contrast to the spirit in Thomas's dream, the Holy Spirit never tells us to depart because we are unworthy. Neither are we to doubt our salvation for scripture tells us repeatedly that those who place their trust in the Son are saved: John 3:36; 5:24; Acts 2:21; 3:19; 4:12; 16:29–34; Rom 3–5; 8:1–4; 1 Cor 1:8; 2 Cor 1:21–22, and more.

Instead of becoming free from the law of "having to do" and being set free in Christ, one who follows after Mary must be "*perseveringly devoted to Mary,*" as Liguori clearly says. (In *The Glories*, Liguori tell readers what this devotion means in the many Rosaries and other prayers, novenas, scapulars to be worn, and dedications of persons, families, and countries to her that appear in his compilation.)

> *As men take pride in having others wear their livery, so the most holy Mary is pleased when her servants*

> *wear her scapular, as a mark that they have dedicated themselves to her service, and are of the number of the family of the mother of God. Modern heretics, of course, ridicule this devotion, but the holy Church has approved it by many bulls and indulgences. And Father Crasset relates, and also Father Lezzana, when speaking of the scapular of Mt. Carmel, that about the year 1251, the holy Virgin appeared to the blessed Simon Stock, an Englishman, and giving him her scapular, said to him that those who wore it should be saved from eternal damnation, in these words: "Receive, oh my very beloved son, this scapular of thy order, the badge of my confraternity, a privilege granted to thee and to all other Carmelites; and anyone who wears this at death shall be delivered from eternal flames."* (Liguori 660)

In the year 1251, scripture was almost completely unavailable for the laity; even then, it was only available in Latin to a small group of clergy. For those unfamiliar with scripture then, it was perhaps excusable for them to believe that a scapular could save their souls when scripture teaches that only faith in God through Christ brings salvation and that the Holy Spirit was given as the *guarantee* of our personal salvation.

> *And Father Crasset still further relates, that Mary appeared at another time to Pope John XXII., and directed him to declare to those who wore the above-mentioned scapular, that they should be released from purgatory on the Saturday after their death; this the same pontiff announced in his bull, which was afterwards confirmed by Alexander V., Clement VII., and others, as the above-named Father Crasset relates in the passage above cited. And as we have remarked in the first part, Paul V. mentions the same,*

> *and appears to explain the bulls of the preceding pontiffs, prescribing in his bull the conditions to be observed in order to gain the indulgences annexed, namely, the observance of chastity according to the state of life, the recitation of the little office of the Virgin, and for him who cannot recite that, the observance, at least, of the feasts of the Church and abstinence from meat on Wednesday. Thus the indulgences that are attached to this scapular of our Lady of Mt. Carmel, as well as to the others of the dolors of Mary, of Mary of Mercy, and particularly to that of the Conception, are innumerable, daily, and plenary, in life and at the article of death. For myself, I have taken all the above-mentioned scapulars.* (Liguori 660–661)

There are, in fact, many different scapulars. Similarly, in the visitations, the children were taught that praying the Rosary was necessary in some cases, such as that of young Francisco for him to get to heaven. Woe then to the apostles and early believers who did not have access to those scapulars and the Rosary since they were unavailable in those days.

In contrast, the apostles taught that we have all we need through the richness of blessings from Christ and His Spirit as will be shown.

> *The glorious St. Bonaventure, in order to revive in the hearts of sinners confidence in the protection of Mary, represents to us the sea in a tempest, in which sinners who have fallen from the bark of divine grace, tossed about by remorse of conscience, and by the fear of divine justice, without light and without a guide, have almost lost the breath of hope, and are nearly sinking in despair.* (Liguori 131)

> *And Mary intended to signify the same when she appeared to St. Gertrude, spreading her mantle to receive all who had recourse to her: at the same time it was given the saint to understand, that the angels are waiting to defend the devout suppliants of Mary from the assaults of hell.* (Liguori 146–147)

The overarching theme in all the above is always that the believer does not already have all that God has given through His Holy Spirit. Since we lack, we need recourse to Mary even for protection from "assaults of hell."

The New Testament carries a very different message when speaking of spirits and demons:

> *You, dear children, are from God and have overcome them, because the one who is in you is greater than the one* (Satan) *who is in the world.* (1 John 4:4)

Liguori on the other hand claims:

> *This divine mother, with her powerful prayers and assistance, has obtained for us paradise, if we place no obstacle to our entrance there. Wherefore <u>those who are servants of Mary</u>, and for whom Mary intercedes, are as secure of paradise as if they were already there. (Liguori 280)*

God's Word teaches us that we *already have <u>all</u>* we require for eternal life *<u>through faith in Jesus</u>*.

The following scriptures, among many others, summarize the good news that we have life with Christ both in this world and in the next when we place our trust in Christ Jesus and His finished work of our salvation:

When the criminal on the cross placed his trust in Jesus, He replied ***"Truly I tell you, today you'll be with me in Paradise."*** (Luke 23:43)

Whoever believes in the Son has eternal life, but whoever rejects the Son will not see life, for God's wrath remains on them. (John 3:36)

Very truly I tell you, whoever hears my word and believes him who sent me has eternal life and will not be judged but has crossed over from death to life. (John 5:24)

Very truly I tell you, the one who believes has eternal life. (John 6:47)

Now this is eternal life: that they know you, the only true God, and Jesus Christ, whom you have sent. (John 17:2–3)

And everyone who calls on the name of the Lord will be saved. (Joel 2:32 and Acts 2:21)

The jailer called for lights, rushed in and fell trembling before Paul and Silas. He then brought them out and asked, "Sirs, what must I do to be saved?" They replied, "Believe in the Lord Jesus, and you will be saved—you and your household." (Acts 16:29–31)

Now to the one who works, wages are not credited as a gift but as an obligation. However, to the one who does not work but trusts God who justifies the ungodly, their faith is credited as righteousness. David says the same thing when he speaks of the blessedness

> *of the one to whom God credits righteousness apart from works: "Blessed are those whose transgressions are forgiven, whose sins are covered. Blessed is the one whose sin the Lord will never count against them."* (Rom 4:4–8)

> *Therefore, since we have been justified through faith, we have peace with God through our Lord Jesus Christ, through whom we have gained access by faith into this grace in which we now stand. And we boast in the hope of the glory of God.* (Rom 5:1–2)

> *Since we have now been justified by his blood, how much more shall we be saved from God's wrath through him! For if, while we were God's enemies, we were reconciled to him through the death of his Son, how much more, having been reconciled, shall we be saved through his life! Not only is this so, but we also boast in God through our Lord Jesus Christ, through whom we have now received reconciliation.* (Rom 5:9–11)

However, what the followers of Mary have done, as documented and promoted by Liguori, is much like what the Pharisees did, which was add new conditions, such as *having to be servants of Mary,* to attain what had already been given us through faith in the sacrifice of Christ Jesus.

> *The holy Virgin, says St. Basil, drew into herself all the graces of the Holy Spirit. Hence she herself said by the mouth of Ecclesiasticus: My abode is in the fulness of saints: "In plenitudine Sanctorum detentio mea," which St. Bonaventure thus explains: I have in fulness all that the other saints have in part.* (Liguori 372)

The verse from the book of Ecclesiasticus (see appendix 3: "The Apocrypha") is from chapter 24, which is written about wisdom and not of Mary. Verse 1 reads: "Wisdom shall praise her own self, and shall be honoured in God, and shall glory in the midst of her people," while the quoted verse 16 says, "And I took root in an honourable people, and in the portion of my God his inheritance, and my abode is in the full assembly of saints."

If, as claimed, Mary had "*all the graces of the Holy Spirit*," then it was as a precursor or type of the post-Pentecost Spirit-filled believer.

St. Paul tells us this believer does not lack any spiritual Gift:

> *I always thank my God for you because of his grace given you in Christ Jesus. For in him you have been enriched in every way—with all kinds of speech and with all knowledge— God thus confirming our testimony about Christ among you. Therefore you do not lack any spiritual gift as you eagerly wait for our Lord Jesus Christ to be revealed.* (1 Cor 1:4–7)

St. Peter tells us this believer has been given everything for life and godliness:

> *His divine power has given us everything we need for a godly life through our knowledge of him who called us by his own glory and goodness. Through these he has given us his very great and precious promises, so that through them you may participate in the divine nature, having escaped the corruption in the world caused by evil desires.* (2 Peter 1:3–4)

And if the believer still *feels* he lacks any gift, Jesus Himself assures us:

> ***So I say to you: Ask and it will be given to you; seek and you will find; knock and the door will***

> ***be opened to you. For everyone who asks receives; the one who seeks finds; and to the one who knocks, the door will be opened.*** (Luke 11:9–10)

If we are Spirit-filled believers—and if we truly follow Christ we ought to be—we should not be looking to Mary as *divinely special in the particular sense of having every gift* (as claimed) but rather simply perhaps as the *first of many.*

Scripture makes it clear the Spirit-filled believer lacks nothing for with the Spirit we have the fullness of life that Jesus promised. (John 10:10).

If God's Spirit in us is *not* enough, then *nothing* will ever be enough, but praise God who has revealed to us that we have been given *all* we will ever need.

> *St. Augustine says, that in order to obtain more certainly and abundantly the favors of the saints, it is necessary to imitate them, for when they see us practising the virtues which they practised, then they are more moved to pray for us. The queen of saints, and our first advocate, Mary, after she has rescued a soul from the grasp of Lucifer, and has united her to God, wishes her to begin to imitate her example, otherwise she will not be able to enrich her, as she would wish, with her graces, seeing her so opposed to her in conduct. Therefore Mary calls those blessed who diligently imitate her life; "Now, therefore, children, hear me; blessed are they that keep my ways."* (Liguori 592–593)

God does not ask us to seek the favor of men whether or not they be canonized saints, dead, or alive. Neither does He ask us to imitate them or any created being. We are rather to walk in the Spirit and commune with Him. To seek to please those who have passed on is to turn our eyes away from our one Savior and Lord.

Our "first" and only advocate on earth is the Holy Spirit; in heaven, that role belongs to Jesus. Jesus Himself called the Holy Spirit the "Advocate" (John 14:16; 14:26; 15:26; 16:7).

The scripture that Liguori attributes to Mary is taken from Proverbs 8:32, which is about wisdom, an attribute of God. That Liguori would choose to attribute it instead *to Mary* is part of a *pattern* that will be examined further in this section.

> *THE servants of Mary are very attentive and fervent in celebrating the Novenas of her Feasts; and during these the holy Virgin, full of love, dispenses to them innumerable and special blessings.* (Liguori 650)

In contrast to this, the Spirit-filled believer who walks in the Spirit is *constantly* in communion with God through His Spirit. This believer does not wait for special feasts but receives gifts from the Spirit who prepares us and knows when to release the right gift as part of the process of molding us into the image of Christ Jesus and seeing the will of the Father done on earth.

> *The reflection which Rupert the abbot makes upon the prodigal son is very beautiful. If the mother of this prodigal son had been living, he would either never have left his father's house or would have returned much sooner. And by this he wished to say, that he who is a child of Mary, either never departs from God, or if for his misfortune he departs, by means of Mary he quickly returns.* (Liguori 95)

The "reflection" by Rupert on the parable, which Jesus Himself told, infers that even God isn't enough since the father in the parable represents God Himself. This shows that such reflections and contemplations are the product of the mind of man (or worse) and not revelations of God.

> *Hence we justly call the Virgin our hope hoping, as Cardinal Bellarmine says, to obtain, by her intercession what we could not obtain by our prayers alone. We pray to her, says St. Anselm, in order that the dignity of the intercessor may supply our deficiencies.* (Liguori 116–117)

The apostles understood and taught us that we have been given all we need from God and that, in Jesus and the Holy Spirit, we have everything. The following are some of what believers have been given:

Righteousness and the Forgiveness of Our Sins

> *Therefore, there is now no condemnation for those who are in Christ Jesus, because through Christ Jesus the law of the Spirit who gives life has set you free from the law of sin and death.* (Rom 8:1–2)

> *And so he condemned sin in the flesh, in order that the righteous requirement of the law might be fully met in us, who do not live according to the flesh but according to the Spirit.* (Rom 8:3–4)

> *For I will forgive their wickedness and will remember their sins no more.* (Heb 8:12)

Spiritual Gifts

> ***All things have been committed to me by my Father.*** (Luke 10:22)

> ***So I say to you: Ask and it will be given to you; seek and you will find; knock and the door will***

be opened to you. For everyone who asks receives; the one who seeks finds; and to the one who knocks, the door will be opened. Which of you fathers, if your son asks for a fish, will give him a snake instead? Or if he asks for an egg, will give him a scorpion? If you then, though you are evil, know how to give good gifts to your children, how much more will your Father in heaven give the Holy Spirit to those who ask him! (Luke 11:9–13)

If you remain in me and my words remain in you, ask whatever you wish, and it will be done for you. This is to my Father's glory, that you bear much fruit, showing yourselves to be my disciples. (John 15:7–8)

Therefore you do not lack any spiritual gift as you eagerly wait for our Lord Jesus Christ to be revealed. (1 Cor 1:7) (The gifts of God are given by the Spirit and described in 1 Corinthians 12:7–11)

Praise be to the God and Father of our Lord Jesus Christ, who has blessed us in the heavenly realms with every spiritual blessing in Christ. (Eph 1:3)

In love he predestined us for adoption to sonship through Jesus Christ, in accordance with his pleasure and will—to the praise of his glorious grace, which he has freely given us in the One he loves. (Eph 1:4–6)

And this is my prayer: that your love may abound more and more in knowledge and depth of insight, so that you may be able to discern what is best and may be pure and blameless for the day of Christ, filled with the fruit of righteousness that comes through Jesus Christ—to the glory and praise of God. (Phil 1:9–11)

Power to Overcome Temptation

So I say, walk by the Spirit, and you will not gratify the desires of the flesh. (Gal 5:16–18)

His divine power has given us everything we need for a godly life through our knowledge of him who called us by his own glory and goodness. Through these he has given us his very great and precious promises, so that through them you may participate in the divine nature, having escaped the corruption in the world caused by evil desires. (2 Pet 1:3–4)

For if we have been united with him in a death like his, we will certainly also be united with him in a resurrection like his. For we know that our old self was crucified with him so that the body ruled by sin might be done away with that we should no longer be slaves to sin—because anyone who has died has been set free from sin. (Rom 6:5–7)

You have been set free from sin and have become slaves to righteousness. (Rom 6:18)

But now that you have been set free from sin and have become slaves of God, the benefit you reap leads to holiness, and the result is eternal life. (Rom 6:22)

An Intercessor in Heaven

We have a High Priest in heaven, Jesus so that none else is needed. (as described in Hebrews 7:1–28)

> *He came and preached peace to you who were far away and peace to those who were near. For through him we both have access to the Father by one Spirit. (Eph 2:17–18)*

> ***And I will do whatever you ask in my name, so that the Father may be glorified in the Son. You may ask me for anything in my name, and I will do it. (John 14:13–14)***

An Advocate on Earth

> ***But the Advocate, the Holy Spirit, whom the Father will send in my name, will teach you all things and will remind you of everything I have said to you.*** (John 14:26)

> ***But when he, the Spirit of truth, comes, he will guide you into all the truth. He will not speak on his own; he will speak only what he hears, and he will tell you what is yet to come.*** (John 16:13)

> *And he who searches our hearts knows the mind of the Spirit, because the Spirit intercedes for God's people in accordance with the will of God.* (Rom 8:27)

Believers who are led by the Spirit seek Jesus and the Father and the Spirit in daily living because we are continually transformed by coming close to Him and seeking His will in our lives. It is by the Spirit that we are molded into the image of Christ Jesus (2 Thess 2:13; Tit 3:3–8; 1 Pet 1:2). He guides us and gives us the spiritual gifts we require as well as the character and strength we need to grow in this life.

When Moses returned from meetings with God, his face glowed so that that he had to wear a veil due to its brightness (Exod

34:33–35). Moses's glow was likely the outward expression of what was happening on the inside.

Like Moses, we too need to approach and meet with God and not Mary in prayer, in order to allow His Spirit to transform us on the inside at every encounter.

Only God can do in us what is required in this life so that we are ready to meet with Him in eternity. For that to happen, we need to come to God continually.

A Fruit: Another Gospel

A significant fruit of the beliefs is that of a *substitute gospel* that Christians have come to accept as being from Christ and His apostles.

Unlike the true Gospel, this "other" gospel, based in tradition, does not place complete faith in the finished redemptive work of Christ. It requires supplementation in various works, such as services, novenas, scapulars, and adorations of tangible elements.

The relationship with the one divine God is replaced with having to go through Mary for intercession, gifts, divine mercy, help, and everything that God has given and continues to give.

Elements of this substitute gospel are examined under the heading "Questions That Must Be Answered," which appears after the following warnings from the apostles.

Warnings from the Apostles

God, in His mercy and kindness, has always forewarned His people (both Jews and Gentiles) of coming things of significance that would affect them. Prophecies in the New Testament were given through Jesus and His disciples. These prophecies include a number concerning how some teachers from within the church would be deceived and would go on to mislead others. It should not surprise believers then that, in every age, there would arise teachers of what St. Paul called a "different" Gospel.

The following are some such scriptural warnings, which are mostly written by the apostle Paul. They tell us that we should not be surprised that such things arise from within the family of believers.

The apostle Paul addressed the elders at Ephesus before he left them:

> *Be shepherds of the church of God, which he bought with his own blood. I know that after I leave, savage wolves will come in among you and will not spare the flock. Even from your own number men will arise and distort the truth in order to draw away disciples after them. So be on your guard! Remember that for three years I never stopped warning each of you night and day with tears.* (Acts 20:28–31)

He also wrote a letter to the churches in Galatia:

> *I am astonished that you are so quickly deserting the one who called you to live in the grace of Christ and are turning to a different Gospel — which is really no Gospel at all. Evidently some people are throwing you into confusion and are trying to pervert the Gospel of Christ. But even if we or an angel from heaven should preach a Gospel other than the one we preached to you, let them be under God's curse! As we have already said, so now I say again: If anybody is preaching to you a Gospel other than what you accepted, let them be under God's curse!* (Gal 1:6–9)

He wrote from prison to the church at Colossae:

> *See to it that no one takes you captive through hollow and deceptive philosophy, which depends on human*

> *tradition and the elemental spiritual forces of this world rather than on Christ.* (Col 2:8)

This is what he wrote to his spiritual son, Timothy:

> *The Spirit clearly says that in later times some will abandon the faith and follow deceiving spirits and things taught by demons. Such teachings come through hypocritical liars, whose consciences have been seared as with a hot iron. They forbid people to marry and order them to abstain from certain foods, which God created to be received with thanksgiving by those who believe and who know the truth. For everything God created is good, and nothing is to be rejected if it is received with thanksgiving, because it is consecrated by the Word of God and prayer.* (1 Tim 4:1–4)

> *Have nothing to do with godless myths and old wives' tales; rather, train yourself to be godly.* (1 Tim 4:7)

Here is his letter to the Hebrews:

> *Remember your leaders, who spoke the Word of God to you. Consider the outcome of their way of life and imitate their faith. Jesus Christ is the same yesterday and today and forever. Do not be carried away by all kinds of strange teachings.* (Heb 13:7–9)

Here is a letter from the apostle Peter:

> *But there were also false prophets among the people, just as there will be false teachers among you. They will secretly introduce destructive heresies, even denying the sovereign Lord who bought them—bringing swift destruction on themselves.* (2 Pet 2:1)

Other scriptures were given as warnings: Mark 7:6–8; 2 Cor 11:12–15; Col 2:16–23.

Questions That Must Be Answered

So far, in this book, I have let scripture answer the question of whether the teachings are of a different Gospel by showing the teachings of men, women, and spirits against the revealed Word of God in scripture. Scripture, the Word of God, is powerful enough to defend itself, and if the reader asked the Holy Spirit to guide them in reading this simple work, then His conviction would surely come.

The following questions are basic to Christianity and to the Gospel. Believers in the true Gospel will answer them very differently from those who follow any substitute gospel.

I pray the Holy Spirit will guide you, the reader, in honestly seeking the answers to these. Most of these have already been answered in the preceding text, but they are summarized here:

- Are we sinners or, as believers, are we the redeemed of God?
- Do we lack anything from God to live full lives in Christ?
- Have we been left as orphans?
- How do we overcome sin and temptation?
- How do we become holy?
- Who is the Holy Spirit and what part should He play in our lives?
- How should believers live their lives?
- What are demons? Do they assail us and have power over us such that we should seek to flee to "mother" or angels for protection?
- What role does Mary play in our present salvation?
    - Is she the advocate of God?
    - Is she the seal and pledge of our salvation?
    - Does she have the power to change us?
    - Can we not find Jesus unless we first go to her?

- Do we overcome the powers of hell by her and by invocation of her name?
- Have we been abandoned by God so that she is our refuge, our help, and our all?
- Does honoring her and putting our trust in her somehow count in our salvation—and are we lost who do not know her or turn to her?
- Does God not hear us that we need to invoke her merits?
- Can we not receive the gifts of God except by going to her?
- Is Mary our backup or fallback if we do not succeed with Christ?

The above questions are posed only because Liguori, the learned men and women he quotes, and the spirits of the visitations have revealed *their* answers to them, which are contrary to the true Gospel. The scriptural answers to these questions have been given throughout this book but are summarized in appendix 14: "Additional Material for Another Gospel."

Note that the answers in this appendix appear mostly only as scriptural references (they point to the books, chapters, and verses of the Bible) and not as entire quotations. Quoting them all would add enormously to this volume. Many fall under the spell of false gospels because they have never taken the time to read God's love letter to them compiled in the books of the Bible.

Jesus said: ***"It is written: 'Man shall not live on bread alone, but on every word that comes from the mouth of God'"*** (Matt 4:4).

A Fruit: God Made to Appear as Angry But Mary as Merciful

One theme running through the teachings and stories about Mary is that we should go to her because she is all goodness and mercy. God, on the other hand, is painted as angry and even harsh with us sinners.

> *She is called a plane-tree: As a plane-tree was I exalted: "Quasi platauus exaltata sum." Sinners may understand by this, that as the plane tree gives a shelter to travellers, where they may take refuge from the heat of the sun, thus Mary, when she sees the anger of divine justice kindled against them, invites them to resort to the shelter of her protection.* (Liguori 133)

The reference to the plane-tree was taken from the book of Ecclesiasticus and, as always, the writing is about wisdom and not about Mary. The interpretation and remark about the "*anger of divine justice*" is Liguori's alone.

> *St. Bonaventure remarks that Isaias, in his day lamented, and said, "Behold, thou art angry and we have sinned there is none that riseth up and taketh hold of thee;" because Mary was not yet born into the world.* (Liguori 133)

St. Bonaventure said that Israel was unable to find protection from the wrath of God because Mary had not yet been born. Yet in the very *same chapter* of *The Glories*, Liguori quotes a different writer who said that King David found protection in the tabernacle that was Mary:

> *Hail! refuge and retreat of sinners, to whom alone they can flee with confidence! And this is what David intended to express, says a certain author, when he said: "He hath protected me in the secret place of his tabernacle."* (Liguori 130)

Both Isaiah and King David lived in the times before Mary and the incarnate Christ. St. Bonaventure and an unnamed author each interpreted scripture written by Isaiah and King David to present completely *contradictory conclusions* regarding alleged protection afforded by Mary, yet Liguori used them to frame his glowing arguments about Mary as though they were truth.

Scripture is true, but the unjustified claims of these writers to attribute verses of apocrypha and scripture as referring to Mary are flawed.

> *But now, if God is offended with any sinner, and Mary undertakes to protect him, she restrains the Son from punishing him, and saves him. Also, continues St. Bonaventure, no one can be found more fit than Mary to place her hand upon the sword of divine justice, that it may not descend upon the head of the sinner. Richard of St. Laurence expresses the same thought, when he says: God lamented, before the birth of Mary, that there was no one to restrain him from punishing the sinner; but Mary being born, she appeases him.* (Liguori 133)

All these speak of a punishing God but a merciful Mary, yet none of this is what the apostles and writers of scripture taught or wrote under the guidance of the Holy Spirit. Instead, these unscriptural teaching glorify not God, but Mary.

> *Oh how many, exclaims the Abbot of Celles, who merits to be condemned by the divine justice, are saved by the mercy of Mary! for she is the treasure of God and the treasure of all graces; therefore it is that our salvation is in her hands. Let us always then have recourse to this mother of mercy, and confidently hope to be saved by means of her intercession; since she, as Bernardine de Bustis encourages us to believe, is our salvation, our life, our hope, our counsel, our refuge, our help.* (Liguori 300)

The abbot is quick to speak of the righteous judgment of God, but he is slow to apply the mercy given by the same God. Bernadine attributes to Mary all the traits and merits that are of God alone.

> *And St. Anselm also says: Thou* (Mary) *dost embrace with maternal love the sinner who is despised by the whole world, neither dost thou leave the wretched until thou has reconciled them to their God. By which he gives us to understand that the sinner, being hated by God, is rendered odious and abominable in the eyes of all creatures; but if he has recourse to the refuge of sinners, Mary not only does not despise him, but affectionately embraces him, and does not abandon him until he is pardoned by her Son and our Judge, Jesus Christ. Then, oh my Lady, if thou art the refuge of all sinners, thou art also my refuge.* (Liguori 746–747)

What is claimed above is patently both unscriptural and untrue.

It claims that the sinner "*is despised by the whole world*" and is "*hated by God.*" Scripture repeatedly reveals the contrary to us; the *righteous* is rejected and despised by the world, but the *sinner* is both <u>*of the world*</u> and is <u>*one with the world*</u>.

Jesus Himself said that the world loves the sinner but hates the righteous:

> ***If the world hates you*** (righteous followers of Christ)***, keep in mind that it hated me first.*** (John 15:18)

> ***If you belonged to the*** (lost and unredeemed) ***world, it would love you as its own. As it is, you do not belong to the world, but I have chosen you*** (as My followers) ***out of the world. That is why the world hates you.*** (John 15:19)

> ***I have told you these things, so that in me you may have peace. In this world you*** (followers of Mine) ***will have trouble. But take heart! I have overcome the world.*** (John 16:33)

> *You adulterous people, don't you know that friendship with the world means enmity against God? Therefore, anyone who chooses to be a friend of the world becomes an enemy of God.* (Jas 4:4)

Scripture addresses God's attitude toward sinners:

> ***It is not the healthy who need a doctor, but the sick. I have not come to call the righteous, but sinners.*** (Mark 2:17)

> ***I tell you that in the same way there will be more rejoicing in heaven over one sinner who repents than over ninety-nine righteous persons who do not need to repent.*** (Luke 15:7)

> *But God demonstrates his own love for us in this: While we were still sinners, Christ died for us.* (Rom 5:8)

> *Here is a trustworthy saying that deserves full acceptance: Christ Jesus came into the world to save sinners—of whom I am the worst. But for that very reason I was shown mercy so that in me, the worst of sinners, Christ Jesus might display his immense patience as an example for those who would believe in him and receive eternal life.* (1 Tim 1:15–16)

> ***What do you think? If a man owns a hundred sheep, and one of them wanders away, will he not***

> ***leave the ninety-nine on the hills and go to look for the one that wandered off? And if he finds it, truly I tell you, he is happier about that one sheep than about the ninety-nine that did not wander off. In the same way your Father in heaven is not willing that any of these little ones should perish.*** (Matt 18:12–14)

God loves the sinner (but not their sin) and gave His most precious Son in order to save them. This is not the action of a God who hates sinners.

A story is related in the example on pages 139–140 of *The Glories* wherein a sinful husband, who had been told by his wife to say a "Hail Mary" every time he passed before her altar, saw the Virgin holding the infant covered in wounds and bleeding. The child turned away from him and did not want to forgive him the sins he had committed to cause the wounds. Finally, the Virgin Mother begged that the child forgive the sinner. See appendix 12: "Additional Material for God Being Made to Appear as Angry but Mary as Merciful" for the full account of this story.

All these non-biblical teachings assert that Mary is willing to forgive while Jesus is not willing.

The essence of the teachings of the spirit behind the apparitions of "Mary" likewise glorify Mary rather than the One who left heaven to come to earth to pay for the sinner's salvation with His very life, the One who is "*the compassionate and gracious God, slow to anger, abounding in love and faithfulness*" (Exo 34:6).

In St. Paul's letter to the Romans, he brought assurance that God is merciful and that we can trust in His mercy:

> *If God is for us, who can be against us? He who did not spare his own Son, but gave him up for us all—how will he not also, along with him, graciously give us all*

> *things? Who will bring any charge against those whom God has chosen? It is God who justifies. Who then is the one who condemns? No one. Christ Jesus who died—more than that, who was raised to life—is at the right hand of God and is also interceding for us.* (Rom 8:31–34)

God Himself said that He is always willing to forgive and even forget:

> *Let the wicked forsake their ways*
> *and the unrighteous their thoughts.*
> *Let them turn to the LORD, and he will have mercy on them,*
> *and to our God, for he will freely pardon.* (Isa 55:7)

> *as far as the east is from the west,*
> *so far has he removed our transgressions from us.* (Ps 103:12)

> *I, even I, am he who blots out*
> *your transgressions, for my own sake,*
> *and remembers your sins no more.* (Isa 43:25)

This is the message of the Gospel—a message telling us of the mercy of God who loves the sinner so much that He sacrificed what was most precious to Him, His Son, so that the wretched might have life, life in abundance, and life eternal with Him. This is not an angry God who needs to be pacified. His willing sacrifice has allowed us to live in a time of His extended mercy:

> *Seek the LORD while he may be found; call on him while he is near.* (Isa 55:6)

The day is coming when judgment will come upon the earth, but *today* is the day to seek Him and to believe in and receive His mercy—not to doubt His love for the sinner or to try to get away from or around Him.

A Fruit: Reassignment of the Positions, Attributes, and Titles of God

Dear children, keep away from anything that
might take God's place in your hearts.
—1 John 5:21[39]

In Liguori's *The Glories*, the positions, attributes, and titles that are of God and His alone are liberally applied instead to Mary. Examples of these have already been shown, such as in the many misquotations of wisdom scripture made to apply to Mary as well as the application of the Holy Spirit's roles as Advocate and Giver of spiritual gifts to Mary.

In this chapter, the positions, attributes, and titles of God that were reassigned to Mary are examined. These include the following:

- omnipotent and eternal
- mercy and compassion
- refuge and protection
- wisdom
- source of divine gifts
- hope and comfort
- advocate
- price of redemption
- object of praise and worship—the only One to whom we bow

[39] Holy Bible, New Living Translation, copyright 1996, 2004, 2015 by Tyndale House Foundation.

Most of the above exclusively belong to God, such as omnipotence, eternal, source of divine gifts, price of redemption, and the only One to whom we bow. Others may apply to worldly things except when applied in the context of divine or spiritual realities, in which case, as in the discussion here, they also belong exclusively to God.

Omnipotent and Eternal

Omnipotence refers to God's sovereign power over all things, material and immaterial.

Eternal refers to God's divine attribute of holding time in His hands. He lives outside of time since He Himself created all things including space and time.

> *Prayer ... Do not say that thou (Mary) canst not aid me, for I know that thou art omnipotent, and dost obtain whatever thou desireth from thy God.* (Liguori 79)
>
> *Thy help is omnipotent, oh Mary: "Omnipotens auxilium tuum, O Maria;" as Cosmas of Jerusalem exclaims. Yes, Mary is omnipotent, adds Richard of St. Laurence, since the queen, by every law, must enjoy the same privileges as the king. For as the power of the Son and mother are the same, the mother by the omnipotent Son is made omnipotent.* (Liguori 202–203)

Firstly, these writers apply what they believe are established rules of earth onto the heavenly realm. The opposite ought to be true: may God's will be done here on earth as it is in heaven and not the other way round.

Secondly, queens do not enjoy equal privileges to kings. This is true in just about every monarchy and is revealed in the kingdoms described in the Bible. For instance, in the book of Esther, King Xerxes dethroned Queen Vashti after she snubbed him at the royal banquet.[40]

Thirdly, in order to apply the queen analogy, these writers believe that Jesus declared Mary to be queen of heaven, which does not appear anywhere in scripture. Furthermore, the queen of heaven in scripture is a deceptive principality who led the children of Israel away from God as previously seen in the chapter "Queen of Heaven" in part I of this book.

> *Hence Guerric, the abbot, represents Jesus thus speaking to Mary: My mother, upon thee I will establish the seat of my kingdom, for through thee will I bestow the graces that are asked of me: thou hast given me the human nature; I will give to thee, as it were, a divine nature, that is, my omnipotence, by which thou canst assist all who invoke thee to obtain their salvation.* (Liguori 248)

Why would an abbot propose to represent the words of Jesus to Mary? Liguori treats these words as though they were scripture when they are an extreme example of "going beyond the written word." Mary is not the one who bestows God's graces on mankind and God Himself, having chosen Mary as mother, He took up the human nature; she did not give it to Him who holds all things in His hands.

> *St. Antoninus asserts the same thing in nearly the same words: As it is impossible that those from whom Mary turns away her eyes of compassion should be saved, so it must be that all those towards whom she turns her eyes, and for whom she intercedes, shall be saved and glorified.* (Liguori 255)

---

40 See also 1 Kgs 2:17–25.

Mary would have to be both omnipresent and omniscient to have her eyes of compassion across the world. To say then that those from whom her "eyes of compassion" are turned away should not be saved is unfounded as she is neither all-powerful nor present everywhere.

> *"Auxilium Christianorum:" Help of Christians. St. John of Damascus calls her: Aid prepared and ready to free us from all dangers. The help of Mary is, as St. Cosmas of Jerusalem declares, omnipotent to save us from sin and from hell. St. Bernard addressed her in these words: Thou art invincible in the defence of thy servants: "Tu bellatrix egregia," doing battle with the demons who assail them.* (Liguori 748)

In the New Testament, it is the Holy Spirit—not Mary—who is called "The Helper." In the Old Testament, God is called the helper: "*Do not hide your face from me, do not turn your servant away in anger; you have been my helper*" (Psalm 27:9).

The Lord God alone is the *Almighty*—in more than three hundred verses of scripture—a description that describes, as fully as human words can convey, His *omnipotence* which is shared with no one.

Mercy and Compassion

Instead of turning to God for mercy and compassion, Liguori teaches believers to turn to Mary for these.

> *Prayer... No, neither in heaven nor on earth can I find one who has more compassion for the miserable, or who can aid me more than you.* (Liguori 79)

> *Every one invoking this mother of mercy may then say, with St. Augustine: "Remember, oh most compassionate Lady! that since the beginning of the*

> *world there never has been any one abandoned by thee. Therefore pardon me if I say that I do not wish to be the first sinner who has sought thy aid in vain."* (Liguori 151)

Liguori's prayer reveals he believes Mary to be more compassionate than God. St. Augustine's writing implies that Mary has been around since the beginning of the world, which clearly is not the case.

> *St. Bernard writes that Mary becomes all things to all men, and opens to all the bowels of her mercy, that all may receive of her; the captive his freedom; the sick man health; the afflicted consolation; the sinner pardon, and God glory: hence there is no one, since she is the sun, who does not partake of her warmth.* (Liguori 246)

What St. Bernard wrote sounds oddly like what Jesus proclaimed of Himself and His mission when He read the scroll of Isaiah in the synagogue (Luke 4:16–19). Only God can do all these things for all men in His compassion since He alone is omniscient, omnipresent, and omnipotent.

> *ST. BERNARD, speaking of the great mercy of Mary for us poor sinners, says that she is the very Land promised by God, flowing with milk and honey. St. Leo says, that to the Virgin has been given such bowels of compassion that she not only merits to be called merciful, but should be called mercy itself.* (Liguori 290)

If we were to call Mary "mercy itself," then how should we address the mercy of God?

> *Mary is that very throne of grace, says St. Antoninus, to which the apostle exhorts us to have recourse with*

> *confidence, that we may obtain the divine mercy, with all needed help for our salvation. To the throne of grace, that is, to Mary, as St. Antoninus remarks. Hence, Mary was called by St. Catherine of Sienna; The dispenser of divine mercy: "Administratrix misericordise."* (Liguori 300–301)

In contrast to what these saints claim:

- The throne of grace is what the Lion and the Lamb, Jesus Christ, occupies for judgment *and* mercy.
- Divine mercy can only be given by God because it is Him against whom sin is committed.
- Only the Judge can be merciful since it is only *in* the act of judgment that one can choose to dispense mercy.
- Jesus alone, who took our punishment for sin, can dispense toward us the mercy *He* paid the price for; it belongs to no one else to give.

God alone said, "*I will have mercy on whom I will have mercy, and I will have compassion on whom I will have compassion*" (Exod 33:19).

In acknowledging God's sovereign mercy, King David wrote, "*Have mercy on me, O God, according to your unfailing love; according to your great compassion blot out my transgressions*" (Ps 51:1).

Refuge, Protection, Hope, and Comfort

> *Prayer … Behold, oh mother of my God, Mary, my only hope, behold at thy feet a miserable sinner, who implores thy mercy. Thou art proclaimed and called by the whole Church, and by all the faithful, the refuge of sinners; thou then art my refuge; it is thine to save me. Oh Mary, I hasten to thee, and in thee I trust.* (Liguori 88–89)

> *It is sufficient for anyone to have recourse to her for protection. "I am the city of refuge for all those who flee to me," as St. John of Damascus says, speaking in her name.* (Liguori 128)

Where did St. John of Damascus get this teaching, which is not in scripture, and why did he believe he could speak on her behalf?

> *Do you not know that she is the only city of refuge, and the only hope of sinners? As St. Augustine has called her, The only hope of sinners: "Unica spes peccatorum." … Hence St. Ephrem says: Thou art the only advocate of sinners, and of those who are deprived of every help; and he thus salutes her: Hail! refuge and retreat of sinners, to whom alone they can flee with confidence.* (Liguori 129)

> *And what more secure refuge can we find, says the devout Thomas a Kempis, than the compassionate heart of Mary? There the poor find shelter; the sick medicine; the afflicted consolation; the doubtful counsel; the abandoned help.* (Liguori 293)

> *Refugium peccatorum: Refuge of sinners. Thus Mary is called by St. Germanus: The refuge, ever ready, for all sinners.* (Liguori 746)

> Spirit at Fatima: *"I will never forsake you. My Immaculate Heart will be your refuge and the way that will lead to God."* (Fatima 69)

God has always been, is, and will always be the *only refuge and Rock for the sinner.* He is the same yesterday, today, and forever (Heb 13:8). Those who seek *another* refuge do not seek Him.

> *The LORD is my rock, my fortress and my deliverer; my God is my rock, in whom I take refuge, my shield and the horn of my salvation. He is my stronghold, my refuge and my savior—from violent people you save me.* (2 Sam 22:2–3)

> *Do not tremble, do not be afraid. Did I not proclaim this and foretell it long ago? You are my witnesses. Is there any God besides me? <u>No, there is no other Rock; I know not one.</u>* (Isa 44:8)

> *God is our refuge and strength, an ever-present help in trouble. Therefore we will not fear, though the earth give way and the mountains fall into the heart of the sea, though its waters roar and foam and the mountains quake with their surging.* (Ps 46:1–3)

> *Whoever dwells in the shelter of the Most High will rest in the shadow of the Almighty. I will say of the Lord, "He is my refuge and my fortress, my God, in whom I trust."* (Ps 91:1–2)

The above verse is followed by a long list of *promises* of God as to the ways He will rescue and protect the one who trusts *<u>in Him</u>*.

> *<u>If</u> you say, "The LORD is my refuge," and you make the Most High your dwelling, no harm will overtake you, no disaster will come near your tent.* (Ps 91:9–10)

Instead, the "devout" Thomas à Kempis says we cannot find a more secure refuge than Mary. His devotion was to Mary when it should have been to God.

> *And if we feel our crosses heavy, let us have recourse to Mary, who is called by the Church: the comforter of the afflicted: "Consolatrix afflictorum;" and by St. John Damascene: The remedy for all sorrows of the heart: "Omnium dolorum cordium medicamentum."* (Liguori 639)

Jesus said the Holy Spirit is *the Comforter* (John 14:16; 14:26; 15:26; 16:7) and even in the Old Testament, scripture reveals the Comforter to be God Himself (Jer 8:18; Isa 51:12).

If God is our Comforter, how could Mary have been given this title by the church?

While these writers and saints choose to place their hope in Mary, scripture speaks to us instead:

> *The LORD is good to those whose hope is in him, to the one who seeks him* (Lam 3:25)

> *For the eyes of the LORD range throughout the earth to strengthen those whose hearts are fully committed to him.* (2 Chr 16:9)

Wisdom

> *She gives us to know that she has with her all the riches of God, that is, the divine mercies, that she may dispense them for the benefit of those who love her. "With me are riches and glory, that I may enrich them that love me."* (Liguori 120–121)

> *"Blessed is the man that heareth me, and that watcheth daily at my gates." Blessed, says Mary, is he who listens to my counsels, and incessantly watches at the door of my mercy, invoking my help and intercession!* (Liguori 142–143)

The above quotations were paraphrased from Proverbs 8:18–21 and 8:34. Chapter 8 is clearly about Wisdom and not Mary.

> Verse 1 of chapter 8 declares, "*Does not wisdom call out?*"
> Verse 12 declares, "*I, wisdom, dwell together with prudence, I possess knowledge and discretion.*"

Wisdom is an attribute of God. Nowhere does scripture say wisdom is Mary.

Just as Jesus revealed that He is "***the Way, the Truth, and the Life,***"[41] scripture tells us about Wisdom:

> *Christ, in whom are hidden <u>all the treasures of wisdom and knowledge</u>. (Col 2:2–3)*

> *You are in Christ Jesus, who has become for us wisdom from God—that is, our righteousness, holiness, and redemption.* (1 Cor 1:30)

Dispenser of Divine Gifts

In part I of this book, in "Mary: The Source of Grace and Gifts from God," scripture has already been shown to reveal the Holy Spirit (and not Mary) is the dispenser of divine gifts.

Advocate

We have examined this subject in "Advocate" in part I, but we will look at a few more instances of where Mary is given the title that divinely belongs only to Jesus and the Holy Spirit.

[41] John 14:6.

> *Hence St. Antoninus encourages us, saying: If Mary is for us, who is against us?* (Liguori 104)

The above might well be blasphemy since St. Antoninus substitutes Mary for God in the following scripture:

> *What, then, shall we say in response to these things? If God is for us, who can be against us? (Rom 8:31)*

Liguori continues:

> *Console yourselves, then, oh ye faint of heart, I will say with St. Thomas of Villanova, take heart, oh miserable sinners; this great Virgin, who is the mother of your judge and God, is the advocate of the human race. Powerful and able to obtain whatever she wishes from God; most wise, for she knows every method of appeasing him; universal, for she welcomes all, and refuses to defend none.* (Liguori 223–224)

"*Advocate of the human race*" and "*most wise*" are terms reserved only for members of the Holy Trinity.

> *Let us rejoice with Mary in the glory with which her God has enriched her; and let us also rejoice for ourselves, for Mary, at the same time was made queen of the world, and appointed our advocate. She is so merciful as advocate, that she consents to defend all sinners who recommend themselves to her; and she is so powerful with our Judge that she gains all the causes which she defends. Oh our queen and advocate, in thy hand is our salvation; if thon dost pray for us, we shall be saved.* (Liguori 756–757)

Scripture teaches us we have an Advocate in heaven, Christ Jesus, and an Advocate-Helper on earth, the Holy Spirit. Followers of Mary, however, appoint her as their advocate and pray to her instead of to God as Jesus taught us.

Price of Redemption, Life, and Salvation

> *He who finds me shall find life, and shall receive from God eternal salvation." Listen, as St. Bonaventure exclaims here upon these words, listen, all ye who desire the kingdom of God; honor the Virgin Mary, and ye shall have life and eternal salvation.* (Liguori 80–81)

The scripture quoted above is taken from Proverbs 8, which speaks of *Wisdom* and not Mary:

> *For those who find me find life and receive favor from the LORD. But those who fail to find me harm themselves; all who hate me love death.* (Prov 8:35–36)

Liguori further claims:

> *He has placed the price of our redemption in the hands of Mary, that she may dispense it at her pleasure.* (Liguori 118)

The Gospel is clear that there is no question of anyone "dispensing the price of our redemption" from their hands since the price was paid in full by Jesus—and all who come to Him are saved.

> *It is true that in this life no one can be certain of his eternal salvation: "Man knoweth not whether he be worthy of love or hatred, but all things are kept*

> *uncertain for the time to come." David asked of God: Oh Lord, who will be saved? "Who shall dwell in thy tabernacle?" St. Bonaventure, writing on these words, answers: Oh sinners, let us follow the footsteps of Mary, and cast ourselves at her blessed feet, and let us not leave her until she blesses us, for her blessing will secure to us paradise. It is enough, oh Lady, says St. Anselm, that thou dost wish to save us, for then we cannot but be saved. St. Antoninus adds, that souls protected by Mary are necessarily saved; those upon whom she turns her eyes are necessarily justified and glorified.* (Liguori 283)

Solomon wrote Ecclesiastes, and King David wrote much of the Psalms, both which are quoted above, long before the atoning death of Christ Jesus. Thus, neither Solomon nor David could have known that our sin was to be covered by the Blood of the Lamb.

Liguori, like each of us, was born in this present season of grace and in the new covenant in the blood of Christ. He says that we cannot be certain of salvation, yet he professes that we *are saved and secure* in our salvation *if* we turn fully to Mary.

Trusting in the finished work of Christ Jesus, as Jesus, the apostles, and as scripture taught, was apparently not security enough for him.

> *"Janua cceli:" Gate of heaven. Mary is called the gate of heaven, because no one can enter into heaven, as St. Bonaventure declares, except through Mary.* (Liguori 744)

It is the likes of St. Bonaventure and Liguori who call Mary the "*Gate of heaven*" and taught others to do so (which is still being done), which is not what Jesus said.

> ***Very truly I tell you, I am the gate for the sheep. All who have come before me are thieves and robbers, but the sheep have not listened to them. I am the gate; whoever enters through me will be saved. They will come in and go out, and find pasture.*** (John 10:7–9)

> ***I am the way and the truth and the life. No one comes to the Father except through me.*** (John 14:6)

Object of Our Praise and Worship

> *THERE are so many reasons why we should love this our loving queen, that if all the earth should praise Mary, and all sermons treat of her alone, and all men should give their lives for Mary, it would yet be little compared to the homage and gratitude we owe her, for the very tender love she bears to all men, even to the most miserable sinners who preserve towards her any feeling of devotion.* (Liguori 215–216)

The phrase "*All the earth praise her, all the sermons treat of her alone, all men give their lives for Mary*" summarizes how those who turn to her end up giving her their all, which rightly belongs only to God.

> *Moreover, Father Auriemma relates, that the blessed Virgin promised St. Matilda a good death, if she recited everyday three "Hail Marys" in honor of her power, wisdom, and goodness.* (Liguori 649)

In exchange for the promise of "a good death," we are taught to pray to Mary. As for her "*power, wisdom and goodness,*" are these not the attributes of God and not a created being?

> *"Virgo praedicanda:" Virgin to be praised. The holy Church sings that this divine mother is worthy of all praise: "Omui laude dignissiina;" for according to St. Ildephonsus, all praise that is given to the blessed Virgin is an honor paid to her Son: "Refuiiditur in filium quod impenditur matri." With reason, then, did St. George of Nicomedia declare that the praises given to Mary God accepts, as if offered to himself. The holy Virgin promises paradise to him who endeavors to make her known and loved.* (Liguori 734)

Worthy of *all* praise? Only God is worthy of all praise.

The teaching that all honor paid to Mary is the same as though it were given to God is unscriptural and is an unconvincing excuse for such activity. The real reason is either that they want to receive the promises the spirit who claims to be her offers—such as paradise—or they are already so far from the knowledge of God and His Spirit that any substitute will do.

> *Fear the LORD your God and serve him. Hold fast to him and take your oaths in his name. He is the one you praise; he is your God, who performed for you those great and awesome wonders you saw with your own eyes.* (Deut 10:20–21)

> *Heal me, LORD, and I will be healed; save me and I will be saved, for you are the one I praise.* (Jer 17:14)

> *But you are a chosen people, a royal priesthood, a holy nation, God's special possession, that you may declare*

> *the praises of him who called you out of darkness into his wonderful light.* (1 Pet 2:9)

The apostle Peter wrote that we were *chosen to praise God* who called use out of darkness and into His wonderful light.

While Liguori and others would say that they do not worship Mary but rather "*honour*" her, the kind of "honour" they give her is indistinguishable from worship—giving her all praise and exaltation, applying to her all of God's attributes, and even casting themselves at her feet. No child would honor their parents in such a way. The Old Testament is replete with examples of those who asked for or demanded such worship, including Satan and King Nebuchadnezzar.

At the temptation of Jesus, when Satan promised Him all the kingdoms of the world and all their splendor if He would bow down to worship him, Jesus replied, ***"Away from me, Satan! For it is written 'Worship the Lord your God, and serve him only.'"***

We would do well to obey Jesus and worship God and serve Him alone—unlike what the *servants* of Mary advocate we do.

The End Fruit: The Substitution of God

Every title, position, and attribute that belongs to God is given instead to Mary by her followers. Further, they teach believers to give to her all that can rightly only belong to God, such as adoration, praise, and even their entire lives.

The consequence of attributing to Mary all that is God's and God's alone is that God is replaced in the minds and devotions of the believers.

Instead of the Holy Spirit

The Holy Spirit is one Person in the Trinity of the Godhead. He appears all throughout scripture—from the creation account right through to Revelation. It was He who hovered over the waters in the beginning, breathed life into Adam, spoke to the prophets, raised Jesus up from the dead, and enters in and remains with Spirit-filled believers all their days. It is He who is our Advocate on earth and who works constantly to transform us into the image of Christ.

Jesus called Him the Advocate, Helper, Counselor, Comforter, Guide, Mediator, Seal, Deposit, and Spirit of Truth. In scripture, He is also called the Spirit of God and the Spirit of Christ.[42]

The titles, positions, and attributes of the Holy Spirit that have been replaced by Mary in the lives and teachings of her followers are:

- our advocate on earth
- our mediator
- our helper
- our comforter
- dispenser of spiritual gifts
- seal and pledge of our redemption
- constant companion until the end of this age

They gave Mary all the above, and the advocates of Mary effectively removed the Holy Spirit from the lives of those who follow their teachings by having *exclusively* given to her what God already gave to His Spirit as clearly declared in scripture.

They did this by using such phrases as *only* Mary, she *alone*, that *every* blessing comes from her, and that she is *the* pledge or seal.

The following examples of these teachings are all taken from Liguori's *The Glories.*

[42] The Spirit of God—Rom 8:9, 14; 2 Cor 3:17–18. Spirit of Christ—John 17:26; Acts 16:7; Rom 8:9; Phil 1:19; 1 Pet 1:11. Spirit of Truth, Wisdom, Revelation, and Prophecy—John 14:16–17; 15:26; 16:13; Eph 1:17; 1 John 5:6; Rev 19:10.

Our Advocate

> *Hence St. Ephrem says: Thou art the only advocate of sinners, and of those who are deprived of every help; and he thus salutes her: Hail! refuge and retreat of sinners, to whom alone they can flee with confidence.* (Liguori 129)

> *Thou art the only advocate of sinners, the secure haven of the shipwrecked ... We have no hope but in thee, oh most pure Virgin!* (Liguori 322)

> *No; let my sins never prevent thee from exercising thy great office of mercy by which thou art the advocate, the mediatrix of reconciliation, the only hope, and the most secure refuge of sinners.* (Liguori 332–333)

> *And where can we find an advocate who is more occupied with our salvation, and who loves us more than Mary? We acknowledge that one alone in heaven is solicitous for us, as St. Augustine says of her.* (Liguori 740)

Our Mediator on Earth

> *Also the Idiot remarks, that every blessing, every help, every grace that men have received or will receive from God, to the end of the world, has come to them, and will come to them, through the intercession and by means of Mary.* (Liguori 119)

> *The glorious St. Cajetan said that we could ask for graces, but we could never obtain them without the intercession of Mary. And St. Antoninus confirms this, expressing himself thus beautifully: Whoever asks*

> *and wishes to obtain graces without the intercession of Mary, attempts to fly without wings.* (Liguori 189)

Our Comforter

> *WE poor children of the unhappy Eve, guilty before God of her sin, and condemned to the same punishment, go wandering through this valley of tears, exiles from our country, weeping and afflicted by innumerable pains of body and soul! But blessed is he who in the midst of so many miseries turns to the consoler of the world, to the refuge of the unhappy, to the great mother of God, and devoutly invokes her and supplicates her!* (Liguori 142)

Our Helper

> *St. Thomas of Villanova says the same thing, calling her our only refuge, help, and protection.* (Liguori 118)

When translated into English, the words *advocate, mediator, comforter,* and *helper* are often interchangeably used in scripture.

In direct contrast to the claims of Liguori and others, scripture teaches:

> ***And I will ask the Father, and he will give you another advocate to help you and be with you forever—the Spirit of truth.*** (John 14:16–17)

> ***But the Advocate, the Holy Spirit, whom the Father will send in my name, will teach you all things and will remind you of everything I have said to you.*** (John 14:26)

> ***When the Advocate comes, whom I will send to you from the Father—the Spirit of truth who goes out from the Father—he will testify about me.*** (John 15:26)

> ***But very truly I tell you, it is for your good that I am going away. Unless I go away, the Advocate will not come to you; but if I go, I will send him to you.* (John 16:7)**

> *In the same way, the Spirit helps us in our weakness. We do not know what we ought to pray for, but the Spirit himself intercedes for us through wordless groans. And he who searches our hearts knows the mind of the Spirit, because the Spirit intercedes for God's people in accordance with the will of God.* (Rom 8:26–27)

Instead of "*we could ask for graces but never obtain them without the intercession of Mary*" (189), Jesus promised (as shown in the chapter "Mary: The Source of Grace and Gifts from God") "***whatever you ask in my name, the Father will give you***" (John 15:16; 16:23; 16–26–28).

Dispenser of Spiritual Gifts

> *Hence the venerable Abbot of Celles exhorts everyone to have recourse to this treasurer of graces, as he calls her: "Thesaurariam gratiarum" for only by her means the world and men are to receive all the good they may hope for.* (Liguori 179)

> *St. Bernardine of Sienna thus addresses her: Oh Lady, since thou art the dispenser of all graces, and we must receive the grace of salvation through thy hand alone, then our salvation depends on thee.* (Liguori 190)

> *Mary, then, having been made the mother of all the redeemed, by the merit of her sufferings, and of the offering of her Son; it is just to believe that only by her hand may be given them the milk of those divine graces, which are the fruits of the merits of Jesus Christ, and the means to obtain life eternal.* (Liguori 469)

In contrast, scripture teaches the following:

> *I always thank my God for you because of his grace given you in Christ Jesus. For in him you have been enriched in every way—with all kinds of speech and with all knowledge— God thus confirming our testimony about Christ among you. Therefore you do not lack any spiritual gift as you eagerly wait for our Lord Jesus Christ to be revealed.* (1 Cor 1:4–7)

> *There are different kinds of gifts, but the same Spirit distributes them. There are different kinds of service, but the same Lord. There are different kinds of working, but in all of them and in everyone it is the same God at work.*

> *Now to each one the manifestation of the Spirit is given for the common good. To one there is given through the Spirit a message of wisdom, to another a message of knowledge by means of the same Spirit, to another faith by the same Spirit, to another gifts of healing by that one Spirit, to another miraculous powers, to another prophecy, to another distinguishing between spirits, to another speaking in different kinds of tongues, and to still another the interpretation of tongues. All these are the work of one and the same*

Spirit, and he distributes them to each one, just as he determines. (1 Cor 12:4–11)

But the fruit of the Spirit is love, joy, peace, forbearance, kindness, goodness, faithfulness, gentleness and self-control. (Gal 5:22–23)

His divine power has given us everything we need for a godly life through our knowledge of him who called us by his own glory and goodness. Through these he has given us his very great and precious promises, so that through them you may participate in the divine nature, having escaped the corruption in the world caused by evil desires. (2 Peter 1:3–4)

Seal and Pledge of Our Redemption

By St. Andrew of Crete, Mary is called "The security of divine pardon." By this is meant, that when sinners have recourse to Mary that they may be reconciled to God, God assures them of pardon, and gives them the assurance by also giving them the pledge of it. And this pledge is Mary, whom he has given us for our advocate, by whose intercession, in virtue of the merits of Jesus Christ, God pardons all sinners who place themselves under her protection. (Liguori 85–86)

Contrary to the above, four separate verses in three books of the New Testament identify the *Holy Spirit* as the pledge given by God, the assurance of the pardon and of what is to come:

Now it is God who makes both us and you stand firm in Christ. He anointed us, set his seal of ownership on

> *us, and put his Spirit in our hearts as a deposit* (pledge), *guaranteeing what is to come*. (2 Cor 1:21–22)

> *Now the one who has fashioned us for this very purpose is God, who has given us the Spirit as a deposit, guaranteeing what is to come.* (2 Cor 5:5)

> *And you also were included in Christ when you heard the message of truth, the Gospel of your salvation. When you believed, you were marked in him with a seal, the promised Holy Spirit, who is a deposit guaranteeing our inheritance until the redemption of those who are God's possession—to the praise of his glory.* (Eph 1:13–14)

> *We know that the whole creation has been groaning as in the pains of childbirth right up to the present time. Not only so, but we ourselves, who have the firstfruits* (pledge) *of the Spirit, groan inwardly as we wait eagerly for our adoption to sonship, the redemption of our bodies. For in this hope we were saved.* (Rom 8:22–24)

No scripture ever identified Mary as the pledge or that the pledge would ever change.

> ***And I will ask the Father, and he will give you another advocate to help you and be with you forever—the Spirit of truth.*** (John 14:16–17)

Guide and Constant Companion until the End of This Age

> *For this reason the great mother is also called by the holy Church: Star of the sea: "Ave, Maris Stella." For as*

> *navigators, says the angelic St. Thomas, are guided to port by means of a star, thus Christians are guided to heaven by means of Mary.* (Liguori 278)
>
> *St. Germanus, recognizing Mary to be the source of every blessing, and the deliverance from every evil, thus invokes her: Oh my Lady, thou alone art my help, given me by God; thou art the guide of my pilgrimage, the support of my weakness, my riches in poverty, my deliverer from bondage, the hope of my salvation: graciously listen, I pray thee to my supplications, take compassion on my sighs, thou my queen, my refuge, my life, my help, my hope, my strength.* (Liguori 119–120)

Spirit of Fatima:

> *I will never forsake you. My Immaculate Heart will be your refuge and the way that will lead to God.* (Fatima 69)

Jesus said of the Spirit of God:

> ***But when he, the Spirit of truth, comes, he will guide you into all the truth. He will not speak on his own; he will speak only what he hears, and he will tell you what is yet to come.*** (John 16:13)
>
> St. Paul's letter to the Romans:
>
> *For those who are led by the Spirit of God are the children of God.* (Rom 8:13)

Liguori and those he quotes sometimes, though rarely, mention the Holy Spirit but then take away from Him all that is His in the lives of believers. In all the roles that are His and His alone, they have convinced others to look instead to Mary.

In *Mary: Model of Disciples, Mother of the Lord*, author John M. Lozano wrote, "One Protestant author who examined a number of Catholic writings confessed her surprise on learning that in all those places where she expected to find references to the Holy Spirit, Catholics referred instead to Mary."

There is, however, no substitute for the Holy Spirit in the lives of any believer. Jesus said that the Father would send Him and that it was *better* for us that Jesus left so the Spirit could come to us.

All through the Old Covenant, the Spirit would often visit or be with those who were to take on special roles in their generations. However, in the New Covenant of grace, ushered in by the sacrifice of Christ Jesus at the cross, the Holy Spirit would thereafter *dwell* in the hearts of all who received Christ into their lives.

> ***Very truly I tell you, no one can enter the kingdom of God unless they are born of water and the Spirit. Flesh gives birth to flesh, but the Spirit gives birth to spirit. You should not be surprised at my saying, "You must be born again."*** (John 3:5–7)

To be born again of the Spirit, one has to believe in and confess the salvation that has come through the sacrifice of Christ Jesus, believing Him to be the Son of God who took our place in death. One also has to know of the Spirit and be open to receiving the Holy Spirit to be their guide.

The difference between having the Spirit being *with* someone and having the Spirit live *in* someone is so great that Jesus described this with these words:

> ***Truly I tell you, among those born of women there has not risen anyone greater than John the Baptist; yet whoever is least in the kingdom of heaven is greater than he.*** (Matt 11:11)

To try to live life as a disciple of Christ without a relationship with the Holy Spirit would be futile since we do not have the capacity to live such a life. This is why He was given to us and why Jesus instructed His followers to wait for the Spirit who was to come. This they did, and the church was born in the upper room on the day of Pentecost.

Each believer has to have his personal day of Pentecost as demonstrated in every salvation witnessed in the book of Acts. It does not necessarily have to be with all manner of visible signs, but nonetheless, it has to be. Jesus said, "***No one can enter the kingdom unless they are born of water and the Spirit.***"

> ***Not everyone who says to me, "Lord, Lord," will enter the kingdom of heaven, but only the one who does the will of my Father who is in heaven. Many will say to me on that day, "Lord, Lord, did we not prophesy in your name and in your name drive out demons and in your name perform many miracles?" Then I will tell them plainly, "I never knew you. Away from me, you evildoers!"*** (Matt 7:21–23)

To invite the Holy Spirit into our lives and live submitted to His rightful Lordship over us is to have Jesus *know* us.

To substitute the Spirit with Mary, as is taught by Liguori and others, is to live a life without the empowering presence of the Spirit who will be with us to the end of the age.

- At the least, such substitution would mean living a powerless Christian life.

- At worst, living without His Spirit's presence risks hearing Jesus one day say, "***I never knew you.***"

Anyone who replaces the Spirit in their teaching of scripture with anything else is like the teachers Jesus warned about: "***Woe to you experts in the law, because you have taken away the key to knowledge***" (Luke 11:52).

Without the Spirit, we cannot hope to understand scripture and be the good soil that receives the seed as spoken by Jesus in the parable of the sower.[43]

Instead of Jesus and God the Father

While it might seem inconceivable to some that the teachings of Liguori and others might take believers away from Jesus and God the Father, in many cases, this is what the beliefs they advocate actually do.

We are told, in scripture, of many of the divine titles, roles, and positions of Jesus and our heavenly Father. Rather than separately list who holds these title, roles, and positions, they are listed in aggregated form below:

- Wisdom of God
- Jesus: Our Advocate in Heaven
- Our Refuge
- Our Hope
- Jesus: Our Salvation
- Jesus: The One to Imitate
- Jesus: Was Given All Authority
- Him to Whom Glory belongs

[43] Luke 8:8.

The Wisdom of God

All through *The Glories*, references in the Bible and the Apocrypha that speak of the wisdom of God are turned instead to point to Mary. For instance,

From the book of Proverbs:

> *In order that we may be preserved in the life of divine grace, spiritual strength is necessary to resist all the enemies of our salvation. Now, this strength can only be obtained by means of Mary: Mine is this strength, says Mary: "Mea est fortitude."* (Liguori 90, citing Prov 8:14)

> *St. Denis the Carthusian asks: Who will ever be saved? Who will ever reign in heaven? They are saved, and will certainly reign, he himself answers, for whom this queen of mercy offers her prayers. And this Mary herself affirms: By me kings reign: "Per me reges regnant."* (Liguori 279, citing Prov 8:15)

> *And in the same sense the holy Church applies to Mary these words of Proverbs: All that hate me love death: "Omnes qui me oderunt, diligunt mortem."* (Liguori 257, citing Prov 8:36)

From Ecclesiasticus:

> *She is called a plane-tree: As a plane-tree was I exalted: "Quasi platauus exaltata sum." Sinners may understand by this, that as the plane tree gives a shelter to travellers, where they may take refuge from the heat of the sun, thus Mary, when she sees the anger of divine justice kindled against them,*

> *invites them to resort to the shelter of her protection.* (Liguori 133, citing Ecclus 24:19)

> *The same holy Church, in the office which she requires to be recited on the Festivals of Mary, applying to her the words of Wisdom, gives us to understand that in Mary we shall find every hope: "In me is all hope of life and virtue."* (Liguori 173–174 citing Ecclus 24:25)

Scripture, speaking of wisdom, says that the Holy Spirit is the Spirit of wisdom and that wisdom can be imparted, just as the Spirit imparted wisdom to each of the judges and prophets. But scripture also says that Jesus Christ is the Wisdom of God come down from heaven.

> *The Spirit of the LORD will rest on him— the Spirit of wisdom and of understanding, the Spirit of counsel and of might, the Spirit of the knowledge and fear of the LORD.* (Isa 11:2)

> *Praise be to the name of God for ever and ever; wisdom and power are his.* (Dan 2:20)

> *But to those whom God has called, both Jews and Greeks, Christ the power of God and the wisdom of God.* (1 Cor 1:24)

> *It is because of him that you are in Christ Jesus, who has become for us wisdom from God—that is, our righteousness, holiness and redemption.* (1 Cor 1:30)

> *But the wisdom that comes from heaven is first of all pure; then peace-loving, considerate, submissive, full of mercy and good fruit, impartial and sincere.* (Jas 3:17)

In scripture, only members of the Trinity or Godhead are described as either Wisdom or the Wisdom of God (the very personification of wisdom).

Our Refuge

> *St. Thomas of Villanova says the same thing, calling her our only refuge, help, and protection.* (Liguori 118)
>
> *Do you not know that she is the only city of refuge, and the only hope of sinners?* (Liguori 129)
>
> *Hence St. Ephrem says: Thou art the only advocate of sinners, and of those who are deprived of every help; and he thus salutes her: Hail! refuge and retreat of sinners, to whom alone they can flee with confidence.* (Liguori 129)
>
> *Let us say with St. Thomas of Villanova: Oh Mary, we poor sinners know no refuge but thee. Thou art our only hope; to thee we intrust our salvation. Thou art the only advocate with Jesus Christ; to thee we all have recourse.* (Liguori 130)
>
> *The devout Blosius also says that she is the only refuge for those who have offended God: the asylum of all those who are tempted and afflicted.* (Liguori 131–132)
>
> *Prayer of St. William, Bishop of Paris: "No; let my sins never prevent thee from exercising thy great office of mercy by which thou art the advocate, the mediatrix of reconciliation, the only hope, and the most secure refuge of sinners. It is thy office to reconcile God to man."* (Liguori 332–333)

Scripture, on the other hand, is clear that God is our only refuge and strength, and at least fifty-five passages confirm Him as our secure refuge.

> *David sang to the LORD the words of this song when the LORD delivered him from the hand of all his enemies and from the hand of Saul. He said: "The LORD is my rock, my fortress and my deliverer; my God is my rock, in whom I take refuge, my shield and the horn of my salvation. He is my stronghold, my refuge and my savior—from violent people you save me."* (2 Sam 22:1–3)

> *God is our refuge and strength, an ever-present help in trouble.* (Ps 46:1)

> *The LORD will rescue his servants; no one who takes refuge in him will be condemned.* (Ps 34:22)

> *The LORD helps them and delivers them; he delivers them from the wicked and saves them, because they take refuge in him.* (Ps 37:40)

To the one willing to trust God alone as his refuge, God Himself *promises* the following:

> *If you say, "The LORD is my refuge," and you make the Most High your dwelling, no harm will overtake you, no disaster will come near your tent.*
>
> *For he will command his angels concerning you to guard you in all your ways; they will lift you up in their hands, so that you will not strike your foot against a stone.*

You will tread on the lion and the cobra; you will trample the great lion and the serpent.

"Because he loves me," says the LORD, "I will rescue him; I will protect him, for he acknowledges my name. He will call on me, and I will answer him; I will be with him in trouble, I will deliver him and honor him. With long life I will satisfy him and show him my salvation." (Ps 91:9–16)

Our Hope

When I saw death drawing near, finding myself laden with sins, and abandoned by all, I turned to the mother of God and said to her, Lady, thou art the refuge of the abandoned, behold me at this hour deserted by all; thou art my only hope, thou alone canst help me; have pity on me. The Holy Virgin obtained for me the grace of making an act of contrition; I died and am saved, and my queen has also obtained for me the grace that my pains should be abridged, and that I should, by suffering intensely for a short time, pass through that purification which otherwise would have lasted many years. (Liguori 36–37)

St. Augustine rightly calls her the only hope of us sinners, since by her means alone we hope for the remission of all our sins. (Liguori 83)

Prayer of St. Ephrem: OH immaculate and wholly pure Virgin Mary! mother of God, queen of the universe, our most excellent Lady, thou art superior to all the saints, thou art the only hope of the Fathers, and the joy of the blessed. (Liguori 322)

> *Prayer: Oh Mary, I trust in thee: in this hope I live, and in this hope I wish to die, repeating always: "Jesus is my only hope, and after Jesus, Mary."* (Liguori 127)

In the above final prayer, Jesus is first said to be Liguori's *only* hope, yet he adds, *"After Jesus, Mary."* One cannot say that for Liguori, he has only *one* hope, but rather that he does *not* place *all his hope* in Jesus.

Scripture has dozens of passages where God is proclaimed as the hope of those who look to Him. Most notable are perhaps the words of Job and those who wrote the various Psalms.

> *Though he slay me, yet will I hope in him.* (Job 13:15)

Jesus Christ is the hope of those who are saved by His blood:

> *The former regulation is set aside because it was weak and useless (for the law made nothing perfect), and a better hope* (apart from the law) *is introduced, by which we draw near to God.* (Heb 7:18–19)

> *Praise be to the God and Father of our Lord Jesus Christ! In his great mercy he has given us new birth into a living hope through the resurrection of Jesus Christ from the dead.* (1 Pet 1:3)

> *To them God has chosen to make known among the Gentiles the glorious riches of this mystery, which is Christ in you, the hope of glory.* (Col 1:27)

> *We remember before our God and Father your work produced by faith, your labor prompted by love, and your endurance inspired by hope in our Lord Jesus Christ.* (1 Thess 1:3)

> *Paul, an apostle of Christ Jesus by the command of God our Savior and of Christ Jesus our hope.* (1 Tim 1:1)

> *In him we were also chosen, having been predestined according to the plan of him who works out everything in conformity with the purpose of his will, in order that we, who were the first to put our hope in Christ, might be for the praise of his glory.* (Eph 1:11–12)

> *Dear friends, now we are children of God, and what we will be has not yet been made known. But we know that when Christ appears, we shall be like him, for we shall see him as he is. All who have this hope in him purify themselves, just as he is pure.* (1 John 3:2–3)

See also 1 Tim 4:10 and 1 Pet 1:18–21.

As with "Refuge," God makes *promises* to those who will make Him their hope:

> *Kings will be your foster fathers, and their queens your nursing mothers. They will bow down before you with their faces to the ground; they will lick the dust at your feet. Then you will know that I am the LORD; those who hope in me will not be disappointed."* (Isa 49:23)

> *Let us hold unswervingly to the hope we profess, for he who promised is faithful.* (Heb 10:23)

Our Advocate, Mediator, and Intercessor in Heaven

> *And St. John Chrysostom repeats the same thing, namely, that sinners receive pardon <u>only through</u> the intercession of Mary.* (Liguori 83–84)

> *Oh Lady! it is true that all the saints desire our salvation and pray for us; but the charity and tenderness which thou dost manifest for us in heaven, by obtaining with thy prayers so many mercies from God, obliges us to confess, that we have in heaven only one advocate, that is thyself, and that thou alone art the only true lover watchful of our welfare.* (Liguori 219)

In the previous chapter, regarding the Holy Spirit, it was shown that the Spirit is our intercessor with us on earth. Scripture reveals to us that we also have an intercessor in heaven (Christ Jesus).

Jesus sits at the right hand of God in heaven,:

> *My dear children, I write this to you so that you will not sin. But if anybody does sin, we have an advocate with the Father—Jesus Christ, the Righteous One. He is the atoning sacrifice for our sins, and not only for ours but also for the sins of the whole world.* (1 John 2:1–2)

> *For there is one God and one mediator between God and mankind, the man Christ Jesus, who gave himself as a ransom for all people.* (1 Tim 2:5–6)

> *Now there have been many of those priests, since death prevented them from continuing in office but because Jesus lives forever, he has a permanent priesthood. Therefore he is able to save completely those who come to God through him, because he always lives to intercede for them.* (Heb 7:23–25)

> *But in fact the ministry Jesus has received is as superior to theirs as the covenant of which he is mediator is*

> *superior to the old one, since the new covenant is established on better promises.* (Heb 8:6)
>
> *For this reason Christ is the mediator of a new covenant, that those who are called may receive the promised eternal inheritance—now that he has died as a ransom to set them free from the sins committed under the first covenant.* (Heb 9:15)
>
> *You have come to God, the Judge of all, to the spirits of the righteous made perfect, to Jesus the mediator of a new covenant, and to the sprinkled blood that speaks a better word than the blood of Abel.* (Heb 12:23–24)

Scripture does not tell of any *other* intercessor in heaven besides Jesus, and it clearly says that He is the *only* One.

Our Salvation

Liguori and others taught that believers must look to Mary for their salvation. They were required to turn to her, pray to her, and ask her for mercy. Without actively seeking her and serving her, they would be lost eternally.

> *Prayer: Behold, oh mother of my God, Mary, my only hope, behold at thy feet a miserable sinner, who implores thy mercy.* (Liguori 88)
>
> *Hence Father Suarez concludes it to be the universal sentiment of the Church at the present day, that the intercession of Mary is not only useful, but necessary.* (Liguori 180)

> *As we have access to the eternal Father only through Jesus Christ, so, says St. Bernard, we have access to Jesus Christ only through Mary.* (Liguori 191)

> *And this is also asserted by others, as the blessed Albertus Magnus: All those who are not thy servants, oh Mary, shall perish: "Gens quse non servierit tibi peribit." St. Bonaventure, too: He who neglects the service of Mary shall die in sin. And in another place: He who has not recourse to thee, oh Lady, will not reach paradise. And on Psalm xcix, the saint goes so far as to say that those from whom Mary turns away her face, not only will not be saved, but can have no hope of salvation. And before this St. Ignatius, the martyr, said the same thing, asserting that a sinner cannot be saved except by means of the holy Virgin, who, on the other hand, saves by her merciful intercession many that would be condemned by the divine justice.* (Liguori 256)

The quotation "He who neglects the service of Mary shall die in sin" is attributed by Liguori to come from Psalm 116. In fact, nothing in Psalm 116 says anything remotely like that. "He who has no recourse to thee, oh Lady, shall not reach paradise" is claimed to be taken from Psalm 86, but it is nowhere found in scripture. Finally, Psalm xcix or 99 is claimed to warn that "those from whom Mary turns away her face, not only will not be saved, but can have no hope of salvation." However, this passage too contains no such verses.

> *Whether or not our names are written in the book of life? If we are true servants of Mary and obtain her protection, we certainly are written there; for, as St. John of Damascus says, God gives the grace of devotion to his holy mother only to those whom he will save; in conformity with this, as the Lord seems*

> *to have declared expressly through St. John: "He that shall overcome, I will write upon him the name of my God, and the name of the city of my God." And who is this city of God but Mary? as St. Gregory explains, commenting on this passage of David: "Glorious things are said of thee, oh city of God."* (Liguori 285)

> *I shall prove, in the fifth chapter of this book, that all graces are dispensed by the hand of Mary alone, and that all those who are saved, are saved solely by means of this divine mother; it may be said, as a necessary consequence, that the salvation of all depends upon preaching Mary, and confidence in her intercession.* (Liguori 19–20)

> *Justly, then, does St. Lawrence Justinian call her the hope of evil-doers, "spes delinquentium," since she alone can obtain their pardon from God.* (Liguori 83)

> *St. Augustine rightly calls her the only hope of us sinners, since by her means alone we hope for the remission of all our sins.* (Liguori 83)

> *St. Bernardine of Sienna thus addresses her: Oh Lady, since thou art the dispenser of all graces, and we must receive the grace of salvation through thy hand alone, then our salvation depends on thee.* (Liguori 190)

Firstly, in quoting St. John of Damascus, Liguori claims that God only saves those to whom He gives the "*grace of devotion to His holy mother.*" He further claims Jesus confirmed this, quoting a passage from Revelation about Jesus writing the name of the city of God on the redeemed and that this city was Mary:

> *The one who is victorious I will make a pillar in the temple of my God. Never again will they leave it. I will write on them the name of my God and the name of the city of my God, the new Jerusalem, which is coming down out of heaven from my God; and I will also write on them my new name.* (Rev 3:12)

It is clear in the very scripture he quoted that the city is the New Jerusalem come down from heaven, which other scriptures describe in some detail including its walls, gates, and roads—and that it will be inhabited by the redeemed. This city is clearly not Mary.

Scripture teaches that, to be saved, one has to believe in the Christ Jesus and that salvation comes from God alone through believing in Him who was sent.

When at the Temple, Simeon saw the infant Jesus, he proclaimed:

> *Sovereign Lord, as you have promised, you may now dismiss your servant in peace. For my eyes have seen your salvation, which you have prepared in the sight of all nations: a light for revelation to the Gentiles, and the glory of your people Israel.* (Luke 2:29–32)

Jesus taught:

> ***"Do not work for food that spoils, but for food that endures to eternal life, which the Son of Man will give you. For on him God the Father has placed his seal of approval."*** *Then they asked him, "What must we do to do the works God requires?" Jesus answered,* ***"The work of God is this: to believe in the one he has sent."*** (John 6:27–29)

The Apostle Peter's Proclamation to the Crowd

> *Salvation is found in no one else, for there is no other name under heaven given to mankind by which we must be saved.* (Acts 4:12)

St. Paul's Messages

> *For God did not appoint us to suffer wrath but to receive salvation through our Lord Jesus Christ.* (1 Thess 5:9)

> *Therefore I endure everything for the sake of the elect, that they too may obtain the salvation that is in Christ Jesus, with eternal glory.* (1 Tim 2:10)

> *And how from infancy you have known the Holy Scriptures, which are able to make you wise for salvation through faith in Christ Jesus.* (1 Tim 3:15)

The Letters to the Hebrews

> *In bringing many sons and daughters to glory, it was fitting that God, for whom and through whom everything exists, should make the pioneer of their salvation* (Jesus) *perfect through what he suffered.* (Heb 2:10)

> *And once made perfect, he became the source of eternal salvation for all who obey him.* (Heb 5:9)

In all His teachings, Jesus always said that we were to come to Him, not through anyone else but directly to Him. He Himself will knock, and we must open the door to Him.

More could be said for other exclusive divine roles, such as authority and subjects such as glory, and if the reader would like to explore more, he or she may choose to look into appendix 13: "Divine Authority."

The End Fruit: Giving Themselves Completely Over to Her

Having exalted Mary to positions far beyond what Holy Spirit-inspired scripture teaches us about her and then imputing the attributes of God to her, the followers of Mary, as a consequence, cast themselves completely to her in a manner that should belong only to God.

This is the end fruit of the beliefs taught about her as well as from the teachings imparted at the visitations and can be seen in the prayers below.

Each prayer is from Liguori's *The Glories* and is not an aberration to those who follow Mary. Indeed, the book was commissioned by Pope Urban VIII and reflects the beliefs of the highest ecclesiastics. These prayers, beliefs, and teachings are as alive today as they ever were, and similar prayers can be found in the various websites that profess Mary.

The version of *The Glories* quoted here was translated from the original Italian into English, having been examined and approved by John, the archbishop of New York, on January 21, 1852.

> *Prayer: Therefore I say to thee with St. Bonaventure, Oh, Lady, I submit myself to thy control, that thou mayest rule and govern me entirely. Do not leave me to myself. Rule me, oh my queen, and do not leave me to myself. Command me, employ me as thou wilt, and punish me if I do not obey thee, for very salutary will be the punishments that come from thy hand. I would esteem it a greater thing to be thy servant than*

Lord of the whole earth. Thine I am, save me! Accept me, oh Mary, for thy own and attend to my salvation, as I am thine own. I no longer will be my own, I give myself to thee. (Liguori 38)

Prayer—Would that my tongue could praise thee with the power of a thousand tongues, in order to make known thy greatness, thy holiness, thy mercy, and thy love, with which thou lovest those who love thee. If I had riches, I would employ them all for thy honor. (Liguori 66)

To thy hands I commit the cause of my eternal salvation. To thee I consign my soul; it was lost, but thou must save it. (Liguori 239–240)

Prayer: Oh great mother of God, and my mother Mary, it is true that I am unworthy to pronounce thy name … Oh Lady, do not delay coming to my help when I call upon thee, since in all the temptations which may assail me, in all the necessities I may suffer, I shall never cease calling upon thee, always repeating Mary, Mary. (Liguori 320–231)

Prayer of St. Ephrem: "OH immaculate and wholly pure Virgin Mary! mother of God, queen of the universe, our most excellent Lady, thou art superior to all the saints, thou art the only hope of the Fathers, and the joy of the blessed. By thee we have been reconciled to our God. Thou art the only advocate of sinners, the secure haven of the shipwrecked. Thou art the consolation of the world, the redemption of captives, the joy of the sick, the comfort of the afflicted, the refuge and salvation of the whole world. Oh great princess! mother of God! cover us with the wings of thy compassion: have pity on us. We have no hope but in thee, oh most pure Virgin! We are given to thee, and consecrated to thy service; we bear the name of thy servants; do not permit Lucifer to draw us down to hell. Oh immaculate Virgin! we are under thy protection; therefore, unitedly we have recourse to thee, and supplicate thee to prevent thy Son, whom our sins have offended, from abandoning us to the power of the devil." (Liguori 322–323)

Prayer of St. Germanus: "OH my only Lady, who art the sole consolation which I receive from God; thou who art the only celestial dew that doth soothe my pains; thou who art the light of my soul when it is surrounded with darkness; thou who art my guide in my journeyings, my strength in my weakness, my treasure in my poverty; balm for my wounds, my consolation in sorrow; thou who art my refuge in misery, the hope of my salvation, graciously hear my prayer, have pity on me, as is befitting the mother of a God who hath so much love for men. Yes, my Lady, my refuge, my life, my help, my defence, my strength, my joy, my hope, make me to come with thee to paradise." (Liguori 325–326)

Prayer of St. Peter Damian: "HOLY VIRGIN, mother of God, succor those who implore thy assistance. Turn to us. But, having been deified, as it were, hast thou for gotten men? Ah, certainly not. Thou knowest in what peril thou hast left us, and the wretched condition of thy servants; no, it is not befitting a mercy so great, to forget so great misery as ours. Turn to us with thy power, because he who is powerful hath given thee omnipotence in heaven and on earth. Turn to us, also, in thy love. I know, oh my Lady, that thou art all kindness, and dost love us with a love that no other love can surpass. How dost thou appease the anger of our Judge when he is on the point of punishing us for our offences!" (Liguori 332)

Prayer: Oh beloved of God! most amiable child Mary! oh, that like thee, who didst present thyself in the temple, and at once and wholly didst consecrate thyself the glory and love of thy God, I might offer to thee to-day the first years of my life, and dedicate myself entirely to thy service, oh my most holy and sweet Lady! (Liguori 409)

Prayer: Into thy hands I entirely abandon myself, and only pray the divine Majesty, that through the merits of my Saviour Jesus, he may grant me those graces that thou dost ask of him for me. Ask, ask then for me, oh most holy Virgin, whatever thou esteemest best. Thy prayers are never rejected. They are the prayers of a mother to a Son, who loves thee so much, and finds his joy in granting whatever thou dost ask of him, thus the more to honor thee, and at the same time, show thee the great love he bears thee. Oh Lady, thus let it be. I will live trusting in thee. Thou must think only on saving me. Amen. (Liguori 457)

Prayer: Oh holy mother of God my mother Mary, didst thou then feel so great care of my salvation that thou didst even consent to offer up to death the object dearest to thy heart, thy beloved Jesus? … To-day, oh my queen, I also, in imitation of thee wish to offer my poor heart to God; but I fear that he will refuse it, seeing it thus filthy and loathsome. But if thou wilt offer it to him, he will not refuse it. All the offerings made him by thy most pure hands he accepts and receives. To thee, then, oh Mary, I present myself to-day, miserable as I am, and to thee I give myself entirely. (Liguori 474)

In heaven thou seest more plainly our miseries, and therefore thou must pity and relieve us the more. Make us on earth thy faithful servants, that we may thus go to bless thee in paradise. On this day, when thou hast been made queen of the universe, we also consecrate ourselves to thy service. (Liguori 514)

I omit other devotions, which are to be found in other books, as the seven joys, the twelve privileges of Mary, and the like, and let us terminate this work with the beautiful words of St. Bernardine: Oh woman, blessed among all women, thou art the honor of the human race, the salvation of our people. Thou hast a merit that has no limits, and an entire power over all creatures. Thou art the mother of God, the mistress of the world, the queen of heaven. Thou art the dispenser of all graces, the glory of the holy Church. Thou art the example of the just, the consolation of the saints, and the source of our salvation. Thou art the joy of paradise, the gate of heaven, the glory of God. Behold, we have published thy praises. We supplicate thee then, oh mother of mercy, to strengthen our weakness, to pardon our boldness, to accept our service, to bless our labors, and impress thy love upon the hearts of all, that after having honored and loved thy Son on earth, we may praise and bless him eternally in heaven. Amen. (Liguori 678)

Oh Mary, most pure; oh Mary, most lovely, thou didst gain the heart of God; take possession of my poor heart also, and make me holy. (Liguori 733)

Oh my queen and mother, I rejoice in thy greatness, and am ready to give my life that thy glory should not be diminished in the least degree, if it were possible that it could be diminished. Oh, that I might give all my blood to cause all the nations of the earth to honor and love thee as the Lady thou art! (Liguori 741)

Let not my sins prevent me from confiding in thee, oh great mother of God; no, I trust in thee, and trust in thee so much, that if my salvation were in my own hands, yet I would place it all in thine. (Liguori 759)

OH queen of heaven, I who once have been a miserable slave of Lucifer, now dedicate myself to thee, as thy servant forever, and offer myself to honor and serve thee for the whole life; accept me, do not refuse me as I merit. (Liguori 765)

OH queen of paradise, who sittest above the choirs of angels, nearest to God; from this vale of misery I, a miserable sinner, salute thee, and pray thee to turn towards me those kind eyes of thine, that dispense graces to all those they look upon. See, oh Mary, in how much danger I now find myself, and must find myself, while I live on this earth, of losing my soul, paradise, and God. In thee, oh Lady, I have placed all hopes. I love thee, and long to come to thee, see thee, and praise thee in paradise. Ah Mary, when will the day come that I shall see myself safe at thy feet, and shall behold the mother of my Lord and my mother, who has been so occupied with my salvation? When shall I kiss that hand which has so many times delivered me from hell and bestowed on me so many graces, when, by my sins, I merited to be hated and abandoned by all? Oh Lady, I have been very ungrateful to thee in my life; but if I come to paradise I will be no more ungrateful. There I will love thee as much as I can, every moment through all eternity, and I will make amends for my ingratitude by blessing thee and thanking thee forever. Above all, I thank God who gives me such confidence in the blood of Jesus Christ and in thee; namely, that thou wilt save me, that thou wilt free me from my sins, and obtain for me light and strength to execute the divine will, and finally conduct me to the port of paradise. All this have thy servants hoped, and none have been deceived. Neither shall I be deceived. Mary, I wish nothing else; thou must save me. Pray thy Son Jesus, as I also pray him, through the merits of his passion, to preserve in me, and always more increase this confidence, and I shall be saved. (Liguori 768–770)

OH my most holy mother, I know what graces thou hast obtained for me, and I see the ingratitude of which I have been guilty towards thee. The ungrateful are no longer worthy of favors; but I will not on this account distrust thy mercy, which is greater than my ingratitude. Oh my great advocate, have pity on me. Thou art the dispenser of all the graces which God grants to us miserable sinners, and for this end he has made thee so powerful, so rich, and so merciful, that thou mightest succor us in our miseries … Thou art the advocate of the most wretched and abandoned sinners who have recourse to thee, defend me also, who recommend myself to thee. Do not tell me that it is difficult to gain my cause, for the most desperate causes are all gained when they are defended by thee. In thy hands, then, I place my eternal salvation, and to thee I commit my soul. (Liguori 771–772)

Oh mistress of all things, saint of saints, our strength and refuge, God, as it were, of the world, glory of heaven, accept those who love thee; hear us, for thy Son honors thee and denies thee nothing. (Liguori 784)

DEDICATION OF ONESELF TO MARY: OH most holy virgin mother of God, Mary, I, N., although most unworthy of being thy servant, yet moved by thy wonderful mercy and by the desire to serve thee, choose thee to-day, in presence of my guardian angel, and of the whole celestial court, for my especial Lady, Advocate, and mother, and make the firm resolution that I always will love and serve thee for the future, and do whatever I can to induce also others to love and serve thee. I pray thee, mother, of God, and my most kind and amiable mother, by the blood of thy divine Son which was shed for me, that thou wilt receive me into the number of thy servants for thy child and servant forever; assist me in all my thoughts, words, and actions, at every moment of my life, that every step and breath may be directed to the greater glory of my God, and through thy most powerful intercession obtain for me that I may never more offend my beloved Jesus, that I may glorify and love him in this life, and that I may also love thee, my most beloved and dear mother, that I may love thee and enjoy thee through eternity in holy paradise. Amen.

My mother Mary, I recommend to thee my soul, especially at the hour of my death. (Liguori 778–779)

DEDICATION OF A FAMILY TO MARY: OH blessed and immaculate Virgin, our queen and mother, refuge and consolation of all those who are in misery, I, prostrate before thy throne with all my family, choose thee for my Lady, Mother, and Advocate with God. I, with all who belong to me, dedicate myself forever to thy service, and pray thee, oh mother of God, to receive us into the number of thy servants, taking us all under thy protection, aiding us in life, and still more, at the hour of our death. Oh mother of mercy, I choose thee Lady and ruler of my whole house, of my relatives, my interests, and all my affairs. Do not disdain to take care of them; dispose of them all as it pleases thee. Bless me, then, and all my family, and do not permit that any of us should offend thy Son. Do thou defend us in temptations, deliver us from dangers, provide for us in our necessities, counsel us in our doubts, console us in afflictions, be with us in sickness, and especially in the agonies of death. Do not permit the devil to glory in having in his chains any of us who are now consecrated to thee; but grant that we may come to thee in heaven to thank thee, and together with thee to praise and love our Redeemer Jesus for all eternity. Amen, thus may it be. (Liguori 779–780)

Every one of the above prayers is a prayer that should only ever be prayed to God and not to *any* created being. Every one of them completely ignores the presence of the Holy Spirit whom God has given us to be our light in this world and the One who prepares for the day we meet with God.

God alone is our salvation, hope, and the one to whom believers should dedicate our lives fully to in obedience to the highest commandments that Jesus taught us:

> ***"Love the Lord your God with all your heart and with all your soul and with all your mind and with all your strength." The second is this: "Love your neighbour as yourself." There is no commandment greater than these."*** (Mark 12:29–31)

Why Has This Happened?

There seem to have been a number of reasons.

Departure from Scripture

Early teachers who mistranslated scripture had done the church of believers a great disservice.

This could have been corrected; instead, it was compounded by those who rather than revert to scripture to check, as the Bereans had done when St. Paul preached, built upon the unscriptural teachings even to the extent of confirming errant beliefs with other errant beliefs and teachings. This has been shown in much of what Liguori wrote. There are numerous more examples from *The Glories* that are omitted here for lack of space.

In contrast, the apostle Paul wrote, *"All Scripture is God-breathed and is useful for teaching, rebuking, correcting and training in righteousness, so that the servant of God may be thoroughly equipped for every good work"* (2 Tim 3:16–17).

Teaching must conform to scripture, and if it deviates, the teaching must be brought to question.

Rather than rely on scripture, Liguori and others taught from often questionable and even discredited material while making up new material from contemplations and "revelations" that were seemingly never questioned or checked against the Word of God. Worse still, in some cases, those who should have known better listened to demons and the devil when they should have listened to Christ. It was Jesus who said that the devil is the father of lies so that nothing from him is to be believed. Examples of these include the teachings about the demons who "fled" when Mary's name was invoked, the dead who still spoke, and the devil who said that "every Hail Mary is blow to the head."

Looking to the Flesh Rather than the Spirit

Jesus was the son of Mary. Without His sonship through Mary, His death on the Cross would not have saved us. It was His kinsman-redeemer relationship to us, *through her*, that allowed Him to be *our* substitute and so take *our* place and pay for *our* sin.[44]

Jesus was also—and is also—the Son of God.[45] He is the eternal Word of God[46] who is unchanging. He alone had two natures—that of being the son of Mary ***and*** the Son of God.

Jesus spoke of those who were to follow Him and would likewise be blessed with the indwelling of the Holy Spirit (and so also have two natures):

> ***Very truly I tell you, no one can enter the kingdom of God unless they are born of water and the Spirit. Flesh gives birth to flesh, but the Spirit gives birth to spirit.*** (John 3:5–6)

[44] Lev 25:44–55; Ruth 4:1–11.

[45] Matt 3:17; 11:27; 16:15–17; 17:5; Mark 9:7; Luke 1:32, 35; 9:35; John 1:14; 3:35; 5:36; 6:46; 2 Pet 1:17; Heb 1:1–3, 8; 4:14.

[46] John 1:1–18.

> ***Do not work for food that spoils, but for food that endures to eternal life, which the Son of Man will give you. For on him God the Father has placed his seal of approval.*** (John 6:27)
>
> ***The Spirit gives life; the flesh counts for nothing. The words I have spoken to you—they are full of the Spirit and life.*** (John 6:63)

In all that he compiled in *The Glories*, Liguori and those he quoted exalted Mary, the source of the human nature of Jesus. Rather than point believers toward the Spirit nature of Jesus who gives life, they pointed believers toward the human nature He inherited from Mary. They even went so far as to say that Mary was given all the graces possible to have been given at the time of *her* conception (what they call the Immaculate Conception) so that she could then pass them onto Jesus:

> *God, having deigned to make her his mother, conferred greater gifts than on all other creatures, as the same Doctor teaches. From her he received his human nature, hence before all others she must have obtained from Christ the fulness of grace; for, being mother, as Father Suarez says, she has a certain peculiar right to all the gifts of her Son. And as, by the hypostatic union, Jesus must of right have the fulness of all graces; thus by the divine maternity, it was meet that Jesus should confer on Mary, as a natural debt, greater graces than those bestowed on all the other saints and angels.* (Liguori 395)

Firstly, the belief that Mary was "full of grace" came from the mistranslation by Jerome.

Secondly, the early history of Mary, including details of her parents and birth, came primarily from the Protoevangelium of James, which even the Catholic Church and its pope had discredited.

Thirdly, Jesus did not receive His grace or power from Mary; it came from His divine origin in the Holy Spirit, who both brought to pass His incarnation on earth and later refilled Him at the start of His ministry. It had always been the plan of God for the Son of Man to appear in His redemptive role for humanity:

> *But when the set time had fully come, God sent his Son, born of a woman, born under the law, to redeem those under the law, that we might receive adoption to sonship.* (Gal 4:4–5)

The main difficulties Jesus experienced when He tried to teach of the Spirit and the kingdom of God were caused by people who looked at His earthly origins and not His Spirit nature:

> *Isn't this the carpenter's son? Isn't his mother's name Mary, and aren't his brothers James, Joseph, Simon and Judas?* (Matt 13:55)

> *But we know where this man is from; when the Messiah comes, no one will know where he is from.* (John 7:27)

> *How can the Messiah come from Galilee? Does not Scripture say that the Messiah will come from David's descendants and from Bethlehem, the town where David lived?* (John 7:41–42)

The learned men and women quoted by and including Liguori himself seemingly sought to find in Mary the spiritual wellsprings for Jesus that instead originated from God. This is also what they taught others to do by always pointing others to seek Mary and never to the Spirit of God for all their spiritual needs.

During Jesus's ministry, whenever followers turned to Mary, Jesus Himself guided them back to looking at Himself and His mission from the heavenly Father.

> *As Jesus was saying these things, a woman in the crowd called out, "Blessed is the mother who gave you birth and nursed you." He replied, **"Blessed rather are those who hear the Word of God and obey it."*** (Luke 11:27–28)

As followers of Jesus, our role is to follow *Him* and do all *He* tells us:

> *Jesus replied, **"Anyone who loves me will obey my teaching. My Father will love them, and we will come to them and make our home with them. Anyone who does not love me will not obey my teaching. These words you hear are not my own; they belong to the Father who sent me."*** (John 14:23–24)

We obey His words when we live by His words as both written in scripture and as spoken to us by His Holy Spirit:

> ***My sheep listen to my voice; I know them, and they follow me.*** (John 10:27)
>
> ***I will not leave you as orphans; I will come to you.*** (John 14:18)
>
> ***All this I have spoken while still with you. But the Advocate, the Holy Spirit, whom the Father will send in my name, will teach you all things***

> ***and will remind you of everything I have said to you.*** (John 14:25–26)

We know that Jesus remains seated at the right hand of God until all things are brought to completion when His enemies are placed under His feet.[47] So when He said that He would never leave or forsake us, He was speaking of the Holy Spirit who would remain with us for all time.

The Father, Son, and Spirit are One. We have Emmanuel, God, with us, and we are never far from Him *if* we choose to set our eyes and hearts to Him.

Looking to a Spirit Other than the Holy Spirit

Before Jesus went to sit at the right hand of God, He told His disciples that it was *better* that He left so that the Holy Spirit could come to be with believers. This is the Spirit who would be all that we would need to lead us through this life and who would prepare us for the next.

This is the same Spirit who spoke through the prophet Joel when God said He would pour out His Spirit on all people. The apostle Peter confirmed this had happened when He preached to the crowd at Pentecost.

The church, though, had long abandoned the Spirit, except in word alone. It does not seek or expect the Spirit to infill believers when they first believe or when baptized or even to lead its services, relying instead on prepared texts that were to be preached regardless of the circumstances of different assemblies everywhere.

When any spirit claiming to be the Mother of God appeared, it was always believed regardless of—whether the message lined up

---

[47] Matt 22:44; Mark 16:19; Luke 22:69; Acts 2:33; 7:55–56; 8:34; Eph 1:20; Col 3:1; Heb 1:3; 8:1, 10:12: 2; 1 Pet 3:22.

with scripture. In turning from the Holy Spirit, it is no wonder that we witness all the fruit described in this part of this book:

- the turning away from full faith in the redeeming work of Christ to instead believe that our salvation is somehow lacking something that needs Mary in it
- the diminishing of perfect goodness and mercy of God to that of any angry god and the elevation of Mary to be merciful
- the reapplication of all of the positions, attributes, and titles that belong only to God to Mary
- the substitution of the Triune God with Mary in worship, adoration, and praise
- the shifting the focus of believers in God alone to be upon Mary, angels, the holy family, scapulars, Rosaries, sacraments, and rites
- the replacement of the servanthood of believers from God to Mary

When He was tempted by the devil, Jesus rebuked him:

> ***Away from me, Satan! For it is written: "Worship the Lord your God, and serve him only."*** (Matt 4:10)

When Jesus was tested by the Pharisee about the greatest commandment, He replied:

> ***"Love the Lord your God with all your heart and with all your soul and with all your mind." This is the first and greatest commandment. And the second is like it: "Love your neighbor as yourself." All the Law and the Prophets hang on these two commandments.*** (Matt 22:37–40)

Endnote

Your word is a lamp for my feet, a light on my path.
—Psalm 119:105

The apostle Paul praised the Bereans to whom he ministered because they checked all that he taught them to see if it all lined up with scripture.[48]

> *My people are destroyed from lack of knowledge.*
> *Because you have rejected knowledge,*
> *I also reject you as my priests;*
> *because you have ignored the law of your God,*
> *I also will ignore your children.* (Hos 4:6)

If Liguori and all the learned teachers he quoted had checked scripture carefully, they would have realized that many of the things they taught were not from scripture. Many of these teachings, in fact, contradicted scripture. They elevated the teachings of men to higher than the word of God and taught countless generations to follow them. The early teachers did not always have the written word available to them; today, we have no such excuse because every teaching can be tested against scripture.

The same is true for those who believe the spirits of the visitations. Every teaching of those spirits can be tested against scripture and be shown to not be in agreement with scripture. Instead, these teachings follow the same patterns that appear in Liguori's work, which is not of the foundation of the true Gospel.

Had the church not departed from living under the Lordship of the Holy Spirit, to follow other spirits, none of this would likely have happened.

---

[48] Acts 17:11.

> ***But when he, the Spirit of truth, comes, he will guide you into all the truth.*** (John 16:13)

Whereas the Bereans were praised by Paul, the opposite was said by him about some of the Jews. What he said about the latter can also be applied to Liguori and all who follow in his footsteps:

> *For I can testify about them that they are zealous for God, but their zeal is not based on knowledge.* (Rom 10:2)

Without living in the clear light of scripture **and** living under the guidance of the Holy Spirit, anyone can be deceived.

Much has been written about Mary that is not scriptural. In fact, much has been written that directly contradicts the clear teachings in scripture.

Christians of all denominations can agree that Mary was given a special role in bringing forth Christ Jesus into this world. Why did Jesus come into the world? What was His mission? This is examined in the next section.

PART IV

JESUS, HIS MISSION, AND HIS KINGDOM

Parts I and II of this book looked at the many existing teachings and beliefs about Mary, the mother of Jesus. The teachings and beliefs, collectively "Marian dogma," together with their apparent sources were examined and contrasted against scripture:

- mistranslations of scripture
- stories such as from the Protoevangelium of James that were propagated by some even though agreed by the ecclesiastical authorities of the church, including the pope, to have been fallacies
- writings emanating from the contemplations of monks
- writings of mystics who were thought to have been able to overhear private conversations in heaven
- misquotations and attributing of scripture to speak of Mary when it actually spoke of God and His attributes
- apparitions of the Lady at Fatima, which is representative of other "visitations"

Much of the above dogma was elevated to the level of scripture—and often higher—since they were taught even when they contradicted revealed scripture.

Part II included a chapter on the Spirit behind the visitations, contrasting "her" against the Mary of the Bible. This spirit who claimed to be both Mary and the queen of heaven also claimed that God wanted mankind to dedicate itself to her, "honoring" her in a manner that can only be described as worship.

Part III looked at the apparent fruit of the dogma—how dogma turned the eyes and ears of believers toward Mary—a Mary quite unlike the mother of Jesus as described in scripture, who never pointed anyone to herself. The beliefs resulted in believers placing their prayers, hopes, and faith in "Mary," with expectations of gifts, blessings, protection, mercy, graces, and even eternal life dispensed from her hands—and not from God.

The result was that God—in the Father, Son, and Holy Spirit—is substituted with Mary in the prayers and hopes of believers who turn their entire lives and all that they have to her.

Having examined what Liguori and the eminent teachers he quoted taught—as well as what the spirit of Fatima spoke—it is time to examine what Jesus Himself did and said. Before we examine His mission and teachings, we need to reflect for a moment on who Jesus was and is.

Jesus: Who He Is

Early in creation, God declared that He would send One who would crush the head of the serpent who would, in turn, bruise His ankle. All through the books of Moses and the prophets, the coming Messiah was foretold, including His birth, places of origin, His kingly authority and righteous character, His dominion, and even His suffering, death, and resurrection. His imminent birth was announced by the archangel Gabriel, and His arrival was announced by a choir of angels to shepherds and shortly afterward to the Magi of the East.

He was revealed to be the Messiah by Simeon and the prophetess Anna at His presentation at the temple at a very young age and again later by the prophet John the Baptist who himself was foretold as the one to prepare the way for Him.

Jesus opened the eyes of the blind, even those born with the affliction, healed the sick, crippled and leprous, multiplied food, expelled demons, calmed storms, and walked on water.

He was called the *Son of God* by God the Father,[49] by angels,[50] demons,[51] His followers the apostles,[52] by outside observers,[53] and by the Holy Spirit.[54] He performed miracles that could only have been done by God, such as raising the dead, showing He held the power of life and death in His hands. He spoke, and the skies and seas obeyed Him, and He both made wine from water and multiplied fishes and loaves, showing He held the power of creation. He showed Himself to be the incarnate God, Immanuel.

Those who knew Him attested that He was the perfect representation of God.[55] This Lamb of God then submitted Himself to hideously painful and gory torture and death—only to arise on the third day, as foretold in scripture and by Himself, after which He was seen by hundreds.

What was the mission of Jesus—and what did Jesus say when He walked the earth?

---

49 Matt 2:15; 3:17; 17:5; Mark 1:11; Luke 3:22; 9:35.

50 Luke 1:32, 35.

51 Matt 8:29; Mark 3:11; 5:7; Luke 4:41; 8:28

52 Matt 14:33; 16:16; John 1:14, 18; 3:16–18, 35–36; 8:27; 20:31; Rev 2:18.

53 Matt 27:54; Mark 1:1; 15:39; John 1:49; 11:27.

54 As all the above scripture was inspired by the Spirit.

55 John 14:6–10; Heb 1:3; Col 1:15–20.

The Mission of Jesus

The mission Jesus undertook was to reconcile man to God.

The break in the relationship had occurred early in history, at the Garden of Eden, when man chose to listen to the deceiving spirit and disobey God. Before then, death was not part of the created order, but it came to be because sin cannot live alongside a holy God. While sin reigned in us, we could not be allowed tó live eternally with God. The alternative would have been to have live eternally without God, which as scripture shows is a darkness[56] of suffering that almost cannot be fathomed.

Death, while being less than desirable in our eyes, was also the means God provided by which mankind would be reunited with God. For Jesus came to "give his life as a ransom for many."[57]

> *For Christ also suffered once for sins, the righteous for the unrighteous, to bring you to God. He was put to death in the body but made alive in the Spirit.* (1 Peter 3:18)

> *He is the atoning sacrifice for our sins, and not only for ours but also for the sins of the whole world.* (1 John 2:2)

> *In fact, the law requires that nearly everything be cleansed with blood, and without the shedding of blood there is no forgiveness.* (Heb 9:22)

Jesus, in fact, did not just die for our sins; He went beyond in that he took the punishment of torture and the painful death so that

[56] 1 Sam 2:9; Ps 88:12; Matt 5:22, 29–30; 8:12; 10:28; 11:23; 13:42, 49–50; 18:19; 22:1–13; 23:33; 25:14–30, 41–46; Mark 9:43, 45, 47; Luke 10:15; 12:5; Luke 16:19–31; John 12:46; Col 1:13; 1 Thess 5:5; 2 Pet 2:4, 17; Jude 1:6, 13; Rev 1:18; 20:13–14.
[57] Mark 10:45.

we would also be free from the curses of sin (sickness, sufferings, diseases, infirmities, and more). This is why, in the name of Jesus, when healing is declared in faith, the sick are healed.

Because of what Jesus and Jesus alone did, we are seen as righteous before God, and we are reestablished into a relationship with God just as Adam and Eve had early in the Garden of Eden.

> *All this is from God, who reconciled us to himself through Christ and gave us the ministry of reconciliation: that God was reconciling the world to himself in Christ, not counting people's sins against them.* (2 Cor 5:18–19)

> *God made him who had no sin to be sin for us, so that in him we might become the righteousness of God.* (2 Cor 5:21)

From the beginning, our salvation as humanity was planned, and for each one saved, Christ alone is both the beginning and completion of this salvation. Our salvation comes from believing in Him who came for us.

> ***The work of God is this: to believe in the one he has sent.*** (John 6:29)

> *Jesus, the pioneer and perfecter of faith. For the joy set before him he endured the cross, scorning its shame, and sat down at the right hand of the throne of God.* (Heb 12:2)

In various translations, Jesus is the pioneer and perfector, the author and finisher, the beginning and the end of our salvation. There is no other apart from the Trinity who has accomplished our salvation—from the events at Calvary, to the planting and nurturing of the very faith we have through to the sealing with the Holy Spirit as a guarantee of the things to come.

From the beginning, we were created in the image of God to be in relationship to Him. The events at Calvary marked the restoration of that relationship that God organized and carried out. It also ushered in the kingdom that Jesus spoke about more than anything else that He taught. It is this kingdom that we will look at next.

The Kingdom of God

The kingdom of God is also called the kingdom of heaven. It is the fulfillment of the mission of Jesus. In almost every sermon that Jesus preached, He spoke of this kingdom. John the Baptist too spoke of its coming and warned his listeners to be ready and to turn from their ways (repent) in preparation for this kingdom.

What then is this kingdom—and how are we to participate in it? Jesus said many times that we must *seek the kingdom* before all else[58] and that those thrown out of the kingdom end up where there is darkness, crying, and gnashing of teeth—the same descriptions He used when He spoke of hell.

What the Kingdom Is

A kingdom, by definition, is where a king rules over his dominion. Thus, there is a king and his subjects.

In the kingdom that Jesus established, the king is God and the subjects are mankind. Jesus, in His teachings, made it clear that the kingdom includes both those who are His loyal subjects, those on the outside,[59] and those who were in the kingdom but planted by the enemy.[60] In His many parables and the explanations of the parables

[58] Matt 6:19–21, 25–33; 7:13–14, 21–27; 8:11–12; 13:24–30, 37–50; 22:1–13; 25:31–46; Luke 12:27–34; 13:23–30; 16:19–31.

[59] Mark 4:11; Luke 8:10.

[60] Matt 13:24–30, 37–43.

given to his disciples, He tells that the kingdom comprises of both but the weeding out of the disloyal and those planted by the enemy will occur at the end of the age.

Scripture tells us that this kingdom was prepared from the beginning of time.[61] In the ministry of John the Baptist and the early ministry of Jesus, the kingdom was "coming near" or "at hand." Jesus later revealed that it had "now arrived."[62] In keeping with the kingdom being already present, He taught His listeners how they ought to live as loyal subjects to the King who is God.[63]

When the Kingdom Was Established

It had always been God's desire to live with and be among His people since our separation at the Garden of Eden. However, because we, His creation, were an unfaithful people and not ready to receive Him, the kingdom was established in stages, which can be seen in the following prophesies that have all been fulfilled:

> *Then I will dwell among the Israelites and be their God. They will know that I am the LORD their God, who brought them out of Egypt so that I might dwell among them. I am the LORD their God.* (Exod 29:45–46)

> *But you are to seek the place the LORD your God will choose from among all your tribes to put his Name there for his dwelling. To that place you must go* (Deut 12:5)

[61] Matt 25:34.

[62] Matt 5:1–10, 17–20; 12:27–28; 18:3–4; 19:14; 21:31; Mark 10:15; Luke 11:20; 12:32; 17:20–21; John 3:5; 4:23.

[63] Matt 5:5–16, 19–7:27; 13:3–23, etc.

See also Deut 12:11; 14:23; 16:2, 11; 26:2.

These prophecies all pointed to the time when God would be present in the tabernacle tent and later the temple. They were written when God was already with them on the journey to the Promised Land. However, even after He lived among His people, He maintained a relationship through His priests because they were still not ready for Him. The people rejected Him to chase after idols, false gods, and a God-less lifestyle.

> *Our parents were unfaithful; they did evil in the eyes of the LORD our God and forsook him. They turned their faces away from the LORD's dwelling place and turned their backs on him.* (2 Chr 29:6)
>
> *The LORD, the God of their ancestors, sent word to them through his messengers again and again, because he had pity on his people and on his dwelling place.* (2 Chr 36:15)

The children of Israel trampled the covenant in the very places God had both promised and given them, and they defamed His name by the way they lived. They lived more wickedly than even those peoples who had been removed from the lands they were given. For this, God finally abandoned them and drove them from the land as He had warned them through Moses and every prophet.

God, however, had a plan for *all* mankind. It was to have a kingdom without gates and walls. This kingdom would come in three stages:

- First, the Son of God would establish it when He appeared on earth.
- Then the Holy Spirit would seal it until the fulfillment of all things.

- God would then step back on earth to dwell forever with His people.

All the preceding stages were in preparation for this.

The Kingdom with Jesus (Stage 1)

When Jesus came to His people, as many as had been prepared by the repentance ministry of John the Baptist were ready to welcome Him although they did not understand the kind of kingdom that would be set up at that stage. Jesus Christ on earth was truly God with His people, but He was here to make the *fullness* of that kingdom a possibility—firstly by taking on our humanity so that He could take our place in death for us and secondly so that the Holy Spirit might be released on as many as would receive Him.

Among the many Old Testament prophecies[64] of this stage of the kingdom is one of Mary and Jesus:

> *Therefore the Lord himself will give you a sign: The virgin will conceive and give birth to a son, and will call him Immanuel.* (Isa 7:14)

About seven hundred years later, the archangel Gabriel confirmed that Jesus was to fulfill this prophecy as well as establish the everlasting kingdom:

> *You will conceive and give birth to a son, and you are to call him Jesus. He will be great and will be called the Son of the Most High. The Lord God will give him the throne of his father David, and he will reign over Jacob's descendants forever; his kingdom will never end.* (Luke 1:30–33)

[64] Ps 2:7–12; 45:6–7; Isa 9:6–7; Mic 5:1–3.

After the Spirit of God descended upon Jesus at His baptism, He started His ministry:

- preaching the good news of the kingdom of God
- healing, blessing, and working miraculous signs and wonders as testimony to who He was and of the hand of God in all He did
- preparing followers who would then continue the mission He undertook
- laying down His life for us all so that the curse of sin, death, and suffering would be overcome.

Jesus's death by crucifixion, after scourging and beating that so altered His appearance such that He hardly looked human, was witnessed by followers, His enemies, and the impartial. As further evidence of all His claims, including that of His overcoming the curse of death over all of us, He came back from the dead on the third day.

In His glorified body, He was seen by more than five hundred to whom He showed evidence that it was truly Him. He then commissioned His disciples to wait for the appearance and empowerment of the Holy Spirit. This was so they could continue His work in the preaching of the good news of salvation with healings, deliverances, signs, and wonders.

Shortly after commissioning His disciples and blessing them, He rose in the sight of many to return again at a promised future time.

The Kingdom with the Holy Spirit (Stage 2)

The Holy Spirit is, in a word, "God" in our presence today. We live in the time of the Holy Spirit, and He will remain with us until the fulfillment of all things (stage 3).

Scripture tells us the Spirit was with the Father and the Son at the beginning of Creation:

> *In the beginning God created the heavens and the earth. Now the earth was formless and empty, darkness was over the surface of the deep, and the Spirit of God was hovering over the waters.* (Gen 1:2)

The Father, the Son, and the Spirit are One, and this is revealed in a number of scriptures:

> *Jesus answered … **"Believe me when I say that I am in the Father and the Father is in me; or at least believe on the evidence of the works themselves."*** (John 14:9, 11)

> *Jesus replied, **"Anyone who loves me will obey my teaching. My Father will love them, and we will come to them and make our home with them.*** (John 14:23)

> ***If you love me, keep my commands. And I will ask the Father, and he will give you another advocate to help you and be with you forever—the Spirit of truth. The world cannot accept him, because it neither sees him nor knows him. But you know him, for he lives with you and will be in you.*** (John 14:15–17)

The Spirit coming to live in us is then the materialization of the promise "***we will come to them and make our home with them."***

> *For who knows a person's thoughts except their own spirit within them? In the same way no one knows the thoughts of God except the Spirit of God.* (1 Cor 2:11)

When Jesus took on our flesh to walk the earth, He could only be in one place at a time because He was limited by the humanity He adopted—the flesh itself. However, after His ascension into heaven, His Father sent us the promised Holy Spirit. This same Spirit can be with *each* of us *wherever* we are as first depicted by the tongues of flame that separated and then rested on all those in the upper room at Pentecost.[65]

> ***But very truly I tell you, it is <u>for your good</u> that I am going away. Unless I go away, the Advocate will not come to you; but if I go, I will send him to you.*** (John 16:7)

Other translations put this as, "***it is best for you,***" "***it is for your benefit,***" "***it is profitable for you,***" or simply "***it is to your advantage.***" With Him *in* us, we *can* live the Christian life, which is impossible without His guidance and empowerment.

As we've seen in the chapter, "*Instead of the Holy Spirit,*" the Holy Spirit is called in scripture *the Spirit of God, the Spirit of Christ,* and *the Spirit of Truth, Wisdom, Revelation, and Prophecy.*

> Before He left, Jesus told His disciples: ***"I am going to send you what my Father has promised; but stay in the city until you have been clothed with power from on high."*** (Luke 24:49)

He spoke of the Spirit who was to come to them, remain *with* them, and be *in* them until the end of the age.

This kingdom was born on Pentecost Sunday in the "upper room" when the faithful who had already put their trust in the risen Christ were filled with the Holy Spirit who had come upon them. This was the new reality for believers now *living in a Covenant relationship with God*—the promise made a reality only by the sacrifice of Christ at the cross and a relationship much greater than any of the prophets could ever have experienced.

---

[65] Acts 2.

> ***Truly I tell you, among those born of women there has not risen anyone greater than John the Baptist; yet whoever is least in the kingdom of heaven is greater than he.*** (Matt 11:11)

The prophets had looked forward to that first day when believers in the one true God could be led by Him and free from sin and its curse, which separated us from Him.

> To single Mary out for her brief experience of having our Creator and Savior Lord in her womb and as her Son is to ignore the greater truth alive in us who are born of the Spirit today—that is, of the Spirit of God Himself living within us.
>
> This is what Jesus would have us focus on and live by in the here and now—not in the past and not of someone else's experience.

The apostles understood that what happened to them at Pentecost was the fulfillment of scripture, including that spoken of by the prophet Joel:

> *In the last days, God says,*
> *I will pour out my Spirit on all people.*
> *Your sons and daughters will prophesy,*
> *your young men will see visions,*
> *your old men will dream dreams.*
> *Even on my servants, both men and women,*
> *I will pour out my Spirit in those days,*
> *and they will prophesy.*
> *I will show wonders in the heavens above*
> *and signs on the earth below,*
> *blood and fire and billows of smoke.*
> *The sun will be turned to darkness*
> *and the moon to blood*

> *before the coming of the great and glorious day of the Lord.*
> *And everyone who calls*
> *on the name of the Lord will be saved.* (Acts 2:17–21 cf Joel 2:28–32)

There was now no separation of believers from God, and each one—even the servants both men and women—could now come to God and not have to go through the intermediaries of the Levitical priests or the ceremonies.

Furthermore, "*everyone who calls on the name of the Lord will be saved.*" The burden of sin with all its guilt and shame was removed. These prophecies were made reality from that moment:

> *As far as the east is from the west, so far has he removed our transgressions from us.* (Ps 103:12)

> *For no matter how many promises God has made, they are "Yes" in Christ. And so through him the "Amen" is spoken by us to the glory of God.* (2 Cor 1:20)

It is no wonder the believers at Pentecost were overjoyed and that those who heard the good news the apostles preached in Christ that day were added to their number. Evidence of this appears in the book of Acts:

> *They devoted themselves to the apostles' teaching and to fellowship, to the breaking of bread and to prayer. Everyone was filled with awe at the many wonders and signs performed by the apostles. All the believers were together and had everything in common. They sold property and possessions to give to anyone who had need. Every day they continued to meet together in the temple courts. They broke bread in their homes and ate together with glad and sincere hearts, praising God and enjoying the favor of all*

> *the people. And the Lord added to their number daily those who were being saved.* (Acts 2:42–47)

The baptism of the Spirit with the fruit of its power also changed the lives of each of the believers. It completely and for all time transformed those previously fearful apostles, who hid from those who had crucified their Lord, into the mighty ministers of faith they then became so that they even stood up to the Sanhedrin and Pharisees. Such was the power and faith that the Spirit in them gave them that they each carried the Gospel with them in signs and power all their days.

Being connected to God *through His Spirit* was what Jesus had previously taught them:

> ***Remain in me, as I also remain in you. No branch can bear fruit by itself; it must remain in the vine. Neither can you bear fruit unless you remain in me.***
>
> ***I am the vine; you are the branches. If you remain in me and I in you, you will bear much fruit; apart from me you can do nothing. If you do not remain in me, you are like a branch that is thrown away and withers; such branches are picked up, thrown into the fire and burned. If you remain in me and my words remain in you, ask whatever you wish, and it will be done for you. This is to my Father's glory, that you bear much fruit, showing yourselves to be my disciples.*** (John 15:4–8)

This connection to God enabled the apostles to walk in power and fruitfulness. Christ had already alluded to this:

> ***Very truly I tell you, whoever believes in me will do the works I have been doing, and they will do even greater things than these, because I am going to the Father.*** (John 14:12)

The apostle Paul summed it up in his letter from prison to the church at Colossae when he wrote about the *mystery* of all ages:

> *Once you were alienated from God and were enemies in your minds because of your evil behavior. But now he has reconciled you by Christ's physical body through death to present you holy in his sight, without blemish and free from accusation—if you continue in your faith, established and firm, and do not move from the hope held out in the gospel. This is the gospel that you heard and that has been proclaimed to every creature under heaven, and of which I, Paul, have become a servant.* (Col 1:21–23)

> *I have become its servant by the commission God gave me to present to you the Word of God in its fullness—the mystery that has been kept hidden for ages and generations, but is now disclosed to the Lord's people. To them God has chosen to make known among the Gentiles the glorious riches of this mystery, which is Christ in you, the hope of glory.* (Col 1:25–27)

"*Christ in you*" is the Holy Spirit living in born-of-the-Spirit believers because Christ, the Spirit, and the Father are One.

"*The hope of glory*" is the guarantee of things to come as scripture tell us:

> *He anointed us, set his seal of ownership on us, and put his Spirit in our hearts as a deposit, guaranteeing what is to come.* (2 Cor 1:21–22)

> *When you believed, you were marked in him with a seal, the promised Holy Spirit, who is a deposit guaranteeing our inheritance until the redemption of those who are God's possession—to the praise of his glory.* (Eph 1:13–14)

The Spirit-filled and Spirit-led believer cannot be any closer to God than he already is because God is in him.

Today, many parts of the church do not live such a reality.

Scripture tells us that the church began to falter by not relying on the Spirit. By the time the book of Revelation was written by the apostle John, a few short decades after Pentecost, God had to remind the seven churches in Asia to listen to what the Holy Spirit was saying to them.[66]

Sadly, this turning away from the Holy Spirit has largely been the history of the church ever since—relying on human wisdom and earthly power and not on the Spirit of God. Without turning to and living under the authority and power of the Spirit, the miracles ceased. Instead of turning back to the Spirit, many in the church taught that the "age of miracles" had passed, even misquoting scripture such as below to justify their arguments:

> *Love never fails. But where there are prophecies, they will cease; where there are tongues, they will be stilled; where there is knowledge, it will pass away.* (1 Cor 13:8)

The verses that follow provide the necessary context:

---

[66] Rev 2:7, 11, 17, 29; 3:6, 13, 22.

> *For we know in part and we prophesy in part, but when completeness comes, what is in part disappears. When I was a child, I talked like a child, I thought like a child, I reasoned like a child. When I became a man, I put the ways of childhood behind me. For now we see only a reflection as in a mirror; then we shall see face to face. Now I know in part; then I shall know fully, even as I am fully known* (1 Cor 13:9–12)

What scripture says then is that the prophecies, tongues, knowledge, and miracles will cease *when completeness comes*—that is the "Stage 3 Kingdom of God" described in Revelation, which speaks of the return of our Lord Jesus Christ to rule and reign forever.

The Spirit never left, but the church had stopped listening to and following the Spirit so that there were no manifestations of the Spirit in signs and wonders. Believers were meant to have continued in the power of the Spirit just as the apostles had and to have moved like Jesus in more power and authority than Elijah, Gideon, and all the mighty men and women of the Old Testament. Instead, unbelief had replaced faith.

Rather than return to the Spirit, the church taught of Mary and her supposed power and pointed believers to her rather than to the living Spirit of God. If, indeed, "Mary" was where the power was, Jesus need never have told His followers to wait for the Spirit. He never pointed them toward following her. Even in our day and age, followers of Mary turn to her when they should be turning to the Spirit who is God with us.

Around the 1970s, the Spirit of God touched communities everywhere—Protestant, Catholic, and Orthodox—in a revival that the Catholic world termed *the Charismatic Renewal.* However, in 1973, at the gathering of the Notre Dame Conference, (Roman Catholic) Cardinal Suenens announced, "*If you want to know where the Holy Spirit is, then look to Mary."* This was greeted with loud cheers.

The Holy Spirit, however, is *not* Mary, and the Spirit-filled believer—which every believer ought to be—need not look for Mary to find the Spirit who should be the ever-present Lord *of* and *in* his life.

One does not find God by going to Mary, despite what Liguori and others would have us believe. God the Spirit is here, waiting for us to turn to Him and acknowledge Him and His right over our lives. He seeks us to love Him and to be loved by Him, which is why He created us in His image.

> *Come near to God and he will come near to you.* (Jas 4:8)

> ***Remain in me, as I also remain in you.*** (John 15:4)

God will come near to you, and if you invite Him in, He will come and dwell in you. When that happens, there is no closer that you can get to God here on earth:

> ***Here I am! I stand at the door and knock. If anyone hears my voice and opens the door, I will come in and eat with that person, and they with me.*** (Rev 3:20)

Ask for His Holy Spirit and for His rightful place over you and you will receive Him:

> ***So I say to you: Ask and it will be given to you; seek and you will find; knock and the door will be opened to you. For everyone who asks receives; the one who seeks finds; and to the one who knocks, the door will be opened.***

> ***Which of you fathers, if your son asks for a fish, will give him a snake instead? Or if he asks for an egg, will give him a scorpion? If you then, though you are evil, know how to give good gifts to your children, how much more will your Father in heaven give the Holy Spirit to those who ask him!*** (Luke 11:9–13)

However, God will not force a relationship with Him on you. In the parable of the prodigal son,[67] the father lets his selfish and wasteful son take the inheritance he demanded and leave. After this son had squandered all the wealth in wild living, he made his way back when hunger and deprivation woke him to his senses. His father, who apparently often scanned the horizon hoping for his return, ran out to meet him halfway when he saw him. This is the picture that Jesus painted of the Father God He intimately knew: His God and our God, His Father and Our Father who respects our freedom to choose whether to draw near to Him or to not want anything to do with Him.

He waits for us to come to Him—ready to embrace us, cloak us with righteousness just as the father did, with the "*best robe*" with "*ring and sandals,*" to take up our position as His children in His kingdom and with a feast for all to celebrate our return.

If and when we return, it is His Spirit who is sent to meet us and then abide in us if we welcome Him in.

> *Jesus replied, "**Anyone who loves me will obey my teaching. My Father will love them, and we will come to them and make our home with them.**"* (John 14:23)

The present kingdom of God is the kingdom of believers who are submitted to Jesus and living under the direction and calling of the Spirit of God.

---

67 Luke 15:11–32.

Jesus spoke of this kingdom life lived with the Spirit of God:

> ***Very truly I tell you, no one can enter the kingdom of God unless they are born of water and the Spirit. Flesh gives birth to flesh, but the Spirit gives birth to spirit. You should not be surprised at my saying, "You must be born again." The wind blows wherever it pleases. You hear its sound, but you cannot tell where it comes from or where it is going. So it is with everyone born of the Spirit.*** (John 3:5–8)

The next chapter examines the role the Holy Spirit graciously takes in the life of the believer in the present kingdom of God.

The Holy Spirit: God with Us, Here and Now

If the Holy Spirit is God with us in the present kingdom, then every believer needs to know the Spirit and be in submission to this Spirit of God.

In this chapter, we will look at what scripture says about five topics:

- the roles of the Holy Spirit in the life of the believer
- how to receive the Holy Spirit
- how to live with the Holy Spirit
- sanctification by the Holy Spirit
- how to always remain in the Spirit

The Roles of the Holy Spirit in the Life of the Believer

Scripture speaks of many roles the Holy Spirit has in the lives of believers. These roles are exclusively His in many respects since only

He can, in our lives, do what an all-knowing and all-present God can do. To recognize the roles is to begin to understand how much we need the Spirit of God in our lives.

The following summaries simply scratch the surface of the involvement the Spirit can have in the lives of believers. The reader is invited to delve more deeply by reading each of the scriptural references given.

To Guide, Instruct, Assign and Test Us

When Jesus walked the earth, He taught and guided His disciples. He also sent them out on assignments to help carry His mission and sometimes tested them so that they would know their own hearts. So too does the Spirit of God do these things in the lives of believers today:

> ***But when he, the Spirit of truth, comes, he will guide you into all the truth. He will not speak on his own; he will speak only what he hears, and he will tell you what is yet to come.*** (John 16:13)

> *On the contrary, we speak as those approved by God to be entrusted with the gospel. We are not trying to please people but God, who tests our hearts.* (1 Thess 2:4)

His guidance sometimes comes in a whisper, a nudge, or a feeling, but at other times, it is a direct word—seemingly if we have developed the habit of listening and obeying often enough or perhaps when the occasion requires it.

> *The Spirit told Philip, "Go to that chariot and stay near it."* (Acts 8:29)

> *While they were worshiping the Lord and fasting, the Holy Spirit said, "Set apart for me Barnabas and Saul for the work to which I have called them."* (Acts 13:2)

Read the following scriptures to learn more of how the Spirit carries out these roles: John 14:26; 16:13; Acts 1:1–2; 8:29; 10:19–20; 11:12; 13:2, 4; 15:28; 16:6–7; 20:22–23, 28; 21:4, 11; 22:10; Rom 15:18–19; 1 Cor 14:3–5; 1 Thess 2:4; 2 Thess 3:5; 2 Tim 1:14; Heb 3:7–11; 9:8; 10:15–17; 1 Pet 1:11–12; 1 John 2:27.

Without our submission to the Spirit for our guidance, instruction and assignment, how can any believer expect to hear and live out the words of Jesus who said,

> ***My sheep listen to my voice; I know them, and they follow me. I give them eternal life, and they shall never perish; no one will snatch them out of my hand.*** (John 10:27–28)

A believer who submits himself or herself to the Spirit's leading will always have fresh testimonies to share of God's recent work in their lives. This is because the Spirit is one with God.

> *Jesus said to them, "**My Father is always at his work to this very day, and I too am working.**"* (John 5:17)

The Holy Spirit Says, "Go!"

Ivan and Jane Mills run a ministry called Christ For All Children. They travel from Australia to different parts of the world to minister to children and train local people to minister to children.

Many years ago, Ivan was planning a trip to Poland. He and his friend Laurie were to be in Poland for five weeks, running outreach programs for children in many different towns and villages.

At the last minute, Ivan received some money so that he could pay for their flights, but he had no other funds to pay for their expenses in Poland for five weeks. Rather concerned about this, Ivan asked the Holy Spirit what he should do. He felt the Holy Spirit saying to him, "Go!"

Ivan responded, "You want me to go to Poland for five weeks with no money?"

Again he felt the Holy Spirit saying, "Go!"

On the day that the two of them were to depart, a lady came to visit and gave them two hundred dollars. That was a wonderful blessing, but they needed about two thousand dollars.

In obedience to the Holy Spirit, they got on the plane.

Now the flight was through Singapore, where they were to stay with their Singaporean friend on Saturday and Sunday nights. Ivan ministered to children on Sunday morning and received a small donation from the local Singaporean church, for which they were very thankful.

They were keen to attend a church service in Singapore. Ivan asked his Singaporean friend whether there were any night services. His friend knew of one, and off they went.

They were warmly welcomed by church people who asked them why they were in Singapore. Ivan and Laurie told them that they were on their way to Poland. They told them what they were planning to do, but they did not mention money.

Somehow, the pastor found out about them, and during the service, he mentioned that there were some Australian visitors there who were on their way to Poland. He invited Ivan to come to the front and tell everyone what he and Laurie were planning to do in Poland. Ivan spoke briefly, again not mentioning anything about money. After he spoke, the pastor decided that the congregation would take up an offering for them!

Ivan and Laurie very gratefully received the offering and left Singapore the following day with two thousand dollars, enough to fund their five weeks of ministry.

Open Us to Understand Things Beyond

God does not want us, who follow Him, to be ignorant of things He will bring to pass or of things that are outside of the "here and now." He does not reveal to us more than we can handle either, but what is useful to build His kingdom of which we are a part or what will encourage us.

> *And he carried me away in the Spirit to a mountain great and high, and showed me the Holy City, Jerusalem, coming down out of heaven from God.* (Rev 21:10)
>
> *One of them, named Agabus, stood up and through the Spirit predicted that a severe famine would spread over the entire Roman world.* (This happened during the reign of Claudius.) (Acts 11:28)

Read also John 14:20; 16:13, 15; Acts 11:28; Rom 9:1; 2 Cor 2:9–13; Eph 1:8–9; 1:17–19; 3:3–6; Col 1:9–10; 2 Pet 1:21; Rev 1:10–11; 21:10.

> ***If you love me, keep my commands. And I will ask the Father, and he will give you another advocate to help you and be with you forever — the Spirit of truth. The world cannot accept him, because it neither sees him nor knows him. But you know him, for he lives with you and will be in you. I will not leave you as orphans; I will come to you. Before long, the world will not see me anymore, but you will see me. Because I live, you also will live. On that day you will realize that I am in my Father, and you are in me, and I am in you.*** (John 14:15–20)

There are mysteries all around us, but perhaps the greatest mystery to be grasped and understood by the believer is that spoken of by Jesus in His last statement above (John 14:20). This can only be understood by the revelation of the Spirit of God.

Testify to Us about Jesus, Reveal Him and Glorify Both Him and the Father

Just as Jesus revealed His Father to us, so too the Holy Spirit reveals Jesus to us. And just as we have access to the Father through Jesus, we also have access to the Father and Jesus through the Spirit who was given to us.

> *I keep asking that the God of our Lord Jesus Christ, the glorious Father, may give you the Spirit of wisdom and revelation, so that you may know him better.* (Eph 1:17–19)

Read also John 15:26; 16:14; 17:26; Acts 2:11; 7:55–56; 2 Cor 4:6; Eph 1:17–19; 3:20–21; Col 1:28–29; 2 Thess 1:11–12; 1 John 5:6–8.

> *The person with the Spirit makes judgments about all things, but such a person is not subject to merely human judgments, for, "Who has known the mind of the Lord so as to instruct him?" But we have the mind of Christ.* (1 Cor 2:15–16)

It is the Spirit of God who reveals God to us, and in the revelation, we are transformed daily more and more into the image of Christ.

If we want to know Christ, we need to commune with His Spirit—for the Spirit is the very presence of Christ in us.

> *I pray that out of his glorious riches he may strengthen you with power through his Spirit in your inner being, so that Christ may dwell in your hearts through faith.* (Eph 3:16–17)

Read also 2 Cor 13:5; Col 1:25–27; 1 John 3:24; 4:13

There is no higher place to which we can go while living on this side of eternity than to have Christ our Creator and Savior live in us. We can only do this through having His Spirit in us.

Help Us Pray to God, Know Him, and Live in His Presence

The Spirit of God guides believers in how and what we are to pray. This is so that the will of God is done in our lives and in the lives of those for whom we pray.

> *We do not know what we ought to pray for, but the Spirit himself intercedes for us through wordless groans.* (Rom 8:27)

> *And pray in the Spirit on all occasions with all kinds of prayers and requests. With this in mind, be alert*

and always keep on praying for all the Lord's people. (Eph 6:18)

Read also Acts 10:44–46; Rom 8:26–27; 1 Cor 14:15–16; Gal 4:6; Eph 2:6, 18; 3:16–19; 5:18–20; 6:18; Col 1:9–12, 3:16; Jude 1:20–21.

If we pray in the way that He leads us, then our prayers cannot but be heard, and He who hears is faithful to do all that is in His will to do.

The following testimony is from Hans Hansma, an Australian who, with his wife, Akkie, ministers in Thailand:

> One morning I was called to the infectious disease hospital located in my leprosy-care village. A widow from my village had become seriously ill. For a living, she collected empty bottles to be recycled. She has one young daughter who depends on her for everything. The workers told me, "Please come quickly to the women's ward and pray." They also mentioned, "She must not die, Hans, because her daughter needs her so very much." I agreed and took a few of my fellow workers with me to pray.
>
> Upon arrival, I saw that she was indeed in a bad way. We lay hands on her and prayed for her in the Name of Jesus Christ. After prayer, I told the people who were with me that I wanted to go back to the base for some more practical work. The double doors to the hallway were wide-open, but when I reached the doorway, I was stopped by a strange invisible force; the doorway had become a wall, preventing me from leaving the ward. I tried three times to push through, but I could not break through it. Realizing I could not leave, I

started to look around me. My eyes were drawn to a woman on a bed close to the doorway, but still within the ward. Instantly, I knew that somehow the invisible wall had some connection to this person on the bed. I could not see much of this person because a blanket completely covered her.

Reaching out, I gently touched her.

Within a second, the blanket was pushed away. I saw a lady with tears streaming down her cheeks looking straight at me. I asked her, "What can I do for you?"

Through her tears, she asked me, "May I tell you something first?"

She explained how she had felt very sick and had covered herself with her blanket that morning. She said, "Then I heard footsteps. Within a minute, I heard a man's voice starting to pray for someone in the room. It was all so real, and I really knew his God heard him. Then, from under the blanket, I whispered from the depths of my heart and said, "Oh, God, of this man. He prayed for this other lady. Please, please make him pray for me too. Make him stay in this room because I need a prayer too."

After hearing this I was amazed at the way God had prevented me from leaving the ward. He truly is the Lord who hears and answers!

After prayer, she was completely healed and believed in the Lord as her Savior.

Bring Conviction of Sin as Well as Assurance of Salvation

Jesus paid the price for our sin by dying on the cross. In doing so, He brought about our salvation by taking the punishment that we had earned by our rebellion against God. Salvation, however, is not automatic as we have to *receive* the gift of life that He gave by *believing* that He redeemed us.

Unless we are made aware of our sinfulness, we will not recognize the need for a Savior. The Holy Spirit is the One who convicts us of this sinfulness.

> ***When he comes, he will prove the world to be in the wrong about sin and righteousness and judgment: about sin, because people do not believe in me; about righteousness, because I am going to the Father, where you can see me no longer; and about judgment, because the prince of this world now stands condemned.*** (John 16:8–11)

> *But if an unbeliever or an inquirer comes in while everyone is prophesying, they are convicted of sin and are brought under judgment by all, as the secrets of their hearts are laid bare. So they will fall down and worship God, exclaiming, "God is really among you!"* (1 Cor 14:24–25)

> *Jesus said:* ***"I am the vine; you are the branches. If you remain in me and I in you, you will bear much fruit; apart from me you can do nothing."*** (John 15:5)

It is Jesus, through His Holy Spirit, in the life of the believer whose Word produces fruit when preached—fruit that brings eternal life to those who receive it. Unless the Word is preached and the Spirit give fruitfulness, who can be saved?

See John 16:8–11; Acts 6:10; 10:44–46; 11:21; 15:8; Rom 10:14–15; 1 Cor 14:24–25; Phil 1:27–28; 1 Thess 1:5; 1 John 3:24; 4:13.

Once saved, it is the same Spirit who then in the life of the believer provides the assurance of salvation, if indeed, they received His Spirit:

> *And this is how we know that he lives in us: We know it by the Spirit he gave us.* (1 John 3:24)

> *And by him we cry, "Abba, Father." The Spirit himself testifies with our spirit that we are God's children.* (Rom 8:15–16)

Without the Holy Spirit, a believer may *hope* for salvation, but with the Spirit alive in him, he has the blessed *assurance* of salvation.

The following is the testimony of an Australian pastor who ministers in Pakistan.

> I was travelling on a bus from the high mountains on a twelve-hour journey to my home in North Pakistan. I had met a young French traveller, and neither of us slept as I shared with him about Christ and His gift of salvation.
>
> When we arrived at our destination, I invited him to come to my place and he agreed. As I shared more of the free gift of salvation, he said quite simply, "I have come to the gift," and so I prayed with him the prayer of commitment. As I was praying, I felt the Lord saying to me, "You are healed." That was really exciting, because I was suffering from severe diarrhoea at the time. My guest left, and I felt the twinges of diarrhoea, but I knew I had the victory, and my heart rejoiced to be well again. From that moment I was healed, but much more importantly, this man was saved and committed to Christ.

Baptize Us and Equip Us in the Gifts of God

The baptism of the Spirit should be one of the first spiritual experiences believers have after putting their faith in the finished work of Christ Jesus. This baptism of power enables believers to be the hands, feet, and mouth of Christ in our world.

The apostles had little power except when Jesus was with them. Peter could only walk on water when Jesus called him. Without Jesus, they all fell apart.

> ***"You will all fall away,"*** *Jesus told them,* ***"for it is written: 'I will strike the shepherd, and the sheep will be scattered.'"*** (Mark 14:27)

After His resurrection, He told them to wait for power to descend upon them. That power was the empowering presence of the Spirit that enabled them to be and do the things Christ did—in His power.

> ***Very truly I tell you, whoever believes in me will do the works I have been doing, and they will do even greater things than these, because I am going to the Father.*** (John 14:12)

> ***Unless I go away, the Advocate will not come to you; but if I go, I will send him to you.*** (John 16:7)

The Spirit enables this by equipping the believer with gifts that will build both the individual as well as the body of believers around them.

For the Individual

This equipping for the individual includes strengths such as supernatural power, boldness, and the power to overcome sin and fear:

> *God also testified to it by signs, wonders and various miracles, and by gifts of the Holy Spirit distributed according to his will.* (Heb 2:4)
>
> *For if you live according to the flesh, you will die; but if by the Spirit you put to death the misdeeds of the body, you will live.* (Rom 8:13)
>
> *For the Spirit God gave us does not make us timid, but gives us power, love and self-discipline.* (2 Tim 1:7)

See also Acts 1:5, 8; 2:4, 17–18, 43; 4:8–11, 31; 5:12; 8:39–40; 13:6–12; 14:3; 19:6, 11–12; Rom 8:5, 9, 13, 15, 26; 15:18–19; 1 Cor 1:8; 2:4; 12:4–13; 1 Cor 14:22; Gal 3:5; 5:16–18, 22; Eph 3:16; Phil 4:6–7, 12–13; Col 1:9–11; 1 Thess 1:5–6; 2 Tim 1:7; 4:17; Heb 2:4; 1 John 3:9; 4:4.

The Spirit also is the divine Helper, Comforter, and Advocate, and He who encourages us.

In these roles, His presence is like that of a strong and dependable father or brother who is there for us in all our trials to bring us through, but He is also there in all our successes to help us not lose our focus of God.

See John 14:16, 26; 15:7; Acts 9:31; 13:52; Rom 8:26–27; Phil 2:1; 1 Thess 2:2; 2 Thess 2:16–17; Rev 14:13.

The Spirit is He who releases in us the promise of Jesus when He said that He came to give us life in its fullness. This fullness includes freedom, joy, peace, and protection.

> *But the Lord stood at my side and gave me strength, so that through me the message might be fully proclaimed and all the Gentiles might hear it. And I was delivered from the lion's mouth. The Lord will rescue me from every evil attack and will bring me safely to his heavenly kingdom. To him be glory for ever and ever. Amen.* (2 Tim 4:17–18)

> *But the fruit of the Spirit is love, joy, peace, forbearance, kindness, goodness, faithfulness, gentleness and self-control.* (Gal 5:22–23)

See also Rom 14:17; 2 Cor 3:6, 17; Gal 5:22–23; Phil 1:19; 2 Thess 3:3, 16; 2 Tim 4:17–18; 1 Pet 1:5; 1 John 5:18

The Spirit of God also is He who makes us children of God. We have no higher family to which we can belong. This belonging comes through the presence of the Spirit in us.

See Rom 8:14–17; Titus 3:5–7.

These are but an outline of the many blessings that come from God who has given them through His Holy Spirit so that the believer might have a life of fullness in Him.

For the Church

For building the body of believers, the equipping includes gifts such as signs and wonders that grow the church and divine virtues that strengthen and bring unity to it.

> ***May they also be in us so that the world may believe that you have sent me. I have given them the glory that you gave me, that they may be one as we are one—I in them and you in me—so that they may be brought to complete unity.*** (John 17:21–23)

> *Since you are eager for gifts of the Spirit, try to excel in those that build up the church.* (1 Cor 14:12)

See also John 17:21–23; 1 Cor 12:12–30; Eph 2:19–22; 4:3–6, 11–13; 5:18–19; Phil 2:1–4; 1 Thess 3:12, 4:9.

Bring to Mind the Scriptures as Well as the Current Words God Has for Us

The Spirit of God spoke through the prophets and inspired the writers of scripture with words meant for us. The same Spirit today awakens these words in us when we need them.

> *Above all, you must understand that no prophecy of Scripture came about by the prophet's own interpretation of things.* (2 Pet 1:20)

> *But the Advocate, the Holy Spirit, whom the Father will send in my name, will teach you all things and will remind you of everything I have said to you.* (John 14:26)

> *Take the helmet of salvation and the sword of the Spirit, which is the Word of God.* (Eph 6:17)

Who is there, among believers, who has not had the need for a word at the right time? Whether it is to build us up, guide us, or humble us, the right word of scripture comes through the Spirit who first inspired it.

Sometimes we need the words to overcome the challenges we face in this life—whether spiritual, material, or other. The Spirit will bring the words we need to sustain us at the very moment we need them. Every Spirit-filled believer experiences such sustenance every day like manna from heaven.

Even as you read these words, the Spirit might be reminding you of other words:

> ***Man shall not live on bread alone, but on every word that comes from the mouth of God.*** (Matt 4:4)

Bring Kingdom Fruitfulness in and through Our Lives

The book of Acts is mostly a documentary of the Spirit of God in action in the newly born church. Most newborns are completely helpless, dependent upon others, and completely unproductive.

The same cannot be said of the newly birthed church, which was more fruitful than perhaps at any other time in history. For instance, on the morning of Pentecost, the 120 or so believers grew by about three thousand. The work of the Spirit enabled all of this fruitfulness to manifest.

> ***I am the vine; you are the branches. If you remain in me and I in you, you will bear much fruit; apart from me you can do nothing.*** (John 15:5)

> ***This is to my Father's glory, that you bear much fruit, showing yourselves to be my disciples.*** (John 15:8)

See also John 15:5, 8; Acts 9:31; Col 1:9–10; 2 Thess 1:11.

The fullness of life that we read about in the previous section is not just for us; it is for all to whom God has sent His Son to die for. It is for all humanity. In the hands of the Holy Spirit, any yielded, faithful, and faith-filled believer can be one of those Jesus spoke of.

> ***But the seed falling on good soil refers to someone who hears the word and understands it. This is the one who produces a crop, yielding a hundred, sixty or thirty times what was sown.*** (Matt 13:23)

Geoff Kingsford, part of the leadership of Youth With a Mission (YWAM), took a team to Hyderabad, India, as part of a Discipleship Training School (DTS) program. He also wrote *Suicidal to Saved.*

> The DTS split into two teams and my team was assigned to a community that was erecting an ablution block. My role was to supervise the installation. If my father was still alive, he would have laughed since he knew I was not good when it comes to plumbing.
>
> For three days, I bluffed my way through what needed to be done. At the end of the third day, I was finished. I went to my leaders and told them, "I can't do this. I have no idea what I'm doing."
>
> Being the wonderful and wise leaders that they were, they said, "Let's pray for Geoff."
>
> "Fat lot of good that will do," I thought.
>
> Anyway I let them pray for me and went to bed that night, hoping for something to change.
>
> The following morning, I work up and we headed to the community to begin work. We were scheduled to meet with the council engineer to check the

construction site. The engineer met us there and began giving the community instructions on what to do.

He told them, "We need to dig three feet down here, and follow this line, and we will connect up to the mains sewerage at the other end."

Without thinking, but with great confidence, I turned to him and said, "No, we need to dig six feet down here and follow this line, because if we don't, the pipe will end up three feet above the ground."

He looked at me and said, "Okay."

And that was it, the decision was made. We followed the directions that God had given me and when we left, the pipe was just about to be connected to the sewerage outlet.

I was told that when they connected it, the pipe literally slotted directly onto the connection at exactly the right height. Somehow God had downloaded into me all the plans needed to help with the construction of the ablution block. I supervised the purchasing of equipment, the laying of the line and requesting permission from individuals for the connection.

Everything that was needed God had given me.

Could I do it again? Who knows? What I do know is that God provided me with the knowledge needed to complete the tasks that He had given me to do.

Seal Us in Christ, Sanctify Us, and Mold Us Daily into the Image of Christ Jesus

This, from our perspective, might be seen as the most significant role of the Spirit in our lives.

First, we are sealed in the Spirit as a *guarantee* of our inheritance of the kingdom of God.

Second, the Spirit earnestly works in us so that we are sanctified and made more and more into the image of the One who died to save us. We are saved by the faith God gave us, but we are made holy by the combination of scripture and the work of the Holy Spirit in our lives.

He does this so we can do the will of God and be prepared for our day of meeting with God—whether it is when He returns or when we pass into eternity. In the latter case, the Holy Spirit will raise us up on that day Jesus returns to this world.

> *But you, dear friends, by building yourselves up in your most holy faith and praying in the Holy Spirit, keep yourselves in God's love as you wait for the mercy of our Lord Jesus Christ to bring you to eternal life.* (Jude 1:20–21)

See also Rom 8:11; 15:16; 1 Cor 6:11; 2 Cor 1:21–22; 3:3, 18; 4:14, 16; 5:5; Gal 5:5; 6:8; Eph 1:13–14; 2:6–7; 4:30; Phil 1:6, 9–11; Phil 1:27–28; 1 Thess 3:13; 5:23–24; 2 Thess 1:11; 2:13; Titus 3:5; Heb 9:14; 1 Pet 1:2; Jude 1:20–21.

The Holy Spirit at work in us will enable us to stand on the day of the Lord. This is the work of He who lives in us.

Just as Moses was transformed when he met with God on the mountain so that his face glowed, so are we transformed when we commune with the Spirit in us.

> *And we all, who with unveiled faces contemplate the Lord's glory, are being transformed into his image with ever-increasing glory, which comes from the Lord, who is the Spirit.* (2 Cor 3:18)

The above list is likely not a complete list of the many ways the Spirit intercedes for us. The Spirit is God, and the Spirit is alive—so who can enumerate all that He does? However, we do know that the Spirit works in these areas in roles that belong exclusively to Him.

For the Christian, *there is no substitute for the Holy Spirit.*

Jesus gave us this warning to His disciples with regard to His return:

> ***At that time the kingdom of heaven will be like ten virgins who took their lamps and went out to meet the bridegroom. Five of them were foolish and five were wise. The foolish ones took their lamps but did not take any oil with them. The wise ones, however, took oil in jars along with their lamps. The bridegroom was a long time in coming, and they all became drowsy and fell asleep.***
>
> ***At midnight the cry rang out: "Here's the bridegroom! Come out to meet him!"***
>
> ***Then all the virgins woke up and trimmed their lamps. The foolish ones said to the wise, "Give us some of your oil; our lamps are going out."***
>
> ***"No," they replied, "there may not be enough for both us and you. Instead, go to those who sell oil and buy some for yourselves."***
>
> ***But while they were on their way to buy the oil, the bridegroom arrived. The virgins who were ready went in with him to the wedding banquet. And the door was shut.***
>
> ***Later the others also came. "Lord, Lord," they said, "open the door for us!"***
>
> ***But he replied, "Truly I tell you, I don't know you."***
>
> ***Therefore keep watch, because you do not know the day or the hour.*** (Matt 25:1–13)

Oil in scripture almost invariably refers to the anointing presence of the Holy Spirit.

The wise virgins were those who were filled with the Spirit of God, while the foolish virgins were those who in *all appearances* were part of the righteous of the kingdom of God but lacked the Spirit who is the seal and guarantee of salvation.

> ***Not everyone who says to me, "Lord, Lord," will enter the kingdom of heaven, but only the one who does the will of my Father who is in heaven. Many will say to me on that day, "Lord, Lord, did we not prophesy in your name and in your name drive out demons and in your name perform many miracles?" Then I will tell them plainly, "I never knew you. Away from me, you evildoers!"*** (Matt 7:21–23)

> *Jesus answered,* ***"Very truly I tell you, no one can enter the kingdom of God unless they are born of water and the Spirit."*** (John 3:5)

To have the Holy Spirit in your life and live submitted to His rightful Lordship over us is to have Jesus *know* us and be made fit to enter the kingdom of heaven.

Receiving the Spirit of God

Just as we have to *receive* the gift of eternal life by placing our trust in Jesus and confessing with our mouths that He is Lord,[68] so too we have to *receive* His Spirit.

Scripture tells us that—in obedience to Jesus's command to wait for the power from on high—the believers waited in the upper

[68] Rom 10:9.

room and on the day of Pentecost, the Spirit came upon them.[69] They were "baptized" in the Holy Spirit just as John the Baptist had prophesized earlier:

> *John answered them all, "I baptize you with water. But one who is more powerful than I will come, the straps of whose sandals I am not worthy to untie. He will baptize you with the Holy Spirit and fire."* (Luke 3:16)

Jesus said that being born of the Spirit was necessary for anyone to enter into the kingdom of God:

> *Jesus replied,* ***"Very truly I tell you, no one can see the kingdom of God unless they are born again."*** (John 3:3)

> *Jesus answered,* ***"Very truly I tell you, no one can enter the kingdom of God unless they are born of water and the Spirit."*** (John 3:5)

On that day of Pentecost, the apostle Peter preached the Word to those outside who had witnessed the sound of the supernatural wind and the disciples speaking in tongues:

> *Repent and be baptized, every one of you, in the name of Jesus Christ for the forgiveness of your sins. And you will receive the gift of the Holy Spirit.* (Acts 2:38)

Receiving the Spirit and being baptized with the Spirit are synonymous, but many equate the latter with visible signs. Not everyone who receives the Spirit experiences visible signs, such as immediately speaking in tongues.

---

[69] Acts 2.

The thief who was beside Jesus at Calvary received the gift of eternal life when He placed his hope in Jesus who promised he would be with Him that very day in paradise. This thief had neither the opportunity for a water baptism nor a sign-filled baptism of the Spirit, yet He was received into the heavenly kingdom—so he must have received the Spirit in those last hours of life.

Placing our trust fully in Jesus and His work alone in taking our punishment will prepare and enable us to receive the Spirit of God. We then simply wait upon the Lord for the impartation of His Spirit to come into us. It is not for us to demand that our baptism be accompanied by signs. Few have had visible tongues of flame come upon them since the day of Pentecost in Jerusalem.

If and when signs accompanying a Spirit baptism do appear, then these are but an outward display of an inward reality and should be received for the blessing that it is.

Such a blessing might occur through the laying of hands. This happened to those who already had accepted Christ as their Savior and Lord:

> *When the apostles in Jerusalem heard that Samaria had accepted the Word of God, they sent Peter and John to Samaria. When they arrived, they prayed for the new believers there that they might receive the Holy Spirit, because the Holy Spirit had not yet come on any of them; they had simply been baptized in the name of the Lord Jesus. Then Peter and John placed their hands on them, and they received the Holy Spirit.* (Acts 8:14–17)

Sometimes, the proclamation and receiving of the Gospel itself was enough to bring about the Spirit's visible baptism—even before the baptism of water:

> *While Peter was still speaking these words, the Holy Spirit came on all who heard the message. The*

> *circumcised believers who had come with Peter were astonished that the gift of the Holy Spirit had been poured out even on Gentiles. For they heard them speaking in tongues and praising God.*
>
> *Then Peter said, "Surely no one can stand in the way of their being baptized with water. They have received the Holy Spirit just as we have." So he ordered that they be* (water) *baptized in the name of Jesus Christ.* (Acts 10:44–48)

Whatever the manner of its arrival, the receiving of the Spirit is both a requisite part in the journey of the believer and an end in itself.

Jesus came to us and paid the price for our sin so that we might have this relationship with God. The *Spirit in us* is this relationship while we are still on this earth. This seems to be why to not have the Spirit is to not belong to the kingdom of God.

> *And you also were included in Christ when you heard the message of truth, the Gospel of your salvation. When you believed, you were marked in him with a seal, the promised Holy Spirit, who is a deposit guaranteeing our inheritance until the redemption of those who are God's possession—to the praise of his glory.* (Eph 1:13–14)

> *You, however, are not in the realm of the flesh but are in the realm of the Spirit, if indeed the Spirit of God lives in you. And if anyone does not have the Spirit of Christ, they do not belong to Christ.* (Rom 8:9)

Living with the Spirit

Spirit-filled believers have already begun their eternity with God while still living in the here and now. It is not a future event that happens when the believer dies:

> ***Father, the hour has come. Glorify your Son, that your Son may glorify you. For you granted him authority over all people that he might give eternal life to all those you have given him. Now this is eternal life: that they know you, the only true God, and Jesus Christ, whom you have sent.*** (John 17:1–3)

The Holy Spirit is Jesus Christ in us,[70] and this Spirit will remain with us until the consummation (completion) of all things. He is the Advocate given us here on earth to intercede for us.[71] He is the seal and pledge of our redemption[72] so that we can have confidence in our being justified by the blood of Christ and of our future with Him. He is also the power[73] through which we can live the Godly life and advance the kingdom here on earth.

Since the Spirit is God, we do not need anything or anyone else for that fullness of life Jesus promised us:

> ***The thief comes only to steal and kill and destroy; I have come that they may have life, and have it to the full.*** (John 10:10)

---

[70] John 14:18; Rom 8:9–10; 1 Cor 15:45; 2 Cor 3:14–18; Gal 4:6–7; Eph 2:22; Phil 1:19; Heb 13:5.

[71] John 14:16–17, 26; 15:26; 16:7–11; Rom 8:26–27.

[72] John 6:27; Rom 8:22–24; 2 Cor 1:21–22; 5:5; Eph 1:13–14.

[73] Mark 9:1; Luke 1:35; 4:14; 24:49; Acts 1:8; Rom 8:11, 13–14; 15:13, 19; 1 Cor 2:4–5; 4:20; 12:4, 7, 8, 10; 2 Cor 1:21; 3:17–18; 6:7; 10:4; Gal 5:16; Eph 3:16; 6:10; Col 1:9–11; 1 Thess 1:5; 2 Tim 1:7; Heb 6:4–6; 2 Pet 1:3.

> *I pray that out of his glorious riches he may strengthen you with power through his Spirit in your inner being, so that Christ may dwell in your hearts through faith ... to know this love that surpasses knowledge—that you may be filled to the measure of all the fullness of God.* (Eph 3:16–19)

> *For in Christ all the fullness of the Deity lives in bodily form, and in Christ you have been brought to fullness.* (Col 2:9–10)

Spirit-filled believers have the fullness of God[74] in them to live as overcomers in this day and age. The Spirit teaches us,[75] guides us,[76] comforts us,[77] gives us all we need,[78] intercedes for us,[79] enables us to overcome temptation,[80] and sanctifies us (see below).

In Him, we have all we need:

> *His divine power has given us everything we need for a godly life through our knowledge of him who called us by his own glory and goodness.* (2 Pet 1:3)

While all these things have been given to us, believers have to remain in relationship with the Spirit—much in the same way as getting married is only the start of a journey together. Marriage itself does not mean much if a partner is ignored, not loved, and not consulted in the decisions of life. The wisdom of the world is faulty and unreliable and shows in the state of the world today. There is the wisdom of God in the written word of God but followers often

---

74 Eph 3:16–19; Col 1:19; 2:9.

75 John 14:26.

76 John 16:14; Gal 5:16–18.

77 John 14:26; 15:26.

78 1 Cor 12:4–11; Gal 5:22–23; 2 Tim 1:7.

79 Rom 8:27.

80 Rom 8:9; 2 Cor 3:14–18; Gal 5:16–18; 2 Tim 1:7.

are unsure how to apply scripture in specific circumstances. Then there is the living wisdom of God in the Holy Spirit who knows each situation long before we encounter it.

> ***When you are brought before synagogues, rulers and authorities, do not worry about how you will defend yourselves or what you will say, for the Holy Spirit will teach you at that time what you should say.*** (Luke 12:11-12)

Call on the Spirit continually, consult with Him in all decisions, drink of the fullness of God, and ask Him for anything you lack.

> *You desire but do not have, so you kill. You covet but you cannot get what you want, so you quarrel and fight. You do not have because you do not ask God. When you ask, you do not receive, because you ask with wrong motives, that you may spend what you get on your pleasures.* (Jas 4:2–3)

> *This is the confidence we have in approaching God: that if we ask anything according to his will, he hears us.* (1 John 5:14)

Sanctification by the Holy Spirit

Scripture tells us that the Spirit is He who is able to make us holy so that we are sanctified by Him to do the will of Father God:

> *He gave me the priestly duty of proclaiming the Gospel of God, so that the Gentiles might become an offering acceptable to God, sanctified by the Holy Spirit.* (Rom 15:16)

> *Neither the sexually immoral nor idolaters nor adulterers nor men who have sex with men nor thieves nor the greedy nor drunkards nor slanderers nor swindlers will inherit the kingdom of God. And that is what some of you were. But you were washed, you were sanctified, you were justified in the name of the Lord Jesus Christ and by the Spirit of our God.* (1 Cor 6:10–11)

> *To God's elect, exiles scattered throughout the provinces of Pontus, Galatia, Cappadocia, Asia and Bithynia, who have been chosen according to the foreknowledge of God the Father, through the sanctifying work of the Spirit, to be obedient to Jesus Christ and sprinkled with his blood: Grace and peace be yours in abundance.* (1 Pet 1:1–2)

In the next chapter, a section entitled "Scripture Is Able to Sanctify Us—to Make Us Holy" reveals that Scripture is the other gift of God that is able to make us holy. Scripture can only make us holy if we allow it to do so. This means we have to read or hear scripture and let it sink in and obey it.

God opens the eyes and ears of our hearts to help us receive and understand scripture.

> *But their minds were made dull, for to this day the same veil remains when the old covenant is read. It has not been removed, because only in Christ is it taken away. Even to this day when Moses is read, a veil covers their hearts. But whenever anyone turns to the Lord, the veil is taken away. Now the Lord is the Spirit, and where the Spirit of the Lord is, there is freedom. And we all, who with unveiled faces contemplate the Lord's glory, are being transformed into his image with*

> *ever-increasing glory, which comes from the Lord, who is the Spirit.* (2 Cor 3:14–18)
>
> *And beginning with Moses and all the Prophets, he* (Jesus) *explained to them what was said in all the Scriptures concerning himself.* (Luke 24:27)
>
> *Then he* (Jesus) *opened their minds so they could understand the Scriptures.* (Luke 24:45)

In our present age of grace, where God is with us and in us through His Spirit, His Spirit opens our minds to receive and understand scripture:

> *The person without the Spirit does not accept the things that come from the Spirit of God but considers them foolishness, and cannot understand them because they are discerned only through the Spirit.* (1 Cor 2:14)
>
> *For the message of the cross is foolishness to those who are perishing, but to us who are being saved it is the power of God.* (1 Cor 1:18)

Without scripture *and* the Holy Spirit to guide us, we might never attain to the fullness of life that Jesus came to give us. For *life in its fullness* is a life walked with the Spirit.

King David rose from young shepherd boy to king and described such a life:

> *The LORD is my shepherd, I lack nothing.*
> *He makes me lie down in green pastures,*
> *he leads me beside quiet waters,*
> *he refreshes my soul.*
> *He guides me along the right paths for his name's sake.*

Even though I walk through the darkest valley,
I will fear no evil,
for you are with me;
your rod and your staff, they comfort me.
You prepare a table before me in the presence of my enemies.
You anoint my head with oil; my cup overflows.
Surely your goodness and love will follow me all the days of my life,
and I will dwell in the house of the LORD forever.
(Ps 23)

We live in a fallen world due to our sin and the sins of our forefathers. As a result, life will always have its challenges even as King David experienced them; his challenges were by no means trivial. Yet David constantly lived a joyous life filled with praise for God because he knew what it was to live in the presence and blessings of God.

To know and walk with the Spirit is to live a life filled with the blessings that come with knowing the Good Shepherd who walks before His sheep. He knows where He is going to take His sheep and clears the path. He often overcomes obstacles that lay before them, mostly which the sheep will never even be aware of and which are removed before they ever reach them.

Even while there might be places passed through that appear terrifying, the Shepherd is the protector—and His mighty hand is more than enough to be relied upon. The sheep need only focus on Him at all times. They have His presence with them as long as they listen to His voice and follow Him where He leads them—even to the end of their days; when He then opens the gate to the life beyond. This is the blessed life of living with the Spirit of God.

Remaining with the Spirit

Receiving the Spirit does not automatically imply that a believer will walk with or remain with the Spirit of God all his or her days. The Spirit is faithful and will not abandon us, but the believer can end up walking a different path from which the Spirit leads if he or she is not vigilant and submitted to the Spirit of God. Like the sheep following the shepherd, the believer has to set his eyes and ears to the ever-present guidance of the Holy Spirit.

Jesus warned of the requirement for vigilance when speaking to his disciples.

> ***Be on guard! Be alert! You do not know when that time will come. It's like a man going away: He leaves his house and puts his servants in charge, each with their assigned task, and tells the one at the door to keep watch. Therefore keep watch because you do not know when the owner of the house will come back—whether in the evening, or at midnight, or when the rooster crows, or at dawn. If he comes suddenly, do not let him find you sleeping. What I say to you, I say to everyone: 'Watch!'*** (Mark 13:33–37)

> ***Be dressed ready for service and keep your lamps burning, like servants waiting for their master to return from a wedding banquet, so that when he comes and knocks they can immediately open the door for him. It will be good for those servants whose master finds them watching when he comes. Truly I tell you, he will dress himself to serve, will have them recline at the table and will come and wait on them. It will be good for those servants whose***

> ***master finds them ready, even if he comes in the middle of the night or toward daybreak. But understand this: If the owner of the house had known at what hour the thief was coming, he would not have let his house be broken into. You also must be ready, because the Son of Man will come at an hour when you do not expect him.*** (Luke 12:35–40)

As with the parable of the wise and foolish virgins (Matt 25:1–13), Jesus's warnings are for believers and not for the unsaved.

The apostle Paul warned the very believers he had raised up and taught:

> *You foolish Galatians! Who has bewitched you? Before your very eyes Jesus Christ was clearly portrayed as crucified. I would like to learn just one thing from you: Did you receive the Spirit by the works of the law, or by believing what you heard? Are you so foolish? After beginning by means of the Spirit, are you now trying to finish by means of the flesh? Have you experienced so much in vain—if it really was in vain? So again I ask, does God give you his Spirit and work miracles among you by the works of the law, or by your believing what you heard?* (Gal 3:1–5)

These Galatians had started their journeys as Christians by submitting to and following the Spirit of God, but they had lapsed into a ritual of following rules of behavior and customs—a form of *spirituality without the Holy Spirit.*

Like the Church in Ephesus described in chapter 2 of the book of Revelation, the Galatians likely worked hard and did many of the right things, "***enduring hardships for my name,***" but they had "***forsaken the love you had at first.***" (Rev 2:1–7)

Being filled and remaining with the Holy Spirit is not a *one-off* event; it is a life of continual resubmission with humility to the Spirit of God. Many great Christian evangelists have fallen because they grew proud or—in their eagerness to do more—became detached from the very One they had earlier served faithfully.

The message Jesus has for all of us who are not close and abiding with His Spirit is the same as what He had for the church in Ephesus:

> ***Consider how far you have fallen! Repent and do the things you did at first. If you do not repent, I will come to you and remove your lampstand from its place.*** (Rev 2:5)

The Power of Scripture: God's Guidebook and Love Letter to Us

In part III of this book, the chapter "Departure from Scripture" summed up how false teachings were accepted by the church when true scripture was not taught, spread, or checked against.

To many believers, scripture is a collection of "Bible stories," teachings of wisdom, and information about things beyond what we can perceive with our eyes and ears. It tells us of things past, present, and future and of realms beyond what we experience with our senses and through the knowledge of the world. Scripture, however, is much more than just these.

The apostles took scripture, especially the Gospel of salvation, seriously. In fact, all of them—except for the apostle John—died deaths as martyrs in spreading the good news. Jesus had told them—and us, by extension—to "***make disciples of all nations . . . teaching them to obey everything I have commanded you***" (Matt 28:19–20). This meant actively taking scripture, especially the words of Jesus, into the world.

The book of Acts documents the beginning of the church and its growth through the mission of the apostles—particularly the apostles Peter and Paul—to take the word into the world. Many miracles are recorded, and these occurred when the Word was preached. God, through His Spirit, confirmed the truth of the Word of God that was preached *through* these miracles.

The Word of God here refers to scripture that was written before that time, the words spoken by Jesus, and the words given by the Holy Spirit to the church. Much of the New Testament consists of the letters of Paul, Peter, and James, the brother of Jesus. The Holy Spirit inspired them to write living scripture.

Scripture Is Flawless

Scripture was spoken and inspired by the Holy Spirit to the prophets and writers of the books of the Bible. This is the reason why each and every prophecy has either come to pass or will come to pass. In fact, many prophecies, including the rebirth of the nation of Israel, have come to pass even within the last century. Every prophecy about Israel and of the Messiah has been fulfilled except those about the final days of this soon-to-end era.

> *Above all, you must understand that no prophecy of Scripture came about by the prophet's own interpretation of things. For prophecy never had its origin in the human will, but prophets, though human, spoke from God as they were carried along by the Holy Spirit.* (2 Pet 1:20–21)

> *Every Word of God is flawless; he is a shield to those who take refuge in him. Do not add to his words, or he will rebuke you and prove you a liar.* (Prov 30:5–6)

Scripture includes those words spoken by Jesus Himself.

> ***Heaven and earth will pass away, but my words will never pass away.*** (Matt 24:35; Mark 13:31; Luke 21:33)

> ***It is easier for heaven and earth to disappear than for the least stroke of a pen to drop out of the Law.*** (Luke 16:17)

Scripture Is Alive and Has Power

It was by the spoken Word of God that all things were called into being. It was by the breath of God that we received life. The Word of God calls things into being and breathes Spirit life into the lives of those who hear the Word and receive it.

Unlike the words of man, the Word of God brings salvation to the hearer.

> *He chose to give us birth through the word of truth, that we might be a kind of firstfruits of all he created … Therefore, get rid of all moral filth and the evil that is so prevalent and humbly accept the word planted in you, which can save you.* (Jas 1:18, 21)

> *For you have been born again, not of perishable seed, but of imperishable, through the living and enduring Word of God.* (1 Pet 1:23)

> *For I am not ashamed of the Gospel, because it is the power of God that brings salvation to everyone who believes: first to the Jew, then to the Gentile. For in the Gospel the righteousness of God is revealed—a*

> *righteousness that is by faith from first to last, just as it is written: "The righteous will live by faith."* (Rom 1:16–17)

> *And we also thank God continually because, when you received the Word of God, which you heard from us, you accepted it not as a human word, but as it actually is, the Word of God, which is indeed at work in you who believe.* (1 Thess 2:13)

> *For the Word of God is alive and active. Sharper than any double-edged sword, it penetrates even to dividing soul and spirit, joints and marrow it judges the thoughts and attitudes of the heart.* (Heb 4:12)

> *But the Word of God continued to spread and flourish.* (Acts 12:24)

> *Do not merely listen to the word, and so deceive yourselves. Do what it says.* (Jas 1:22)

This doing is completely conditional on the believers first reading or listening to the Word and allowing it to take root and grow in their hearts.

As Jesus said, in explaining the parable of the sower:

> ***But the seed falling on good soil refers to someone who hears the word and understands it. This is the one who produces a crop, yielding a hundred, sixty or thirty times what was sown.*** (Matt 13:23)

Only those who have read and continue to read scripture under the direction of the Spirit of God can begin to understand and experience the power of scripture. As in the book of Acts, miracles are experienced today when the Word of God is preached in settings where the Spirit of God is welcomed to move in power.

As always, God graciously does not force His presence or will upon us. He waits to be invited in.

Scripture Is Able to Guide Us and Direct Our Ways

This power in scripture includes day-to-day guidance and also correction. This power works in those who allow the Spirit of God to work in them and reveal what He wants to bring to the one who receives.

> *Your word is a lamp for my feet, a light on my path.* (Ps 119:105)

> *My son, keep my words and store up my commands within you. Keep my commands and you will live; guard my teachings as the apple of your eye. Bind them on your fingers; write them on the tablet of your heart.* (Prov 7:1–3)

> ***It is written: "Man shall not live on bread alone, but on every word that comes from the mouth of God."*** (Matt 4:4)

Most, if not all, Spirit-filled believers have experienced the Spirit of God bringing to mind a scripture that they needed for a particular situation they have found themselves facing. Often, had it not been a verse they recognized as being from scripture, they would have brushed off that leading of the Spirit as emanating from their own thoughts. The Spirit confirms His leading by using scripture.

Scripture Is Able to Equip Us and Help Us Overcome

Even though believers who are saved have the presence of the Holy Spirit, life still has its challenges and its many valleys, plains, and mountaintops. Quite apart from the usual challenges that come from living in the fallen world, Satan and his angels seem to like to throw difficulties our ways in order to turn our attention from God and from living His will.

With the guidance of Scripture coupled with the presence of His Spirit, we can overcome many of the spanners that life and Satan throws at us along our journey. For instance, many of the problems that face us are often of our own doing, through bad decisions often based on incorrect understanding or just plain foolishness. The Word of God helps us see things from the correct perspective—God's eyes—so that we are able to navigate through life with wisdom.

When Satan throw issues our way, we can, with discernment, rebuke him and his schemes just as Jesus did when He was tempted after His forty days of fasting. Jesus showed us how to handle many of the curses brought about by the fall, including how to heal, cast out demons, and call upon God for our needs. All of this is written for our benefit in scripture:

> *All Scripture is God-breathed and is useful for teaching, rebuking, correcting and training in righteousness, so that the servant of God may be thoroughly equipped for every good work.* (2 Tim 3:16–17)

> *I write to you, dear children, because you know the Father. I write to you, fathers, because you know him who is from the beginning. I write to you, young men, because you are strong, and the Word of God lives in you, and you have overcome the evil one.* (1 John 2:14)

> *Take the helmet of salvation and the sword of the Spirit, which is the Word of God.* (Eph 6:17)

Scripture Is Able to Sanctify Us to Make Us Holy

On this side of eternity, there are very few things that can make the believer holy. Scripture tells us what these are in the New Covenant of the Blood of Christ. One of these is scripture itself.[81]

> ***Sanctify them by the truth; your word is truth.*** (John 17:17)
>
> ***You are already clean because of the word I have spoken to you.*** (John 15:3)
>
> *Now I commit you to God and to the word of his grace, which can build you up and give you an inheritance among all those who are sanctified.* (Acts 20:32)
>
> *Husbands, love your wives, just as Christ loved the church and gave himself up for her to make her holy, cleansing her by the washing with water through the word, and to present her to himself as a radiant church, without stain or wrinkle or any other blemish, but holy and blameless.* (Eph 5:25–27)
>
> *But as for you, continue in what you have learned and have become convinced of, because you know those from whom you learned it, and how from infancy you have known*

[81] The others being faith in Christ Jesus (John 17:19; Acts 26:18; 1 Cor1:2; 6:11; 7:14; Heb 10:29) and the work of the Holy Spirit (Rom 15:16; 1 Thess 5:23; 2 Thess 2:13; 1 Pet 1:2).

> *the Holy Scriptures, which are able to make you wise for salvation through faith in Christ Jesus.* (2 Tim 3:14–15)

In *The Glories*, Liguori often quoted scripture, but as has been shown in the preceding chapters, many of his quotations wrongly attributed the object of those scriptures to being Mary. He also referenced the many contemplations and teachings of others—elevating them to the level of scripture—even when those teachings were contrary to scripture. Rather than verifying such teachings against God's Word, he chose to use them to confirm other similar teachings.

The spirit behind the visitations on the other hand has never quoted scripture or directed anyone toward scripture or to the diligent study of the Word that God gave us for our edification (building up).

Jesus quoted scripture and taught extensively from it during His years of ministry. Upon His resurrection, He showed the two followers on the road to Emmaus and then His disciples[82] how He had fulfilled scripture by all He had done and gone through.[83]

At the start of His ministry, He used scripture to thwart Satan:

> ***It is written: "Man shall not live on bread alone, but on every word that comes from the mouth of God."*** (Matt 4:4)

Jesus clearly attached great weight to scripture and to its teaching because of its great power to save. Everywhere He went, He taught scripture and proclaimed the coming kingdom of God.

If scripture is all that it is said to be, why did those who studied it most in Jesus's day fail to recognize the Messiah when He came?

---

[82] Luke 24:27, 44–47.

[83] He also fulfilled scripture through all the circumstances of His life that He seemingly had no control over, such as the circumstances of His birth and relocations as a Child.

Worse still, why did these "*experts in the law*"[84] (called as such even by Jesus) oppose Him the most and then band together to plot His death by crucifixion?

Jesus spoke to those leaders:

> ***You study the Scriptures diligently because you think that in them you have eternal life. These are the very Scriptures that testify about me, yet you refuse to come to me to have life.*** (John 5:39–40)

When Stephen, was about to be martyred, he said a similar thing to the high priest and the Sanhedrin:

> *You stiff-necked people! Your hearts and ears are still uncircumcised. You are just like your ancestors: You always resist the Holy Spirit! Was there ever a prophet your ancestors did not persecute? They even killed those who predicted the coming of the Righteous One. And now you have betrayed and murdered him—you who have received the law that was given through angels but have not obeyed it. (Acts 7:51–53)*

The very people to whom scripture was entrusted and who had even studied it diligently did not understand—or perhaps *want* to understand—the core tenets of scripture. As a result, they went against everything scripture was meant to teach them.

An expert in the law tested Jesus and asked, "Teacher, which is the greatest commandment in the Law?"

Jesus summarized all of scripture when He answered the expert:

> ***"Love the Lord your God with all your heart and with all your soul and with all your mind." This***

[84] Matt 22:35; Luke 7;30; 10:25, 37; 11:45–52; 14:3.

> ***is the first and greatest commandment. And the second is like it: "Love your neighbor as yourself." All the Law and the Prophets hang on these two commandments.*** (Matt 22:36–40)

Aside from not practicing what they taught,[85] the experts of the law failed to learn from scripture for many reasons:

- They were greedy and self-indulgent.[86]
- In their pride, they refused to bend to God's will.[87]
- They thought they were not sinners, thus not needing salvation.[88]
- They failed to learn that we are called and commanded firstly to *love.*
- This call to love is firstly to be directed toward God.
- Secondly, we are to love everyone else

Had they understood scripture, they might have recognized the embodiment of love when He walked among them. They would have seen that all He did was done out of love.

Scripture is meant to lead us to love and to God. If we fail to recognize that simple truth, then all the study will be worse than fruitless. The apostle Paul understood this:

> *If I have the gift of prophecy and can fathom all mysteries and all knowledge, and if I have a faith that can move mountains, but do not have love, I am nothing. If I give all I possess to the poor and give over my body to hardship that I may boast, but do not have love, I gain nothing.* (1 Cor 13:2–3)

---

[85] Matt 23:1–4.

[86] Matt 23:25; Mark 12:38–40.

[87] Luke 7:29–30.

[88] Luke 16:1–2.

Paul knew exactly what he was writing about since he had once been one of the blind Pharisees[89] who, diligent in studying scripture, had nonetheless failed to grasp its meaning. He had been one of those who had persecuted Jesus[90] even though he had not met Him when He walked the earth.

We are commanded to love because God is love and because He first loved us.[91]

Scripture is God's love letter to us because it tells of the love God has poured out toward us since creation. Indeed, He created us to love Him and to be loved by Him. No matter how much He did for us, we always eventually revert to sinful rebellion against Him. Finally, He sent His Son to die for us so that our sin nature could die in us. When Jesus died for us, He broke the shackles of sin that bound rebellion in our hearts for all who have chosen to receive His gift of life.

In this new freedom, in exchange for the gift of His life in us, He took our death.

The Spirit AND the Word

The Spirit and the Word of God working *together* bring about salvation. The Holy Spirit is, after all, called the Spirit of Christ,[92] and Christ Jesus is the living Word of God.[93]

> *With great power the apostles continued to testify to the resurrection of the Lord Jesus. And God's grace was so powerfully at work in them all that there were no needy persons among them.* (Acts 4:33–34)

---

89 Matt 23:26.

90 Acts 9:4; 22:7; 26:14.

91 1 John 4:8, 16.

92 Spirit of Christ—John 17:26; Acts 16:7; Rom 8:9; Phil 1:19; 1 Pet 1:11.

93 The Living Word of God: John 1:1, 14; Rev 19:13.

> *Those who had been scattered preached the word wherever they went. Philip went down to a city in Samaria and proclaimed the Messiah there. When the crowds heard Philip and saw the signs he performed, they all paid close attention to what he said. For with shrieks, impure spirits came out of many, and many who were paralyzed or lame were healed. So there was great joy in that city.* (Acts 8:4–8)

> *While Peter was still speaking these words, the Holy Spirit came on all who heard the message.* (Acts 10:44)

> *So Paul and Barnabas spent considerable time there, speaking boldly for the Lord, who confirmed the message of his grace by enabling them to perform signs and wonders.* (Acts 14:3)

The Spirit of God confirms the truth and authority of scripture by releasing signs and wonders when the Gospel is proclaimed. The miracles enable people to see that there is a realm of truth and reality beyond what they experience through the senses. God confirms the truth of the Gospel of salvation in Christ Jesus. Miracles are not meant to impress; they are meant to lead people into a direct relationship with God.

We need the Holy Spirit because He brings into our hearts the recognition of God's love for us. When we read scripture, He helps us understand so that we will not be like the teachers of the law who could not see the love of God in all that was written. Instead of love, they only saw rules that required works to fulfill instead of faith.[94] Instead of believing the promises of God—as Abraham, Moses, and all the faithful had done—they chose to live through a set of rituals to which they added even more.

The Spirit of God stays the course with us and guides us through

[94] Rom 9.

our entire journey through life. It cannot be easy for the Spirit who is averse to sin because, by remaining with us, He has to witness the many times we fall into and commit sin. He then counsels us and lifts us up.

When a believer ministers to others in acts such as preaching the Gospel, the Holy Spirit is working in and through that believer. The Spirit moves the hearer-recipient so that the love of God is understood. When the Word is preached, the Spirit moves in the heart of the hearer because "*faith come from hearing and hearing the Word of God.*"[95]

If believers are to be fruitful, then—like entering into the waters of baptism—they must immerse themselves in the study of scripture while welcoming the Holy Spirit to open them to understanding and His guidance.

> ***God is spirit, and his worshipers must worship <u>in the Spirit</u> and <u>in truth</u>.***[96]
>
> ***Sanctify them by the truth; your word is truth.***[97]

There are several keys to allowing scripture to work in a believer's life:

- We must allow the Spirit of God—the Author of scripture—to lead us when reading scripture. He will open our understanding to the words and to the God behind those words.
- We must obey the words with the underlying intention of submission to God—not trying to earn salvation through the effort but simply to please God—just as a son or

[95] Rom 10:17.
[96] John 4:24.
[97] John 17:17.

daughter wishes to please their parent or a spouse wishes to please their loved one.[98]

- We must discover God and His heart in all scripture.

Scripture Did Not Come to Us without a Price

Today, in many parts of the developed world, scripture can be readily accessed via the printed word, audio, the internet, and mobile phones, tablets, and other devices. Through some of these channels, it is even available without cost to the reader or listener. There are free websites, mobile sites, and other apps that host the Bible. Through *The Gideons International* and other organizations, even print versions are made available without cost to recipients. As a result, many believers today underestimate the true value and cost of scripture. Being the Word of God, it is priceless as far as its value is concerned. The cost, on the other hand, is the price paid for it to come to each one of us.

If scripture is available to us free today, it is because someone else paid the price to make it available in that way. There are those who generously give to organizations like *The Gideon*s and to the numerous other custodians of websites and apps. Some sites and apps, on the other hand, receive income through advertising. Most have to pay royalties to publishers who hold the copyright for certain translations and versions of the Bible.

Missionaries who have independently translated scripture into indigenous languages have also distributed untold numbers of Bibles or parts thereof. This they did in obedience to the command of Christ Jesus who told us to make disciples of all nations and to teach them to obey all that He commanded us.

In many parts of the world, where the Word is not freely available, believers who live under severe persecution still meticulously copy scripture by hand just as they did in the days of the early church soon

[98] Such a demeanor results in joy—to both the giver and the receiver.

after the resurrection of Christ. The price for being caught with the Bible is, in some cases, death.

The Bible is available in the major languages of the world today mainly because the early reformers translated the texts from Latin, Greek, and Aramaic into the languages of the masses. Convicted by the Spirit of the urgency of spreading the good news, these translators-publishers did this from around the time the printing press was invented. Many, such as William Tyndale and others, were burned at the stake by the ruling church authorities and powers of their day for their efforts.

Our debt to these faithful translators cannot be measured; what they did began the movement that brought scripture to us all.

The ruling church had, at that time, become like the teachers of the Law in Jesus's day. They ignored both scripture and the Spirit and made others live instead by rituals. It was only when the translations by the sacrificial faithful continued to spread, to the extent they could not be stopped, that the church was forced to accept this turn of events and remedy the tide by bringing out their own versions.

Before then, there was a long period of time when very few were exposed to the Word of God. Instead, the Word remained hidden in monasteries and places of higher learning where monks copied the word by hand. The masses had no exposure to the Word, and few were literate. They were, instead, exposed to tiny snippets of scripture that the ecclesiastical authorities had thought worthy to release through the sermons of their clergy.

In the early days of the church, believers would copy—by hand—scripture that came in the form of letters of the apostles and early church leaders. This was a widespread practice since there was no other means by which to duplicate text. This practice enabled the early believers to study and spread scripture and the faith.

The apostles and many early disciples went out on missions to spread the good news of the kingdom. Except for the apostle John, each of the apostles died the harrowing deaths of martyrs to bring the Gospel to the world. We are the recipients of the word today *because* they first spread the Word wherever they went. Before them, Jesus Christ paid the price at the Cross for us to believe in Him. No higher price was paid for anything by anyone.

Given that the Word of God is His message to us and the cost of it took to come to us, we really have no reason to not give it the attention it deserves in our lives.

> ***It is written: "Man shall not live on bread alone, but on every word that comes from the mouth of God."*** (Matt 4:4)

> ***Anyone who loves me will obey my teaching. My Father will love them, and we will come to them and make our home with them. Anyone who does not love me will not obey my teaching. These words you hear are not my own; they belong to the Father who sent me.*** (John 14:23–24)

A follower of Jesus will supernaturally have a hunger for His Word. The believer who does not know the Bible and read it diligently—as the Bereans did—will likely be seduced by any and every deception and distraction, including works put forward by those who claim to have spiritual authority.

When you are on the journey of studying and living scripture, the truth and power of it will begin to become a reality in your life. Its effect is truly transformative. Undertake the diligent study of scripture yourself:

> ***If you hold to my teaching, you are really my disciples. Then you will know the truth, and the truth will set you free.*** (John 8:31–32)

Obedience to the Word

Jesus does not want any of His followers to stumble on our journey toward eternity. He does not hide any of the keys to the fullness of life that He gave us. There are no secret teachings or instructions; everything we need is given in His Word and through His Spirit.

Scripture reveals the following about the teachings of Jesus:

> ***Why do you call me, "Lord, Lord," and do not do what I say?*** (Luke 6:46)

> *We know that we have come to know him if we keep his commands. Whoever says, "I know him," but does not do what he commands is a liar, and the truth is not in that person. But if anyone obeys his word, love for God is truly made complete in them. This is how we know we are in him: Whoever claims to live in him must live as Jesus did.* (1 John 2:3–6)

> *Do not merely listen to the word, and so deceive yourselves. Do what it says. Anyone who listens to the word but does not do what it says is like someone who looks at his face in a mirror and, after looking at himself, goes away and immediately forgets what he looks like. But whoever looks intently into the perfect law that gives freedom, and continues in it—not forgetting what they have heard, but doing it—they will be blessed in what they do.* (Jas 1:22–25)

When writing of obedience to the Word, it is necessary to point out to those unfamiliar with scripture that many Old Testament requirements were fulfilled for us by Christ at the cross. These fulfilled rules were necessary at a time for different reasons, but they were deemed not binding on the New Testament believer by the apostles at the Council of Jerusalem. A brief explanation of these laws is included in appendix 16: "Old and New Covenant Laws."

Jesus Christ is the embodiment of the Word of God.[99]

> ***Therefore everyone who hears these words of mine and puts them into practice is like a wise man who built his house on the rock. The rain came down, the streams rose, and the winds blew and beat against that house; yet it did not fall, because it had its foundation on the rock. But everyone who hears these words of mine and does not put them into practice is like a foolish man who built his house on sand. The rain came down, the streams rose, and the winds blew and beat against that house, and it fell with a great crash.*** (Matt 7:24–27)

> ***Heaven and earth will pass away, but my words will never pass away.*** (Mark 13:31)

What did Jesus teach? In summary, He taught that God is love and that we are to love God above all things, including life itself, and to love our neighbor just as we love ourselves. We are to follow Him and in faith to remain faithful to Him who would and did die for us. To follow Him is not a matter of lip service; we must repent of living in sin, put His commands to practice, and die to ourselves in

[99] Luke 1:2; John 1:1, 14; 5:24; 6:68; 8:51; 1 John 1:1; Rev 19:13.

order to live for Him and for His kingdom. We can do this with a joyful heart, free from fear and worry, through living by His Spirit.

The words Jesus spoke regarding the above can be examined in appendix 17: "What Jesus Taught." In some cases, such as in prayer, He taught His disciples more by how He lived than by simply using words.

Without the Holy Spirit, it is not possible to live in obedience to the Word. Only He can enable the believer to live a God-directed and empowered life. Trying to live the words of the Sermon on the Mount[100] without the Spirit should convince anyone that this is so.

[100] Often called "The Beatitudes," Matt. 5–7.

PART V

CONCLUSIONS AND CHOICES

Summary

> *We demolish arguments and every pretension that sets itself up against the knowledge of God, and we take captive every thought to make it obedient to Christ.* (2 Cor 10:5)

In this book, we have looked at:

- Many teachings and beliefs that have grown around Mary since the first century, some of their apparent origins, and how far removed they are from what the Holy Spirit reveals in scripture.
- How these teachings and beliefs have led believers to look to Mary in ways that the apostles would never have taught. Believers have turned their eyes to her instead of to the Holy Spirit who was left to indwell, guide, and empower us to live the Christian life. Without the daily submission to the Spirit, we have only our flesh and willpower to try to live

such a life, which is unattainable by any means apart from the Spirit.

- The expectation of being led by Mary opened the way for believers to expect her to manifest. This opened up the way for deceiving spirits to appear to those least equipped to discern the spirits. The idea existed—and perhaps still persists—that little children are innocent and therefore able to see visions.

  In actuality, it is only those who confess their sin, turn over their lives to the lordship of Jesus Christ, submit to the Holy Spirit, and study and allow the Word of God to wash them clean who can discern if spirits are from God or otherwise. They do so by listening to the Spirit of God.
- The spirit who continually appeared showed that she could take many different forms. She also taught many beliefs that have no origin in the Gospel message and led believers to turn to her rather than to the Holy Spirit in the roles that God exclusively gave to the Spirit.
- The consequences of the propagated beliefs and from the apparitions were shown from Liguori's testimonies; in the end, Mary's followers have placed their entire lives and hopes in her.

  Every prayer and every form of worship directed toward her should have been directed toward God. This is easily seen when you take any of those prayers and replace her name with "God." The result is a prayer that is compatible with scripture. In their original forms, with Mary as the object, they would have been prayers that neither the apostles nor Mary, the mother of Jesus, would have condoned.

The net result are churches that have a form of godliness but that deny its power.[101] A church that does not turn over control to

[101] 2 Tim 3:5.

the Holy Spirit for its leading and guidance does not lead its people into a relationship with God. The power of the church of God is found in the Spirit of God.

Jesus died on the cross to restore the broken relationship we had with God. Regardless of its history, a church whose people do not submit to the Holy Spirit is one where its people risk hearing the warning words of Jesus when He said, "***I never knew you.***"[102]

No church or congregation can rest on its history. Jesus warned five out of seven churches that, in the book of Revelation, they risked losing their lampstands.[103] These were churches that were birthed by the apostles yet had strayed and not remained true to their calling even while the apostle John was still alive.

God Is Sufficient

God has always been enough for each and every one of us.

> *The Lord is my shepherd, I lack nothing.* (Ps 23:1)
>
> *Therefore you do not lack any spiritual gift as you eagerly wait for our Lord Jesus Christ to be revealed.* (1 Cor 1:7)
>
> *And my God will meet all your needs according to the riches of his glory in Christ Jesus.* (Phil 4:19)

Each of us is only aware of what we need from our limited insight. A child is not aware that he needs knowledge and understanding in order to get by in this world. By ourselves, we can only know what we know.

---

[102] Matt 25:41.

[103] Rev 2–3.

God, in His wisdom and grace, has made provision for all our needs. This is in every area of our lives and is why He has many names:

- Jehovah Jireh — God will Provide
- Jehovah Rophe — My Healer
- Jehovah Mekadesh — The Lord who Sanctifies
- Jehovah Tsidkenu — The God of my Righteousness
- Jehovah Shalom — The Lord is Peace
- Jehovah Rohi — God my Shepherd

Even beyond that, throughout the ages, He has made promises for those who seek to know Him. These promises include freedom from fear and addictions; deliverance from sin, evil, depression and anxiety; health, healing, strength; comfort and hope; protection and rest; and abundance and salvation. Every one of those promises is given to and received by those who, in faith, believe God at His Word:

> *For no matter how many promises God has made, they are "Yes" in Christ. And so through him the "Amen" is spoken by us to the glory of God.* (2 Cor 1:20)

This faith is not that which is blind to only believe without understanding or evidence. Rather, it is a faith that is built upon earnest seeking and choosing to know truth above preconception, prejudice, or what the world says for what the world says is truth is that which is forever changing.

Faith is, in part, searching for the many evidences God has put for each of us to find.

It is seeking Him in His Word and what He has done over the ages. It is calling out to Him who is only as far as the door to your heart, waiting to answer and provide tangible proof of His existence and presence. It is checking out—without prejudice—the many proofs of His visit to our world where He lived, suffered, and died at our hands in just the way He foretold through the many witnesses over the ages. The evidence for His life and death were documented by His followers, His enemies, as well as the unaffiliated, including in the records of the governing Romans.

It is the faith that comes from seeking and then finding:

> ***Ask and it will be given to you; seek and you will find; knock and the door will be opened to you. For everyone who asks receives; the one who seeks finds; and to the one who knocks, the door will be opened.*** (Matt 7:7–8)

> *And without faith it is impossible to please God, because anyone who comes to him must believe that he exists and that he rewards those who earnestly seek him.* (Heb 11:6)

> *But if from there you seek the LORD your God, you will find him if you seek him with all your heart and with all your soul.* (Deut 4:29)

We have been left great and wonderful promises, and He has sealed these promises in blood. It is not just any blood; it is the blood of Christ Jesus. Faith is believing God at His Word. Call to Him who promised:

> *The LORD looks down from heaven on all mankind to see if there are any who understand, any who seek God.* (Ps 14:2)

> *The LORD is near to all who call on him, to all who call on him in truth. He fulfills the desires of those who fear him; he hears their cry and saves them.* (Ps 145:18–19)

> *Come near to God and he will come near to you.* (Jas 4:8)

> ***Here I am! I stand at the door and knock. If anyone hears my voice and opens the door, I will come in and eat with that person, and they with me.*** (Rev 3:20)

Seek Him for who He is. Seek Him even if you simply want to know if the words of this book are true. Call on Him and He will answer.

> *To you, O people, I call out; I raise my voice to all mankind.* (Prov 8:4)

> *I love those who love me, and those who seek me find me.* (Prov 8:17)

> *For those who find me find life and receive favor from the LORD.* (Prov 8:35)

God is—and always has been—enough. His Word is precious because it comes from Him and has been given to us for our benefit. We do not need to turn to any created being in heaven or on earth for life and holiness.

What Should One Do Now?

Part III of this book maintains that the end fruit of the false teachings of both man and spirits has been the worship of one other than God, and the cause of this has been the result of the disregard for scripture and the neglect of living in relationship with the Holy Spirit.

Those who have followed after the image of Mary fashioned from false teachings may want to repent of their actions. This repentance might include confessing of sin, returning to the study of scripture and being obedient to its instruction, and submitting to the Holy Spirit and His guidance.

Confession of Sin

Confession of sin is a requisite part of the Christian walk. Anyone who repents should confess so as to be free of any burden of sin.

The followers of John the Baptist confessed before receiving their water baptism[104] as did the disciples.[105]

Scripture instructs us how to confess and tells us the fruit of this confession:

> *Therefore confess your sins to each other and pray for each other so that you may be healed. The prayer of a righteous person is powerful and effective.* (Jas 5:16)
>
> *If we confess our sins, he is faithful and just and will forgive us our sins and purify us from all unrighteousness.* (1 John 1:9)

Read also Jas 5:13–16; 1 John 1:8–10, which put the above into context.

The Study of Scripture

There are many means available today through which to study scripture. In many places, there are group Bible studies conducted in small groups by local churches. There are also online studies and study Bibles that can aid in the understanding of scripture.

Regardless of the means, a believer should have a complete Bible and should lean into the Holy Spirit to open up the reader (or

---

[104] Matt 3:6; Mark 1:5.

[105] Acts 19:18.

listener) to understand. He will guide Christians into all wisdom. If you have no one to aid you in reading and understanding the Bible, start at the Gospel of John. After completing it, go through the entire New Testament before beginning again at the Old Testament.

Scripture is meant to point one to God. Seeking to understand the person of Jesus and the love of God will aid your understanding of scripture.

Submission to the Holy Spirit

If you have not already done so, call on God. His Spirit searches for those who will seek Him, and He is never far away.

If you are a believer but have not experienced any of the blessings of the Spirit of God (as outlined in the chapter "The Holy Spirit—God with Us, Here and Now"), ask God to give you His Spirit.

> ***Which of you fathers, if your son asks for a fish, will give him a snake instead? Or if he asks for an egg, will give him a scorpion? If you then, though you are evil, know how to give good gifts to your children, how much more will your Father in heaven give the Holy Spirit to those who ask him!*** (Luke 11:11–13)

God is both faithful to forgive and generous to give of His Spirit, and He knows that you need Him throughout your journey of life. The Holy Spirit is God with you now. Earnestly ask God and then wait as the disciples waited.

After you have asked for the Spirit of God, wait until you have had some sign of His presence. Subsequently, do not ever act as though He has not been given or that you have not received Him. A believer who does not walk with the Spirit grieves Him for then He is unable to do the things He wants to do in the life of the believer.

Once you have been started on your journey with the Spirit, it becomes a living relationship, and as with any relationship, regular communication is the way to keep it alive. This communication with God in His Spirit is called prayer. It is not a one-way street, and as you pray from your heart to Him about anything, be prepared to listen. He will guide you.

Do what He directs you to do, but be aware that even as He guides you, you still need to feed on the Word of God. He speaks to you just as Jesus said, while scripture is alive and will speak life into you.

A word of caution: When you ask for the Holy Spirit, be mindful that it is for the will of God in your life. You may receive great and wonderful ideas that you feel inspired to act upon immediately. Remember that the Spirit is given for the will of God and for the building of His body on earth, including you.

Great and wonderful ideas are sometimes the distractions the "other spirit" sends to take you on a different journey: achieving great things for yourself and not for God. Examine the ideas and see if they glorify God or yourself and if they result in eternal kingdom purposes or things that only last this side of eternity. Always place God first, and He will look after you better than you ever could for yourself.

Find a place where the full Word of God is preached and where the Spirit of God is given room to lead.

Pray. Speak to God. Ask Him what His will is in whatever circumstance you find yourself in. Practice praying for others. Be in fellowship with mature Christians. Die to self and live for Christ. This we can do—but *only* in the power of the Holy Spirit.

> ***Whoever finds their life will lose it, and whoever loses their life for my sake will find it.*** (Matt 10:39)

Also see Matt 16:25–26; Mark 8:35–37; Luke 9:23–25; 17:33; John 12:24–26.

Endnote

To those who follow after Mary, if you wish to honor her, then do what she did, which was to turn her eyes to the one and only Savior-Redeemer. He died to save all mankind.

Honor the Mary foretold in the Old Testament and written of in the Gospels and book of Acts.

Honor the Mary the Holy Spirit once foreshadowed. Honor her by reading those words of scripture He inspired and not the writings, contemplations, and dreams of people who had already given their hearts and all to the image they held of "her." Follow not after spirits who claim to be her and who taught all manner of teachings contrary to the Gospels and of the apostles. Hold not onto the fine-sounding arguments of men whose teachings were shown to have no basis in scripture and whose arguments are easily shown to carry no weight in truth when closely examined.

Seek Him who desires a deep relationship with you. Allow the Spirit and Word to take root, grow in you, and transform you; the fullness of life will then open to you.

I thank you for having read this far into this book; I know it has been difficult.

To those who do not follow after Mary, pray that the Holy Spirit will bring the clarity of truth in scripture to all believers, including those who follow after Mary. Thank you for having read this book on a subject that must have seemingly appeared out of left field and irrelevant for Christians. A lot more could have been added to this book on related subjects, but it would have been too lengthy to have examined those subjects in order to do them justice.

To the unbeliever, this may all seem a bit strange—that people would hold such strong beliefs in things that seem to make little sense in the "real world." What I have tried to distinguish is the spiritual reality from the counterfeit. As with anything real and counterfeit, there could never be a counterfeit unless one of genuine value exists—and usually of *great* value. Why go through all the trouble of mimicking something unless there is real value in it? I pray the eyes of your heart be opened and that the understanding of things deeper than the physical eyes can perceive be made known to you. You too are of great value, especially to the One who formed you and gave you life.

Ask God if He is real. Sincerely ask—and then wait for the answer.

To all readers, I pray you allow the Spirit of God to lead you in every decision in your life. I pray your lives will be mightily fruitful while being lived with the leading of the Spirit of God and His Holy Word.

I pray we someday meet in the heavenly kingdom that He prepared for those who love and obey Him; meanwhile, I wish for peace and rest for your souls.

APPENDIX 1

MARY AS SHE APPEARS IN THE HOLY BIBLE

The Bible tells us of Mary, the mother of Jesus, in a way that is somewhat similar to that written of Jesus. Scripture foretold of her long before she was born and then documented parts of her life. Unlike Jesus, there is nothing said about her after her life on earth—although some might disagree with this statement (as we shall see).

Around seven hundred years before it happened, the prophet Isaiah wrote about her:

> *Hear now, you house of David! Is it not enough to try the patience of humans? Will you try the patience of my God also? Therefore the Lord Himself will give you a sign: Behold, a virgin will be with child and bear a son, and she will call His name Immanuel.* (Isa 7:13–14)

In the Gospel of Luke, we read about how this sign is, in the fullness of time, confirmed to Mary herself by the angel Gabriel:

> *In the sixth month of Elizabeth's pregnancy, God sent the angel Gabriel to Nazareth, a town in Galilee, to a virgin pledged to be married to a man named Joseph, a descendant of David. The virgin's name was Mary. The angel went to her and said, "Greetings, you who are highly favoured! The Lord is with you."*
>
> *Mary was greatly troubled at his words and wondered what kind of greeting this might be. But the angel said to her, "Do not be afraid, Mary; you have found favor with God. You will conceive and give birth to a son, and you are to call him Jesus. He will be great and will be called the Son of the Most High. The Lord God will give him the throne of his father David, and he will reign over Jacob's descendants forever; his kingdom will never end."*
>
> *"How will this be," Mary asked the angel, "since I am a virgin?"*
>
> *The angel answered, "The Holy Spirit will come on you, and the power of the Most High will overshadow you. So the holy one to be born will be called the Son of God. Even Elizabeth your relative is going to have a child in her old age, and she who was said to be unable to conceive is in her sixth month. For no word from God will ever fail."*
>
> *"I am the Lord's servant," Mary answered, "May your word to me be fulfilled." Then the angel left her.* (Luke 1:26–38)

Saint Paul wrote a letter to the believers in Galatia:

> *But when the set time had fully come, God sent his Son, born of a woman, born under the law, to redeem those under the law, that we might receive adoption to sonship.* (Gal 4:4–5)

After the encounter with the angel, Mary visited her elder cousin:

> *At that time Mary got ready and hurried to a town in the hill country of Judea, where she entered Zechariah's home and greeted Elizabeth. When Elizabeth heard Mary's greeting, the baby leaped in her womb, and Elizabeth was filled with the Holy Spirit. In a loud voice she exclaimed: "Blessed are you among women, and blessed is the child you will bear! But why am I so favoured, that the mother of my Lord should come to me? As soon as the sound of your greeting reached my ears, the baby in my womb leaped for joy. Blessed is she who has believed that the Lord would fulfil his promises to her!"* (Luke 1:39–45)
>
> *And Mary said:*
> *"My soul glorifies the Lord*
> *and my spirit rejoices in God my Saviour,*
> *for he has been mindful*
> *of the humble state of his servant.*
> *From now on all generations will call me blessed,*
> *for the Mighty One has done great things for me—*
> *holy is his name.*
> *His mercy extends to those who fear him,*
> *from generation to generation.*
> *He has performed mighty deeds with his arm;*
> *he has scattered those who are proud in their inmost thoughts.*
> *He has brought down rulers from their thrones*
> *but has lifted up the humble.*
> *He has filled the hungry with good things*
> *but has sent the rich away empty.*
> *He has helped his servant Israel,*
> *remembering to be merciful*

to Abraham and his descendants forever,
just as he promised our ancestors."
Mary stayed with Elizabeth for about three months and then returned home. (Luke 1:46–56)

Matthew told how Joseph came to accept the child of Mary, his betrothed:

> *This is how the birth of Jesus the Messiah came about: His mother Mary was pledged to be married to Joseph, but before they came together, she was found to be pregnant through the Holy Spirit. Because Joseph her husband was faithful to the law, and yet did not want to expose her to public disgrace, he had in mind to divorce her quietly.*
>
> *But after he had considered this, an angel of the Lord appeared to him in a dream and said, "Joseph son of David, do not be afraid to take Mary home as your wife, because what is conceived in her is from the Holy Spirit. She will give birth to a son, and you are to give him the name Jesus, because he will save his people from their sins."*
>
> *All this took place to fulfil what the Lord had said through the prophet: "The virgin will conceive and give birth to a son, and they will call him Immanuel" (which means "God with us").*
>
> *When Joseph woke up, he did what the angel of the Lord had commanded him and took Mary home as his wife. But he did not consummate their marriage until she gave birth to a son. And he gave him the name Jesus.* (Matt 1:18–25)

Luke told of the birth of Jesus as having taken place during the census of Caesar Augustus:

And everyone went to their own town to register.

So Joseph also went up from the town of Nazareth in Galilee to Judea, to Bethlehem the town of David, because he belonged to the house and line of David. He went there to register with Mary, who was pledged to be married to him and was expecting a child. While they were there, the time came for the baby to be born, and she gave birth to her firstborn, a son. She wrapped him in cloths and placed him in a manger, because there was no guest room available for them. (Luke 2:3–7)

So they (the shepherds) *hurried off and found Mary and Joseph, and the baby, who was lying in the manger. When they had seen him, they spread the word concerning what had been told them about this child, and all who heard it were amazed at what the shepherds said to them. But Mary treasured up all these things and pondered them in her heart.* (Luke 2:16–19)

In laying out the genealogy of Jesus, the apostle Matthew mentioned Mary in his Gospel:

This is the genealogy of Jesus the Messiah the son of David, the son of Abraham:
Abraham was the father of Isaac,
Isaac the father of Jacob,
Jacob the father of Judah and his brothers,
Judah the father of Perez and Zerah, whose mother was Tamar,
. . .
and Jacob the father of Joseph, the husband of Mary, and Mary was the mother of Jesus who is called the Messiah. (Matt 1:1–16)

The Magi from the East had journeyed to Israel in search of the child destined to be the king of the Jews:

> *On coming to the house, they saw the child with his mother Mary, and they bowed down and worshiped him.* (Matt 2:11)

King Herod, upon finding that the Magi had left his lands without telling him where the child-king was, set about searching for the Child so that he might destroy Him.

> *When they* (the Magi) *had gone, an angel of the Lord appeared to Joseph in a dream. "Get up," he said, "take the child and his mother and escape to Egypt. Stay there until I tell you, for Herod is going to search for the child to kill him."*
>
> *So he got up, took the child and his mother during the night and left for Egypt, where he stayed until the death of Herod. And so was fulfilled what the Lord had said through the prophet: "Out of Egypt I called my son."* (Matt 2:13–15)

Matthew then related the return of the holy family from Egypt:

> *After Herod died, an angel of the Lord appeared in a dream to Joseph in Egypt and said, "Get up, take the child and his mother and go to the land of Israel, for those who were trying to take the child's life are dead."*
>
> *So he got up, took the child and his mother and went to the land of Israel.* (Matt 2:19–21)

According to the Mosaic Law, parents were required to present a first-born son to God. Luke wrote of the presentation of Jesus at the temple in Jerusalem:

> *When the time came for the purification rites required by the Law of Moses, Joseph and Mary took him to Jerusalem to present him to the Lord (as it is written in the Law of the Lord, "Every firstborn male is to be consecrated to the Lord"), and to offer a sacrifice in keeping with what is said in the Law of the Lord: "a pair of doves or two young pigeons."* (Luke 2:22–24)

The sacrificial offering here was that for a sin offering for the mother as prescribed by the Law (Lev 12:6–8).

> *When the parents brought in the child Jesus to do for him what the custom of the Law required, Simeon took him in his arms and praised God.* (Luke 2:27–28)

> *The child's father and mother marvelled at what was said about him. Then Simeon blessed them and said to Mary, his mother: "This child is destined to cause the falling and rising of many in Israel, and to be a sign that will be spoken against, so that the thoughts of many hearts will be revealed. And a sword will pierce your own soul too."* (Luke 2:34–35)

> *When Joseph and Mary had done everything required by the Law of the Lord, they returned to Galilee to their own town of Nazareth.* (Luke 2:39)

Luke related the story of young Jesus at the Temple:

> *Every year Jesus' parents went to Jerusalem for the Festival of the Passover. When he was twelve years old, they went up to the festival, according to the custom. After the festival was over, while his parents were returning home, the boy Jesus stayed behind in*

> *Jerusalem, but they were unaware of it. Thinking he was in their company, they travelled on for a day. Then they began looking for him among their relatives and friends. When they did not find him, they went back to Jerusalem to look for him. After three days they found him in the temple courts, sitting among the teachers, listening to them and asking them questions. Everyone who heard him was amazed at his understanding and his answers. When his parents saw him, they were astonished. His mother said to him, "Son, why have you treated us like this? Your father and I have been anxiously searching for you."*
>
> ***"Why were you searching for me?"*** *he asked.* ***"Didn't you know I had to be in my Father's house?"*** *But they did not understand what he was saying to them.*
>
> *Then he went down to Nazareth with them and was obedient to them. But his mother treasured all these things in her heart. And Jesus grew in wisdom and stature, and in favour with God and man.* (Luke 2:41–52)

At the start of Jesus's ministry, when He had some disciples, they all attended a wedding at Cana:

> *On the third day a wedding took place at Cana in Galilee. Jesus' mother was there, and Jesus and his disciples had also been invited to the wedding. When the wine was gone, Jesus' mother said to him, "They have no more wine."*
>
> ***"Woman, why do you involve me?"*** *Jesus replied.* ***"My hour has not yet come."***
>
> *His mother said to the servants, "Do whatever he tells you."* (John 2:1–5)

> *After this he went down to Capernaum with his mother and brothers and his disciples. There they stayed for a few days.* (John 2:12)

The Gospel accounts of Matthew, Mark, and Luke describe a particular event that reveals that the family that Jesus grew up in doubted his divine calling:

> *Then Jesus entered a house, and again a crowd gathered, so that he and his disciples were not even able to eat. When his family heard about this, they went to take charge of him, for they said, "He is out of his mind."* (Mark 3:20–21)
>
> *Then Jesus's mother and brothers arrived. Standing outside, they sent someone in to call him. A crowd was sitting around him, and they told him, "Your mother and brothers are outside looking for you."*
>
> ***"Who are my mother and my brothers?"*** *he asked.*
>
> *Then he looked at those seated in a circle around him and said,* ***"Here are my mother and my brothers! Whoever does God's will is my brother and sister and mother."*** (Mark 3:31–35)
>
> *While Jesus was still talking to the crowd, his mother and brothers stood outside, wanting to speak to him. Someone told him, "Your mother and brothers are standing outside, wanting to speak to you."*
>
> *He replied to him,* ***"Who is my mother, and who are my brothers?"*** *Pointing to his disciples, he said,* ***"Here are my mother and my brothers. For whoever does the will of my Father in heaven is my brother and sister and mother."*** *(Matt 12:46–50)*

Now Jesus's mother and brothers came to see him, but they were not able to get near him because of the crowd. Someone told him, "Your mother and brothers are standing outside, wanting to see you."

He replied, ***"My mother and brothers are those who hear God's word and put it into practice."*** (Luke 8:19–21)

The very town He grew up in also disbelieved him, and Jesus Himself confirms both the disbelief of his townspeople as well as those of his family as written by both Matthew and Mark:

Coming to his hometown, he began teaching the people in their synagogue, and they were amazed. "Where did this man get this wisdom and these miraculous powers?" they asked. "Isn't this the carpenter's son? Isn't his mother's name Mary, and aren't his brothers James, Joseph, Simon and Judas? Aren't all his sisters with us? Where then did this man get all these things?" And they took offense at him.

But Jesus said to them, ***"A prophet is not without honour except in his own town and in his own home."*** (Matt 13:53–57)

"Where did this man get these things?" they asked. "What's this wisdom that has been given him? What are these remarkable miracles he is performing? Isn't this the carpenter? Isn't this Mary's son and the brother of James, Joseph, Judas and Simon? Aren't his sisters here with us?" And they took offense at him. (Mark 6:2–4)

Jesus said to them, ***"A prophet is not without honour except in his own town, among his relatives and in his own home."*** (Mark 6:2–4)

His relationship with his immediate family was foretold by King David. The king wrote prophetically of the suffering and rejected Savior and the family into which he would be born:

> *I am a foreigner to my own family, a stranger to my own mother's children.* (Ps 69:8)

Luke related the story of the woman who called out to Jesus:

> *As Jesus was saying these things, a woman in the crowd called out, "Blessed is the mother who gave you birth and nursed you."*
>
> *He replied, "**Blessed rather are those who hear the Word of God and obey it.**" (*Luke 11:27–28)

Mary was present at the crucifixion as told by the apostle John who was also there:

> *Near the cross of Jesus stood his mother, his mother's sister, Mary the wife of Clopas, and Mary Magdalene. When Jesus saw his mother there, and the disciple whom he loved standing nearby, he said to her, "**Woman, here is your son,**" and to the disciple, "**Here is your mother.**" From that time on, this disciple took her into his home.* (John 19:25–27)

Shortly before Jesus ascended to heaven, He told his disciples to wait in Jerusalem for the coming of the Holy Spirit. After He had ascended, the book of Acts tells us that Mary was among those who gathered; she would have been there on the Day of Pentecost:

> *They all joined together constantly in prayer, along with the women and Mary the mother of Jesus, and with his brothers.* (Acts 1:14)

The above are the scriptural verses that directly or indirectly include references to Mary, the mother of Jesus. They tell of God's vessel chosen to bring His Messiah into the world. While Mary is the chosen mother and was given the revelation as to His special nature, she apparently did not understand His divine calling. In the later scriptures (Luke 2:41–52; John 2:1–5; Mark 3:31–35; Matt 12:46–50; Luke 8:19–21; 11:27–28), including when Jesus had begun His ministry, He appears to have somewhat distanced Himself from her so He could live out His calling.

A few other scriptures are often cited by certain Orthodox churches as referring to Mary, and these are shown below:

Early in Creation as Related in the Genesis Account

> *And I will put enmity*
> *between you and the woman,*
> *and between your offspring and hers;*
> *he will crush your head,*
> *and you will strike his heel.* (Gen 3:15)

In the above verse, God speaks to the serpent after he has deceived Adam and Eve into eating the fruit of the tree of the knowledge of good and evil. The reference clearly refers to Christ being the offspring who will crush the head of the serpent. Since Eve was the only woman in creation at this time, we know this is the woman who is described. However, some have chosen to have taken the woman to be Mary.

The Apostle John's End-Time Vision

> *A great sign appeared in heaven: a woman clothed with the sun, with the moon under her feet and a*

crown of twelve stars on her head. She was pregnant and cried out in pain as she was about to give birth. Then another sign appeared in heaven: an enormous red dragon with seven heads and ten horns and seven crowns on its heads. Its tail swept a third of the stars out of the sky and flung them to the earth. The dragon stood in front of the woman who was about to give birth, so that it might devour her child the moment he was born. She gave birth to a son, a male child, who "will rule all the nations with an iron sceptre." And her child was snatched up to God and to his throne. The woman fled into the wilderness to a place prepared for her by God, where she might be taken care of for 1,260 days.

Then war broke out in heaven. Michael and his angels fought against the dragon, and the dragon and his angels fought back. But he was not strong enough, and they lost their place in heaven. The great dragon was hurled down—that ancient serpent called the devil, or Satan, who leads the whole world astray. He was hurled to the earth, and his angels with him.

Then I heard a loud voice in heaven say:
"Now have come the salvation and the power
and the kingdom of our God,
and the authority of his Messiah.
For the accuser of our brothers and sisters,
who accuses them before our God day and night,
has been hurled down.
They triumphed over him
by the blood of the Lamb
and by the word of their testimony;
they did not love their lives so much
as to shrink from death.
Therefore rejoice, you heavens

> *and you who dwell in them!*
> *But woe to the earth and the sea,*
> *because the devil has gone down to you!*
> *He is filled with fury,*
> *because he knows that his time is short."*

> *When the dragon saw that he had been hurled to the earth, he pursued the woman who had given birth to the male child. The woman was given the two wings of a great eagle, so that she might fly to the place prepared for her in the wilderness, where she would be taken care of for a time, times and half a time, out of the serpent's reach. Then from his mouth the serpent spewed water like a river, to overtake the woman and sweep her away with the torrent. But the earth helped the woman by opening its mouth and swallowing the river that the dragon had spewed out of his mouth. Then the dragon was enraged at the woman and went off to wage war against the rest of her offspring—those who keep God's commands and hold fast their testimony about Jesus.* (Rev 12:1–17)

The above passages appear to cover a vast span of time from before the incarnation of Christ on the earth until the very last days preceding His Second Coming. The woman is regarded by some Orthodox churches as Mary, while others see the woman as representing Israel. The former view is supported by her being the mother of the Messiah and is reinforced by the appearance of the lady who gives birth to a son who will rule with an iron scepter.

The latter view being of Israel, on the other hand, is supported by the twelve stars being representative of the twelve tribes out of whom the Messiah was born. Furthermore, the reference to the time, times, and time and a half support the view that this refers to both the persecution by the Antiochus Epiphanes in the second century

BC and prefigures the very end-times spoken of by Daniel—both times that do not include Mary's life. The latter also cannot be Mary since it is interpreted as alluding to the tribulation and Rapture when Israel is given refuge by God Himself. In any case, there are no Gospel accounts of Mary being taken into the wilderness or the devil attacking her in the manner described in the text. However, the fact that some in the Orthodox churches over the centuries have held onto the view that the woman is Mary has had consequences as explained in the chapter "Queen of Heaven."

The apostle John saw the vision and wrote Revelation, and he described what he saw as a *sign* in heaven. It was not, as some say, that he saw Mary in her glory in heaven, which would not have been called a *sign*. He, in fact, never described who he saw as Mary and would have done so had he seen her since he knew her well. He would have known her from early on in the ministry of Christ (both were at the wedding at Cana) to the time he took her in as his mother at the crucifixion and at Pentecost and after.

APPENDIX 2

ADDITIONAL MATERIAL FOR MARY—THE SOURCE OF GRACE AND GIFTS FROM GOD

St. Bernard assigns the reason for this by saying: Behold, oh man, the design of God, a design arranged for our benefit, that he may be able to bestow upon us more abundantly his compassion; for, wishing to redeem the human race, he has placed the price of our redemption in the hands of Mary, that she may dispense it at her pleasure. (Liguori 118)

Mater divinaegratiae: Mother of divine grace. Mary is called by St. Anselm: Mother of all graces: "Mater omnium gratiarura." And by the Idiot: Treasurer of divine grace: "Thesauraria gratiarum." Hence St. Bernardine of Sienna writes: All the graces which we receive from God are dispensed by the hand of Mary, and are dispensed to whom Mary will, when she will, and as she will. (Liguori 730)

In St. Paul's letter to the Corinthians, he wrote of the gifts of the Holy Spirit. He described each gift and the source of the gifts:

> *All these are the work of one and the same Spirit, and he distributes them to each one, just as he determines.* (1 Cor 12:11)

It can be seen that the saints quoted by Liguori directly contradict scripture—even having chosen words that are similar but attributing the work of the Holy Spirit instead to Mary.

> *Wretched should we be, if we had not this mother of mercy, mindful and solicitous to help us in our miseries! "Where there is no wife," says the Holy Spirit, "he mourneth that is in want." This wife, remarks St. John Damascene, is certainly Mary, without whom the sick man suffers and mourns. So, indeed, it is, since God has ordained that all graces should be dispensed by the prayers of Mary: where these are wanting, there is no hope of mercy, as our Lord signified to St. Bridget, saying to her: "Unless Mary interposes by her prayers, there is no hope of mercy."* (Liguori 293)

The scripture referred to by St. John Damascene is taken from the book of Ecclesiasticus, which appears in the Catholic Bible but not the Jewish or Protestant versions. Ecclesiasticus, which should not be confused with the canonical Ecclesiastes, was written in the period between the Old and New Testaments, which was the period of four hundred years before Christ appeared when the Holy Spirit was not heard from.

Still, St. John Damascene attributes this non-canonical verse to the Holy Spirit and then used this as evidence of Mary—who was not even born at the time. Liguori used this as further evidence that God ordained that all graces should be dispensed by the prayers of Mary when, in fact, all gifts (graces) are dispensed by the Holy

Spirit as written and evidenced throughout the New Testament. In any case, it is a stretch to take it that the wife refers to Mary and that, without turning to Mary, the believer has no hope of mercy. The revelations to St. Bridget and others will be covered elsewhere.

> *God ordered Moses to make a propitiatory of the purest gold ... A certain author explains this propitiatory to be Mary, through whom the Lord speaks to men, and dispenses to them pardon, graces, and favors.* (Liguori 118)

The "propitiatory" was, in fact, the Ark of the Covenant. If representative of anything, it would have been of the Holy Spirit through whom the Lord spoke to men and dispensed gifts, blessings, and powers as testified throughout the books of both the Old and New Covenants. Nowhere in these same books was it shown that such gifts were also dispensed through Mary.

> *St. Basil ... says: Oh sinner, be not timid, but in all thy necessities flee to Mary, invoke her aid, and thou wilt always find her ready to assist thee, for it is the divine will that she should aid all men in all their necessities.* (Liguori 134)

Jesus taught on the other hand, ***"Come to me, all you who are weary and burdened, and I will give you rest."*** (Matt 11:28)

> *Let us then approach God's throne of grace with confidence, so that we may receive mercy and find grace to help us in our time of need.* (Heb 4:16)

Liguori on the other hand taught:

> *We shall consider to-day, in the present discourse, how the divine mother is the treasurer of all graces.*

We shall divide the discourse into two points. In the first, we shall prove that he who desires graces must have recourse to Mary. In the second, that he who has recourse to Mary, should be certain of obtaining the graces that he desires.

Point First

For at her first entrance, and at that first salutation, Elizabeth was filled with the Holy Spirit, and John was delivered from guilt and sanctified, and therefore gave that sign of joy, exulting in the womb of his mother; for he wished in this way to make known the grace received by means of the blessed Virgin; as Elizabeth herself declared: "As soon as the voice of thy salutation sounded in my ears, the infant in my womb leaped for joy." So, as Bernardine de Bustis observes, in virtue of the salutation of Mary, John received the grace of the Divine Spirit, who sanctified him: When the blessed Virgin saluted Elizabeth, the voice of the salutation entering through her ears, descended to the child, by virtue of which salutation he received the Holy Spirit.

Now if these first-fruits of the redemption all passed through Mary, and she was the channel by means of which grace was communicated to the Baptist, the Holy Spirit to Elizabeth, the gift of prophecy to Zachary, and so many other blessings to that house, which were the first graces that we know to have been given upon earth by the Word, after he had become incarnate; we have great reason to believe that God, even from that time, had constituted Mary a universal channel, as St. Bernard calls her, through which thenceforth should be dispensed to us all the other graces which the Lord wishes to bestow

> *on us, as it was said in p. 1 c. 5, of this work.* (Liguori 437–439)

Mary may have been a conduit as the Holy Spirit was with her. This is much the same as Peter and the apostles having "brought" the Spirit to the new believers as written in the Acts of the Apostles.

In actuality, it is the Holy Spirit who orchestrated and brought together each of the participants in each of these encounters and graced them with His presence. It is this same Spirit who now dwells in us: "***But you know him, for he lives with you and will be in you***" (John 14:17.) Liguori's point then that Mary had been the channel or instrument of the Holy Spirit—while perhaps true—is reflected in Spirit-filled and Spirit-led believers now being such channels and instruments of the Holy Spirit who abides in them.

It is a disservice to the Holy Spirit to ignore His presence and leadings in the daily experiences He brings us to and instead look to Mary who, at a point in time, was His instrument. This is akin to new believers saying they wish they were there two thousand years ago when Jesus walked the earth; Jesus Himself said it is *better* that He return to the Father and we have the presence of the Holy Spirit (John 16:7).

> *And why should Jesus Christ ever have placed in the hands of this his mother all the riches of the mercies which he wishes to use for our benefit, if not that she may enrich with them all her servants who love and honor her, and with confidence recur to her? With me are riches … that I may enrich them that love me: "Mecum sunt divitise … nt ditem diligentes me." Thus the Virgin herself speaks in this passage, which the holy Church applies to her on so many of her festivals.* (Liguori 443–444)

Liguori asks why "Jesus ever placed in the hands of his mother" when there is nothing in scripture to indicate this, but much on the contrary is written that the Holy Spirit dispenses grace and gifts. The verse he and the Holy Church attribute to Mary is from Proverbs 8, which is written of Wisdom and not Mary.

> *Let our confidence, then, ever revive, oh devoted servants of Mary, as often as we have recourse to her for graces. And to revive this confidence, let us ever remember the two great privileges which this good mother possesses, namely: the desire she has to do us good, and the power she has with her Son to obtain whatever she asks. That we may know the desire Mary has to aid all, it would be sufficient only to consider the mystery of the present festival, namely, the visit of Mary to Elizabeth ... But this did not prevent the blessed Virgin, tender and delicate as she then was, and not accustomed to such efforts, from immediately setting forth moved by what? moved by that great charity with which her most tender heart was ever filled, to go and commence from that time her great office of dispenser of graces.* (Liguori 446–447)

Scripture tells us she went to visit and help her elder cousin who was previously barren as told by the angel—not to fulfill "her great office of dispenser of graces."

> *Mary, then, having been made the mother of all the redeemed, by the merit of her sufferings, and of the offering of her Son; it is just to believe that only by her hand may be given them the milk of those divine graces, which are the fruits of the merits of Jesus Christ, and the means to obtain life eternal. And it is to this that St. Bernard alludes, when he says that*

> *God has placed in the hands of Mary the whole price of our redemption. By which the saint gives us to understand, that by means of the intercession of the blessed Virgin, the merits of the Redeemer are applied to souls, as by her hand these graces are dispensed, which are precisely the price of the merits of Jesus Christ.* (Liguori 469)

"*It is just to believe*" is another of Liguori's "it was fitting" arguments that raise human reasoning to the level of the authority of scripture. It is not that her "intercession" caused the merits to be applied to souls. In truth, the merits of our Redeemer in the sacrifice at the cross were *always* meant to be applied to souls for this is why our Savior came to this earth—to save souls of which Mary's was one.

> *"Tun-is eburnea;" Tower of ivory. Thus Mary is also called: Thy neck is as a tower of ivory: "Collum tuum sicut turns eburnea." Mary is called the neck, for she is the mystic neck through whom from the head, Jesus Christ, are transmitted to us the faithful, who are the members of the mystic body of the Church, the vital spirits, namely, the divine help which preserves in us the life of grace. In the words of St. Bernardine: Through the Virgin, the life giving graces flow from Christ, the head, into his mystic body. The saint adds, that from the time when Mary conceived in her womb the incarnate Word, she received from God such honor, that no one could receive any grace except through her hands. (Liguori 741–742)*

The term *Tower of Ivory* was taken from the Song of Solomon (Song 7:4) where it describes the prince's daughter. St. Bernadine and others have taken it to mean Mary. The teaching that Mary is the "mystic neck" through which Jesus is transmitted to the faithful is a *false teaching* since the Holy Spirit was given to us, resides in us, and directs our ways.

Thus, we need no created intermediary through which to come to God since the Spirit is one with God. This was clearly revealed by God when the veil that separated the holy of holies from the rest of the temple was torn from top to bottom when Jesus died—signifying there is now no separation, and we can come directly to God.

> *And the saint (Bernard) exhorts us, whenever we desire and ask any favor, to recommend ourselves to Mary, and trust that we shall obtain it through her intercession. For, says the saint, if you do not deserve from God the favor you ask, Mary, who asks it in your behalf, merits to obtain it. Hence the same Bernard exhorts us each and all, that, whatever we offer to God, whether works or prayers, we recommend all to Mary, if we wish our Lord to accept them.* (Liguori 196)

Faith, among other things, is knowing we do ***not*** deserve any favor from God, but we can trust His grace and goodness toward us so that we can ask in faith. His Word tells us we can boldly approach His throne of grace.

> *Therefore, since we have a great high priest who has ascended into heaven, Jesus the Son of God … Let us then approach God's throne of grace with confidence, so that we may receive mercy and find grace to help us in our time of need.* (Heb 4:14–16)

> Jesus said: ***"And I will do whatever you ask in my name, so that the Father may be glorified in the Son. You may ask me for anything in my name, and I will do it."*** (John 14:13–14)

To live otherwise is to live outside of faith, believing that either we merit favor or that God is not gracious. To go to *another* for favor, when He has covered all our sin through the sacrifice of His Son at the Cross and told us to go to Him, is also not faith.

> *And without faith it is impossible to please God, because anyone who comes to him must believe that he exists and that he rewards those who earnestly seek him.* (Heb 11:6)

Note how the scripture says, "*those who earnestly seek Him*" and not "seek to go through His mother." This absence of faith can be seen in the following prayer:

Prayer to the Most Holy Mary to Obtain Her Patronage

> *OH my most holy mother, I know what graces thou hast obtained for me, and I see the ingratitude of which I have been guilty towards thee. The ungrateful are no longer worthy of favors; but I will not on this account distrust thy mercy, which is greater than my ingratitude. Oh my great advocate, have pity on me. Thou art the dispenser of all the graces which God grants to us miserable sinners, and for this end he has made thee so powerful, so rich, and so merciful, that thou mightest succor us in our miseries ... Thou art the advocate of the most wretched and abandoned sinners who have recourse to thee, defend me also, who recommend myself to thee. Do not tell me that it is difficult to gain my cause, for the most desperate causes are all gained when they are defended by thee. In thy hands, then, I place my eternal salvation, and to thee I commit my soul.* (Liguori 771–772)

The only reason one asks for the patronage of another is because one is *unsure of* or *unwilling to* trust in the absolute judge over all. God has Himself already given us a Savior and an Advocate. To turn to another is to not fully trust both Savior and Advocate. Therefore, come such prayers as "*In thy hands, then, I place my eternal salvation, and to thee I commit my soul*" when all the faithful through the ages have placed their trust entirely in God—as scripture teaches.

APPENDIX 3
THE APOCRYPHA

The Apocrypha are a collection of writings that were not part of the Hebrew Masoretic Text or Hebrew Bible. Many of the writings, including *Ecclesiasticus* (not to be confused with *Ecclesiastes,* which was written by King Solomon), were written in the Intertestamental period, which was the four-hundred-year period until Christ came to this earth as Son of Man.

It was during this time that the Holy Spirit was not heard from, and this is one of the reasons why both the Jews and Christians (excluding Catholics) do not consider these writings inspired by God. Another reason is both Jesus Christ and the apostles both quoted and referred to the books of Moses (Genesis, Exodus, Leviticus, Numbers, and Deuteronomy), Psalms (Job, Psalms, Proverbs, Ecclesiastes, and Song of Solomon), and the Prophets (the remaining twenty-nine books of the Old Testament) but never taught that the other writings were sacred.

Long before the fourth century AD, the sixty-six books of the Bible were already accepted as the authoritative canon of scripture.

Ecclesiasticus

This book was written by Ben Sira, who lived in Jerusalem around 200 BC, and much of the book was written with the subject being "wisdom," which is a trait of God. Liguori and others quoted many of the verses and attributed them to Mary. Instead, these writings spoke unequivocally of Wisdom and not of Mary.

The Wisdom of Solomon

This book was dated in the Intertestamental period, around the mid-first century BC, long after the time of King Solomon.

The Protoevangelium of James

Also referred to as the "Gospel of James," this work was compiled sometime around the second century AD. It is a collection of stories about Mary, including her miraculous conception (in the womb of her mother), her infancy and childhood, her marriage, and more. It also asserts her perpetual virginity.

Liguori and others quote from it and treat it as though it were scripture—even though it was condemned by their pope (Pope Innocent I in AD 405) and church councils as being non-scriptural and unreliable.

Even relatively recent authors, such as the staunch Mariologist Rene Laurentin in *A Year of Grace with Mary: Rediscovering Her Presence,*[106] referred to the Protoevangelium:

> *The Protoevangelium of James testifies not only to great fervour towards Mary, but also to a profound insight into her holiness and her virginity ... It is totally unlikely that a little girl of three years of age could have*

[106] *A Year of Grace with Mary: Rediscovering Her Presence*, Rene Laurentin, Veritas Publications, 1989.

> *been reared there (in the temple of Jerusalem)—let alone the holy of holies, reserved for priests on solemn occasions.* (Laurentin)

If the Protoevangelium cannot be relied upon in its descriptions of Mary having been raised in the Holy of Holies given the strictness of Jewish law, how could this same document be relied upon for "*insight into her holiness and virginity*"?

Maccabees

The book of Maccabees covers the revolt by led by Judas Maccabeus against the Romans. It was not part of the accepted Hebrew Bible. Like the early Christian Bible, it was included only as supplemental text (such as today we find with *Maps*), but it was not inspired scripture.

APPENDIX 4

ADDITIONAL MATERIAL FOR MARY WAS BORN WITHOUT ORIGINAL SIN

The following are further examples of Liguori's justification for the belief that Mary was without original sin. Note that the term "Immaculate Conception" does not refer to Mary's conception of Jesus by the Holy Spirit but rather the belief that Mary herself was born of the Holy Spirit free of sin in the womb of her mother.

> *Ah, that God who is wisdom itself well knew how to prepare upon the earth a fit dwelling for him to inhabit: "Wisdom hath built herself a house," "The Most High hath sanctified his own tabernacle." "God will help it in the morning early." The Lord, says David, sanctified this his habitation in the morning early; that is, from the beginning of her life, to render her worthy of himself; for it was not befitting a God who is holy to select a house that was not holy: Holiness becometh thy house: "Domum tuum decet sanctitudo."* (Liguori 252)

The first quotation is taken from Proverbs 9:1-4:

Wisdom has built her house;
she has set up its seven pillars.
She has prepared her meat and mixed her wine;
she has also set her table.
She has sent out her servants, and she calls
from the highest point of the city,
"Let all who are simple come to my house!" (Prov 9:1–4)

When only the first half of the first verse is read, it might be believed that this refers to Mary; however, when read more completely, it does not appear to allude to her.

"*The Most High hath sanctified his own tabernacle*" is curious since Liguori claims it is from Psalm 45:56, but Psalm 45 only has seventeen verses. The Column to the Immaculate Conception built by Pope Pius IX in Rome quotes the same verse as being Psalm 45:4, which it is not. Instead, the Latin verse "Sanctificavit tabernaculum suum altissimus" is found in verse 5 of Psalm 46. Verses 4–5 are rendered in English as "*There is a river whose streams make glad the city of God, the holy place where the Most High dwells. God is within her, she will not fall; God will help her at break of day*" (Ps 46:4–5). Again, these verses do not appear to refer to Mary. The river and "her" appear similar to references to the Holy Spirit and the New Jerusalem in the book of Revelation—and not the early life of Mary.

> *"And if he himself declares that he will never enter into a malicious soul, and into a body subject to sins"; how can we think that the Son of God would have chosen to inhabit the soul and body of Mary without first sanctifying her and preserving her from every stain of sin? for, as St. Thomas teaches us, the eternal Word*

> *inhabited not only the soul, but the body of Mary.* (Liguori 352–353)

"*For wisdom will not enter into a malicious soul, nor dwell in a body subdued by sin*" comes from the "Wisdom of Solomon" (see appendix 3: "The Apocrypha"). In any case, it speaks of a malicious soul and one subdued by sin rather than a believer in God who overcomes sin by allowing the sanctifying work of the Holy Spirit.

While it is likely true that God would first sanctify Mary before inhabiting her, this does not necessarily infer that such sanctification need occur before birth. This is true in both the Old and New Covenant. In the Old Covenant, prophets and kings were anointed, and some had the Spirit come to sanctify and guide them for their tasks of guiding the people. In the New Covenant, the spirit-filled believers were sanctified by faith and then received God in His Holy Spirit as testified in the book of Acts and beyond.

He prepares and equips us for the task <u>*after*</u> we have agreed to participate. If this were not so, no one could receive the Holy Spirit:

> *That Son would, indeed, commit a sin, says Father Thomas d Argentina, an Augustinian, who, being able to preserve his mother from original sin, should not do so; now that which would be sinful in us, says the same author, <u>cannot be esteemed befitting</u> the Son of God, namely, if he should not have created his mother immaculate when he was able to do so.* (Liguori 354)

This is yet another of the "it was fitting" arguments that man constructs by which he determines what God should do and then judges God.

The main reason for the argument for Immaculate Conception of Mary is that the pious believe that Jesus should not bear to have a mother under the curse of original sin. But as pointed out, pushing the sinless birth back a generation does not overcome her mother also needing to be sinless—all the way back to Eve. Further, Jesus did not come to earth to preserve us from original sin but to break the curse of original sin over us.

> *And as there are two modes of redeeming, as St. Augustine teaches, one by raising the fallen; the other, by preventing from failing; doubtless, the latter is the most noble. More nobly, says St. Antoninus, is he redeemed who is prevented from falling, than he who is raised after failing; because in this way is avoided the injury or stain that the soul always contracts by a fall. Therefore we ought to believe that Mary was redeemed in the nobler manner, as became the mother of a God, as St. Bonaventure expresses it; for Frassen proves the sermon on the assumption to have been written by that holy doctor. We must believe that by a new mode of sanctification the Holy Spirit redeemed her at the first moment of her conception, and preserved her by a special grace from original sin, which was not in her, but would have been in her. On this subject Cardinal Cusano has elegantly written: Others have had a deliverer, but the holy Virgin had a predeliverer; others have had a Redeemer to deliver them from sin already contracted, but the holy Virgin had a Redeemer who, because he was her Son, prevented her from contracting sin.* (Liguori 355–356)

These authors used the phrases "*we ought to believe*" and "*we must believe*" only because they knew it was not in any scripture and so had no scriptural justification to believe so.

On the other hand, scripture teaches us something else:

> *Do not go beyond what is written.* (1 Cor 4:6)

> *Every Word of God is flawless; he is a shield to those who take refuge in him. Do not add to his words, or he will rebuke you and prove you a liar.* (Prov 30:5–6)

> *I warn everyone who hears the words of the prophecy of this scroll: If anyone <u>adds</u> anything to them, God will add to that person the plagues described in this scroll.* (Rev 22:18)

Liguori on the other hand writes:

> *Now, if an excellent painter were allowed to choose a bride as beautiful or as deformed as he himself might paint her, how great would be his solicitude to make her as beautiful as possible! <u>Who, then, will say that the Holy Spirit has not dealt thus</u> with Mary, and that, <u>having it in his power</u> to make this his spouse as beautiful as it became her to be, <u>he has not done so</u>? Yes, <u>thus it was fitting he should do</u>, and thus he did, as the Lord himself attested when praising Mary; he said to her: "Thou art all fair, oh my love; and there is not a spot in thee;" which words, as we learn from a Lapide, St. Ildephonsus, and St. Thomas, explain as properly to be understood of Mary. The Holy Spirit signifies the same thing, when he called this his spouse: "A garden enclosed, a fountain sealed up." Mary, says St. Jerome, was properly this enclosed garden and sealed fountain; for the enemies never entered to harm her, but she was always uninjured, remaining holy in soul and body.* (Liguori 357–358)

These are yet more "it was fitting" arguments, this time regarding earthly beauty when God Himself says, "*The LORD does not look at the things people look at. People look at the outward appearance, but the LORD looks at the heart"* (1 Sam 16:7). The remaining quotations regarding "art all fair" and "the garden enclosed" were taken from Song of Solomon 4 and likely do not refer to Mary for it says the bride is from Lebanon.

In his very insightful and readable book, *No God But One, Allah or Jesus*, the late Nabeel Qureshi tells of meeting a Muslim lady who asked, "How can you believe Jesus is God if he was born through the birth canal of a woman and that he had to use the bathroom? Aren't these things below God?"* Her question has parallels to Liguori's argument that God could not have entered the body of one who inherited Adam's sin.

As part of the answer Nabeel gave her, he asked her to imagine being on time for a very important ceremony, dressed in her finest. She was then asked to imagine seeing her own daughter drowning in a pool of mud. When asked if she would jump in to save her daughter, in spite of her finery and what others would think, she says she would.

Nabeel then said, "If you, being a human, love your daughter so much that you are willing to lay aside your dignity to save her, how much more can we expect God, if He is our perfectly loving Father, to lay aside His majesty to save us?"[108]

This is our great and loving God.

*A few early theologians proposed their own answer to the question: That Jesus did not pass through the birth canal but was miraculously delivered. Their proposition appeared to have been more to preserve the dignity of Mary and the belief in her perpetual virginity than to preserve the dignity of Jesus.

[107] *No God But One, Allah or Jesus?* Nabeel Qureshi, Zondervan, 89, 92.

APPENDIX 5

ADDITIONAL MATERIAL FOR PARDON FROM JUDGMENT AND MERCY FOR SINNERS

> *St. Bernard assigns the reason for this by saying: Behold, oh man, the design of God, a design arranged for our benefit, that he may be able to bestow upon us more abundantly his compassion; for, wishing to redeem the human race, he has placed the price of our redemption in the hands of Mary, that she may dispense it at her pleasure.* (Liguori 118)

The true Gospel is clear that the price of redemption was the life of our Lord at the cross. This was a price paid for all—that all are saved who, in faith, trust that their lives were redeemed by our Savior. There is no question of anyone "*dispensing the price of our redemption*" from his or her hands as the price was paid in full and all who come to Him are saved.

> *Jesus says,* ***"Here I am! I stand at the door and knock. If anyone hears my voice and opens the door, I will come in and eat with that person, and they with me."*** (Rev 3:20)

> *All praise to the God and Father of our Lord Jesus Christ. He is the source of every mercy and the God who comforts us.* (2 Cor 1:3)

Jesus always invited all by saying "***Come to Me***" because He is the Source and Giver of all good things:

> ***Come to Me, all you who labour and are heavy laden, and I will give you rest.*** (Matt 11:28)

> ***Let the little children come to Me.*** (Matt 19:14, Mark 10:14, and Luke 18:16)

> ***If anyone thirsts, let him come to Me and drink.*** (John 7:37)

> ***All that the Father gives Me will come to Me.*** (John 6:37)

> ***No one can come to Me unless the Father who sent Me draws him.*** (John 6:44)

> ***But you are not willing to come to Me that you may have life.*** (John 5:40)

Liguori and those he quotes would instead rather that we go to Mary.

> *And why should Jesus Christ ever have placed in the hands of this his mother all the riches of the mercies which he wishes to use for our benefit, if not that she*

may enrich with them all her servants who love and honor her, and with confidence recur to her? With me are riches … that I may enrich them that love me: "Mecum sunt divitise … nt ditem diligentes me." Thus the Virgin herself speaks in this passage, which the holy Church applies to her on so many of her festivals. (Liguori 443–444)

As covered in appendix 2, Liguori asks why "*Jesus ever placed* ('graces') *in the hands of his mother*" when there is nothing in scripture to indicate this, but much on the contrary it is written that the Holy Spirit dispenses grace and gifts. The verse Liguori and the *Holy Church* attribute to Mary is from Proverbs 8, which is written of Wisdom and not of Mary.

"He that shall find me, shall find life, and shall have salvation from the Lord." Blessed is he who having recourse to me finds me, says our mother. He will find life, and will find it easily; for, as it is easy to find and draw water (as much as one wishes) from a great fountain, so it is easy to find graces and eternal salvation by going to Mary. A holy soul hath said, we have only to ask graces of our Lady and we shall have them. And St. Bernard says, that before Mary was born, the world was without this abundance of graces, that now are overflowing the earth, because this desirable channel (Mary) was wanting. But now that we actually have this mother of mercy, what graces can we not obtain, if we cast ourselves at her feet? I am the city of refuge, thus St. John of Damascus makes her to say, for all those who have recourse to me: come, then, my children, and you will obtain from me graces, in greater abundance than you can imagine. (Liguori 445–446)

The scripture *"He that shall find me ..."* is taken from Proverbs 8:35, which is about Wisdom and not Mary. The cities of refuge that God designated in the Old Covenant were a precursor to and *type* of Christ and not Mary. We are told to bow only before God, but Liguori repeatedly teaches that we should cast ourselves at the feet of Mary.

Liguori wrote a series of prayers to be recited over the course of a week in a chapter entitled *"Prayers to the Divine Mother."* The titles of these prayers for each day are as follows:

> *Sunday: Prayer to the most holy Mary to obtain the pardon of sins*
> *Monday: Prayer to the most holy Mary to obtain holy perseverance*
> *Tuesday: Prayer to Mary most holy to obtain a good death*
> *Wednesday: Prayer to Mary most holy to obtain deliverance from hell*
> *Thursday: Prayer to the most holy Mary to obtain paradise*
> *Friday: Prayer to the most holy Mary to obtain love towards her and Jesus Christ*
> *Saturday: Prayer to the most holy Mary to obtain her patronage*

Three of the days then are devoted to prayers to obtain mercy (pardon of sins, deliverance from hell, and obtaining paradise).

In scripture, we are never asked to pray to any apart from God. The believer who in faith has placed his hope and trust in Christ has already received pardon from their sin. To turn to another in the hope of gaining *more* is itself sin because it is treating Christ's sacrifice as insufficient and their sin as greater. Scripture (paraphrased) teaches us:

- Jesus gave his life as a ransom for many (Mark 10:45). He sacrificed for our sins once for all when He offered Himself (Heb 7:27).

- The work of God is to believe in the One He sent (John 6:27–29). He who believes has everlasting life (John 6:47).
- We have been justified freely by His grace through faith in Jesus Christ (Rom 3:24–25).
- Our transgressions are forgiven, our sins are covered, and the Lord will never count our sins against us (Rom 4:7–8).
- Since justified, we have peace with God (Rom 5:1–2).
- Justified by (His) blood, we are saved from God's wrath (Rom 5:9–11).
- Therefore, if anyone is in Christ, the new creation has come: The old has gone, the new is here! All this is from God, who reconciled us to himself through Christ and gave us the ministry of reconciliation: that God was reconciling the world to himself in Christ, not counting people's sins against them (2 Cor 5:17–18).

There are many more scriptures that proclaim the same salvation message, which is why the Gospel is called the good news. All these scriptures and more point believers to Jesus—and never to Mary—as their source of mercy.

APPENDIX 6

ADDITIONAL MATERIAL FOR MARY AS ADVOCATE AND INTERCESSOR

All nations shall call thee blessed, because all thy servants by thy means shall obtain the life of grace and eternal glory, "In thee sinners find pardon, and the just perseverance, and afterwards life eternal." (Liguori 85)

The Need We Have of the Intercession of Mary for our Salvation — To invoke and pray to the saints, especially to the queen of saints, most holy Mary, that they may obtain for us, by their intercession, the divine favor, is not only a lawful but a useful and holy practice, and this is of faith, being established by the Councils, against heretics, who condemn it as injurious to Jesus Christ, who is our only mediator; but if a Jeremias, after his death, prays for Jerusalem; if the elders of the Apocalypse present to God the prayers of the saints; if a St. Peter promises his disciples to remember them after his death; if a St.

> *Stephen prays for his persecutors; if a St. Paul prays for his companions; if, in a word, the saints pray for us, why may we not implore the saints to intercede for us? St. Paul commends himself to the prayers of his disciples: Pray for us: "Orate pro nobis." St. James exhorts the Christians to pray for each other: "Pray for one another, that ye may be saved." We may then do likewise.* (Liguori 168–169)

The claim that the prophet Jeremiah prayed for Jerusalem is taken from the book of Maccabees, which is included as scripture in the Catholic Bible and was written over four hundred years after his life —but not in others, including the Jewish Bible. It is part of the Apocrypha (see appendix 3). The "saints" referred to in true scripture speak of the living faithful, whereas many of the traditional churches have a man-made tradition of electing, exalting, and later referring to their chosen departed as "saints." Indeed, they do not recognize saints as the living faithful as in their understanding, these cannot truly be called "saints" until the days of their lives are completed, lest one be recognized as a "saint" and then fall short before death.

In scripture, we are exhorted to pray *for* our fellow saints, the *living* faithful believers, whereas what Liguori advocates is something quite different. He uses scripture to advocate that we pray *to* the departed saints, which is never taught in scripture where we are told to pray to God.

When His disciples asked Jesus how to pray, He taught them the manner of praying to God. When Paul asked for his disciples to pray for him, he meant while he was still on this earth and not after. Scripture, in fact, warns us to never seek or approach the dead as though they were living, and this was most clearly shown in the first book of Samuel when King Saul called upon the spirit of the prophet Samuel to divine the outcome of the battle that was to take place. Samuel then rebuked him.

"Why should we not implore the saints to intercede for us?" The answer is that to do so is simply to be practicing a lack of faith in the mercy of our Savior who died for us. We are told in scripture to *"approach God's throne of grace with confidence, so that we may receive mercy and find grace to help us in our time of need"* (Heb 4:16) and *"In Him* (Jesus) *and through faith in Him we may approach God with freedom and confidence"* (Eph 3:12). Instead, Liguori and others teach believers to implore Mary and the saints, bypassing God in an attempt to seek favor.

The teachings of Liguori regarding approaching Mary instead of God have echoes in Haman begging Queen Esther (Esth 7:7–8) and Adonijah approaching King Solomon's mother Bathsheba (1 Kgs 2:13–25)—in both cases to bypass the reigning kings. Both of these are examples of what *not* to do since they both ended badly for the ones seeking favors.

APPENDIX 7

ADDITIONAL MATERIAL FOR MARY AS OUR ONLY ADVOCATE

Mary was, then, the mediatrix of men, someone will say, but can she be called also the mediatrix of angels? Many theologians are of opinion that Jesus Christ obtained by his merits the grace of perseverance also for the angels; so that as Jesus Christ was their mediator de condigno Mary may also be called their mediatrix de congruo, having hastened by her prayers the coming of the Redeemer. At least, having merited de congruo to be chosen for the mother of the Messias, she merited for the angels the restoration of their seats which had been lost by the demons. Then, at least, she merited for them this accidental glory; hence, Richard of St. Victor says: Every creature by her is restored, the ruin of the angels by her is repaired, and human nature is reconciled. And St. Anselm before had said: All things by this Virgin are reclaimed and restored to their pristine state. (Liguori 382–383)

Scripture does not say anything of Jesus being mediator for the angels—much less Mary. In fact, scripture is blunt about the fallen angels not being under the New Testament covenant,[108] and this might be because they were in the presence of God in all His glory and yet chose to rebel.

Scripture also says nothing of Mary having "*hastened by her prayers the coming of the Redeemer.*" Instead, scripture tells us that "*when the set time had fully come*" (Gal 4:4), Christ was revealed, which was predestined since it was revealed to Daniel exactly when this would be (Dan 9:25–26). There is nothing in scripture that backs up the words of both Richard of St. Victor and St. Anselm.

---

[108] Matt 25:41

APPENDIX 8

ADDITIONAL MATERIAL FOR ATTRIBUTING SCRIPTURE TO MEAN MARY WHEN THEY MEANT OTHERWISE

In Liguori's *The Glories*, various writers, including popes and Liguori himself, often attributed scripture to refer to Mary. A few of these are shown below.

Mary as the Moon

There are many references in *The Glories* to Mary being a *type* of the moon:

> *AFTER God had created the earth he created two lights, the greater and the less: the sun to give light by day, and the moon to give light by night. The sun, says Cardinal Hugo, was the type of Jesus Christ, in whose light the just rejoice who live in the daylight of divine*

> *grace; but the moon was the type of Mary, by whom sinners are enlightened, who are living in the night of sin. Mary, then, being the moon, so propitious to miserable sinners, if any unhappy person, says Innocent III. finds that he has fallen into this night of sin, what must he do? Since he has lost the light of the sun, by loosing divine grace, let him turn to the moon, pray to Mary, and she will give him light to know the misery of his condition, and strength to come forth from it.* (Liguori 127–128)

> *St. Bonaventure applies to the blessed Virgin the words spoken to Ruth: "Blessed art thou, my daughter, and thy latter kindness has surpassed the former." Meaning, as he afterwards explains, that if the pity of Mary for the unhappy was great when she lived on earth, much greater is it now when she is reigning in heaven. And he adds, that as the splendor of the sun exceeds that of the moon, so the mercy of Mary, now that she is in heaven, exceeds the mercy she had for us when she was upon the earth.* (Liguori 244)

> *Of thee the Holy Ghost speaks when he says: Who is she that arises like the dawn, fair as the moon, bright as the sun? Thou art, then, come into the world, oh Mary, as a resplendent dawn, preceding, with the light of thy sanctity, the coming of the Sun of Justice. The day in which thou didst appear in the world may truly be called the day of salvation, the day of grace. Thou art fair as the moon; for as there is no planet more like the sun, so there is no creature more like God than thou art.* (Liguori 324–325)

In the first quotation above, the sun is described as a *type* of Jesus and the moon as a *type* of Mary. In both the second and third descriptions, the sun and moon are taken to be Mary—a contradiction. The quotation from Ruth is about Naomi, and to say that it applies to Mary could equally well be said to apply to any other female person in scripture. The verse quoted in the third description was taken from Song of Solomon and describes the Shulamite from Lebanon. This means she is neither a Jewess nor from the line of David.

In scripture, God is our salvation from beginning to end.

He is the Author and Finisher of our faith[109]—the very faith that causes us to believe in His promises and to receive them. There is no *second rung* upon which we are told to anchor our faith as proposed by Cardinal Hugo. God made the Way so that all who come to *Him* in true repentance are saved.

[109] Heb 12:1–2.

APPENDIX 9

PRAYER TAUGHT BY THE ANGEL AT FATIMA

The angel, who claimed to be the guardian angel of Portugal, taught the cousins a prayer in 1916. Lucia described the scene as follows:

> *He was holding a chalice in his left hand, with the Host suspended above it, from which some drops of blood fell into the chalice. Leaving the chalice suspended in the air, the Angel knelt down beside us and made us repeat three times: "Most Holy Trinity, Father, Son and Holy Spirit, I adore You profoundly, and I offer You the most precious Body, Blood, Soul and Divinity of Jesus Christ, present in all the tabernacles of the world, in reparation for the outrages, sacrileges and indifference with which He himself is offended. And, through the infinite merits of His most Sacred Heart, and the Immaculate Heart of Mary, I beg of You the conversion of poor sinners."*
>
> *Then, rising, he took the chalice and the Host in his hands. He gave it the Sacred Host to me, and shared the Blood from the chalice between Jacinta and Francisco, saying as he did so: "Take and drink*

the Body and Blood of Jesus Christ, horribly outraged by ungrateful men! Make reparation for their crimes and console your God."

Once again, he prostrated on the ground and repeated with us, three times more, the same prayer "Most Holy Trinity ..." and then disappeared.

We remained a long time in this position, repeating the same words over and over again. When at last we stood up, we noticed that it was already dark, and therefore time to return home. (Liguori 64–65)

APPENDIX 10

DEHYDRATION PRACTICED BY THE COUSINS AT FATIMA

The following extract is taken from Lucia's book.[110]

> *We were parched with thirst, and there wasn't a single drop of water for us to drink! At first, we offered the sacrifice generously for the conversion of sinners, by after midday, we could hold out no longer.*
>
> *As there was a house quite near, I suggested to my companions that I should go and ask for a little water. They agreed to this, so I went and knocked on the door. A little old woman gave me not only a pitcher of water, but also some bread, which I accepted gratefully. I ran to share it with my little companions, and they offered the pitcher to Francisco, and told him to take a drink.*
>
> *"I don't want to." He replied.*
>
> *"Why?"*
>
> *"I want to suffer for the conversion of sinners."*

[110] *Sr Mary Lucia, Fatima in Lucia's Own Words*, 10th edition, 32.

"You have a drink, Jacinta!"

"But I want to offer this sacrifice for sinners too."

Then I poured the water into a hollow in the rock, so that the sheep could drink it, and went to return the pitcher to its owner. The heat was getting more and more intense. The shrill singing of the crickets and grasshoppers coupled with the croaking of the frogs in the neighbouring pond mad an uproar that was almost unbearable. Jacinta, frail as she was, and weakened still more by the lack of food and drink, said to me with that simplicity which was natural to hear:

"Tell the crickets and the frogs to keep quiet! I have such a terrible headache."

The Francisco asked her:

"Don't you want to suffer this for sinners?"

The poor child, clasping her head between her two little hands, replied:

"Yes, I do. Let them sing!"

APPENDIX 11
THE ROSARY

The Rosary is both a physical prayer accessory consisting of threaded beads along a string and the collection of prayers recited with the use of the device. Physically, it resembles the prayer beads used by some Eastern (non-Christian) religions to count recited prayers.

The prayers recited with the use of the Rosary are organized in a specific arrangement, and the Rosary can be recited alone, in a pair, or in a group. If recited by more than one person, the prayers are usually recited with one leading and the others following. For instance, the beginning half of a prayer is spoken by the leader, and the remaining verses are recited in response by the group.

The prayers recited consist of the following in order of frequency:

- fifty-three Hail Marys
- six Lord's Prayers (Our Father)
- six Glory Bes
- five different introductions, depending on the church annual calendar of "seasons" to the five "decades" consisting of one Lord's Prayer and ten Hail Marys each
- one Apostle's Creed

The sequence of prayer is as follows:

- The Apostle's Creed
- one Lord's Prayer
- three Hail Marys
- one Glory Be
- five decades consisting of an Introduction (called a Mystery), one Lord's Prayer, ten Hail Marys, and one Glory Be

Various other recited prayers often either precede or follow the Rosary.

Hail Mary

Hail Mary
Full of grace
The Lord is with thee
Blessed art thou amongst women
And blessed is the Fruit of thy womb, Jesus

Holy Mary
Mother of God
Pray for us, sinners
Now and at the hour of our death
Amen.

The recitation of the Rosary is usually accompanied by the "saying" (recitation) of various other long prayers, including asking for Mary and various departed saints to "pray" for those who pray these prayers. A complete "saying" of the Rosary can take ten to fifteen minutes, and believers are encouraged to say many Rosaries each day to cover the needs of themselves and the sins of others and to reduce the time in purgatory for their loved ones.

Brief History

Rene Laurentin, a devout Marian follower, wrote many books praising the virtues of Mary. In a chapter entitled "Prayer with Mary, By Mary, To Mary" in his *A Year of Grace with Mary*, he wrote that the Dominicans brought the Hail Mary prayer to it final and current form. Author John M Lozano wrote that toward the end of the twelfth century, the Council of Paris ordered that the Hail Mary be taught to the faithful along with the Our Father and the Apostle's Creed.

With the subsequent Renaissance and the increasing interest in the arts, Mary and the Rosary became popular as a devotion. Those who did not read or know Latin took the Rosary to be "a kind of popular liturgy." Note that these people who were taught to place their hopes in and to follow Mary were not familiar with scripture since it was still confined to the libraries of the monasteries. Pope Leo XIII (1810–1903) fostered devotion to the Rosary as a powerful antidote to satanic attacks on the church.

Why People Recite the Rosary

There are many reasons why the Rosary is recited today:

- Firstly, it is a firmly entrenched "tradition" in some denominations to pray this prayer, and it is often handed down in the family as *the* way in which to pray.
- It is promoted within some denominations. For instance, Liguori and others have made many claims as to its efficacy. Today, it is still promoted in churches and by various para-church organizations.
- It was advocated by the spirit behind the apparitions with various promises from that spirit. For instance, the spirit promoted the Rosary at every meeting. This spirit also

advocated "world devotion to my Immaculate Heart" as a wish of God Himself—with the Rosary as a means by which many souls will be saved.
- It has been promoted as a blessing, a cover of protection, and a means to save souls from the torments of Purgatory. The spirit behind the Rosary said, "Anyone who goes to Mary and prays the Rosary cannot be touched by Satan."
- The spirit behind the apparitions also claimed that some could only go to heaven (in the case of Francisco) and that others could only be healed or have their petitions met if they prayed this prayer sufficiently.

Other Claims of the Benefits of the Rosary

Apart from the benefits extolled by Liguori and those he quoted—as well as by the spirits that appeared in the many visitations—there are many claimed benefits of the Rosary. The "benefits" of reciting the Rosary have been explained by the Catholic Church:

- It can be prayed for others, especially departed loved ones, as a means by which to reduce their time spent in Purgatory where they are said to remain while being purged of their sins
- It is a means toward peace for the world.
- It is a meditation centered on Christ.

During an exorcism, Gabriele Amorth, chief exorcist of the Vatican, was quoted as having said, "Satan told me, through the possessed person, 'Every Hail Mary of the Rosary is a blow to the head for me; if Christians knew the power of the Rosary, it would be the end of me!'" Elsewhere, it is written that he did not actually witness such a thing. Instead, he may have said, "One day, a colleague of mine heard the devil say those words during an exorcism."

Why the chief exorcist of the Vatican would believe the words of the devil and teach others to rely on those words is extraordinary given what Jesus Himself revealed about the devil.

Jesus talked about those who considered themselves righteous simply on account of their heritage:

> ***You belong to your father, the devil, and you want to carry out your father's desires. He was a murderer from the beginning, not holding to the truth, for there is no truth in him. When he lies, he speaks his native language, for he is a liar and the father of lies.*** (John 8:44)

Every word of the devil is to be distrusted; he wants believers to place their trust in anyone and anything *except* God and His Word.

There are all types of further claims, such as when the prayer is recited, Mary herself comes to join those who pray and further that she brings angels, Jesus, and the Trinity with her. This is in contrast to the teachings of Jesus:

> ***Anyone who loves me will obey my teaching. My Father will love them, and we will come to them and make our home with them.*** (John 14:23)

The book of Acts, which tells us the beginning of the church, tells of how unbelievers first came to know God through the witness of the apostles. Both Jews and Gentiles were taught that Jesus had fulfilled all that was prophesized from ages past. He died for our sins, was buried, was raised on the third day, and was seen by the twelve apostles and about five hundred others. All who believed, had repented, and had confessed their faith in the finished work of Christ were filled with the Holy Spirit—the Spirit of God. This is both the *example* and the *family* to which we are heirs. What was true then is true today.

They did not need to pray the Rosary and then wait for Mary to appear with angels and the Trinity of God. Instead, God met them and us where we are.

Examination of the Rosary

A simple look at the prayers of the Rosary shows that for every prayer addressed to God, there are about eight to nine times as many prayers addressed to Mary—principally the *Hail Marys.* The only other prayers are the six *Lord's Prayers* and the six *Glory Bes*. The Apostle's Creed is a statement of faith and is not really a prayer since prayers are a way for us to speak to and praise God.

The Hail Mary

A significant part of the Rosary is taken up by the Hail Mary, which we have briefly examined. This prayer constitutes 80 percent of the prayers of the Rosary.

The Hail Mary is often said as penance after confession to a priest. In writings used to promote the prayer, it is claimed that a young boy told his Protestant mother that the Hail Mary can be found in the Bible. While it is true that the first part of the prayer is in the Bible, it is simply an address and message from the angel to Mary. It was not a prayer, and nothing else that is similar in the Bible is used like that. There are many comparative words from scripture:

> The Lord's call to Abram to leave his country and people and to go to a distant land: *"I will make you into a great nation, and I will bless you; I will make your name great, and you will be a blessing. I will bless those who bless you, and whoever curses you I will curse; and all peoples on earth will be blessed through you."* (Gen 12:2–3)

The beginning of the angel's address to Gideon: *"The LORD is with you, mighty warrior."* (Judg 6:12)

What we have not done was to have made those words into prayers as has been done with the angel's address to Mary.

Further, the second part of the prayer is not from the Bible—and it contains many very unscriptural messages.

The first part of the prayer, from "*Hail Mary*" until "*Blessed is the Fruit of thy womb, Jesus,*" recounts the words of the angel Gabriel in his address to Mary. This address was to announce the first coming of our Lord Jesus, as a human, to this earth, which He created, and the special role Mary was given in His incarnation.

Jesus's incarnation was a one-time event—as was the angel Gabriel's address to Mary. This address was never meant to have been turned into a prayer for followers of Jesus.

"*Hail Mary*" was the greeting or salutation more in the way of "*Greetings, Mary*" or "*Rejoice, Mary*" rather than "*Hail Caesar,*" which would have been made by commoners while bowing down to one who was superior.

"*Full of grace*" is more correctly translated as "*highly favoured one*" or "*you who have been graced with much favour,*" which attribute the favor as coming from God.

"*The Lord is with thee*" and "*Blessed art thou amongst women*" reflect the favor that God had bestowed upon Mary in choosing her for the incarnation of Christ Jesus. The term "blessed" was used to describe the special position and favor God had given her as one who is blessed by God. Its meaning has changed over time so that many who pray this prayer seem to use the term to mean "worthy of adoration, worship, or honor," especially in praying the Rosary.

"*Blessed is the fruit of thy womb, Jesus*" has been the experience of all faithful believers since Pentecost.

God's Word says that each believer who has surrendered to the Lordship of Jesus becomes in-filled with the Holy Spirit when he is born of the Spirit. Scripture also says that this spirit is Christ in us.[111] Many Christians seem to fail to accept this basic yet entirely profound truth of the Christian experience. To know and live by the Spirit is a radically life-changing experience, which Jesus described as being "born again" and "born of the Spirit."[112] With Christ in her from the time the Spirit covered her until the birth of Christ, Mary was the precursor and example of what each member of the born-again church was to be: a carrier of Christ in the world.

Believers were never expected to spend time looking back into the past to someone else's experience of having God within them—even if it was Mary.

Unlike the first part of the prayer, the second part is not taken from scripture. This part begins with the words "*Holy Mary*."

Jesus had replied to the man who had called Him good, "***There is only One who is good. If you want to enter life, keep the commandments"*** (Matt 19:17). In the prayer that Jesus taught us, we address and rightly give honor to God the Father when we say, "***Our Father in heaven, hallowed be your name"*** (Matt 6:9). God's name—and His name alone—is holy.

The following verse, "*Mother of God,*" was a title conferred to Mary in AD 431 at the Council of Ephesus—to which not all agreed. Jesus, in His *human nature,* did not have an earthly father; Jesus, in His *divine nature,* did not have a heavenly mother.

Finally, the last verse "*Pray for us sinners, now and at the hour of our death, amen,*" is far removed from scripture. The only reference in scripture to there being prayer from heaven to those on earth is when we are told that Jesus intercedes for us to His Father in heaven. He is the One mediator between man and God. In the new covenant in His blood, we are no longer referred to as *sinners;* we are "the redeemed." It is written of those saved by the blood of the

[111] Acts 16:7; Rom 8:9; Phil 1:19.

[112] John 3:5–8.

Lamb that God remembers our sin no more—as far as the East is from the West. In the Hail Mary, though, we are still called sinners.

To continue praying this prayer is to deny our status as the redeemed paid for by the blood of Christ and to surrender to our fallen, unredeemed state as sinners:

> *Once you were alienated from God and were enemies in your minds because of your evil behaviour. But now he has reconciled you by Christ's physical body through death to present you holy in his sight, without blemish and free from accusation—if you continue in your faith, established and firm, and do not move from the hope held out in the gospel. This is the gospel that you heard and that has been proclaimed to every creature under heaven, and of which I, Paul, have become a servant.* (Col 1:21–23)
>
> *So if the Son sets you free, you will be free indeed.* (John 8:36)[113]

In truth, the Hail Mary is just one of many prayers directed toward Mary. The chapter "*Giving Themselves Completely Over to Her,*" in part III of this book, shows what going down the road of praying to her leads to: you could take every prayer and substitute the name Mary with Jesus, and it would still be recognized as a legitimate prayer. The fact that such substitution could be done shows these to be idolatrous prayers because, in the prayers, Jesus and His preeminent and exclusive position and authority *is* substituted with Mary.

[113] Further scriptures that confirm this truth include Rom 4:7–8; Rom 5:1–2, 9–11; Rom 8:1–4; 1 Cor 1:8; 2; Cor 3:14–18; Gal 5:16–18; Eph 1:4–8; Col 1:20; Heb 10:22; 2 Pet 1:3.

Honoring Mary

Adherents to the Rosary use the argument that all prayers directed to Mary are simply "*honoring*" her. However the kind of "honoring" that is carried out is indiscernible from worship. We honor our parents, but we would never think of honoring them the way that Mary is "honored" because it is "worship" under the cloak of the catchword "honor."

> *Jesus said to him, **"Away from me, Satan! For it is written: 'Worship the Lord your God, and serve him only.'"*** (Matt 4:10)

Scripture explicitly warns us not to bow down to worship any men or angels:

> *As Peter entered the house, Cornelius met him and fell at his feet in reverence. But Peter made him get up. "Stand up," he said, "I am only a man myself."* (Acts 10:25–26)

> *At this I fell at his feet to worship him* (an angel). *But he said to me, "Don't do that! I am a fellow servant with you and with your brothers and sisters who hold to the testimony of Jesus. Worship God! For it is the Spirit of prophecy who bears testimony to Jesus."* (Rev 19:10)

> *But the LORD, who brought you up out of Egypt with mighty power and outstretched arm, is the one you must worship. To him you shall bow down and to him offer sacrifices.* (2 Kgs 17:36)

A Meditation Centered on Christ

Believers are taught that the Rosary "is a prayer centered on Christ." This is the title of an article published by the *National Catholic Register*, a national Catholic newspaper of the United States based on writings from the Vatican Archives of November 9, 2003.[114] Pope John Paul II proclaimed October 2002 to the following October to be "the Year of the Rosary." While JPII might not have claimed the Rosary to be the meditation centered on Christ, it did not stop the Vatican or Catholic newspapers from making the claim.

By simply counting the number of prayers in the Rosary, it can be seen that the Rosary centers on Mary, rather than God, and the *Hail Mary* prayer is the main part.

To His followers and any who would follow Him, Jesus said, "***Come to Me.***"[115] He is the source of life and the embodiment of God Himself. Mercy comes from His mercy seat, which is occupied by Him alone.

Writers such as Dave Armstrong (Biblical Evidence for Catholicism),[116] when questioned about the "Marian-centric aspect of the Rosary," claim 90 percent of the Rosary is "90 percent Christ, 10 percent Mary." The reasoning behind this is that the believer, while piously reciting each "decade" (consisting of the preliminary Introduction called a "Mystery," one Lord's Prayer, ten Hail Marys, and one Glory Be), is meant to "meditate" on the Mysteries while mouthing the words of the decade, which principally consists of Hail Marys.

These introductions, also called "Mysteries," are listed below. There are five decades in the Rosary, and there are five separate introductions. For each "season" of the church calendar year, there

---

[114] https://www.ncregister.com/site/article/the_Rosary_a_prayer_centered_on_christ.

[115] Matt 11:28; 19:14; Mark 10:14; Luke 18:16; John 5:40; 6:37, 44, 65; 7:37.

[116] Is the Rosary Christ-Centred https://www.patheos.com/blogs/davearmstrong/2016/05/is-the-Rosary-christ-centered.html.

are separate sets of Mysteries. Each set consists of five Mysteries, corresponding to the five decades that are to be recited.

For instance, at Advent (toward Christmas), while reciting the first decade (one Our Father followed by ten Hail Marys and one Glory Be), the one who prays is meant to imagine the event of the angel Gabriel announcing to Mary that she has been chosen as the vessel for the birth of a Chosen One of God.

These introductions are as follows and depend on the season the church has deemed them to be:

Season 1: The Joyful Mysteries (Advent)

- The Annunciation: by the Angel Gabriel of the chosen place Mary has in the entry of the Redeemer into this world
- The Visitation: of Mary to her cousin Elizabeth when she was pregnant with the prophet John the Baptist
- The Nativity: the birth of Jesus
- The Presentation: of the child Jesus at the temple for the first time
- The Finding in the Temple: when Jesus was lost and was found by Joseph and Mary to be teaching the rabbis

Season 2: The Luminous Mysteries

- The Baptism in the Jordan: when the Father declared Jesus to be His beloved Son
- The Wedding at Cana: when Christ performs His first public miracle of turning the water into wine
- The Proclamation of the Kingdom: when Jesus tells the kingdom of God is near and calls on people to repent and believe
- The Transfiguration: of Christ at the Mount of Transfiguration
- The Institution of the Eucharist: when Jesus has the Last Supper with His disciples

Season 3: The Sorrowful Mysteries (Easter)

- The Agony in the Garden: when Jesus suffers when praying the night before the first Good Friday.
- The Scourging at the Pillar
- The Crowning of Thorns
- The Carrying of the Cross
- The Crucifixion

Season 4: the Glorious Mysteries

- The Resurrection
- The Ascension
- The Descent of the Holy Spirit
- The Assumption: of Mary into heaven. This was a belief that was only defined as dogma by the Catholic Church as recently as 1950
- The Coronation: when Mary is crowned queen of heaven and earth

These introductions are supposedly meant to lead those who pray to meditate on the subject matter while praying the decades. So, those who pray the Rosary are supposed to somehow be meditating on the subjects of the introduction while their lips recite the prayers. This is the basis of the claim that the Rosary centers on Christ. No prayer in scripture follows such a model:

- The believer is supposed to pray to a created being.
- The believer is supposed to pray based on recitation rather than being led by the Spirit in the moment. When His disciples asked Jesus *how* to pray, He taught them according to *how* and not *what*, giving them the example we now refer to as the Lord's Prayer.

- One speaks words while trying to hold in one's mind aspects from the Gospels and beyond that are disconnected from the words.
- It is not about communicating with God in the here and now; it is about imagining a past event while reciting words of a prayer.

What's the Harm in Praying the Rosary?

It is Prayer Centred on A Created Being

All Scripture Teaches That We Should Only Pray to God

God created us in His image and likeness to be in relationship with Him. In Adam, He made mankind to rule over all of His creation and to spend time with Him as He demonstrated by walking and conversing with Adam and Eve in the garden. Even when mankind fell, He was patient and prepared the way for His Son to redeem us and restore us into right relationship with Him. From Him, we came—and to Him, we return.

Prayer is spending time relating to God in the first relationship we ever had and will ever have.

When the disciples asked Jesus to teach them how to pray, He taught them the prayer we now know as the Lord's Prayer, which is sometimes called the "Our Father." Jesus taught His disciples the prayer as an example and as a perfect structure of prayer of opening up to God; it was not simply a prayer to be learned by rote and repeated. Over the centuries, it was turned to rote, and it was even reduced to a rite of penance to be repeated (akin to punishment) after confession of sin.

The Lord's Prayer appears six times in the sequence of prayers recited in the Rosary, but the Hail Mary is recited almost nine times as often. Each time someone prays to one other than God, it is time and petition that is taken away from God.

Scripture Warns Us Never to Pray or Bow Down to Any Created Being

Prayer was never taught in the Bible to be directed to any created being, and such a practice is called *idolatry*, which was strictly forbidden by God.

There are many times when God has warned us not to address those who have passed on or to bow down before any created being. The warning covers both the natural and the supernatural. King Saul's attempt to seek divination from the prophet Samuel who had already died is an example of such prayer in the natural (1 Sam 28:13–19; 1 Chr 10:13–14). The apostle John's encounters with angels in the heavenly realm is an example of such bowing down in the supernatural (i.e. in the vision of John). In response, the angel warns John not to do such a thing (Rev 19:10; Rev 22:8–9).

However, Liguori repeatedly gave examples of some of such idolatrous teachings in *The Glories*:

> *And who can describe, says Blosius, the goodness, the mercy, the fidelity, and the charity with which this our mother strives to save us, when we invoke her aid? Let us prostrate ourselves, then, says St. Bernard, before this good mother, let us cling to her sacred feet, and leave her not until she gives us her blessing, and accepts us for her children.* (Liguori 74–75)

> *If my boldness is great, greater still is thy goodness, which seeks the most miserable to console them. In this, thy goodness, I trust. May it be to thy eternal glory that thou hast saved from hell a miserable wretch, and brought him to thy kingdom, where I hope to console myself by being always at thy feet to thank, bless, and love thee throughout eternity. Oh Mary, I wait for thee, do not leave*

me then disconsolate. Come, come. Amen, amen. (Liguori *114)*

Numerous examples of such prayers are documented in part III of this book in the chapters "The End Fruit: The Substitution of God" and "The End Fruit: Giving Themselves Completely Over to Her."

We Should Never Try To Get Around God

One reason why believers pray to the spirit they believe to be Mary is that, by doing so, many hope to get a *more favorable response* than what they imagine they might get from God Our Father. In the chapters "Mary as Our Only Advocate" and "Advocate Preferable to Jesus", Liguori quoted many teachings that expressly advocated approaching Mary as preferable to approaching Jesus.

This was a teaching that did not originate from the Word of God but rather from man.

Here are a couple of examples from *The Glories*:

> *What fear, says St. Bernard, can the wretched have of going to this queen of mercy since she never shows herself terrible or austere to those who seek her, but all sweetness and kindness? Mary not only gives, but she herself presents to us milk and wool: the milk of mercy to inspire us with confidence, and wool to shield us from the thunderbolts of divine justice!* (Liguori 32)

> *Oh, wretched are those who do not love thee, and who, having it in their power to seek help of thee, do not trust in thee! He who does not implore the aid of Mary is lost: but who has ever been lost that had recourse to her?* (Liguori 136)

So, many turn to Mary in prayer because many teachers have portrayed God as a hard-to-please judge who is not generous with His mercy. Mary, on the other hand, is portrayed as all sweetness and mercy as shown in the chapter "God Made to Appear as Angry but Mary as Merciful."

A Holy Spirit-led believer, on the other hand, will recognize that God is love and that all righteousness and mercy proceed from Him—even the righteousness of Mary.

It is our fallen human nature that always seeks to avoid facing up to admitting our mistakes and sin. Adam, Cain, and King David demonstrated this. Our only hope is going to God and confessing our sin:

> *If we confess our sins, he is faithful and just and will forgive us our sins and purify us from all unrighteousness.* (1 John 1:9)

Jesus Always Told His Followers to Come to Him and Pray to His Father

Jesus never taught anyone to seek His mother. He taught His followers to pray to God numerous times and that whoever saw Him saw the Father. Hence, we can pray to God, Father, and Son. He did not say to go to any other but Him because *in Him,* we have *all things.*

Jesus Also Pointed Us to a Relationship with the Holy Spirit and Not to His Earthly Mother

He told His followers to wait for the Holy Spirit who would come and give them power and be with them until the end of age. He did not tell them to wait for His mother.

We are told that the Holy Spirit is the one we are to walk with, receive guidance from, and receive God's gifts from. All the teachings about Mary place her as *the one* with whom our relationship should be and not the Holy Spirit. This is covered more fully in the chapter "Instead of the Holy Spirit" in part III of this book.

Focusing on the Past Experience of Another and Not on the Here and Now

Each prayer to Mary exalts her in a way that completely ignores the place we have in Christ.

Repeating the Rosary is analogous to a child constantly saying that his elder brother John is especially loved by his mother and father. Each day he might say, "Dad loves John, and Mom loves John. John is specially chosen by Dad and Mom. No one is closer to Dad and Mom than John." In doing so, he fails to realize that in Dad and Mom's eyes, he is just as much loved as John.

Mary having Christ in her womb was foretold in the angel's message: "blessed is the fruit of your womb." This one-time event likely foreshadowed New Testament believers (today's believers included) having the Holy Spirit in them. Believers have "carried" the Lord in them ever since.

"Blessed is the fruit of thy womb, Jesus" is recognition of the one-time event when Mary bore Jesus. Today, every *born-again by the Spirit* believer carries the Holy Spirit in them in a way foreshadowed by Mary carrying Jesus.

To recognize this is to realize the incredible gift we have been given; something the Old Testament prophets hoped for but never received. Jesus foretold this when He said, ***"I tell you, among those born of women there is no one greater than John; yet the one who is least in the kingdom of God is greater than he"*** (Luke 7:28).

To constantly go back to the one-time event of the first century and not recognize that, today and now, we have the responsibility and have been given the privilege of hosting the Holy Spirit and living in gratitude is to miss out on living our gifted birthright as New Covenant believers.

Believers today are meant to be fully conscious, receptive, and obedient to this Holy Spirit in them. This is called "walking in the Spirit." When followers recite the Hail Mary, they look back at the past and take their eyes off what should be their present experience of "blessed is the Spirit in them."

Replacement of True Prayer

The main problem with the Rosary, however, is that it replaces true communication with God.

In any loving relationship, communication is likely the most important ingredient. Love is patient and kind, but if love is not communicated, how does the recipient know there is love? Jesus died to save mankind, but unless the Gospel of His love was preached, how could mankind know of and respond to the love of a God who sacrificed Himself for us?

Prayer is communicating with God. As with all two-way communication, it is a two-way conversation. A marriage where a man, instead of conversing with his wife daily, recites to her an unvarying litany prepared by someone else is doomed to failure. This is regardless of how poetic or meaningful the words may be. We would never think of doing this to our spouses, children, or others, yet many do this to God who in the cool of the evening visited with Adam daily to talk with him.

When I am told of someone who underwent a severe crisis and then, in their despair, protested to God of the unfairness of it all even in anger, I eagerly await the rest of the story. Invariably, from the stories told to me at least, the stories end with an epiphany for the person: God meeting them in some unexpected way and them being either comforted or humbled. This only happens when the one who is upset approaches God honestly with all their pain laid bare and does not vent to others as the ancient children of Israel did with their grumblings.

The Rosary replaces honest and sincere communication—whether praise from the heart, joy, self-doubt, anguish, or sorrow. When we pray from the heart, we come into the presence of God, and as we share from our hearts, He responds.

> *Come near to God and He will come near to you.*
> (Jas 4:8)

Honest, heartfelt communication results in the Holy Spirit moving in us who are Spirit-filled believers. The Holy Spirit is a person and should be treated with at least such dignity and reverence and not bombarded with countless recitations.

One who recites the Rosary believes that it actually is prayer, and so the one who is devoted spends much time in such practice rather than pouring out their hearts and souls to the Lord in open and honest communication.

Instead, each prayer recited of the Rosary is one prayer less that should have been directed to God. Every moment meditating on the merits of Mary is another moment that should have been spent allowing the Holy Spirit to mold and transform a believer into the image of Christ.

> ***True worshippers will worship the Father in the Spirit and in truth, for they are the kind of worshippers the Father seeks. (John 4:23)***

We tend to not think of God as One who seeks worship yet Jesus who knew the Father intimately taught us that God seeks our intimacy. *In Spirit* and *in truth* embodies honest and heartfelt one-to-one communication; not the kind of mental or spiritual gymnastics required to be saying one thing while holding a different thought.

APPENDIX 12

ADDITIONAL MATERIAL FOR GOD BEING MADE TO APPEAR AS ANGRY BUT MARY AS MERCIFUL

The example story at the end of the chapter appears below in full:

> *The blessed John Erolto, who, through humility, called himself the disciple, relates, that there was once a married man who lived in disgrace in the sight of God. His wife, a virtuous woman, not being able to induce him to abandon his vicious courses, entreated him that at least, while he was in so miserable a condition, he would offer this devotion to the mother of God, namely, to say a "Hail Mary" every time he passed before her altar. He accordingly began to practise this devotion.*
>
> *One night, when he was about to commit a sin, he saw a light, and, on closer observation, perceived that it was a lamp burning before a holy image of the blessed Virgin, who held the infant Jesus in her arms. He said a "Hail Mary" as usual; but what did he*

see? He saw the infant covered with wounds, and fresh blood flowing from them. Both terrified and moved in his feelings, he remembered that he himself too had wounded his Redeemer by his sins, and began to weep, but he observed that the child turned away from him. In deep confusion, he had recourse to the most holy Virgin, saying: "Mother of mercy, thy Son rejects me; I can find no advocate more kind and more powerful than thou, who art his mother; my queen, aid me, and pray to him in my behalf." The divine mother answered him from that image: "You sinners call me mother of mercy, but yet you do not cease to make me mother of misery, renewing the passion of my Son, and my dolors." But because Mary never sends away disconsolate those who cast themselves at her feet, she began to entreat her Son that he would pardon that miserable sinner. Jesus continued to show himself unwilling to grant such a pardon, but the holy Virgin, placing the infant in the niche, prostrated herself before him, saying: "My Son, I will not leave thy feet until thou hast pardoned this sinner."

> *"My Mother," answered Jesus, "I can deny thee nothing; dost thou wish for his pardon? for love of thee I will pardon him. Let him come and kiss my wounds." The sinner approached, weeping bitterly, and as he kissed the wounds of the infant, they were healed. Then Jesus embraced him as a sign of pardon. He changed his conduct, led a holy life, and was ever full of love to the blessed Virgin, who had obtained for him so great a favor.* (Liguori 139–140)

Scripture tells us that Jesus is at the right hand of God the Father in heaven.[117] Believers have no reason to doubt that Mary is in heaven too.

[117] Matt 22:44; Mark 16:19; Luke 22:69; Acts 2:33; 7:55–56; 8:34; Eph 1:20; Col 3:1; Heb 1:3; 8:1, 10:12: 2; 1 Pet 3:22.

Heaven in not a place of tears or wounds. The King of kings and Lord of lords is not at the mercy of our sin to be inflicted with wounds each time we sin. At Calvary, He willingly received the wounds to cover the penalty for our sin as well as our sicknesses and infirmities. He paid that price *once and for all.*[118] Upon completing His sacrifice, He said, "***It is finished***" (John 19:30).

118 Rom 6:8–10; Heb 7:27; 9:12, 25; 10:10; 1 Pet 3:18.

APPENDIX 13
DIVINE AUTHORITY

> *In order to comprehend, the greatness to which Mary was elevated, it would be necessary to comprehend the sublime majesty and grandeur of God. It is sufficient, then, only to say, that God made this Virgin his mother, to have it understood that God could not exalt her more than he did exalt her. Rightly did St. Arnold Carnotensis affirm, that God, by making himself the Son of the Virgin, established her in superior rank to all the saints and angels: "Maria constituta est, -super oranem Creaturam." So that, next to God, she is incomparably higher than the celestial spirits, as St. Ephrem asserts: "Nullacomparatione caeteris superis est gloriosior." St. Andrew of Crete confirms this, saying: God excepted, she is the higest (sic) of all: "Excepto Deo, omnibus est altior." And St. Anselm also says: Oh Lady, there is none equal to thee, because every other, is above or beneath thee; God alone is superior to thee, and all others are inferior.* (Liguori 423)

God did exalt Mary by giving her the singular position of mother in His incarnation—a position that could never be challenged or equaled—but this does not necessarily mean she was given *authority* over all of creation as these writers assert.

Liguori and the others conclude that so little is written about Mary in the Gospels because, with regard to her merits, *"it was not necessary for them to describe each separately"* (Liguori 424).

> *So great is the authority of mothers over their children that although they may be monarchs, having absolute dominion over all the persons in their kingdom, yet their mothers can never become subject to them.* (Liguori 200)

> *St. Ambrose even says, that Jesus Christ having deigned to make Mary his mother, was obliged as her son to obey her. And therefore, observes Richard of St. Laurence, it is said of the other saints, that they are with God; but of Mary alone can it be said, that not only was it her lot to be subject to the will of God, but that God was also subject to her will. And as it is said of the other holy virgins, as the same author remarks, that they follow the divine lamb wherever he goes: "seqmmtur agnum quocumque ierit" of the Virgin Mary it may be said, that the divine Lamb followed her on this earth, having become subject to her.* (Liguori 200–201)

Jesus allowed Himself to be subject to the will of Joseph and Mary in His youth. The Gospels appear to show that He separated Himself from the mothering of Mary during His ministry years. This was written of the event when Mary together with his brothers came to bring Him home—evidently believing He was out of his mind as documented in Mark 3: 20–21, 31–35. The same event is also written in Matthew 12:46–50 and Luke 19–21.

> *A woman in the crowd called out, "Blessed is the mother who gave you birth and nursed you." He*

*replied, "**Blessed rather are those who hear the Word of God and obey it.**"* (Luke 11:27–28)

Liguori:

> *Hence we may say, that though Mary is in heaven, and can no longer command her Son, yet her prayers will ever be the prayers of a mother, and therefore most powerful to obtain whatever she asks. Mary, says St. Bonaventure, has this privilege with her Son, that she is most powerful to obtain by her prayers whatsoever she will. And wherefore? Precisely for the reason which we have before mentioned, and which we will now examine more fully, namely, because the prayers of Mary are the prayers of a mother. And therefore, says St. Peter Damian, the Virgin has all power in heaven as on earth, being able to raise to the hope of salvation even the most despairing. And then he adds, that when the mother asks any favor for us of Jesus Christ (called by the saint the altar of mercy where sinners obtain pardon from God), the Son has so great regard for the prayers of Mary, and so great a desire to please her, that when she prays, she seems to command rather that request, and to be a mistress rather than a handmaid. Thus Jesus would honor this his dear mother, who has honored him so much in her life, by granting her immediately whatever she asks and desires. St. Germanus beautifully confirms this by saying to the Virgin: Thou art mother of God, omnipotent to save sinners, and needest no other recommendation with God, since thou art the mother of true life. St. Bernardine of Sienna does not hesitate to say that all obey the commands of Mary, even God himself; signifying by these words, that God listens to her*

> <u>prayers as though they were commands</u>. (Liguori 201–202)

Richard and others assume that the same relationships, including motherhood, apply in heaven as they do on earth. Jesus, however, teaches us that this is not so when the Sadducees tried to ask which of seven brothers would a woman who had married all in turn be the wife of in heaven:

> ***At the resurrection people will neither marry nor be given in marriage; they will be like the angels in heaven.*** (Matt 22:23–32 and Mark 12:18–27).

Likewise, it is never written that we, as believers, are God's grandchildren or great-grandchildren. Instead, we are all *His children*.

There are, apparently, different relationship dynamics operating in heaven than on earth. To elevate Mary to a position where her Creator accedes to her every request is beyond unjustified. The Creator, Jesus, is unique and above all in every way:

> *Before me was one like a son of man, coming with the clouds of heaven. He approached the Ancient of Days and was led into his presence. He was given authority, glory and sovereign power; all nations and peoples of every language worshiped him. His dominion is an everlasting dominion that will not pass away, and his kingdom is one that will never be destroyed.* (Dan 7:13–14)

> *Then Jesus came to them and said,* ***"All authority in heaven and on earth has been given to me."*** (Matt 28:18)

All things have been committed to me by my Father. No one knows who the Son is except the Father, and no one knows who the Father is except the Son and those to whom the Son chooses to reveal him. (Luke 10:22)

After Jesus said this, he looked toward heaven and prayed: ***"Father, the hour has come. Glorify your Son, that your Son may glorify you. For you granted him authority over all people that he might give eternal life to all those you have given him. Now this is eternal life: that they know you, the only true God, and Jesus Christ, whom you have sent."*** *(John 17:1–3)*

He raised Christ from the dead and seated him at his right hand in the heavenly realms, far above all rule and authority, power and dominion, and every name that is invoked, not only in the present age but also in the one to come. And God placed all things under his feet and appointed him to be head over everything for the church, which is his body, the fullness of him who fills everything in every way. (Eph 1:20–23)

For in Christ all the fullness of the Deity lives in bodily form, and in Christ you have been brought to fullness. He is the head over every power and authority. (Col 2:9–10)

For as in Adam all die, so in Christ all will be made alive. But each in turn: Christ, the firstfruits; then, when he comes, those who belong to him. Then the end will come, when he hands over the kingdom to God the Father after he has destroyed all dominion, authority

> *and power. For he must reign until he has put all his enemies under his feet.* (1 Cor 15:22–25)

> *To the only God our Savior be glory, majesty, power and authority, through Jesus Christ our Lord, before all ages, now and forevermore! Amen.* (Jude 1:25)

As God is above His creation, He is not limited to operating within time and space as we are. This is why prophecy always revealed that which was to come—both because God is able to direct events but also because He sees the end from the beginning. We can read the book of Revelation today of things that have not yet come to pass but will come to pass.

Biblical prophecy does not in any way agree with what Liguori and others claim about Mary. This is especially so in their descriptions of her throne, authority, and glory, but it paints a vivid picture of the complete authority, wisdom, and power of our loving God. He is forever to be praised.

APPENDIX 14

ADDITIONAL MATERIAL FOR ANOTHER GOSPEL

The following are some of the answers found in scripture for the "Questions that Must be Answered."

Are We Sinners or—as Believers—Are We the Redeemed of God?

Those who have placed their trust in the finished work of Christ Jesus and walk with His Spirit are already the redeemed of God.

> ***Very truly I tell you, whoever hears my word and believes him who sent me has eternal life and will not be judged but has crossed over from death to life.*** (John 5:24)

> *Therefore, there is now no condemnation for those who are in Christ Jesus, because through Christ Jesus the law of the Spirit who gives life has set you free from the law of sin and death. (Rom 8:1–2)*

See also John 3:36; 6:47; Acts 2:21; 16:29–34; Rom 1:16–17; 5:1–2; 6:5–7, 22–23; 8:1–4, 14–17; 2 Cor 1:21–22; 4:14; 5:1–5; Gal 4:4–7; Eph 1:13–14; 2:4–8; Col 3:1–4; Heb 9:12; 10:8–10, 14–18; 1 John 1:8–10.

How Can We Know We Are the Redeemed?

God spoke to us in our hearts when we believed and assured us by placing His Spirit as the seal of our redemption (see preceding scriptures). Believing God—who has spoken all these promises—we live by faith in His Word (both in scripture and when He speaks to us through His Spirit telling us we can call Him Father).

> *Being confident of this, that he (God) who began a good work in you will carry it on to completion until the day of Christ Jesus.* (Phil 1:6)

> *Now faith is confidence in what we hope for and assurance about what we do not see.* (Heb 11:1)

> *However, to the one who does not work but trusts God who justifies the ungodly, their faith is credited as righteousness.* (Rom 4:5)

It is never a question of how *much* faith we have—but rather we are to *exercise* the faith He has placed in us, which will thereby grow. God put in us the faith we have, so what faith we have is sufficient for our journey thus far, and if we allow scripture and the Holy Spirit to work in us, then our faith will grow.

> *And let us run with perseverance the race marked out for us, fixing our eyes on Jesus, the pioneer* (or author) *and perfecter of faith.* (Heb 12:1–2)

And without faith it is impossible to please God, because anyone who comes to him must believe that he exists and that he rewards those who earnestly seek him. (Heb 11:6)

Can We Successfully Complete the Race Set before Us?

We can successfully complete the race by submitting our lives to Him, keeping our eyes fixed on Him, allowing His Word and His Spirit to guide us in all things, and following all He instructs us to do.

So then, just as you received Christ Jesus as Lord, continue to live your lives in him, rooted and built up in him, strengthened in the faith as you were taught, and overflowing with thankfulness. (Col 2:6–7)

So, as the Holy Spirit says: "Today, if you hear his voice, do not harden your hearts as you did in the rebellion, during the time of testing in the wilderness, where your ancestors tested and tried me, though for forty years they saw what I did." (Heb 3:7–9)

Therefore, since we are surrounded by such a great cloud of witnesses, let us throw off everything that hinders and the sin that so easily entangles. And let us run with perseverance the race marked out for us, fixing our eyes on Jesus, the pioneer and perfecter of faith. For the joy set before him he endured the cross, scorning its shame, and sat down at the right hand of the throne of God. Consider him who endured such opposition from sinners, so that you will not grow weary and lose heart. (Heb 12:1–3)

Do We Lack Anything from God to Live Full Lives in Christ?

As the redeemed of God, we have been given everything we need for a life of fullness in Christ. We even have the very Spirit of God in us. With that we need no other spirit.

> *His divine power has given us everything we need for a godly life through our knowledge of him who called us by his own glory and goodness.* (2 Pet 1:3)

See also 1 Cor 1:4–7; 2 Pet 1:3–4; Luke 11:9–10; John 10:10; Eph 1:3

Have We Been Left as Orphans?

With God as our Father and with the Spirit of God in us, we are sons and daughters of the Most High. (See Rom 8:14–16, 23; Eph 1:5; Gal 3:26–27; 4:5; Phil 2:15; 1 John 3:1–2.)

Since we have His Spirit with us until the end of the age, we are never alone. (See John 14:16; 2 Cor 13:5; Gal 4:6; Eph 3:16–19; 5:18–20; 2 Tim 1:14; 1 John 3:24; 4:13; Heb 13:5.)

In the most direct language possible, Jesus said that He would not leave us as orphans. (See John 14:15–21.)

How Do We Overcome Sin and Temptation?

We overcome sin and temptation by fixing our eyes on Jesus and walking with His Spirit.

> *So I say, walk by the Spirit, and you will not gratify the desires of the flesh.* (Gal 5:16)

See also Rom 6:11–14; 7:15–8:2, 9; 1 Cor 1:4–9; Gal 5:16–18, 22–23; 2 Tim 1:7; Heb 12:1–2; 1 John 1:9.

We overcome sin and temptation by resisting the devil whenever he tempts:

> *Submit yourselves, then, to God. Resist the devil, and he will flee from you. Come near to God and he will come near to you. Wash your hands, you sinners, and purify your hearts, you double-minded.* (Jas 4:7–8)

How Do We Become Holy?

We do not become holy by striving or keeping the commandments. Instead, it is by faith in the finished work of Christ. This faith comes from God; He is both Author and Finisher of our salvation.

> *For it is by grace you have been saved, through faith—and this is not from yourselves, it is the gift of God—not by works, so that no one can boast.* (Eph 2:8–9)

See also Rom 3:20–25, 27–31; 5:1–2; 9:30–33; Gal 2:15–16, 21

Holiness is a product of dying to ourselves, abiding in His Spirit, and living in the way of His guidance.

> *Now the Lord is the Spirit, and where the Spirit of the Lord is, there is freedom. And we all, who with unveiled faces contemplate the Lord's glory, are being transformed into his image with ever-increasing glory, which comes from the Lord, who is the Spirit.* (2 Cor 3:17–18)

See also Rom 7:6; 8:1–11; 1 Cor 1:8; 2 Cor 1:21–22; 3:14–18; 7:1; Gal 3:1–3; Eph 2:19–22; Phil 1:6; 2 Thess 2:13–14; Heb 12:1–3; 1 Pet 1:1–2; 2 Pet 1:3; 1 John 1:9.

We become holy by believing, reading and living in His Word.

> *For I am not ashamed of the gospel, because it is the power of God that brings salvation to everyone who believes: first to the Jew, then to the Gentile. For in the gospel the righteousness of God is revealed—a righteousness that is by faith from first to last, just as it is written: "The righteous will live by faith."* (Rom 1:16–17)

See also John 17:17; Acts 20:32; Eph 5:25–27; Col 1:22–23; Heb 10:26–27.

Living in His Word means following what He tells us to do. The primary commandment He told us was to love God and our neighbors. Having died to sin, we are to live for God out of love and not because we are trying to earn our salvation.

See Mark 12:29–31; 2 Cor 5:9–10, 15; Eph 2:8–9.

Who Is the Holy Spirit and What Part Should He Play in Our Lives?

Please see the chapter "The Holy Spirit—God with Us."

How Should Believers Live Their Lives?

As followers of Jesus, we should firstly follow the commands He gave us. Jesus never told us anything that He Himself did not do.

> ***Why do you call me, "Lord, Lord," and do not do what I say?*** (Luke 6:46)

His commands also come with promises:

> ***If you keep my commands, you will remain in my love, just as I have kept my Father's commands and remain in his love. I have told you this so that my joy may be in you and that your joy may be complete.*** (John 15:10–11)

See also Matt 7:21–23, 24–27; 12:49–50; 18:17; 25:34–40; 28:19–20; Mark 3:35; 16:15–18; Luke 6:46–49; 8:21; 11:27–28; 12:42–48; John 6:29, 40; 7:17–19; 8:31–32, 51; 12:47–50; 13:12–17, 34–35; 14:15, 21, 23–24; 15:10, 12–14, 17, 27; Acts 3:22–23.

Be baptized by water and be born again of the Spirit.

> *Jesus answered,* ***"Very truly I tell you, no one can enter the kingdom of God unless they are born of water and the Spirit. Flesh gives birth to flesh, but the Spirit gives birth to spirit."*** (John 3:5–6)
>
> ***Whoever believes and is baptized will be saved, but whoever does not believe will be condemned.*** (Mark 16:16)

"Baptised with Water" See also Matt 3:6–7, 11, 13–17; 21:31–32; 28:19; Mark 1:4–5, 8–10; Luke 3:3, 7, 12, 16, 21–22; 7:29–30; John 1:24–34; 3: 22–26.

"Filled with or Born of the Spirit" See also Luke 1:11–15, 35, 41, 67; 2:25; 3:16; 4:1; 11:11–13; 12:11–12; 24:49; John 1:33; 3:3–8; 4:10, 13–14, 24; 6:53–63; 7:37–39; 12:24–25; 14:16–20, 26; 15:26; 16:7, 13–15, 27; 20:22.

Love God and love your neighbor.

> *One of them, an expert in the law, tested him with this question: "Teacher, which is the greatest commandment in the Law?"*
>
> *Jesus replied: "'**Love the Lord your God with all your heart and with all your soul and with all your mind.' This is the first and greatest commandment. And the second is like it: 'Love your neighbor as yourself.' All the Law and the Prophets hang on these two commandments."*** (Matt 22:35–40)

See also Matt 5:5–10, 21–28, 38–48; 6:2–4, 12–15; 7:12; 18:4–5, 21–35; 19:16–19; 24:12; Mark 8:1–10; 12:28–31; 12:41–44; Luke 6:27–38; 7:40–48; 10:25–37; John 8:42; 10:17–18; 13:1, 3–17, 34–35; 14:15, 21, 23–24; 15:9–17; 17:20–23–26; 21:15–17.

This includes forgiving one another:

> ***For if you forgive other people when they sin against you, your heavenly Father will also forgive you. But if you do not forgive others their sins, your Father will not forgive your sins.*** (Matt 6:14–15)

See also Matt 6:12; 18:21–35; Mark 11:25–26; Luke 6:27, 35, 37; 11:4; 17:3–4; 23:34; John 20:23.

Repent of your old life.

> ***"The time has come,"*** *he said.* ***"The kingdom of God has come near. Repent and believe the good news!"*** (Mark 1:15)

See also Matt 3:1–2; 4:17; 11:20–24; 12:41; 21:32; Mark 1:4; 2:17; 6:12; Luke 1:16–17; 3:3, 8, 10–14; 6:31–38, 41–42; 7:36–50; 10:13–15; 11:29–32; 13:2–8; 15:; 16:30; 17:3–4; 24:47; John 5:14; 8:11.

Die to living for ourselves.

> *Then Jesus said to his disciples,* ***"Whoever wants to be my disciple must deny themselves and take up their cross and follow me. For whoever wants to save their life will lose it, but whoever loses their life for me will find it. What good will it be for someone to gain the whole world, yet forfeit their soul? Or what can anyone give in exchange for their soul?"*** (Matt 16:24–26)

See also Matt 10:35–39; 16:23–26; 19:29; 23:11; Mark 8:33–38; 10:29–31; 14:36; Luke 5:11, 27–28; 9:23–26; 14:25–35; 17:30–33; 18:29–30; 22:42; John 5:30; 6:38; 10:11, 14–18; 12:24–27; 15:20.

In almost three chapters of the Gospel of Matthew, from chapter 5:1–7:27, Jesus tells us how to live for others.

Live fearlessly, holding firmly to faith in God.

> ***Peace I leave with you; my peace I give you. I do not give to you as the world gives. Do not let your hearts be troubled and do not be afraid.*** (John 14:27)

See also Matt 6:25–34; 8:26; 10:26–31; 14:27; 14:31; 17:6–7; 24:6; 25:24–30; 28:10; Mark 4:40; 5:33–34, 36; 6:50; Luke 1:12, 74; 2:9–10; 8:36–37, 50; 9:45; 12:4–7, 11–12, 22–26, 32–34; 21:9, 14–15; 24:37–38; John 6:20; 14:1, 27.

This includes remaining steadfast and being always prepared.

See Matt 10:22; 32–33; 38–39; 24:12–13; 24:42–51; 25:13; Mark 13:5–23, 33–37; Luke 12:35–48; 21:8–19, 28–36; John 15:1–10.

Pray always and be thankful for all God has given us.

With prayer and thankfulness, Jesus demonstrated such a life with His disciples.

For prayer, see Matt 6:5–13; 7:7–11; 9:37–38; 18:19; 21:13, 16, 21–22; Mark 1:35; 6:46; 9:25–29; 11:17, 22–26; 13:18; 14:32, 35–36, 39; Luke 5:16; 6:12, 28; 9:16, 18, 28–29; 11:1–13; 18:1–8; 19:46; 21:36; 22:32, 40–46; John 6:23–24, 26; 17:1–26.

For thankfulness, see Mark 8:7; 14:22–23; Luke 2:38; 17:12–18; 19:1–9; 22:17, 19; John 6:11, 23; 1 Thess 5:18.

Seek the kingdom of God.

> ***But seek first his kingdom and his righteousness, and all these things will be given to you as well.*** (Matt 6:33)

> ***Not everyone who says to me, "Lord, Lord," will enter the kingdom of heaven, but only the one who does the will of my Father who is in heaven.*** (Matt 7:21)

See also Matt 4:17; 5:6, 7; 8:10–12, 22; 10:37–39; 12:25–28; 16:27–28; 18:1–4; 19:12, 14, 16–30; 20:20–28; 22:1–14; 23:1–14; 25; Mark 1:15; 8:34–38; 9:1, 33–36, 43–48; 10:13–15, 23–31, 42–45; 12:34; Luke 4:43; 6:20–49; 7:28; 12:16–40; 13:18–30; 15:16; 17:20–37; 18:16–30; 19:1–27; 21:12–19, 31, 34–36; 22:15–18; John 3:3–8.

Be fruitful and advance the kingdom of God.

> ***Therefore go and make disciples of all nations, baptizing them in the name of the Father and of the Son and of the Holy Spirit, and teaching them to obey everything I have commanded you. And surely I am with you always, to the very end of the age.*** (Matt 28:19–20)

> ***Then the King will say to those on his right, "Come, you who are blessed by my Father; take your inheritance, the kingdom prepared for you since the creation of the world. For I was hungry and you gave me something to eat, I was thirsty and you gave me something to drink, I was a stranger and you invited me in, I needed clothes and you clothed me, I was sick and you looked after me, I was in prison and you came to visit me."*** (Matt 25:34–36)

See Matt 3:10; 4:19; 7:19; 9:37–38; 10:7; 13:3–12, 18–33, 37–52; 20:1–16; 21:28–43; 24:13, 45–51; 25:14–30; 34–46; Mark 1:17; 4:2–32; 11:12–14, 20–21; Luke 3:8–9; 5:10; 8:1, 5–18; 9:1–6, 10, 23–25, 27, 59–62; 10:8–12; 11:2, 23; 12:6–9, 16–40, 42–48; 13:6–9; 19:11–27; 22:25–30; John 4:35–38; 12:24; 15:1–8, 16, 18–21; 16:1–4.

Set your eyes on God and your permanent home above—not on earthly things that pass.

> *Then Jesus said to his disciples,* ***"Whoever wants to be my disciple must deny themselves and take up their cross and follow me. For whoever wants to save their life will lose it, but whoever loses their***

> ***life for me will find it. What good will it be for someone to gain the whole world, yet forfeit their soul? Or what can anyone give in exchange for their soul?"*** (Matt 16:24–26)

See Matt 5:19–21, 24; 10:32–33, 40–42; 16:24–27; 19:21, 27–30; Mark 10:21, 29–31; Luke 6:22–23, 27–38; 12:8–9, 14–21, 32–34, 35–40, 42–48; 14:12–14; 16:1–13; 18:18–30; 21:1–4, 34–36; John 6:26–29; Heb 12:1–2; 10:19–27.

Meet Together in Unity of Fellowship.

> *And let us consider how we may spur one another on toward love and good deeds, not giving up meeting together, as some are in the habit of doing, but encouraging one another—and all the more as you see the Day approaching.* (Heb 10:24-25)

See John 10:16; 17:11,21-22; Acts 2:1,42,44-47; 3:32-35; 12:12; 13:44; 14:27; 15:30; 20:7; 1 Cor 11:17-26; 33-34.

What are demons? Do they assail us and have power over us such that we should seek to flee to either "mother" or angels?

Demons are fallen angels who took the side of Lucifer when he rebelled against God. While they are powerful, they have no authority over the redeemed of God. We should not fear them.

The main power they have that they employ is fear. That fear causes some to turn to angels or to "Mother Mary" as an alleged buffer against those demons. By giving in to fear, we allow people, spirits, and circumstances to overwhelm us. Scripture, however, teaches us otherwise:

We should not fear anything or anyone. Jesus Himself told us to neither fear nor worry.

See Matt 6:25–34; 8:26; 10:26–31; 14:27; 14:31; 17:6–7; 24:6; 25:24–30; 28:10; Mark 4:40; 5:33–34, 36; 6:50; Luke 1:12, 74; 2:9–10; 8:36–37, 50; 9:45; 12:4–7, 11–12, 22–26, 32–34; 21:9, 14–15; 24:37–38; John 6:20; 14:1, 27.

We have been given God's power over these demons.

See Matt 7:22; 10:5–8; 16:19; 17:16–21; 18:18; Mark 3:14–15; 6:7, 13; 9:17–29, 38–39; 16:17; Luke 9:1, 49–50; 10:17–20.

The Spirit in us is greater than Satan whom the demons follow (2 Cor 3:11).

The Spirit gives us power over fear (Rom 8:15).

And if our faith is still lacking (despite all the above), we have refuge in God our stronghold.

See Dt 33:27; Ru 2:12; 2Sam 22:3; Ps 9:9; 14:6; 28:8; 46:1, 7, 11; 57:1; 59:16; 62:7, 8; 71:3, 7; 92:2, 4, 9; 94:22; 141:8; 142:5; 144:2; Jer 16:19.

What role does Mary play in our present salvation?

Is she the Advocate of God?

> *For there is one God and one mediator between God and mankind, the man Christ Jesus, who gave himself as a ransom for all people.* (1 Tim 2:5–6)

See also John 14:16;26; 15:26; 16:7; Rom 8:27; 1 John 2:1–2; Heb 7:23–25; 8:6; 12:23–24

Our advocate with us on Earth is the Holy Spirit. Scripture does not tell of any other intercessor in heaven but Jesus, and it clearly says that He is the only One.

Is she the seal and pledge of our salvation?

> *Now the one who has fashioned us for this very purpose is God, who has given us the Spirit as a deposit, guaranteeing what is to come. (2 Cor 5:5)*
>
> *And you also were included in Christ when you heard the message of truth, the gospel of your salvation. When you believed, you were marked in him with a seal, the promised Holy Spirit, who is a deposit guaranteeing our inheritance until the redemption of those who are God's possession—to the praise of his glory.* (Eph 1:13–14)
>
> *And do not grieve the Holy Spirit of God, with whom you were sealed for the day of redemption.* (Eph 4:30)

See also 2 Cor 1:21–22; 3:3; Rom 8:22–24.

No scripture ever identified Mary as the pledge or said that the pledge would ever change. Jesus confirmed this:

> ***And I will ask the Father, and he will give you another advocate to help you and be with you forever — the Spirit of truth.*** *(John 14:16–17)*

Does she have the power to change us?

There is nothing in scripture to even suggest that Mary can change us. Scripture does, however, tell us that we are changed by the Holy Spirit and the Word of God.

> *So I say, walk by the Spirit, and you will not gratify the desires of the flesh.* (Gal 5:16)
>
> *I pray that out of his glorious riches he may strengthen you with power through his Spirit in your inner being, so that Christ may dwell in your hearts through faith … to know this love that surpasses knowledge—that you may be filled to the measure of all the fullness of God.* (Eph 3:16–19)
>
> *For in Christ all the fullness of the Deity lives in bodily form, and in Christ you have been brought to fullness.* (Col 2:9–10)

See John 15:3; 17:17; Acts 20:32; Rom 1:16–17; 8:9, 11; 1 Cor 1:8; 6:11; 2 Cor 3:17–18; Gal 5:16–18; Eph 5:25–27; Phil 1:6; 1 Thess 2:13; 2 Tim 3:14–15; 1 Pet 1:1–2; 2 Pet 1:3; 1 John 1:7.

Can we not find Jesus unless we first go to her?

Jesus always taught that we are to come to Him and that He alone is the Way to God. Every time someone spoke of His human parentage, He redirected them toward the things of God.

> ***Come to me, all you who are weary and burdened, and I will give you rest.*** (Matt 11:28)

See also Matt 11:28–30; 12:46–50; 13:53–57; 19:14; Mark 3:31–35; 10:14; Luke 8:19–21; 11:27–28; 18:16; John 5:39–40; 6:37–40, 44; 7:37; 14:6; 16: 22–24; Heb 4:16.

Do we overcome the powers of hell by her and by invocation of her name?

The "powers" of hell have no authority over the born-again, Spirit-led Christian who places all his hopes in the finished work of Christ Jesus. Scripture addresses the spirit of the antichrist and his demonic spirits:

> *You, dear children, are from God and have overcome them, because the one who is in you is greater than the one who is in the world.* (1 John 4:4)

See Matt 16:18; Acts 2:21; 4:12; Rom 8:1; 10:13; Eph 1:18–23; Phil 2:9–10; Col 2:15.

Have we been left alone by God so that she is our refuge, our help, and our all?

See the topic "*Have We Been Left as Orphans*" in this appendix.

Does honoring her and putting our trust in her somehow count in our salvation? Are we lost who do not know her or turn to her?

There is nothing in scripture to suggest that a believer who does not practice devotion to Mary is lost. There is not even any suggestion that anyone should be devoted to her. Glory and honor belong to God alone.

Much of this is covered in part III.

See also John 3:36; 5:24; Rom 4:7–8; 5:9–10; 11:36; Acts 4:12; 1 Cor 10:31; 1 Thess 5:9; 1 Tim 3:15; 2 Tim 2:10; Heb 2:10; 5:9; 1 Pet 4:11; Jude 1:25; Rev 5:13.

Does God not hear us that we need to invoke her merits?

See "Merits of Mary" in part I of this book.

> ***But when you pray, go into your room, close the door and pray to your Father, who is unseen. Then your Father, who sees what is done in secret, will reward you. And when you pray, do not keep on babbling like pagans, for they think they will be heard because of their many words. Do not be like them, for your Father knows what you need before you ask him.*** (Matt 6:6–8)

See also Matt 7:7–11; 18:19; 21:21–22; Mark 11:22–26; Luke 11:5–13; 18:1–8; John 14:11–14; 15:7–8; 16:23–24.

Can we not get the gifts of God except by going to her?

God has already given us all we need through His Holy Spirit. Anything we lack is only because we have not asked.

See 1 Cor 1:4–7; 12:4–11; 2 Pet 1:3–4; Luke 11:9–10; John 10:10; Gal 5:22–23; Eph 1:3; 2 Tim 1:7; Heb 2:3–4; 2 Pet 1:3; Jas 4:2.

Is Mary our backup or fallback if we do not succeed with Christ?

> *Jesus answered,* ***"I am the way and the truth and the life. No one comes to the Father except through me."*** (John 14:6)

Apart from Jesus, there is no way to God. His sacrifice in taking our place in death fully paid the price of sin. Believers are saved by the faith they place in His finished work and are reconciled with God.

See also Mark 10:45; Rom 6:7–10; 8:3–4; Eph 2:14–19; Heb 2:15; 7:1–28; 8:12; 9; 10:10, 17, 18, 26–31; 1 Pet 3:18; 1 John 2:2.

APPENDIX 15

UNITY OF THE TRINITY IN SCRIPTURE

Scripture tells us the Spirit was already there at the beginning of Creation.

> *In the beginning God created the heavens and the earth. Now the earth was formless and empty, darkness was over the surface of the deep, and the Spirit of God was hovering over the waters.* (Gen 1:2)

Jesus tells us that the Father and He were there too before all was made:

> ***And now, Father, glorify me in your presence with the glory I had with you before the world began.*** (John 17:5)
>
> ***Father, I want those you have given me to be with me where I am, and to see my glory, the glory you have given me because you loved me before the creation of the world.*** (John 17:24)

The Father, the Son, and the Spirit are revealed as One in numerous scriptures:

> ***But when they arrest you, do not worry about what to say or how to say it. At that time you will be given what to say, for it will not be you speaking, but the Spirit of your Father speaking through you.*** (Matt 10:19–20)

> *Jesus answered . . .* ***"Believe me when I say that I am in the Father and the Father is in me; or at least believe on the evidence of the works themselves."*** (John 14:9, 11)

> *Jesus replied,* ***"Anyone who loves me will obey my teaching. My Father will love them, and we will come to them and make our home with them."*** (John 14:23)

> ***Holy Father, protect them by the power of your name, the name you gave me, so that they may be one as we are one.*** (John 17:11)

> ***I pray also for those who will believe in me through their message, that all of them may be one, Father, just as you are in me and I am in you. May they also be in us so that the world may believe that you have sent me. I have given them the glory that you gave me, that they may be one as we are one—I in them and you in me—so that they may be brought to complete unity.*** (John 17:20–23)

> ***If you love me, keep my commands. And I will ask the Father, and he will give you another advocate to help you and be with you forever—the Spirit***

> ***of truth. The world cannot accept him, because it neither sees him nor knows him. But you know him, for he lives with you and will be in you.*** (John 14:15–17)

The Spirit coming to live in us is then the materialization of "*we will come to them and make our home with them.*"

> *For who knows a person's thoughts except their own spirit within them? In the same way no one knows the thoughts of God except the Spirit of God.* (1 Cor 2:11)

The following are some of the many verses that show that the Spirit is the Spirit of Christ and the Spirit of Father God.

> ***Whenever you are arrested and brought to trial, do not worry beforehand about what to say. Just say whatever is given you at the time, for it is not you speaking, but the Holy Spirit.*** (Mark 13:11)
>
> ***But make up your mind not to worry beforehand how you will defend yourselves. For I will give you words and wisdom that none of your adversaries will be able to resist or contradict.*** (Luke 21:14–15)
>
> ***But when they arrest you, do not worry about what to say or how to say it. At that time you will be given what to say, for it will not be you speaking, but the Spirit of your Father speaking through you.*** (Matt 10:19–20)

APPENDIX 16

OLD AND NEW COVENANT LAWS

For someone unfamiliar with the Bible, a reading of scripture from Genesis will reveal many laws that appear to not be followed by devout Christians today. This does not include the nonnegotiable laws on murder, adultery, blasphemy, or similar rules, but they include rules on eating, observance of holy days, the "eye for an eye, tooth for a tooth" laws, and the like.

Jesus Christ fulfilled many of the laws for us by paying the price of them at the cross so that we have been set free from the law.

For instance, there are many Old Testament laws concerning what can be eaten. Today, we eat many of the prohibited items and recognize them as foods, including prawns, pork, and crab. This is likely confusing for the new believer, especially if they come from what some might refer to as *legalistic* religions.

Regarding foods, New Testament Scripture reveals many things:

> *Again Jesus called the crowd to him and said, "**Listen to me, everyone, and understand this. Nothing outside a person can defile them by going into***

them. Rather, it is what comes out of a person that defiles them."

*After he had left the crowd and entered the house, his disciples asked him about this parable. "**Are you so dull?**" he asked. "**Don't you see that nothing that enters a person from the outside can defile them? For it doesn't go into their heart but into their stomach, and then out of the body.**" (In saying this, Jesus declared all foods clean.)*

*He went on: "**What comes out of a person is what defiles them. For it is from within, out of a person's heart, that evil thoughts come—sexual immorality, theft, murder, adultery, greed, malice, deceit, lewdness, envy, slander, arrogance and folly. All these evils come from inside and defile a person.**"* (Mark 7:14–23)

The apostle Peter had a vision from heaven:

> *Starting from the beginning, Peter told them the whole story: "I was in the city of Joppa praying, and in a trance I saw a vision. I saw something like a large sheet being let down from heaven by its four corners, and it came down to where I was. I looked into it and saw four-footed animals of the earth, wild beasts, reptiles and birds. Then I heard a voice telling me, 'Get up, Peter. Kill and eat.'*
>
> *"I replied, 'Surely not, Lord! Nothing impure or unclean has ever entered my mouth.'*
>
> *"The voice spoke from heaven a second time, 'Do not call anything impure that God has made clean.' This happened three times, and then it was all pulled up to heaven again.* (Acts 11:4–10)

The apostle Paul wrote:

> *Accept the one whose faith is weak, without quarreling over disputable matters. One person's faith allows them to eat anything, but another, whose faith is weak, eats only vegetables. The one who eats everything must not treat with contempt the one who does not, and the one who does not eat everything must not judge the one who does, for God has accepted them.* (Rom 14: 1–3)
>
> *Therefore let us stop passing judgment on one another. Instead, make up your mind not to put any stumbling block or obstacle in the way of a brother or sister. I am convinced, being fully persuaded in the Lord Jesus, that nothing is unclean in itself. But if anyone regards something as unclean, then for that person it is unclean.* (Rom 14:13–14)

> *Eat anything sold in the meat market without raising questions of conscience, for, "The earth is the Lord's, and everything in it." If an unbeliever invites you to a meal and you want to go, eat whatever is put before you without raising questions of conscience.* (1 Cor 10:25–27)

> *The Spirit clearly says that in later times some will abandon the faith and follow deceiving spirits and things taught by demons. Such teachings come through hypocritical liars, whose consciences have been seared as with a hot iron. They forbid people to marry and order them to abstain from certain foods, which God created to be received with thanksgiving by those who believe and who know the truth. For everything God created is good, and nothing is to be rejected if it is received with*

> *thanksgiving, because it is consecrated by the Word of God and prayer.* (1 Tim 4:1–5)

Jesus and the apostles taught that when we give thanks for the food we eat, these foods are sanctified so that we may consume them. Certain kinds of foods, however, are harmful and are to be avoided, such as certain kinds of sea and predator birds. Meat, such as pork, that would have been dangerous to eat back in the Old Testament days are now harmless if the animals are reared in the right conditions and cooked sufficiently to destroy any potential parasites.

Old Testament laws were meant to point mankind to Jesus. He is the source of life. The Law was given to make us conscious of sin,[119] its seriousness, and its consequences. After the righteousness of Christ was revealed, we are to look to Him rather than to the Law, which could never remove our sin.

Moses himself wrote about Christ:

> *The LORD your God will raise up for you a prophet like me from among you, from your fellow Israelites. You must listen to him.* (Deut 18:15)

God confirmed this:

> *A voice came from the cloud, saying, "This is my Son, whom I have chosen; listen to him."* (Luke 9:35)

> *For the law was given through Moses; grace and truth came through Jesus Christ.* (John 1:17)

---

[119] Rom 3:19–20.

The fulfillment of the Law and what it means to New Testament believers is revealed in the following scriptures, including details of what became known as the "Jerusalem Council" at which the apostles discussed and decreed what rules were binding on non-Jewish believers: Acts 10; 13:39; 15:5–20; Romans 3:19–22, 28; 5:13, 18–21; 6:14–18, 22–23; 7:1–8:17; 10:4; 13:8–10; Galatians 2:16, 19–21; 3:10–13, 19, 23–24; 4:4–5; 5:2–6, 14, 18; 6:2; Ephesians 2:14–15; Hebrews 10:1–31.

Anyone unfamiliar with scripture will want to study the above texts.

APPENDIX 17
WHAT JESUS TAUGHT

God Is Good

Jesus knew God the Father as His Father, and He revealed the nature of God by His presence,[120] by everything He did, and through His words:

> ***Be perfect, therefore, as your heavenly Father is perfect.*** (Matt 5:48)
>
> ***No one is good—except God alone.*** (Mark 10:18)
>
> ***Be merciful, just as your Father is merciful.*** (Luke 6:36)
>
> ***My Father is always at his work to this very day, and I too am working.*** (John 5:17)

See also Matt 6:28–32; 7:11; 10:28–31; 18:14; Luke 11:13: 12:22–31; 15:11–32; 18:1–8; John 6:32–33, 38–40; 10:29; 14:21, 23–26; 16:25–27; 17:1–17.

---

[120] John 14:6–10; Heb 1:3; Col 1:15–20.

Love God and Love Your Fellow Man

Jesus never neglected to teach from scripture that loving God is our foremost duty followed by loving our neighbor.

> ***The most important … is this: "Love the Lord your God with all your heart and with all your soul and with all your mind and with all your strength." The second is this: "Love your neighbor as yourself." There is no commandment greater than these.*** (Mark 12:29–31)

> ***It is written: "Worship the Lord your God and serve him only."*** (Luke 4:8)

> ***So in everything, do to others what you would have them do to you, for this sums up the Law and the Prophets.*** (Matt 7:12)

See also Matt 7:12; 22:39; Luke 6:31; John 15:12–13.

Loving God is not some abstract philosophy; it is an active life of communicating with God in worship, prayer, thanksgiving, and serving Him. Jesus demonstrated this in all He did, including laying His life on the cross.

Prayer and Worship

> ***But when you pray, go into your room, close the door and pray to your Father, who is unseen. Then your Father, who sees what is done in secret, will reward you.*** (Matt 6:6)
>
> *Then Jesus told his disciples a parable to show them that they should always pray and not give up.* (Luke 18:1)

See also Matt 5:5–13; 6:5–13; 7:7–11; 9:37–38; 18:19; 21:13, 16, 21–22; Mark 1:35; 6:46; 9:25–29; 11:17, 22–26; 12:18; 13:18; 14:32, 35–36, 39; Luke 1:13; 5:16; 6:12, 28; 9:16, 18, 28–29; 11:1–13; 18:1–8; 19:46; 21:36; 22:32, 40–46; John 6:23–24, 26; 17:1–26.

Thanksgiving

As with prayer, Jesus demonstrated it more by action than by words (see Mark 8:7; 14:22–23; Luke 2:38; 17:12–18; 19:1–9; 22:17, 19; John 6:11, 23).

To Be Baptized with Both Water and the Spirit

Jesus commanded His disciples to be baptized and to baptize with both water and His Spirit.

Be Water Baptized

Water baptism was a requisite, and scripture tells us that it is a baptism of repentance:

> *He* (John the Baptist) *went into all the country around the Jordan, preaching a baptism of repentance for the forgiveness of sins.* (Luke 3:3)

The fruit of this baptism is revealed in the following passage:

> *All the people, even the tax collectors, when they heard Jesus' words, acknowledged that God's way was right, <u>because they had</u> been baptized by John. But the Pharisees and the experts in the law rejected God's purpose for themselves, <u>because they had not</u> been baptized by John.* (Luke 7:29–30)

> *Jesus answered,* ***"Very truly I tell you, no one can enter the kingdom of God unless they are born of water and the Spirit."*** (John 3:5)

> ***Therefore go and make disciples of all nations, baptizing them in the name of the Father and of the Son and of the Holy Spirit.*** (Matt 28:19)

> *He said to them,* ***"Go into all the world and preach the Gospel to all creation. Whoever believes and is baptized will be saved, but whoever does not believe will be condemned."*** (Mark 16:15–16)

See also Matt 3:11, 13–17; Mark 1:8–10; Luke 3:16, 21–22; 7:29–30; John 1:24–34; 22–26; 4:1–2.

Be Born of the Spirit

Jesus came, suffered, and died for us so that our sin would be covered just as the blood of the lamb on the doorposts covered the sin of the Israelites when the angel passed over them in Egypt.[121] He also came to establish His kingdom of followers who were to be born of the Spirit of God.

> *Jesus replied,* ***"Very truly I tell you, no one can see the kingdom of God unless they are born again."*** (John 3:3)

> *Jesus answered,* ***"Very truly I tell you, no one can enter the kingdom of God unless they are born of water and the Spirit. Flesh gives birth to flesh, but the Spirit gives birth to spirit. You should not be surprised at my saying, 'You must be born***

[121] Exod 12:1–30.

again.' The wind blows wherever it pleases. You hear its sound, but you cannot tell where it comes from or where it is going. So it is with everyone born of the Spirit." (John 3:5–8)

See also Matt 10:19–20; 11:11; Luke 3:16; 11:11–13; 12:11–12; 24:49; John 3:3–8; 4:10, 13–14, 24; 6:53–63; 7:37–39; 14:16–20, 26; 15:26; 16:7, 13–15; 20:22.

The baptism by the Spirit is that miraculous event that fills believers with the Spirit of God. It is the fulfillment of the promise of God to dwell with His people, to be with them, to guide them all their days, and to empower them to live and to be His witnesses throughout the earth.

The many fruits of the Spirit can *then* be enjoyed by the believer. Among these fruits are power, love, and a sound mind—a life free of anxiety in a world where there will be trouble until the fulfillment of all things.

To Live Free from Fear and Worry

Therefore I tell you, do not worry about your life, what you will eat or drink; or about your body, what you will wear. Is not life more than food, and the body more than clothes? (Matt 6:25)

Therefore do not worry about tomorrow, for tomorrow will worry about itself. Each day has enough trouble of its own. (Matt 6:34)

Peace I leave with you; my peace I give you. I do not give to you as the world gives. Do not let your hearts be troubled and do not be afraid. (John 14:27)

See also Matt 6:25–34; 8:26; 10:26–31; 14:27; 14:31; 17:6–7; 24:6; 25:24–30; 28:10; Mark 4:40; 5:33–34, 36; 6:50; Luke 1:12, 74; 2:9–10; 8:50; 9:45; 12:4–7, 11–12, 22–26, 32–34; 21:9, 14–15; 24:37–38; John 6:20; 14:1.

To Advance the Kingdom and Remain True to Him

Following Jesus is not just a matter of internal changes but doing what He did, which was to reach out to a lost world. We can only do this in the power and by the direction of His Spirit.

Be Fruitful and Advance the Kingdom of God

> ***I am the vine; you are the branches. If you remain in me and I in you, you will bear much fruit; apart from me you can do nothing. If you do not remain in me, you are like a branch that is thrown away and withers; such branches are picked up, thrown into the fire and burned. If you remain in me and my words remain in you, ask whatever you wish, and it will be done for you.*** (John 15:5–7)

> ***But seek first his kingdom and his righteousness, and all these things will be given to you as well.*** (Matt 6:33)

> ***Therefore go and make disciples of all nations, baptizing them in the name of the Father and of the Son and of the Holy Spirit, and teaching them to obey everything I have commanded you.*** (Matt 28:19–20)

See also Matt 3:10; 4:19; 7:19; 13:3–12; 18–33; 21:28–43; 24:45–51; 25:14–30, 34–46; 28:19–20; Mark 1:17; 4:2–9, 13–20; 10:13–15,

23–31, 42–45; 11:12–14, 20–21; Luke 3:8–9; 5:10; 8:15; 9:1–6, 59–62; 10:8–11; 11:23; 12:6–9, 27–34; 13:6–9, 18–30; 18:16–30; 19:11–27; John 4:35–38; 12:24; 15:1–8; 16.

Remain Steadfast in Our Love for Him and to Keep Watch

> ***Be dressed ready for service and keep your lamps burning, like servants waiting for their master to return from a wedding banquet, so that when he comes and knocks they can immediately open the door for him. It will be good for those servants whose master finds them watching when he comes. Truly I tell you, he will dress himself to serve, will have them recline at the table and will come and wait on them. It will be good for those servants whose master finds them ready, even if he comes in the middle of the night or toward daybreak. But understand this: If the owner of the house had known at what hour the thief was coming, he would not have let his house be broken into. You also must be ready, because the Son of Man will come at an hour when you do not expect him.*** (Luke 12:35–40)

See also Matt 10:22;32–33;38–39; 24:12–13; 24:42–51; 25:13; Mark 13:5–23, 33–37; Luke 12:35–48; 21:8–19, 28–36; John 15:1–10.

To Follow Him

Jesus came to give us eternal life, He alone is the Light and Life for the world, and He taught that we must follow Him to receive of His life:

> *When Jesus spoke again to the people, he said, "**I am the light of the world. Whoever follows me will***

never walk in darkness, but will have the light of life." (John 8:12)

When he has brought out all his own, he goes on ahead of them, and his sheep follow him because they know his voice. (John 10:4)

My sheep listen to my voice; I know them, and they follow me. (John 10:27)

Whoever serves me must follow me; and where I am, my servant also will be. My Father will honor the one who serves me. (John 12:26)

See also Matt 4:19; 8:22; 9:9; 10:38; Mark 1:17, 20; 2:14; 10:21; Luke 5:10–11, 27; 9:59; 18:29–30; John 21:19, 22.

What Following Jesus Means

Following Jesus involves turning from our own ways (repentance), dying to ourselves and our selfish desires, forgiving one another, and putting into practice all His words and commands.

Repent and Change Both Your Direction and Your Ways

Woe to you, Chorazin! Woe to you, Bethsaida! For if the miracles that were performed in you had been performed in Tyre and Sidon, they would have repented long ago, sitting in sackcloth and ashes. But it will be more bearable for Tyre and Sidon at the judgment than for you. And you, Capernaum, will you be lifted to the heavens? No, you will go down to Hades. (Luke 10:13–15)

> ***The men of Nineveh will stand up at the judgment with this generation and condemn it, for they repented at the preaching of Jonah; and now something greater than Jonah is here.*** (Luke 11:32)

> ***Do you think that these Galileans were worse sinners than all the other Galileans because they suffered this way? I tell you, no! But unless you repent, you too will all perish. Or those eighteen who died when the tower in Siloam fell on them—do you think they were more guilty than all the others living in Jerusalem? I tell you, no! But unless you repent, you too will all perish.*** (Luke 13:1–5)

See also Matt 3:1–2, 11; 4:17; 5:1–7:27 (changing how we live); 11:20–24; 12:41; 21:32; Mark 1:4, 15; 2:17; 6:12; Luke 1:16–17; 3:3, 8, 10–14; 5:31; 6:31–38, 41–42; 7:36–50; 11:29–32; 13:2–8; 15:; 16:30; 17:3–4; 24:47; John 5:14; 8:11.

Dying to Self

> ***Whoever wants to be my disciple must deny themselves and take up their cross and follow me. For whoever wants to save their life will lose it, but whoever loses their life for me will find it. What good will it be for someone to gain the whole world, yet forfeit their soul? Or what can anyone give in exchange for their soul?*** (Matt 16:24–26)

> ***And everyone who has left houses or brothers or sisters or father or mother or wife or children or***

> ***fields for my sake will receive a hundred times as much and will inherit eternal life.*** (Matt 19:29)
>
> ***Very truly I tell you, unless a kernel of wheat falls to the ground and dies, it remains only a single seed. But if it dies, it produces many seeds. Anyone who loves their life will lose it, while anyone who hates their life in this world will keep it for eternal life. Whoever serves me must follow me; and where I am, my servant also will be. My Father will honor the one who serves me.*** (John 12:24–26)

See also Matt 10:35–39; 16:23–26; 23:11; Mark 8:33–38; 10:29–31; Luke 5:11, 27–28; 9:23–26; 14:25–35; 17:30–33; 18:29–30; 22:42; John 5:30; 12:24–26; 15:20

Jesus has never asked us to do what He Himself was not willing to do, and He demonstrated this shortly after speaking the following words:

> ***"Abba, Father,"*** *he said,* ***"everything is possible for you. Take this cup from me. Yet not what I will, but what you will."*** (Matt 14:36)

> ***Now my soul is troubled, and what shall I say? "Father, save me from this hour"? No, it was for this very reason I came to this hour.*** (John 12:27)

> ***For I have come down from heaven not to do my will but to do the will of him who sent me.*** (John 6:38)

> ***I am the good shepherd. The good shepherd lays down his life for the sheep.*** (John 10:11)

See also John 10:14–18.

Forgive One Another

> ***For if you forgive other people when they sin against you, your heavenly Father will also forgive you. But if you do not forgive others their sins, your Father will not forgive your sins.*** (Matt 6:14–15)
>
> ***And when you stand praying, if you hold anything against anyone, forgive them, so that your Father in heaven may forgive you your sins.*** (Mark 11:25–26)

See also Matt 6:12; 18:21–35; Luke 6:27, 35, 37; 11:4; 17:3–4; 23:34; John 20:23.

Put His Words into Practice and Obey God

> ***Not everyone who says to me, "Lord, Lord," will enter the kingdom of heaven, but only the one who does the will of my Father who is in heaven.*** (Matt 7:21)
>
> ***Therefore go and make disciples of all nations … teaching them to obey everything I have commanded you.*** (Matt 28:19–20)
>
> *Then they asked him, "What must we do to do the works God requires?"*
>
> *Jesus answered, "**The work of God is this: to believe in the one he has sent.**"* (John 6:27–29)
>
> ***If you keep my commands, you will remain in my love, just as I have kept my Father's commands and remain in his love.*** (John 15:10)

Very truly I tell you, whoever obeys my word will never see death. (John 8:51)

See also Matt 7:21–23, 24–27; 12:49–50; 18:17; 25:34–40; Mark 9:50; 16:15–18; Luke 6:46–49; 8:21; 11:27–28; 12:16–21, 42–48;13:1–5; 21:34–36; John 6:29, 40; 7:17–19; 8:31–32; 13:12–17, 34–35; 14:15, 21, 23–24; 15: 12–14, 17; Acts 3:22–23.

True repentance, forgiveness of others, and dying to oneself are things that are difficult to do. However, with the Spirit of God, believers do these because, with God, all things are possible when we keep our eyes on the Master, our Lord Jesus Christ.

See also the chapter "How Should Believers Live Their Lives?" in appendix 14: "Additional Material for Another Gospel."

ABOUT THE AUTHOR

Joey grew up in a traditional Roman Catholic family that prayed the Rosary every night. His father was instrumental in setting up and leading Legion of Mary chapters in churches he attended in Malaysia and later in Sydney.

During his teens, Joey adopted Buddhism and had intended on becoming a monk following in the footsteps of his uncle. Later, however, he became a born-again believer who diligently examined scripture seeking the Christianity of the Apostles.

Following on from a family pilgrimage to Lourdes, Fatima, Garabandal and then the Holy Land, he started work on this book which took around 2 decades to research and complete. Trained in both Computing and Journalism, he worked primarily as a software developer - a career he held till retirement.

Printed in the United States
by Baker & Taylor Publisher Services